Comparative Literature: Matter and Method

Comparative Literature: Matter and Method

Edited with Introductions by
A. OWEN ALDRIDGE

UNIVERSITY OF ILLINOIS PRESS
Urbana   Chicago   London

CONTENTS

GENERAL INTRODUCTION

The Purpose and Perspectives
of Comparative Literature

The essays which comprise this book are all taken from the first five volumes of the journal *Comparative Literature Studies*. They have been collected both for their inherent value as literary studies and for their practical value as examples of the best scholarly tradition of comparative literature, a discipline which to many students still appears confusing or elusive.

It is now generally agreed that comparative literature does not compare national literatures in the sense of setting one against another. Instead it provides a method of broadening one's perspective in the approach to single works of literature — a way of looking beyond the narrow boundaries of national frontiers in order to discern trends and movements in various national cultures and to see the relations between literature and other spheres of human activity. The study of comparative literature is fundamentally not any different from the study of national literatures except that its subject matter is much vaster, taken as it is from more than one literature and excluding none which the student has the capacity to read. The comparatist, instead of being confined to the wares of a single nation, shops in a literary department store. Briefly defined, comparative literature can be considered the study of any literary phenomenon from the perspective of more than one national literature or in conjunction with another intellectual discipline or even several. The terms "comparative law," "comparative philology," and "comparative folklore" are parallel to "comparative literature," and the latter should be considered as no more than a convenient label to describe literary studies which transcend national boundaries.

The earliest scholarship in the discipline was devoted primarily to literary history and to the relations between literature and society. In a sense the pioneer comparatist was Mme de Staël, who wrote two world-famous books concerning international literary relations: *De la Littérature considérée dans ses rapports avec les institutions sociales,* 1800; and *De l'Allemagne,* 1813. The journal *Revue de littérature comparée* published the correspondence of Mme de Staël with Thomas Jefferson in its second volume, 1922, and Irving Babbitt remarked during this same era that she has "done more than anyone else to help forward the study of comparative literature as we now understand it."

Embodying a more esthetic point of view, Friedrich Schlegel in 1798 incorporated the cosmopolitanism associated with comparative literature in his concept of *Universalpoesie.* In his words, "romantic poetry is a progressive universal poetry." By universal, Schlegel did not mean uniform in the sense of expressing attitudes felt by everyone or in exercising an appeal broad enough to be responded to by everyone. He meant instead a comprehensive subject matter embracing virtually every aspect of human experience. The poet or novelist, in other words, should not exclude from his work any nuance of character or emotion which awakens his interest.

Goethe a quarter of a century later enunciated the concept of *Weltliteratur,* embodying geographical as well as psychological and esthetic characteristics. Goethe believed that the spiritual needs of all nations could be satisfied through knowledge of "a Universal World-Literature." By this he meant the common heritage represented by the efforts of the best poets and esthetic authors of all nations directed toward the universal in humanity. Comparative literature in the best sense combines the all-embracing psychological perspective of Schlegel's *Universalpoesie* with the concern for esthetic excellence reflected in Goethe's *Weltliteratur.*

To be sure, some critics object to the concept of world literature on the grounds that it is equivalent to the study of "great books" or "world masterpieces" as individual artifacts without consideration of their relations to each other or to the historical traditions of literature and culture. Others object because in practice World Literature has been treated as merely Western Literature to the exclusion of the traditions of Asia and Africa. These objections are valid, but they should be applied only to inadequate applications of the theory of world literature rather than to the principle itself. Certainly the study of comparative literature should embrace every subject of importance to human life which has been successfully treated in written works of the imagination, should relate individual works to similar creations in other national traditions, and should include the literature of the East as well as the West. The only reason that most comparatists neglect Eastern literatures is that they lack the linguistic competence required for tackling them.

In both Europe and America the terms *general literature* and *comparative literature* are sometimes used interchangeably. A distinction exists, but as frequently happens, scholars cannot agree on the nature of the distinction. One might, however, relate general literature to the theories of Schlegel and Goethe concerning universalism — that of theme in Schlegel and that of esthetic response in Goethe. In this sense, general literature would comprise studies of themes, genres, and masterpieces without explicit reference to time or period. Comparative literature would comprise both literary history (including movements, periods, and influences) and the relations of literature to the social, political, and philosophical background. In the sense of this distinction, general literature would completely transcend national boundaries; whereas comparative literature would focus on the relations between one particular literature and others which it touches. So much for the distinction. In practice, the two tendencies usually merge, and even when they do not the term *comparative literature* is widely used for both.

Comparison may be used in literary study to indicate affinity, tradition, or influence. Affinity consists in resemblances in style, structure, mood, or idea between two works which have no other connection. As an example, the Russian novel *Oblomov* may be compared to *Hamlet* because each work is a character study of indecision and procrastination. Tradition or convention consists in resemblances between works which form part of a large group of similar works held together by a common historical, chronological, or formal bond. Goethe's *Die Leiden des jungen Werther* may be compared to the epistolary novels of Richardson and Rousseau because of the first person perspective and the untrammelled expression of sentiment in all three works. For an example of influence, we may turn to the Italian historical novel *I promessi sposi* of Manzoni, which in many ways was directly inspired by the preceding English works of Walter Scott.

To those who advocate an emphasis on the historical point of view, the Golden Age of Comparative Literature was that between the two world wars. In the major studies published during this period, the literary relations noted were precise and concrete and supported by exact bibliographical evidence; minor works were considered along with major ones; and social and philosophical backgrounds were frequently brought into play. In historical studies of literature, the concept of influence is of primary concern, and attention is given to emitters, receivers, and intermediaries (rather awkward terms usually reserved for bibliographical headings). A study of Goethe and England for example, could be devoted to the influence of English life and literature in the works of the German author: English authors would be considered as emitters, Goethe himself would be the receiver, and his English correspondents or anglophile German friends would be intermediaries. If the perspective were reversed in a study of the influence of Goethe in England, Goethe would of course be the emitter; English authors and the English reading public would be receivers; and translations, editions, and reviews of Goethe's works would be intermediaries along with English travelers to Germany and Goethe's English correspondents. More general studies which concentrate on themes and types may show influence, but they do so only incidentally. Emphasis in studies of the classic themes or legends, for example, those of Faust and Don Juan, is on the psychology, morality, philosophy, and other aspects of individual works rather than on authors or national origins.

The emphasis on influence has been attributed, wrongly I believe, to the scientifically-oriented nineteenth century, presumably dominated by a concern for genetics. Critics are supposed to have viewed literature as a scientific organism, growing and evolving almost like a biological specimen. In other words, *Literaturwissenschaft* is supposed to have adopted the methods of *Naturwissenschaft*. The seeking of influences dates well back into the eighteenth century, however, and in English literature at least it is closely associated with textual criticism of the Bible, in which seeking parallels between the Old and New Testament was standard procedure. The method was stimulated moreover by the close relationship betwen poetry and the Latin classics, the poets themselves frequently printing parallel passages or pointing out resemblances in footnotes. T. S. Eliot's notes in *The Waste Land* belong to this tradition.

In recent years the esthetic perspective has been increasingly dominant among comparative literature scholars, and studies have been favored which show resemblances or affinities instead of influence. The method of *rapprochement,* which resembles comparative law in pointing to "analogies without contact" permits a concentration on major works, offers an opportunity for aesthetic analysis, and may provide an insight into the process of artistic creation.

Influence studies may be criticized for depending too much on minor characteristics and minor works, and affinity studies may be criticized for relying too greatly upon subjectivism and impressionism. The first may seem to have too rigid a method, the second, not method enough. According to some scholars, the establishing of sources and influences may be comparative, but it is not literature; according to others, the revealing of parallels through mere rapprochement may be literary comparison, but it is not comparative literature. Each is, nevertheless, valuable in its own way in promoting an increased understanding and enjoyment of literature.

Because of the vastness of material and multiplicity of problems encountered in comparative literature there exists no ideal method or model for study. The grouping of essays in this collection is designed to reveal that methodological terminology is at best ambiguous, and that several different methods may be used even in the study of a single problem. In other words, method is less important than matter.

There is nothing traditional about the five main categories in which the essays in this volume are classified. The first category of Literary Criticism and Theory, the application of esthetic values to literature, is an essential part of the study of both national literatures and comparative literature. Literary Movements in the second category refer to marked psychological, intellectual, or stylistic tendencies in particular chronological periods which are so dominant and penetrating that they characterize the entire age in which they appear. Literary Themes in the third category represent both personalities and abstract ideas which have been presented in many versions and from several points of view in various literatures. Faust and Don Juan are examples of personality themes; suicide is an example of an abstract theme. Literary Forms in the fourth category are also known as genres. They refer to the structure of literary works according to conventional patterns and represent such forms as the sonnet, the epic, or the novel. In the seventeenth and eighteenth centuries, works were supposed to conform to quite rigid requirements for many genres. Present requirements are no longer rigid, but it is still possible to describe the structure of particular specimens of drama, fiction, and poetry as they exist in the twentieth century. The study of Literary Relations, the fifth category, provides an almost inexhaustible variety of methods for the examination of literary phenomena. The two most important of these are the tracing of sources and influence and the portrayal of connections between literature and other aspects of human knowledge.

Comparative Literature Studies while stressing relationships between authors, literatures, and movements, has upheld the principle that the most important of all literary relationships is that between literature and life.

I

Literary Criticism and Theory

The foremost classics of literary theory are Aristotle's Τέχνη Ποιητική, Horace's *Ars poetica,* and Boileau's *l'Art poétique.* It is significant that all three titles are based on some grammatical form of the word *poet,* which in the original Greek meant *maker.* Until the middle of the eighteenth century, all written works with esthetic pretensions were ordinarily classified as belonging to poetry, the word *literature* still not being used in the sense of *belles lettres.* Samuel Johnson, for example, instead of writing the history of English literature, chose to treat the *Lives of the English Poets.* When Alexander Pope undertook his *Essay on Criticism,* in the tradition of Horace and Boileau, he combined literary theory and criticism by including virtually all of the subject matter of his predecessors concerning abstract rules for belles lettres along with practical advice for evaluating particular texts.

In the twentieth century, it is almost impossible to write pure literary theory. Most work which passes for theory is actually either the history of literary theory or polemics concerning some phase of it. Literary tradition in our times comes about in a pragmatic manner, and new theories merely describe methods of successful writing which have been previously adopted experimentally. Whatever may have been the situation in the time of Aristotle, formulae in the modern world come after practice. For example: the Southern Gothic novel of Faulkner and the *nouveau roman* of Robbe Grillet were obviously not constructed to conform to a previously established theory unless it was to one of the author. Critics may pontificate about novels such as these under the illusion that they are formulating theory, but they are, of course, doing no more than generalizing about concrete manifestations. They are not critical realists, but critical nominalists.

Of the following articles, the first, by René Wellek, which summarizes and classifies recent American criticism, is an article *about* literary criticism, not *of* literary criticism, and as such it is really closer to literary history than to either criticism or theory. The article by Ihab Hassan, however, represents literary theory to the degree in which such a phenomenon may be a distinct entity as it argues against the extreme estheticism in post-war criticism. By and large, Hassan's article supports the position of *Comparative Literature Studies* that "the most important of all literary relationships is that between literature and life."

The article on Italian criticism by Rocco Montano is primarily literary history, but it is highly colored by the author's expressed conviction that "criticism can only be the history of art." The final article, by Allan Rodway, is also primarily historical — an analytical treatment of the various aspects of what the author labels English New Criticism. The articles of Hassan, Rodway, and Montano are taken from two special issues of *Comparative Literature Studies* devoted to recent literary criticism in the major areas of Europe and the Western Hemisphere. Each article taken singly seems to be concerned with only a national literature, but when the articles are read as a group they clearly reveal common ideas, cross currents, and influences operating in several literatures.

RENÉ WELLEK

Philosophy and Postwar American Criticism*

CRITICISM is discrimination, judgment, and hence applies and implies criteria, principles, concepts, and thus a theory and aesthetic and ultimately a philosophy, a view of the world. Even the criticism written "with the least worry of head, the least disposition to break the heart over ultimate questions"[1] takes a philosophical position. Even skepticism, relativism, impressionism appeal, at least silently, to some version of naturalism, irrationalism or agnosticism.[2]

American criticism since the end of the second World War is no exception. One could even say that compared to the critics who wrote up to about 1914, or even up to about 1932, American critics have become more clearly conscious of their philosophical affiliations and assumptions. Increasingly, one comes across such statements as that of Elder Olson: "Criticism," he tells us, "is a department of philosophy. A given comprehensive philosophy invariably develops a certain view of art";[3] or, in a new reversal of traditional views, criticism is simply considered as philosophy and even a form of theology, an all-inclusive system, a world hypothesis. Thirty years ago criticism was a lowly day-by-day activity of the reviewer or a little corner of academic concern; today it often makes the most grandiose claims, which far exceed even Arnold's hope for its salutary influence on the preservation of culture. It is serious praise that "criticism, ceasing to be one of several intellectual arts, is becoming the entire intellectual act itself" and that the critic is a "prophet, announcing to the ungodly the communication of man with ultimate reality."[4]

In my own experience of the American academic scene, the contrast between the Princeton of 1927–8, where even eminent scholars seemed hardly aware of the issues of criticism, and the Yale of 1962, where criticism and its problems are our daily bread and tribulation, is striking, and such an impression can

* Mr. Wellek's paper has already been published in his collection of essays, *Concepts of Criticism* (Yale University Press, 1963).

easily be substantiated by a similar contrast between *The American Mercury* of 1927, a satirical organ devoted to muck-raking and the advancement of the naturalistic novel, and the 1962 quarterlies: *The Kenyon, The Hudson, The Sewanee, Criticism,* etc.

We could describe and analyze this change in a chronological order, expound, for instance, the doctrine of the New Criticism at the end of the war and then trace the diverse reactions against it and the alternatives offered for it: myth criticism, existentialism, and so forth. I have tried to do this, in an international context, in an article, "The Main Trends of Twentieth Century Criticism," and again in a long contribution to a German Encyclopedia of World Literature.[5] There, necessarily, little room was left for recent developments in America: an expansion of the older treatments might be in order. But I shall try a somewhat different approach which, I hope, will illuminate from a new angle the lay of the land, and make the features of the landscape stand out in a stronger relief.

I propose to take the history of Western philosophy in its main representatives and currents—Plato, Aristotle, Thomism, British Empiricism, Kant, Schelling, Hegel, etc.—in their chronological order and ask how far recent American critics profess allegiance to any of them or implicitly accept any of their general positions. In the short space at my disposal I shall not be able to discuss all the important critics and books of the seventeen years since the War. I am aware that I can do little more than indicate the main types and trends and assign individual critics rather brusquely to one or the other position, without being able to make the necessary qualifications. Philosophical commitments in criticism, I realize, are often half-hearted: critical books are often hybrid and beset even by confusions and obscurities. Still, I hope to show the continuities of the main philosophical traditions, demonstrate some survivals from the past, point out some kinships and enmities of the mind. I want to achieve a "perspective by incongruity," the "sudden view of things from their reverse, usually unnoticed side" which Edward Bullough required for "psychical distance," and thus for all art.[6] I want what Pound calls "making strange" and Brecht *Verfremdung*.

Coleridge proclaimed that "every man is born either an Aristotelian or a Platonist," and Alfred North Whitehead has called the history of philosophy "a series of footnotes to Plato." [7] We could try separating the American critics into Platonists and Aristotelians, idealists and realists. But we would not get very far with such a simple dichotomy, and there are no Platonists left in a strict sense and very few Aristotelians. But for my purpose I like to think of the American Neo-Humanist movement as Platonic, as certainly Paul Elmer More was a close student of Plato. The Neo-Humanist movement is defunct today, but its outlook survives in one American critic of stature, Yvor Winters. I am aware that Winters, in his youth, contributed to an anti-Humanist symposium,[8] but since then he has expressed his admiration for Irving Babbitt,[9] and he has, in general terms, restated the moralism and anti-Romanticism of that group. Most of Winters' work precedes 1945, but he has summarized his view in a long essay, *The Function of Criticism* (1957), and has applied anew his principles to Hopkins, Yeats, and Robert Frost, "the spiritual drifter." [10] Winters asserts a firm belief in absolute values. "I am aware," he says, "that my absolutism implies a theistic position, unfortunate as this admission may be. If experience appears to indicate that absolute truths exist, that we are able to work toward an approximate apprehension of them, but that they are antecedent to our apprehension and that our apprehension is seldom or perhaps never perfect, then there is only one place in which these truths may be located, and I see no way to escape this conclusion." [11] A poem, he asserts over and over again, is "a rational statement about a human experience. It is a method for perfecting the understanding and the moral discrimination." [12] It is judged by the rationality of its argument and the morality of its meaning, though morality is seen as a balance of form and content, classical order, control, equilibrium, and not as a bald didactic message. There is some harsh truth and hard common sense in Winters' attack on Emerson, Poe, Whitman, Hawthorne and many other American writers as "obscurantists." Winters asserts a surprisingly modern taste in his appreciation of Valéry, Emily Dickinson, Bridges, and many of the less obvious Elizabethan poets, or in his reflections on prosody. But no American critic has indulged so unrestrainedly in the game of ranking: Elizabeth Daryush is "the finest British poet since T. Sturge Moore," Sturge Moore is a better poet than W. B. Yeats, and Adelaide Crapsey "certainly is an immortal poet," etc. [13] The epic and drama are dead, we are told. The novel is dying rapidly. History writing takes their place. Macaulay, oddly enough, appears as the great master. [14] Only the short reflective poem, like Valéry's *Ebauche d'un serpent,* has any future. There is no recourse against such dogmatism.

It is easy to find professed Aristotelians. A whole group of scholars at the University of Chicago during the 1940's called themselves Neo-Aristotelians, and Aristotle's influence is felt even outside of the group. Gerald F. Else has written a voluminous commentary on the *Poetics* (1957). Francis Fergusson, whose central conception of tragedy is rather mythic, constantly appeals to Aristotle's analysis of dramatic structure. He has drawn up an elaborate scheme to reconcile Aristotle's analysis of *Oedipus Rex* with the ritual forms of Greek drama as reconstructed by Gilbert Murray and his school. [15] Philip Wheelwright and Kenneth Burke have Aristotle constantly in mind. The Chicago Aristotelians, we should realize, do not commit themselves, in theory, to anything so crude as a doctrinaire acceptance of Aristotle's system. R. S. Crane, in his introduction to the programmatic volume, *Critics and Criticism* (1952), rather proclaims "a pluralistic and instrumentalist view of criticism," considers their Aristotelianism "a strictly pragmatic and not exclusive commitment" and admits even that his or any other interpreter's Aristotle "may not be Aristotle at all." [16] But in practice, the "method of multiple hypotheses" [17] is constantly abandoned by the Chicago Critics in favor of a dogmatic scheme which serves as a polemical instrument against the New Criticism and the propounders of symbolist and mythic interpretations of literature. Plot, character, genre are the central concepts, while language is relegated to the lowly position of a mere material cause or occasion of poetry. The Chicago Critics often embrace concepts common in Renaissance Aristotelianism. Language is to them inert matter like stone for the sculptor, and genre becomes a rigid scheme of definitions and exclusions. Elder Olson, in *Tragedy and the Theory of Drama* (1961), tells us that "the greater, and the chief part, of playwriting has nothing to do with words." [18] The *Divine Comedy* is classified as not "mimetic" but "didactic," not "symbolical" but only "allegorical." [19] I am not denying that the Chicago Critics have scored many points against the over-readings of the New Critics, especially against Robert Heilman's interpretations of *King Lear* and *Othello*. [20] One must, besides, be impressed by the extensive learning in the history of criticism shown particularly by R. S. Crane, Richard McKeon and Bernard Weinberg. We owe to Weinberg a fully documented *History of Literary Criticism in the Italian Renaissance* (1961). But judged as an instrument of living criticism, the Chicago Aristotelianism seems to me, ultimately, only an ultra-academic exercise. The best practical application of the principles is Wayne Booth's *The Rhetoric of Fiction* (1961), which argues persuasively against the Jamesian dogma of the disappearance of the author from the novel, but ends with a distressingly Philistine plea for a sound and sane morality, to be clearly and publicly announced by the novelist. The only other book of practical criticism of the Chicago School is, oddly enough, devoted to *The Poetry of Dylan Thomas* (1954). Elder Olson, who had attacked Empson for his ambiguities and ingenuities, indulges there enthusiastically in the same game, without any embarrassment at the contradiction. One can understand why other critics lose patience with the scientific pretensions of the Chicago School, and occasionally even with their innocent godfather. Reuben Brower, a sensitive reader of poetry and close student of Alexander Pope, has even voiced the suspicion that "this excellent geometrician did not know what poetry was." [21] It simply won't do to make Aristotle again the master "di color che sanno." Too many things have happened since.

Surprisingly enough, there is no Neo-Thomist criticism in the United States, though its founder, Jacques Maritain, lives among us and published, in English, *Creative Intuition in Art and Poetry* (1953). His new book could be interpreted as deserting Thomism for an almost Bergsonian intuitionism which, in practice, exalts French symbolism and even surrealism. There is, however, a strong intellectual ferment among Roman Catholics in the United States, and professed Catholics take part in literary criticism. Father William J. Lynch, for instance, in *Christ and Apollo* (1960), devised "dimensions" of the imagination which include the analogical, the theological, and the Christian in a scheme modeled on the fourfold method of medieval exegesis. Allen Tate, who is the most speculative mind among the Southern Critics, had, even before his conversion to Roman Catholicism (1956), applied Maritain's doctrine of "angelism" to a confrontation between Dante's "symbolic" and Poe's "angelic imagination." [22] In Tate the hatred of science, the nostalgia for an organic society and religious view of the world, is combined with a somewhat paradoxical preoccupation with writers who reflect the dissolution of the tradition, with Poe, Emily Dickinson, T. S. Eliot, W. B. Yeats and Hart Crane, a personal friend whose tragic fate documents for Tate the disintegration of any artist unsupported by a coherent tradition. But neither of these critics is a Thomist: Roman Catholicism rather provides a framework for a radical rejection of naturalism and positivism and a view of poetry as providing not only "complete knowledge" but revelation, absolute truth, even beatific vision.

These three philosophers, Plato, Aristotle and Thomas Aquinas, represent the old world of ideas about art and poetry. The new world arose in the eighteenth century, when neo-classical orthodoxy broke down and empiricism, sensualism, associationism and their variants replaced it, at least in England. I don't want to suggest that anybody today embraces British eighteenth-century empiricism in its original form, but certainly a broad stream of aesthetic and critical thinking descends from there. Utilitarianism and positivism were its immediate heirs early in the nineteenth century, pragmatism followed closely, and behaviorism and logical positivism would hardly deny their ancestry. In its epistemological assumptions much literary scholarship and discussion is still positivistic, relying on a naive precritical conception of "fact" and assuming a simple mechanistic concept of cause in biographical circumstances, literary influences and social and historical backgrounds. The bulk of conventional academic scholarship is confined within this horizon even today. It hardly needs discussion in a survey of criticism. But later forms of positivistic thought have assumed a great importance for the development of recent American criticism. J. C. Ransom, in *The New Criticism* (1941), starts his chapter on I. A. Richards by saying, "The new criticism very nearly began with him"; [23] and certainly a good argument can be put up for the view that the New Criticism *is* a peculiar combination of Richards and T. S. Eliot. But Richards is an Englishman—though he has been at the other Cambridge for thirty years—and most of his writings precede 1945. Neither his only new critical book, *Speculative Instruments* (1955), nor a few scattered articles constitute a substantial change in his point of view.[24] Richards has merely recognized that his earlier trust in the advances of neurology was irrelevant: he still expounds the view of art as a sort of emotional therapy, of the work as a pattern of impulses, of poetry as emotive language, pseudo-statement, or myth. Richards, like Dewey, denies any difference between aesthetic and ordinary experience and upholds a radical psychologism and hedonistic naturalism. Richards' interest in the meaning of meaning, in semantics, has proved his most fruitful contribution to criticism proper. Such a critic as Cleanth Brooks, who does not share Richards' philosophical assumptions, still uses his key-terms: attitudes, tensions, ambiguities and irony.

The main attempt to erect a pragmatic and semantic philosophy of criticism since Richards has been made by Kenneth Burke. He resembles Richards in general orientation, but he tries to combine semantics with Marxism, Freudianism and the philosophy of the "act" as expounded by George Herbert Mead, a follower of Dewey. Most of Burke's literary criticism belongs to his earlier years. Recently he has been engaged in devising a philosophical system which includes *A Grammar of Motives* (1945), *A Rhetoric of Motives* (1955), and *A Rhetoric of Religion* (1961). I cannot pretend to be able to follow Burke's acrobatics between the different activities of man; but I understand enough to see that a literary work is considered a "symbolic act," a personal ritual of purification which sublimates the poet's subconscious drives and affects society by its model "strategy" of "encompassing situations." [25] Literary criticism as judgment is completely lost sight of: no distinction between trash and Shakespeare is possible. The difference between literature and life, work and action is abolished. Burke's charts, hierarchies, pentads, bureaucracies have nothing to do with literature. When in recent years Burke has engaged a specific poetic text, he has produced only fanciful or heavy-footed Marxist or psychoanalytical interpretations. For instance, the "socioanagogic" interpretation of *Venus and Adonis* amounts to reducing this witty and sensual poem to a "concealed social allegory." The goddess represents a noblewoman in love with a commoner: the poem is "social lewdness" expressed in sexual terms.[26] In "Beauty is truth, truth beauty" Burke professes to find a punning scatological sense.[27] The Albatross in the *Ancient Mariner* is "a synecdochic representative of Coleridge's Sarah," and the whole poem "a ritual for the redemption of his drug." [28] Burke has ceased to be a critic, and has set himself up as an oracle of an abstruse philosophy.

The same thing has happened to Richard P. Blackmur, except that we cannot be sure that there is any philosophy behind the oracular manner. Blackmur also began as an ingenious analyst of texts, but in his recent essays he has become vaguer and vaguer, talking teasingly in the cobwebby style of the very latest stage of Henry James. Even a fervent admirer spoke eleven years ago of his "hidden ball play," [29] and the ball has become even more hidden as the years go by. Blackmur has voiced dissatisfaction with the limitations of the New Criticism, but has been unable to formulate a comprehensible theory of his own. He comes nearest to a general statement when he speaks of "language as gesture." Gesture is a term combining symbol and expression, symbol is a "cumulus of meaning" which is achieved by all the devices of poetry: punning, rhyme, meter, tropes.[30] But most of the new essays collected in *Language as Gesture* (1952) and *The Lion and the Honeycomb* (1955) show a disconcerting loss of contact with any text and a random experimentation with many different terms and their contraries: symbol, myth, imagination, behavior, gesture, and even silence and "the grasp of unreason." [31] Blackmur, just because of his subtlety and versatility, illustrates the predicament of much recent American criticism: its involvement in a private world of concepts and terms, a groping toward a general philosophy of life or even theology by the avenue of literature and a distrust of traditional methods which leads to a reliance on purely personal combinations and associations. In some of Blackmur's essays the privacy of terms and feelings has reached a fuzziness and blur so extreme that it seems impossible to keep up any interest in the solution of the metaphorical riddles propounded or to care for the opaque mysteries which are only pointed or hinted at. It seems odd that a basically naturalistic philosophy should lead to such obeisances to the ultimate darkness. But naturalism and agnosticism, pragmatism and irrationalism go together: William James was not averse to the occult.

Another main strand of American criticism descends rather from German idealism: from Kant, Schelling and Hegel. But we must make distinctions on this point. Kantian aesthetics survives only as a most general attitude: as a recognition of the distinction between the true, the good and the beautiful, of the autonomy of art, a basic insight which is lost or rather purposely obliterated by Dewey, Richards, and their followers. Actual Kantianism is alive only in the modernized version of the German philosopher Ernst Cassirer, who died in New York in 1945. But a kind of neo-Kantian expressionism flourishes today. One influential aesthetician, Susanne K. Langer, has developed, in *Feeling and Form* (1953), a theory of art as representational symbolism which draws on Cassirer's *A Philosophy of Symbolic Forms*. Mrs. Langer, though largely concerned with music and the fine arts, formulates a view of poetry as the creation of symbols of feeling, a world of illusory experience, of "semblance," of metaphor and myth. And Eliseo Vivas, in his essays *Creation and Discovery* (1955), is not very far removed from this point of view. "Poetry uniquely reveals a world which is self-sufficient," a world constituted by means of a symbolic process.[32] Imitation and expression theories and all naturalistic explanations are rejected. Literature does not give us knowledge in the narrow sense of the word. It is rather prior "in the order of logic to all knowledge: constitutive of culture." [33] Vivas elaborates a theory of the "intransitivity" of aesthetic experience [34] which seems a restatement of Kant's "disinterested satisfaction," but he is by no means only engaged in a discussion of aesthetic generalities: he has written well of Dreiser, Henry James, Kafka and Dostoevsky and has recently devoted a book to *D. H. Lawrence* (1960) which tries to distinguish between the shoddy ideology and the good art. The neo-Kantianism of Mrs. Langer and Eliseo Vivas is not, of course, unmixed. Vivas describes himself as an "axiological realist," and if I understand him correctly he has approached a position close to that of Allen Tate.[35]

Oddly enough, the most influential philosopher among the German idealists is Schelling, though his actual works are not read and little is available in translation. It is all due to Coleridge, who transmitted, digested and combined his ideas with many other *motifs* of thought. Coleridge's paper "On Poesy and Art" which is being quoted constantly is hardly more than a translation of a speech of Schelling given at the Munich Academy, and central passages in *Biographia Literaria,* on the two imaginations, on the reconciliation of opposites, paraphrase Schelling very closely.[36] We don't have to make up our minds about the degree of Coleridge's dependence on Schelling to recognize that through Coleridge the central conceptions of German romantic criticism entered the American tradition: creative imagination, the reconciliation of opposites, art as an analogue of nature, the poem as an organic whole, symbol in contrast to allegory, and so forth. These ideas filtered down to American critics through many intermediaries; but T. S. Eliot especially quoted the crucial passages from Coleridge, and Richards, in *Coleridge on Imagination* (1934), tried to translate Coleridge into terms acceptable to a naturalist. The Coleridgean point of view is today most clearly represented by Cleanth Brooks. It is a precarious position: how can one reconcile a contextualist view of the work of art with its self-containedness, its organicity with a meaningful relation to reality? Brooks analyzes poems as structures of opposites, tensions, paradoxes and ironies with unparalleled skill. Paradox and irony are terms used by him very broadly. Irony is not the opposite of an overt statement, but "a general term for the kind of qualification which the various elements in a context receive from the context." [37] It indicates the recognition of incongruities, the union of opposites which Brooks finds in all good, that is, complex, "inclusive" poetry. Poetry must be ironic in the sense of being able to withstand ironic contemplation. The method works best when applied to Donne and Shakespeare, Eliot and Yeats, but in *The Well Wrought Urn* (1947), Brooks has shown that even Wordsworth and Tennyson, Gray and Pope yield to this kind of technique. Brooks attacks the "heresy of paraphrase," all attempts to reduce the poem to its prose content, and he has defended a well-defined absolutism: the need of judgment against the flaccid surrender to relativism and historicism. But in a number of essays, largely devoted to poems from the seventeenth century, Brooks has taken special pains to demonstrate that his absolutism of values is not incompatible with a proper regard for history.[38] Brooks joined forces with W. K. Wimsatt in writing *Literary Criticism: A Short History* (1957). Wimsatt, in the Epilogue, formulates a syncretic creed which belies the "argumentative" concern voiced in the Preface. Poetry, he concludes, is a "tensional unity of making with seeing and saying." All three major theories of poetry, the mimetic or Aristotelian, the emotive or Richardsian, and the expressionistic or Crocean must be respected: only metaphor is the pervasive principle of all poetry.[39] In his earlier work, collected as *The Verbal Icon* (1954), Wimsatt was primarily concerned with the objective structure of the work of art. He sharply dismissed the reliance on the intention of the author as "The Intentional Fallacy" and disparaged criticism according to the emotional effect of the work of art as "The Affective Fallacy." He uses the term "Icon" suggested by Charles Morris as an alternative for the poetic symbol. In one brief passage of the Epilogue of *Literary Criticism* Wimsatt suggests a parallel between his literary theory and the dogma of the Incarnation,[40] but it is an error committed by some reviewers who know of Wimsatt's Roman Catholicism to describe his critical position as religious or specifically Thomist. Both Wimsatt and Brooks, in difference from many of their fellow-critics who have Arnoldian hopes for poetry replacing religion, keep a sharp distinction between aesthetics and theology and refuse to accept poetry as a substitute for religion. Quite rightly, they are not included in Richard Foster's *The New Romantics* (1962), which treats Richards, Vivas, Blackmur and Tate as so many disguised Arnoldians. Brooks and Wimsatt have the peculiar merit of holding firmly to the aesthetic fact, of aiming at a theory of literature which will be literary.

On the whole, the relation of modern American criticism to the idealist tradition is puzzling. They draw, like Eliot, Brooks or Wimsatt, concepts and terms from the Romantic idealists, but these have somehow lost their metaphysical moorings in the new context. Benedetto Croce's aesthetic must have had some influence in transmitting idealist conceptions, since it was expounded early by Joel Spingarn under the title of *The New Criticism* (1910). But Spingarn's version of Croce is diluted: it is simply a negation of rhetorical categories, of style, of genres, of the distinction between the arts and, in practice, a defense of impressionism. Richards dismissed Croce haughtily as appealing "exclusively to those unfamiliar with the subject, to the man of letters and the dilettante." [41] Only recently an Italian émigré scholar, G. N. G. Orsini, has written a full exposition of *Benedetto Croce* (1961) which does justice to his intricate system and to the wide range of his criticism. Hegel came to America directly from Germany in the nineteenth century, and a Hegelian movement was still represented early in this century by the commanding figure of Josiah Royce. From England, Hegelian *motifs* came with A. C. Bradley's *Shakespearean Tragedy* and Bernard Bosanquet's writings on aesthetics. A book such as Richard Sewall's *Vision of Tragedy* (1959) expounds the Bradleian view substantially unchanged. Wimsatt adopts the Hegelian term "concrete universal," [42] but Hegel's dialectical method, not to speak of the details of the aesthetics, is entirely unknown in the United States.

The same is true of Marxism, at least in criticism. There was a Marxist movement in the thirties, and Marxist *motifs* and terms occur in the writings of Edmund Wilson and Kenneth Burke. But today no genuine Marxist criticism seems to be written in the United States. This is not, I think, due to McCarthyism or to anti-Soviet bias. It seems rather ignorance or lack of interest in the kind of criticism practiced by Georg Lukács or T. W. Adorno with such great acclaim on the Continent.

Social criticism in the United States is rather anchored in a concern for the American liberal tradition and for an Arnoldian concept of culture. Genuine socialist affiliations are rare: F. O. Matthiessen professed a Christian socialism, though he was, in practice, a defender of Soviet policies even at the take-over of Czechoslovakia.[43] His only book within our purview, the posthumous study of *Dreiser* (1951), elaborately explains Dreiser's "symbolic" joining of the Communist party and sympathetically studies a writer who must appear as the antipode of his early favorite, T. S. Eliot.

But the other social critics are liberal defenders of a free, critical, tolerant society which they want to preserve both against the evils of our vulgar mass-culture and against reaction. Lionel Trilling, in his collections of essays, *The Liberal Imagination* (1950) and *The Opposing Self* (1955), is worried about the gulf between the rationality of his political convictions and the insights of modern literature represented by Proust, Joyce, Eliot, Kafka, Rilke, Gide and others. A man of modern sensibility, with a taste for Henry James and E. M. Forster and a dislike for naturalism, Trilling can only state his problem but not solve it, as he believes that ideas are emotions and that politics permeates literature. He has come to recognize the "fortuitous and the gratuitous nature of art, how it exists beyond the reach of the will alone," [44] an insight buttressed by his understanding of Freud. The essay on Keats [45] shows his growing feelings for selves in opposition to general culture, for the alienation of the artist as a necessary device of his self-realization. A new essay, "The Modern Element in Modern Literature" (1961), raises again, in very personal terms, the question of the bitter hostility of the artist to civilization, puzzling over the American phenomenon that students will take it all as a matter of course and will engage in the "acculturation of the anti-cultural, or the legitimization of the sub-versive." [46]

This seems an admirable phrase for what has happened to all the irrationalistic philosophies of Europe which came to the United States: romantic historicism, Schopenhauer, Nietzsche, Bergson, Freud, Jung, and Existentialism. With few exceptions they became, at least in criticism, assimilated to the prevailing rationalist or pragmatist temper of the nation and certainly were rarely pushed to their irrationalist and often obscurantist extremes.

Much American criticism, especially criticism of American literature, assumes an attitude of romantic historicism. It is ultimately derived from the body of ideas developed by Herder and his successors, who looked for the organicity and continuity of literature as an expression of the national spirit, the folk. In America these ideas were early assimilated to the tradition of the Enlightenment which promoted the Revolution and were adapted to the particular conditions of the new Continent: the classless society, the frontier, etc. Many recent critics are concerned with defining the nature of the American, the Americanism of American literature, often only dimly aware of how much is common to man, modern man, and common to Europe and America. Old ideas about national character are combined today with concepts derived from the prevalent theories about myth or even from existentialist phraseology. Old questions such as that concerning types in the novel or the image of ideal man in literature are thus refurbished to the new taste. There is a whole spate of such books on American literature. Matthiessen's *American Renaissance* (1941), which precedes our era, is the initiating book: it combines an Eliotic concern for language and diction, symbolism and myth, with a fervent belief in the possibilities of democracy in America. The central theme has been approached by different authors from different angles. Charles Feidelson, in *Symbolism and American Literature* (1953), uses Cassirer, Susanne Langer and Whitehead. Literature is a verbal construct with hardly any relation to immediate social reality. Symbolism is conceived so broadly that no distinction between the early romantic Emersonian and Eliotic view can be made. The symbolistic method of Emerson, Melville, Hawthorne, Poe and Whitman is their title to literary independence, the glory of American literature. Marius Bewley, in a book on Hawthorne and Henry James entitled *The Complex Fate* (1952), is preoccupied rather with the question of the American writer in Europe, his fate of "being an American, fighting against a superstitious valuation of Europe." [47] A second book, *The Eccentric Design* (1959), is concerned with the unhappy plight of the American writer, his isolation and rootlessness in his own country. Harry Levin's study of Hawthorne, Poe and Melville, *The Power of Blackness* (1958), revolves around the somber title theme, which is studied sensitively and soberly. Richard W. B. Lewis, in *The American Adam* (1955), pursues the brighter theme of Paradise, innocence and the recovery of youth. In a flamboyant book, *Love and Death in the American Novel* (1960), Leslie A. Fiedler labors a psychoanalytical and social thesis: "the failure of the American writer to deal with adult heterosexual love and his consequent obsession with death, incest and innocent homosexuality." [48] All these writers focus on what has been called the American

Gothic fiction, "nonrealist, sadist and melodramatic—a literature of darkness and the grotesque in a land of light and affirmation." [49] A book devoted to *The Continuity of American Poetry* (1961) by Roy Harvey Pearce uses cultural anthropology and existential terms for what, in the upshot, seems a high-minded romantic nationalism. The proposed aim of a fusion between the "Adamic" and the "mythic" means little more than the old aspiration to reconcile the individual and society, innocence and experience. Pearce's book simply ignores the fact that American poetry is English poetry, or rather, comfortably relegates this basic problem of a history of American poetry to the extraneous field of "comparative literature." Pearce's programmatic essay, "Historicism Once More," [50] illustrates the current confusion between historicism, existentialism, and anthropology. Historicism means little more than a feeling for the actual existence of the past: its presence among us.

In Kantian, Coleridgean and historistic criticism we find "myth" used in the most diverse ways, but "myth" is also the central term for a type of criticism which has its antecedents in Nietzsche, Frazer, the Cambridge Greek scholars and in Carl Jung. "Myth" thus has today so wide a range of meanings that it has become difficult to argue about it with any clarity of reference. The term appeals to many because it allows the discussion of themes and types, topics usually considered part of the "content" and thus not quite respectable to formalist critics. Huck Finn floating down the Mississippi with Jim is a "myth," and so is any truth which is generally accepted by its society. "Myth" can be simply a synonym for ideology. Richard Chase's *Quest for Myth* (1949) identifies all good, sublime literature with myth. The term may assume, however, more specific value for literary study when it refers to a system of archetypes recoverable in rituals and tales or to a scheme of metaphors, symbols and gods created by a poet such as Blake or Yeats. From Jung comes the dangerously occult idea of a collective unconscious, of a racial memory of which all literature is supposed to be a disguised expression. Myth criticism achieves its purpose when it shows the hidden pattern underlying every work of literature: e.g. the descent into hell, the purgatorial stair, the sacrificial death of the God. But one wonders whether anything important for literary criticism has been achieved by such a discovery. All literature is reduced to a few myths. "After decoding each work of art in these terms one is left with a feeling of monotony and futility. Poetry is revelation, but what does it reveal?" [51]

We must, however, make distinctions among the myth-critics. There are the allegorizers, who find the story of redemption all over Shakespeare or discover Swedenborgianism in the novels of Henry James. There are others who have preserved an aesthetic sense and judgment. Francis Fergusson's *Idea of a Theatre* (1949) uses the results of the Cambridge school to consider the theater of all ages, from Sophocles to T. S. Eliot, as ritual. Even *Hamlet* appears as such a ritual performance in conflict with improvisation, while the drama of Racine and much modern theater is criticized as arbitrary invention, as rationalistic contrivance with no proper relation to society. Fergusson has used this approach also for a very personal and somewhat tenuous interpretation of the *Purgatorio* as *Dante's Drama of the Mind* (1953).

Fergusson remains in many ways a man of the theater, of a poetic symbolist theater. Philip Wheelwright, in *The Burning Fountain* (1954), combines, rather, myth interest with semantics. Wheelwright is a student of Heraclitus, Aristotle and Buddhism. Aesthetic contemplation, he tells us, is and should be "but a halfway house to mysticism." [52] Wheelwright is, fortunately, interested in the beginning of the journey: what he calls the "plurisignation" of the poetic work, the ascent from literal meaning through metaphor and symbol to myth. In his new book, *Metaphor and Reality* (1962), the sequence is elaborated, and in the chapters of *The Burning Fountain* devoted to the *Oresteia* and *The Waste Land* thematic and mythic patterns are studied sensitively.

An all-embracing scheme is proposed in Northrop Frye's *Anatomy of Criticism* (1957). Frye began with an excellent interpretation of Blake's private mythology, *Fearful Symmetry* (1947). In *Anatomy of Criticism* literature is conceived as "existing in its own universe, no longer a commentary of life and reality, but containing life and reality in a system of verbal relationships." Literature "imitates the total dream of man," the "order of nature is imitated by a corresponding order of words." Criticism which clarifies this order should succeed in "reforging the links between creation and knowledge, art and science, myth and concept." [53] In practice Frye devises an enormously intricate scheme of modes, symbols, myths and genres for which, however, the Jungian archetype is the basic assumption. Frye is not interested in causal explanation and rejects the collective unconscious as an unnecessary hypothesis. What concerns him is mostly a new theory of genres, of which there are four: comedy, romance, tragedy and satire; and these correspond to the four seasons: spring, summer, autumn, and winter, the rhythm of nature. The method leads to the most surprising confrontations: thus, in comedy the myth of spring is recapitulated, and such completely different works as *Winter's Tale, Bleak House, Pamela* and *The Rape of the Lock* are interpreted as variants of the Proserpine myth. All literature is finally part of the *Urmythos*. In Frye all distinctions of artistic value disappear: the simplest folk-tale will fit just as well as *Hamlet*. In a "Polemical Introduction" Frye has excluded value judgment from his concept of criticism, as criticism "should show a steady advance toward undiscriminating catholicity." [54] But Frye, in practice, is a sensitive reader and ingenious theorist who imposes the fearful symmetry of his system by his power of discrimination and combination. One cannot help thinking that criticism, in Frye, has overreached itself and that a more modest concept of its aim would be wiser. Frye quotes, with apparent approval, Mallarmé's saying, "Tout, au monde, existe pour aboutir à un livre," [55] but Frye's book is, we know all the time, his own *Anatomy*. The trouble with his speculations is that they are completely uncontrollable. On the analogy of the Freudian dream-interpretation, they allow all manner of substitutions, condensations and identifications. As Frye admits, "The literary universe is a universe in which everything is potentially identical with everything else." [56]

This method is also the bane of Freudian criticism which has "scientific" pretensions and a rationalistic philosophical basis. Freudian criticism, much more than Jungian criticism, is frighteningly obtuse to the text and dreary in its search for sexual symbolism. In the books of Arthur Wormhoudt, writing is spilling of mother's milk. Domes, mountains, pyramids, cups, and even trees and birds are all breast symbols.[57] In Charles Neider's book on Kafka, *The Frozen Sea* (1948), every protuberance and opening is read as male or female. But such total Freudians exist only on the fringes of literary criticism. No strictly Freudian critic has won any reputation. Freudian *motifs* and insights have provided tools for other critics, who see the limitations of the method but use it as a technique of reading below the surface, as an unmasking. Freudian concepts or preconceptions organize many literary biographies and psychological interpretations. Even in this connection, however, Lionel Trilling, who praises Freud for having done "more for our understanding of art than any other writer since Aristotle," [58] has stated convincingly the differences between art and neurosis, artistic creation and day-dreaming.

Bergsonism is another European philosophy which has had important bearings on American criticism. I would class John Crowe Ransom, the supposed Father of the New Criticism, as, at least originally, a Bergsonian. Ransom studied Greats at Oxford and knows much about Kant, Hegel, and Croce. Allen Tate, in an illuminating aside, has protested against the view that Ransom taught his disciples (Tate, R. P. Warren, Cleanth Brooks) the knowledge of good and evil. Rather, he taught them "Kantian aesthetics and a philosophy of dualism, tinged with Christian theology, but ultimately derived from the Nicomachean ethics." [59] But surely Bergson made the greatest impression on the early Ransom: Ransom's criticism of abstraction, his distinction between structure and the "irrelevant" texture of a poem, his attack on Platonic poetry in favor of a poetry of things, is Bergsonian (though some of it may come through T. E. Hulme and Imagism). After World War II, however, Ransom tried different approaches; at one time, for instance, he adopted a Freudian analogy for his distinction between structure and texture: the poem as structure, as thought-work, as prose-value belongs to the *ego;* the latent or suspected content, the texture, belongs to the *id.*[60] But Ransom seems later to have dropped these ideas and in his most recent writings has returned to his more rational defense of the concrete, of texture, of things and nature. He clings to a dualism of form and content and keeps his theory of poetry resolutely secular. The early attempt to set up a God with Thunder seems abandoned. In his rejection of organistic aesthetics Ransom preserves a very individual and isolated position in American criticism.

A new *motif* of American criticism in recent years is Existentialism. I am not sure whether we can speak of a genuinely existential criticism. A concrete, knowing relation to either Heidegger or Sartre does not seem to exist. Existential criticism is a vocabulary, a mood, an attitude, or it should be described rather as "phenomenology," as the attempt to reconstruct the author's "consciousness," his relation to time and space, nature and society in the manner which has been demonstrated so successfully by recent French critics such as Georges Poulet and Jean-Pierre Richard. Geoffrey Hartman, in his *Unmediated Vision* (1954), studies poems by Wordsworth, Hopkins, Valéry and Rilke in order to trace the dialectic of perception and consciousness, the process of "how an

image before the eye becomes an idea in the mind." [61] In J. Hillis Miller's
Charles Dickens: The World of his Novels (1959) a "preexistent psychological
condition" of the writer is assumed by which he "apprehends and in some
measure creates himself." [62] The interior landscape, the search for identity are
the leading themes of an analysis of Dickens' fictional world.

In R. W. B. Lewis' *Picaresque Saint* (1959) the existential theme, the sense
of nothingness, is shown to be transcended, in several modern novelists, by an
"agonized dedication to life." [63] The type of the saintly rogue seems often
forced on the authors selected: Moravia, Camus, Silone, Faulkner and Graham
Greene. Lewis' motivation is really religious and political: optimistic in its conclusions. On the other hand, Ihab Hassan's *Radical Innocence: Studies in the
Contemporary American Novel* (1962) looks only for anti-heroes, victims,
pariahs. "They all share a vision of absurdity despite their radical apprehension
of the Self." Hassan solemnly discusses such an inconsequential romp as Tru-
man Capote's *Breakfast at Tiffany's* and returns again to the question of Americanism. The book concludes with a dusty answer: "Everyone must rediscover
America for himself—alone." [64] The theme of loneliness and despair informs
also Murray Krieger's *The Tragic Vision* (1960). There the protagonist of
tragedy is taken deliberately out of the context of tragedy as structure. The
tragic hero (or rather "visionary") is the man of the "sickness unto death," of
modern nihilism. Even Dostoevsky's Idiot is assimilated to this concept, and
there is less trouble with the heroes of Kafka, Camus, Thomas Mann and
Melville. Krieger, who had before written an acute analysis of the New
Criticism, *The New Apologists for Poetry* (1956), now advocates "thematics"
as a supplement to formal criticism. A new dualism of form and content is
adapted to a metaphysical dualism, a "vision of a final cosmic disharmony."
Literature becomes the "only form of existential philosophy": [65] philosophizing
in existential terms is actually impossible, he asserts. You can convey the
existential vision only in fictional terms. But one may ask how it can be conveyed, then, in terms of criticism? The irrationalistic argument fits existential
criticism as well as philosophy: only a mood, an attitude remains.

If we look back at this panorama, or rather listen to the confusion of tongues
in the new Tower of Babel, we cannot be surprised at a growing feeling of
bewilderment and incomprehension. A facile resignation, a crude anti-intellectualism and anti-criticism is in the air. It can be frankly and grossly Philistine;
it can be a blithe defense of amateurism, impressionism, enthusiasm; it can be
the skepticism and historical relativism of the scholar who sees critical theories
as so many rationalizations for a transient sensibility; or it can be simply the
disgust of poets and writers with the critics' ubiquity and pretentiousness.
Randall Jarrell, in *Poetry and the Age* (1955), complained that "Criticism, which
began by humbly and anomalously existing for the work of art, and was in part
a mere by-product of philosophy and rhetoric, has by now become, for a good
many people, almost what the work of art exists for." [66] Karl Shapiro, in a crude
attack on what he considers the obnoxious clique of Eliot and Pound, called
In Defense of Ignorance (1960), wants the critic to have "no system" and to
leave philosophy alone. He observes that "literary criticism hardly exists in our

time; what we have is culture criticism or theology, ill concealed. The critic today uses literature only as a vehicle for ideas; he has bigger fish to fry than poets." [67] There is some justice in this observation. At every point recent criticism slides over into psychology, sociology, philosophy and theology. Only those who adhere to either the German idealist tradition, in the Kantian or Coleridgean version, or those who rediscover Aristotle, still keep a grasp on the nature of art, and recognize the necessity of an aesthetic and the ideal of a study of literature as literature. But they are today a small minority divided in itself. "Vision" is momentarily the fashionable key-term, as "myth" was a little while ago, and "ambiguity" and "irony" even earlier. I have no sympathy with amateurism and anti-intellectualism, as I am concerned with the theory of literature, with the development of a method or even methodology adequate to deal with literature and its values. I can understand that criticism needs constantly to draw on neighboring disciplines and needs the insights of psychology, sociology, philosophy and theology. But I can also sympathize with a protest against the unlimited expansion of criticism and the abandonment of its central concern: the art of literature. It does seem to me an oddity of our time that "art" and "aesthetic" are sometimes considered to be outside of reality, life and humanity: as if art were not part of life and did not give life coherence and meaning. But recent criticism—and not only criticism in America—looks constantly elsewhere, wants to become sociology, politics, philosophy, theology and even mystical illumination. If we interpret philosophy in the wide sense, our title has announced a tautology or equation. Literary criticism has *become* philosophy. I wish, however, that criticism may preserve its original concern: the interpretation of literature as distinct from other activities of man. In short I hope our phrase will remain: "Philosophy *and* literary criticism."

NOTES

1. H. W. Garrod, *Poetry and the Criticism of Life* (Oxford, 1931), pp. 156–157.

2. Cf. Benedetto Croce, "La critica letteraria come filosofia," *Nuovi Saggi di estetica* (Bari, 1919).

3. *Critics and Criticism*, ed. R. S. Crane (Chicago, 1952), p. 547. Cf. Philip Blair Rice, *On the Knowledge of Good and Evil* (New York, 1955), p. 217: "To the extent that the critic has a consistent point of view, he is tacitly presupposing an aesthetic theory, whether he acknowledges the fact or not."

4. R. W. B. Lewis, "Casella as Critic: A Note on R. P. Blackmur," *Kenyon Review*, XIII (1951), 470, 473–474.

5. *Yale Review*, LI (1961), 102–118 and *Lexikon der Weltliteratur im 20. Jahrhundert*, Vol. II (Freiburg, 1961), 178–261.

6. "Psychical Distance as a Fact in Art and an Aesthetic Principle," *Aesthetics*, ed. E. M. Wilkinson (London, 1957), p. 95.

7. Coleridge, *Table Talk* (London, 1851), p. 100. A. N. Whitehead, *Process and Reality* (New York, 1929), p. 63.

8. "Poetry, Morality and Criticism," *Critique of Humanism*, ed. C. H. Grattan (New York, 1930).

9. *In Defense of Reason* (Denver, 1947), pp. 385–387, 568–569; *The Function of Criticism* (Denver, 1957), pp. 11–13, 75.

10. *Function*, pp. 157ff.

11. *Essays in Criticism*, XII (1962), 79.

12. *Function*, p. 139.

13. *In Defense of Reason*, pp. 105, 490, 568.

14. *Function*, pp. 74, 63ff., 49ff.

15. *Aristotle's Poetics*, Introduction by Francis Fergusson (New York, 1961), p. 40.

16. *Critics and Criticism*, pp. 9, 12–13, 17.

17. *The Languages of Criticism and the Structure of Poetry* (Toronto, 1953), p. 237.

18. Detroit, 1961, p. 9.

19. *Critics and Criticism*, pp. 590ff.

20. *This Great Stage* (Baton Rouge, 1948); *The Magic in the Web* (Lexington, Ky., 1956).

21. "The Heresy of Plot," *English Institute Essays 1951* (New York, 1952), p. 59.

22. Essays in *The Forlorn Demon* (Chicago, 1953).

23. Norfolk, Conn., 1941, p. 3.

24. See "Emotive Language Still," *Yale Review*, 1949, "Poetic Process and Literary Analysis," *Style in Language*, ed. Thomas A. Sebeok (New York, 1960), and "The Future of Poetry," *The Screens and Other Poems* (New York, 1960).

25. *The Philosophy of Literary Form* (Baton Rouge, 1941), p. 1.

26. *A Rhetoric of Motives* (New York, 1955), pp. 212–221.

27. *Ibid.*, p. 204.

28. *The Philosophy of Literary Form*, pp. 72, 96.

29. R. B. W. Lewis, "Casella as Critic," 463.

30. *Language as Gesture* (New York, 1952), p. 16.

31. See "The Language of Silence," *Sewanee Review*, LXIII (1955), 382–404, and "The Great Grasp of Unreason," *Hudson Review*, IX (1956–7), 488–503.

32. New York, 1955, pp. 73–4.

33. *Ibid.*, p. 127.

34. See Appendix to *D. H. Lawrence: The Failure and The Triumph of Art* (Evanston, Ill., 1960).

35. See the fervid tribute to Allen Tate: "Mi ritrovai per una selva oscura," *Sewanee Review*, LXVII (1959), 560–566.

36. See my *History of Modern Criticism* (New Haven, 1955), Vol. II, 152ff.

37. *The Well Wrought Urn* (New York, 1947), p. 191.

38. E.g., "Literary Criticism," *English Institute Essays 1946* (New York, 1947). "The Quick and the Dead," *The Humanities*, ed. Julian Harris (Madison, Wis., 1950).

39. New York, 1957, pp. 749, 750, 755.

40. *Ibid.*, p. 746.

41. *The Principles of Literary Criticism* (London, 1924), p. 255n.

42. See "The Concrete Universal," *The Verbal Icon* (Lexington, Ky., 1954), pp. 69–83.

43. Cf. *From the Heart of Europe* (New York, 1948), esp. pp. 142ff.

44. *The Liberal Imagination* (New York, 1950), p. 280.

45. In *The Opposing Self* (New York, 1955).

46. *Partisan Review*, XXVIII (1961), 31.

47. A quotation from Henry James's letter to Charles Eliot Norton (February 4, 1872), cited in *The Letters of Henry James*, Vol. I (New York, 1920), 13. I am grateful to Professor Leon Edel for this reference.

48. New York, 1960, p. xi.

49. *Ibid.*, p. xxiv.

50. *Kenyon Review*, XX (1958), 554–591.

51. Austin Warren in Wellek and Warren, *Theory of Literature* (New York, 1949), p. 217.

52. Bloomington, Indiana, 1954, p. 61.

53. Princeton, N. J., 1957, pp. 118, 119, 122, 354.

54. *Ibid.*, p. 25.

55. *Ibid.*, p. 122.

56. *Ibid.*, p. 124.

57. *The Demon Lover* (New York, 1949), pp. 6, 13. *The Muse at Length* (New York, 1953). *Hamlet's Mouse Trap* (New York, 1956).

58. *Liberal Imagination*, p. 161.

59. "A Southern Mode of the Imagination," *A Carleton Miscellany*, I (1960), 12.

60. "Poetry: The Final Cause," *Kenyon Review*, IX (1947), 654.

61. New Haven, 1954, p. 123.

62. Cambridge, Mass., p. viii.

63. Philadelphia, 1959, p. 27.

64. Princeton, 1962, pp. 332, 336.

65. New York, 1960, pp. 245, 247.

66. "The Age of Criticism," *Poetry and the Age* (New York, 1953); (Vintage Book ed., 1955), p. 84.

67. New York, 1960, p. 8.

I H A B   H A S S A N

Beyond a Theory of Literature:
Intimations of Apocalypse?

I BEGIN WITH AN ASSUMPTION: that literature defines our concepts of criticism or else it defies them, and that life constantly challenges the pieties of both art and thought. What I shall attempt here, then, could not be considered an authoritative review of postwar criticism. It should be understood, rather, as a partial statement on the gathering mood of American criticism, an intimation of a trend which the facts of literary history in the past two decades (colored inevitably by my own sense of fact) may help to clarify.

The admission that I neither hold nor accept a definitive view of criticism should not be too shocking. In England, where the empiric temper prevails in the name of common sense or urbanity, and even in France, where questions of methodology yield to a lively concern with new writing, such an admission would seem fairly innocuous. It is otherwise in America. Among us, the notion that criticism must become a rigorous, quasi-scientific activity in order to justify its name still finds wide support. Not long ago—or is it really ages past?—most students of literature, myself included, recognized the elegance of René Wellek's formulation of the destiny of criticism: "the interpretation of literature as distinct from other activities of man."[1] Coming from Professor Wellek, the emphasis on interpretation rather than on literary theory seemed unduly self-effacing. Be that as it may, the formula appealed then to the common rage for order, and seemed also to aver the dignity of the humanities on terms that the age demanded. With the years, however, the formula seems, to me at least, to have lost in elegance as it has gained in naïveté. The breed of technicians it has unwittingly sanctioned may have found a truer consummation of their hopes in the laboratories of Oak Ridge. Literature as a distinct activity of man? Criticism as a distinct response to a distinct activity of man? What is man that we should be so little mindful of him, so arbitrary with the complexities of his mind? From Surrealism to Absurdism, literature itself suggests that a distinct aesthetic response may be defined only at the risk of deadly discrimination.

Yet my object is not to engage in polemics. The point can be stated with some equanimity: a new breed of American critics are anxious to assert themselves against the rigors and pieties they have inherited. Their mood is restless, eclectic, speculative; sometimes, it is even apocalyptic. Those who feel out of sympathy with them may wish to apply different epithets: romantic, primitivist, existential, amateurish, or plain anti-intellectual. (The usefulness of these tags, dispensed usually with contumely, is as doubtful as their accuracy.) Others, however, may recognize the creative possibilities of this new mood, troubled, vague, or disruptive as it may seem.

Evidence of the new mood is various though one senses behind it the enduring search for wholeness and vitality in the literary response. One senses, too, the paradoxical desire to appropriate literature to the dream life of men, and then again to implicate it in the widest sphere of their daily actions. Is not the secret task, for poet and critic alike, to participate in that magic process whereby the word is turned into flesh?

The critic therefore feels the need for commitment; he wants to testify. And what is to prevent him? The encounter with an authentic work of art is a bruising experience, full of strange knowledge and hidden pleasure, of the kind we usually spend a life-time resisting. The critic knows that he himself is on trial, and that the act of literary criticism is above all an act of self-judgment. Since his business is to speak of literature, speech in his case must ultimately take the form of self-revelation. But the need for self-revelation is not only a private or existential need. It is also a social function of the critic. "Is art always an outrage—must it by its very nature be an outrage?" Durrell asks.[2] The question haunts the critic even more than it does the oafish censors of our time. For should the critic insist on his dubious right to privacy or detachment, his deepest knowledge of literature would remain locked, a private outrage, an inner wound. Yet literature, we know, acts through language; it is a communal call, there where words and experience are one, as it is solitary subversion, where words begin to fail. In the act of testimony, therefore, the critic admits the *relevance* of the buried power of literature; he offers himself to the harsh task of mediating between society and vision, culture and anarchy. Only thus can he give to outrage wider reference, give it a meaning beyond itself. There is the risk, of course, that such mediation may rob both culture and outrage of their particular force. Yet from that loss a new life in history may be gained, a new consciousness of self and society may be born. This is precisely the gain, implicit in the discomforts of critical commitment, which Lionel Trilling, in his otherwise subtle essay, "On the Modern Element in Modern Literature," seems to ignore.[3]

Commitment, however, is but a single impulse of the new critical attitude; it simply prepares the ground for dialogue. Another impulse may be defined as the refusal wholly to objectify the work of literature. The art work, of course, has been long considered as an *object,* an object for dissection or knowledge, idolatry or classification. Yet the encounter between critic and work is neither entirely objective nor purely aesthetic; it may be a "dialogue" of the kind

Martin Buber has proposed. In Buber's sense, the work of art resists identifica-
tion with the insensible It; for the work demands answer and response, and it
requires a meeting. Is it then so perverse to ask the critic, whether he subscribes
to Buber's theology or not, that he "turn toward" the work and confess with
Buber, "in each instance a word demanding an answer has happened to me"?[4]
Nothing is mystical in this statement, nothing inimical to the spirit of poetry.
The statement, in fact, points to some rather mundane questions which Walter
J. Ong, theologian of another faith, happily raises. In his original essay, "The
Jinnee in the Well-Wrought Urn," Father Ong states: "Creative activity is
often . . . powered by the drive to accomplish, in terms of the production of an
object of art, an adjustment or readjustment in certain obscure relationships
with other persons." What does this mean? Quite obviously, it means that
behind every work of art lurks and strains a human being; less obviously, perhaps, it means that the voice of the human creator, raging heart and feet of
clay, is not entirely silenced in his art. The jinnee cannot be exorcised from
the urn it inhabits, however shapely the latter may prove; the artifact still
comes to life with voices unknown. And indeed this is what we, as readers,
require. Once again, Father Ong sees the point clearly: "as a matter of full,
serious, protracted contemplation and love, it is unbearable for a man or woman
to be faced with anything less than a person. . . ."[5] This is precisely what critics,
compelled by the difficult reciprocities of love, may now want to face: not an
object but a presence mediated cunningly, incomprehensibly, by language. Such
a presence is not simply human. It is the presence, moving and participating in
reality, which Owen Barfield, in *Saving the Appearances,* has shown us to
lie at the heart of the symbolic process. In facing such a presence, critics may
hope to recover the primal connection with a universe mediated increasingly
by abstractions. But they may also hope to recover something more modest: a
spontaneity of judgment which reaches outward, reaches beyond itself. Holden
Caulfield, we recall, was moved to call on an author whose work he had much
enjoyed. In such naïveté there may be a parable for critics as well as an occasion
for derision.

   If some postwar critics are loth to consider the literary work merely as an
object, they are equally reluctant to believe that contemplation is the sole reaction to it. Beyond testimony, beyond participation or dialogue, the critic now
wishes to entertain the possibility that *action* may be a legitimate response to
art. By this, of course, I do not mean that he rushes to the barricades after
reading *The Conquerors,* or that he develops tuberculosis after reading *The
Magic Mountain.* I mean that the experience of a literary work does not leave
him unchanged. To the extent that he is altered in the recesses of his imagination, indeed of his being, to that extent he must act differently in daily life.
For if literature is both cognitive and experiential, as we have been so often
told, then how can new knowledge but prompt new action? We may have
accepted the Thomist notion of *stasis* in art much too uncritically. The counter-
statement is boldly presented in Sartre's essay, "Qu'est Ce Que la Littérature?"
"Parler c'est agir:" Sartre claims, "toute chose qu'on nomme n'est déjà plus tout
à fait la même, elle a perdu son innocence." Sartre continues: "L'œuvre d'art est

valeur parce qu'elle est appel."⁶ The appeal, above all, is to that act of self-definition which the work persuades its reader to perform, an act of definition and also of freedom. For in a sense, the work itself is "created" by the freedom of the reader to give it a concrete and, ultimately, personal meaning. The work, that is, finally enters the total existence of a man, not simply his dream life or aesthetic consciousness; and in doing so, it becomes subject to the total judgment of human passions. This is precisely what an existential writer of a different breed, Camus, meant when he wrote, "To create today is to create dangerously. Any publication is an act, and that act exposes one to the passions of an age that forgives nothing. . . ."⁷ But if the writer must create dangerously these days, the critic cannot afford to criticize timorously. Dangerous criticism assumes that final and somewhat frightening responsibility which some critics naturally resist; namely, the willing suspension of aesthetic judgment in the interests of right action.

I quite realize the enormity of this assertion. For one thing, it brings the critic dangerously close to the posture of the censor—the commissar, the propaganda helot, the prurient chief of police—who requires that every work of art display its social credentials or else stand convicted. No doubt, the redemption of man is a more momentous task than the creation of beauty, and virtue and goodness are not to be scoffed at. Yet redemption, one suspects, does not lie in the grasp of regulators; nor does virtue depend on the degradation of art by power. How, then, can the critic hope to transcend the aesthetic domain of literature without seeming to capitulate to dogma or authority, without seeming to endorse a vulgar or repressive utilitarianism?

There are many answers to this question, though all are equally provisional, for in this as in other literary matters, tact not theory comes to our aid. We can begin, however, by making two observations. First, serious literature offers great resistance to political expediency; other forms of propaganda are far more effective. The basic affinity of modern literature particularly is with vision and outrage. By vision, I mean neither doctrine nor even revelation, but simply a concrete projection of the imagination into the conduct of life. Henry Miller has such an idea in mind when he says: "The role which the artist plays in society is to revive the primitive, anarchic instincts which have been sacrificed for the illusion of living in comfort"; or when he says again: "I do not call poets those who make verses, rhymed or unrhymed. I call that man poet who is capable of profoundly altering the world."⁸ Both these statements reveal the artist's conception of himself as visionary actor; both attest to his hope that prophecy may find its incarnation, beyond language, in action. Emboldened by such statements—and they are by no means restricted to Miller—the critic may feel justified in participating in the action that the work initiates. This is to say that the critic becomes himself part of the devious process by which a writer's vision penetrates culture. The character of this devious process is closer to the character of pedagogy than of social reform. This leads me to the second observation. Since the process is indeed devious, subject to all the ambiguities of modern culture, the critic cannot really maintain a purely pragmatic, a purely political view of literature. This is salutary for the activist critic who finds in the visionary or subversive power of literature an inner check on his propensity for dogma, his penchant for expediency.

This critical ideal is not nearly as pretentious as it may sound; nor does it always require the critic to make his home in the midst of chaos. It may require him, however, to heed certain *thematic* questions which were once considered beneath notice. A number of critical works of the last decade reflect this emergent concern. In *The Tragic Vision,* for instance, Murray Krieger pertinently asks, "But how, if we limit ourselves to technical literary definitions, can we find for the tragic any meaning beyond that of Aristotle? The answer is, by moving from formalistic aesthetics to what I would term 'thematics.' " Krieger's analysis of that term cannot be summarized easily, but the implications of his method are stated succinctly enough. He concludes thus: "All. of which is perhaps to say only that a literary theory must be adequate to the literary experiences for which it is to account and that we trust our way of experiencing literature only as it is adequate to the life out there, which cries for a way of being organized literarily that will yet leave it preserved intact."[9] If the insistence on "the life out there" does not necessarily force the critic into a study of "thematics," it does persuade him to dwell on precisely those formal matters that invoke the larger aspects of reality and may even engage religious thought. Thus the essays of James E. Miller, Jr., Karl Shapiro, and Bernice Slote, in *Start With the Sun,* explore the relation of Dionysian poetry to cosmic consciousness, mystery, and apocalypse. "Start with the sun:" Miss Slote ends, taking her cue from a noble phrase of Lawrence, "Perhaps then we may be absolved from the poetry of mirrors."[10] Parallel explorations of fiction lead R. W. B. Lewis, in his fine study, *The Picaresque Saint,* to distinguish between the generation of Proust, Joyce, and Mann, in whose world the aesthetic experience was supreme, and the generation of Silone, Faulkner, Camus, and Greene, in whose world "the chief experience has been the discovery of what it means to be a human being and to be alive." Lewis continues: "Criticism, examining this world, is drawn to the more radically human considerations of life and death, and of the aspiring, sinful nature of man."[11]

Perhaps I have spoken long enough of certain interests of postwar criticism, though I feel I have spoken of them only tangentially. If one were to search for the theoretical basis of these interests—a task which I must leave to more philosophical critics—one might be inclined to develop a view of literature that does not put the idea of form as its center. By this I do not simply mean a redefinition of the concept of form so that it may account, say, for the plays of Beckett or the novels of Burroughs. I would plead for a more radical view. From Kant to Cassirer, from Coleridge to Croce and down to the New Critics, the idea of organic form has been a touchstone of value and a cornerstone of theory in literary study. We assume, and indeed we believe, that the imagination incarnates itself only as an aesthetic order, and that such an order is available to the analytic mind. We believe more: that aesthetic order defines the deepest pleasures of literature and conveys its enduring attractions. I am not at all secure in these beliefs. Indeed, I am willing to take the devil's part and entertain the notion that "structure" is not always present or explicable in literary works; and that where it reveals itself, it is not always worth the attention we give it. Such works as *Hamlet* and *Don Quixote* are not diminished by the discovery that their form, whatever it may be, is less organic than we expect the form of great works to be. Even that supreme artifact of our century, that total structure of symbols, puns, and cross-references, that city of words full of secret alleys and connecting catacombs, even Joyce's *Ulysses,* may prove to the keen, fresh eye of a critic more of a labyrinth, dead ends and ways without issue, than Dublin itself which encloses the nightmare of history. This is precisely what Robert Martin Adams concludes in his fascinating study, *Surface and Symbol.* Adams inspects minutely the wealth of details in the novel, and finds that many of them serve to blur or confuse rather than to sustain patterns: "The close reading of *Ulysses* thus reveals that the meaningless is deeply interwoven with the meaningful in the texture of the novel. . . . It is a book and an antibook, a work of art particularly receptive to accident. It builds to acute and poignant states of consciousness, yet its larger ambition seems to be to put aside consciousness as a painful burden."[12] Nothing catastrophic to the future of criticism is presaged by this statement. Quite the contrary: criticism may derive new vitality from some attention to the unstructured and even random element in literature. For is not form, after all, best conceived as a mode of awareness, a function of cognition, a question, that is, of epistemology rather than ontology? Its objective reality is qualified by the overpowering reality of human *need.* In the end, we perceive what we need to perceive, and our sense of pattern as of relation is conditioned by our deeper sense of relevance. This is why the aesthetic of the future will have to reckon with Freud, Nietzsche, and even Kierkegaard, who have given us, more than Marx himself, compelling economies of human needs.[13]

I could not persist in suggesting the theoretical implications of postwar criticisms without falling into the trap which I have myself described. We do not always need a theoretical argument to bring forth a new critical attitude; we only need good critics. But perhaps we need, more than anything else, to regard literature in a more oblique fashion, regard it even in the slanting light of its own absurdity. We might then see that the theoretical solemnity of modern criticism ignores the self-destructive element of literature, its need for self-annulment. What Camus said of his own work applies, in various ways, to all literature: the act of creation is akin to chance and disorder, to which it comes through diversity, and it constantly meets with futility. "Creating or not creating changes nothing," Camus writes. "The absurd creator does not prize his work. He could repudiate it." And again: "The absurd work illustrates thought's renouncing of its prestige and its resignation to being no more than the intelligence that works up appearances and covers with images what has no reason. If the world were clear, art would not exist."[14] Perhaps the function of literature, after all, is not to clarify the world but to help create a world in which literature becomes superfluous. And perhaps the function of criticism, as I shall argue later, is to attain to the difficult wisdom of perceiving how literature is finally, and *only* finally, inconsequential.[15]

The foregoing remarks limn certain trends in postwar criticism; they are not intended to define a school or movement. Still, I feel it wise to anticipate some objections before concluding this mock survey.

It may be argued, for instance, that many of the attitudes I have described are not so novel as I make them out to be. Richards' emotive theories, Burke's concept of action, Leavis' cultural vitalism, Trilling's depth-view of manners and imagination, Blackmur's metaphors of silence in literature, and above all, Herbert Read's sympathy for the anarchic spirit, certainly open the way to the speculations of younger critics. The latter, however, still distinguish themselves by a certain quality of passion, a generosity toward the perversities of spirit, and a sense of crisis in man's fate. Two recent books of criticism, R. W. B. Lewis' *The American Adam* and Leslie Fiedler's *Love and Death in the American Novel,* seem quite disparate in tone and method; yet both, I think, stand in this respect closer to Lawrence's seminal work, *Studies in Classic American Literature,* than to Matthiessen's *American Renaissance.*

Then again, it might be argued that my use of the terms, "form" and "theory," appears tendentious; that, ideally speaking, neither of these terms excludes larger commitments; and that, in any case, there are so many concepts of "form" and "structure" in modern criticism as to make a general condemnation of them irresponsible. I should like to think that there are more wicked uses of irresponsibility than in the criticism of criticism. What an ideal formalist theory may contribute to our appreciation of literature is not in dispute; what it has contributed in the past by way of practical criticism is also very considerable. Still, do we not all sense the growing inertness of the Spirit of criticism beneath the weight of the Letter? One sometimes feels that in another decade or two, the task of criticism may be safely performed by some lively computing machine which, blessed with total recall, would never misquote as some critics are reputed to do.

I speak, of course, hyperbolically. Perhaps I can make the point clearer, and sharpen thereby the distinction between two generations of critics, by referring to two eminent theoreticians of literature. Both René Wellek and Northrop Frye are men of vast erudition; both have shaped the course of literary studies in America. This, I think, is entirely as it should be; the timely authority of such works as Wellek and Warren's *Theory of Literature* or Frye's *Anatomy of Criticism* deserves nothing less. Yet at the risk of seeming ungracious, it is to their later, and perhaps lesser, works that I wish to refer. After all, the question still remains: what lies beyond formalist theory?

In *Concepts of Criticism,* Professor Wellek shows himself to be somewhat out of love with the directions of contemporary criticism. "It seems to me that in spite of the basic truth of the insight of organicism, the unity of content and form, we have arrived today at something like a deadend," he states.[16] His dissatisfaction, however, is of short duration. Professor Wellek sees the way out in the doctrine of "structuralism," evolved by the Prague Linguistic Circle— alas, now defunct! "Such a concept of the literary work of art avoids two pitfalls," Professor Wellek hopes, "the extreme of organicism which leads to a lumpish totality in which discrimination becomes impossible, and the opposite danger of atomistic fragmentation."[17] The way out, as it turns out, comes very close to the ancient ideal of the golden mean. This is judicious. But is it really judiciousness which prompts him in two later chapters, "Philosophy and Postwar American Criticism" and "Main Trends of Twentieth-Century Criticism," to deride all recent criticism? The brilliant and inventive concern with American literature in the last two decades is deplored as an example of "romantic historicism," and mythic and existential criticism are condemned as an instance of "the irrationalistic philosophies of Europe" adapted to the pragmatic temper of the United States.[18] Professor Wellek sadly concludes: "Only those who adhere to either the German idealist tradition, in the Kantian or Coleridgean version, or those who rediscover Aristotle, still keep a grasp on the nature of art and recognize the necessity of an aesthetic and the ideal of a study of literature as literature."[19] Having defined literature in formalist terms, it is no wonder that Professor Wellek *still* believes formalist theory to be the most rewarding view of literature. Thus is the rigor of tautology achieved.

The Well-Tempered Critic, which is not wrought in the massive architectural manner of Professor Frye's earlier work, is too urbane to be tautological. Its urbanity expresses a fine subtlety of mind in the final chapter of the book, and the subtlety itself disguises a somewhat chilly view of literature. Professor Frye acknowledges the distinction between the classic and romantic tempers in criticism, and proceeds to discover the correlatives of each. The classic temper, he informs us, is aesthetic, the romantic is psychological; the former views art as artifact, the latter as expression; the one derives from Aristotle, the other from Longinus. I do not quarrel with these distinctions, particularly when categorical distinctions make the very basis of the geometric edifices Professor Frye likes to erect. "The first step to take here," he argues, "is to realize that just as a poem implies a distinction between the poet as man and the poet as verbal craftsman, so the response to a poem implies a corresponding distinction in the critic."[20] For both Northrop Frye and René Wellek, we see, the critical act rests on the *separation* of certain human faculties from the continuum of felt life. There are few critics willing to speak professionally for the ancient female principle, acceptance and fusion, and the enveloping wholeness of things, few willing to speak for the fourfold vision of Blake. Yet carried far enough, distinctions become the source of the mind's alienation, the Cartesian madness of the West.

Again, Professor Frye views criticism not as the experience of literature but, more discretely, as an area of knowledge. This leads him to the hard-boiled conclusion, so repugnant to visionary educators, that "the values we want the student to acquire from us cannot be taught: only knowledge of literature can be taught."[21] Can knowledge be dissociated from value, and criticism forego its aspiration to wisdom? Apparently so. "The fundamental act of criticism is a disinterested response to a work of literature in which all one's beliefs, engagements, commitments, prejudices, stampedings of pity and terror, are ordered to be quiet," he continues.[22] Ordered to be quiet! Who listens, then, and who speaks instead? The imagination never demanded such frozen void, nor do the supreme fictions of the mind reject the earth they transmute. We have seen criticism gaze long enough on the world with the quiet eyes of Apollo. Shall we ever see it partake again of the sacred flesh of Dionysus?

I do not wish to suggest that the Dionysiac vision is bound to penetrate literary criticism the world over. I do sense, however, a movement in contemporary letters which must force us to revise our tenets or else accept the charge of theoretical isolationism in America. It is doubtful, for instance, that the plays of Beckett or Genet or Artaud, the novels of William Burroughs, Maurice Blanchot, or Alain Robbe-Grillet, the later stories of Salinger, the poetry of Charles Olson, Blaise Cendrars, or Dylan Thomas—and I cite these names quite at random—can be illuminated brightly by the critical terms of Professors Wellek and Frye. Nathalie Sarraute's latest book, *The Golden Fruits,* and Marc Saporta's "shuffle novel," *Number 1,* deny the conventional idea of structure. The first is a novel about a novel which cancels itself in the very act of reading; the second is a stratagem which accepts the principle of chance as an integral part of the literary experience. As for Burroughs' *The Soft Machine,* it applies—to what extent, no one will know—the "cut up method of Brion Gysin," a method which combines collage and montage. If these works possess a form, it is probably a "non-telic" form of the kind recently reflected in painting and music.[23] Must we then dismiss such works as faddish freaks, of more interest to literary gossip than literary history?

In France, where criticism has been long associated with the spirit of lucidity, critics take a different stand. A quick look at some of their statements may persuade us that their view of literature is not too far from the view I have proposed. The common theme of Claude Mauriac's *The New Literature* is stated thus: "After the silence of Rimbaud, the blank page of Mallarmé, the inarticulate cry of Artaud, a literature finally dissolves in alliteration with Joyce. The author of *Finnegans Wake* in fact creates out of whole cloth words full of so many diverse overtones that they are eclipsed by them. For Beckett, on the contrary, words all say the same thing."[24] The theme of Roland Barthes' *Le Degré Zéro de L'Ecriture* is similar: the avatar of the new literature is absence. Barthes writes: "dans ces écritures neutres, appelées ici 'le degré zéro de l'écriture,' on peut facilement discerner le mouvement même d'une négation, comme si la Littérature, tendant depuis un siècle à transmuer sa surface dans une forme sans hérédité, ne trouvait plus de pureté que dans l'absence de tout signe, proposant en fin l'accomplissement de ce rêve orphéen: un écrivain sans Littérature."[25] Likewise, for Maurice Blanchot literature is moving toward "l'ère sans parole." This movement may lead to a form of writing that is incessant sound; or it may lead, as Blanchot states in *Le Livre à Venir,* quite in the other direction: "la littérature va vers elle-même, vers son essence qui est la disparition."[26] Both directions, we can surmise, end in the dissolution of significant form, the abdication of language. Is this silence at the heart of modern literature the definition of outrage, a subjective correlative of our terror? Or is the monstrous language of action, which Bachelard[27] believes to be pointing, beyond Lautréamontism, toward "une réintegration de l'humain dans la vie ardente . . .," a closer correlative of that terror? We can only observe that from Sade and Lautréamont to Kafka and Beckett, the twin dark streams of poetry, the poetry of action and the poetry of silence, have been flowing toward some unknown sea wherein some figure of apocalypse, man or beast, still lies submerged.

Critics, however, are of many ilks, and for some the mantic role is as foreign as Elijah's. I wish to force no prophesies in the mouths of students of literature. Still, it is not unreasonable to ask that criticism evolve a method which takes deeper cognizance of the evolving character of life as of literature. The point is almost too obvious: contemporary letters can be judged as little by the standards of pure formalism as, let us say, Romantic poetry can be evaluated by the strict conventions of neo-Classicism.

The problem of criticism, however, must not be left to the indolent spirit of literary relativism. Indeed, the problem may not prove to be one of literary method at all. The problem of criticism is always the challenge of awareness, full awareness of human existence in time and in place, but also outside of both, in the dream world which antecedes all responsibilities. In the end, perhaps, the problem of critics and poets alike is one of human destiny. To say less is to confuse cowardice with modesty.

If there is an underlying theme in recent American criticism, it is the implicit theme of crisis, a crisis not merely of literary method but of literature itself, which means of culture and consciousness. The crisis, as Nicolas Berdyaev knew, is not the crisis of humanism but of humanity itself. In the past, periods of crisis have often bred visions of apocalypse.[28] Such visions may come our way again. They may even lurk in a critic's perplexity. Here is how Krieger put the question: "Or is it, perhaps, that the Kierkegaardian version is right and that our world has itself become the tragic visionary in its unbelief using self-destructive crises to force itself finally to confront the absurdities of earthly reality . . .? Which is to ask, fearfully and even unwillingly, whether we have not been beguiled by aesthetic satisfactions and whether the utterly stripped tragic vision may not after all be less illusory than the fullness which shines through tragedy."[29]

This is no time to sit in judgment on the world or to interpret its modern tragedy. From the Revelation of St. John the Divine to Norman O. Brown's extraordinary PBK address, entitled "Apocalypse," men have envisioned the destruction of the world and foreseen its resurrection. "Blessed and holy *is* he that hath part in the first resurrection: on such the second death has no power . . .," St. John says.[30] But we are not at the first resurrection yet; we are not even beyond madness. Thus from Norman O. Brown: "The alternative to mind is certainly madness. . . . Our real choice is between holy and unholy madness: open your eyes and look around you—madness is in the saddle anyhow."[31] What task will criticism perform, wavering between holy and unholy madness? What bootless task?

Criticism is no country for old men of any age. Criticism, which was born to behold literature, must still do so and look beyond itself. Tact and rigor may attend all our words, but our words will avail nothing if man prevails not. What lies beyond criticism? D. H. Lawrence knew. This is what he says in his *Apocalypse*: "O lovely green dragon of the new day, the undawned day, *come come* in touch, and release us from the horrid grip of the evil-smelling old Logos! Come in silence, and say nothing. Come in touch, in soft new touch like a spring-time, and say nothing."[32]

WESLEYAN UNIVERSITY

NOTES

1. René Wellek, *Concepts of Criticism*, ed. Stephen G. Nichols, Jr. (New Haven, 1963), p. 343.

2. Lawrence Durrell and Alfred Perles, *Art and Outrage: A Correspondence about Henry Miller* (New York, 1961), p. 9.

3. Lionel Trilling, "On the Modern Element in Modern Literature," *The Partisan Review Anthology*, ed. William Phillips and Philip Rahv (New York, 1962), pp. 267 ff.

4. Martin Buber, *Between Man and Man* (Boston, 1955), p. 10.

5. Walter J. Ong, S.J., *The Barbarian Within* (New York, 1962), pp. 19, 25.

6. Jean-Paul Sartre, *Situations II* (Paris, 1948), pp. 72, 98.

7. Albert Camus, *Resistance, Rebellion, and Death* (New York, 1961), p. 251.

8. Henry Miller, *The Cosmological Eye* (Norfolk, Conn., 1939), p. 156; and *Time of the Assassins* (Norfolk, Conn., 1956), pp. 38 ff.

9. Murray Krieger, *The Tragic Vision* (New York, 1960), pp. 2, 244.

10. James E. Miller, Jr., Karl Shapiro, and Bernice Slote, *Start With the Sun* (Lincoln, Neb., 1960), p. 238.

11. R. W. B. Lewis, *The Picaresque Saint* (Philadelphia and New York, 1959), p. 9.

12. Robert Martin Adams, *Surface and Symbol: The Consistency of James Joyce's Ulysses* (New York, 1962), pp. 245, 253.

13. In recent criticism, certain works have already begun to reflect this particular concern. Besides the works by R. W. B. Lewis and Murray Krieger already cited, one might mention Geoffrey Hartman, *The Unmediated Vision* (New Haven, 1954), Ihab Hassan, *Radical Innocence* (Princeton, 1961), Frederick J. Hoffman, *The Mortal No* (Princeton, 1964), and Arturo B. Fallico, *Art and Existentialism* (Englewood Cliffs, N. J., 1962).

14. Albert Camus, *The Myth of Sisyphus* (New York, 1959), pp. 72 ff.

15. These heretical statements are developed more fully in my essay "The Dismemberment of Orpheus," *American Scholar*, XXXII (Summer 1963), pp. 463-484.

16. Wellek, p. 65.

17. *Ibid.*, p. 68.

18. *Ibid.*, pp. 333 ff.

19. *Ibid.*, p. 342.

20. Northrop Frye, *The Well-Tempered Critic* (Bloomington, Ind., 1963), p. 123.

21. *Ibid.*, p. 136.

22. *Ibid.*, p. 140.

23. See Leonard B. Meyer, "The End of the Renaissance," *Hudson Review*, XVI (Summer 1963), pp. 169-186.

24. Claude Mauriac, *The New Literature* (New York, 1959), p. 12.

25. Roland Barthes, *Le Degré Zéro de L'Ecriture* (Paris, 1959), p. 12.

26. Maurice Blanchot, *Le Livre à Venir* (Paris, 1959), p. 237.

27. Gaston Bachelard, *Lautréamont* (Paris, 1963), p. 154.

28. H. H. Rowley, *The Relevance of Apocalyptic*, rev. ed. (New York, n.d.), pp. 150-178.

29. Krieger, p. 21.

30. Revelation xx.6.

31. Norman O. Brown, "Apocalypse," *Harper's* (May 1961), p. 47.

32. D. H. Lawrence, *Apocalypse* (Florence, 1931), pp. 233 ff.

Crocean Influence
and Historicism
in Italy

THERE WAS A RATHER PARADOXICAL SITUATION in Italy during the Fascist dictatorship with regard to Croce and the influence of his philosophy. Croce himself was the acknowledged leader of the opposition to Mussolini. Yet his ideas, his method, and his personal work remained incontestably influential throughout the two decades of Fascist domination. In the academic world, in the actual production of criticism, in the activity of the publishing houses, and in the literary reviews, Croce's authority was undisputed. Luigi Russo, a close disciple, was the most active figure in academic life during the two decades. Besides him there were F. Flora, A. Momigliano (a critic of exquisite taste whose work, although independent, conformed to some particular trends of Croce's system), M. Fubini, and U. Bosco. The *Enciclopedia Italiana,* the proud testimony of the regime in the field of culture, was the work of these and other scholars with the same orientation.

The reason for this apparently strange situation may be found in the fact that the Fascist movement stemmed from a cultural situation of which Croce's idealism was already a central part. Gentile, the brain of the Fascist "revolution," the philosopher who was responsible for the Fascist ideology and its ascendancy over Italian intellectuals, had worked for more than twenty years so closely with Croce as co-editor of his review, *La Critica,* that very often it is hard to decide between them about the paternity of many ideas. Some essential features of Croce's system, by confession of the philosopher himself, had their origin in Gentile's speculation. It is true that Croce had a firm personal dislike for the roughness and violence of the Fascists. He was a defender of the parliamentary system. Yet he also asserted most clearly that politics is a matter of force, thoroughly apart from morality. Furthermore, the liberty of which he spoke was the unconquerable liberty of all human history, of which dictatorship is no less an essential moment than the electoral system.

Substantially no significant objections to the Fascist regime could be deduced from Croce's philosophy. The review which he published was more an alibi for the dictator, who could always claim that he was allowing his major adversary to publish his own review, than a real organ of opposition.

We do not intend to speak of politics, of course. Our idea is that in dealing with Croce's methodology, which constituted the basis of almost all Italian literary activity between the two World Wars, one cannot fail to realize that there were essential aspects of that system which conformed to the exigencies of dictatorship and which explain some later developments. We refer especially to the basic distinction that Croce made among four autonomous activities in the life of the human spirit: art, thought, economy, and morality. In connection with this systematization, as it is known, art was conceived as a pure vision preceding every conscious activity of the mind and every interference of the will. Croce's word was *intuition*. He spoke of it as a kind of creative imagination and a starting moment in the life of the spirit to which previous emotional conditions could be only a kind of kindling.

This meant that knowledge of the sentimental life or the ideas of the artist could not give any real indication about the new creative act. The work of art could only be relived. The critic's task, therefore, was to be an act of intuition, a way of participating, through the suggestions of the poet's language, in his vision. The work was supposed to speak for itself. It was all a question of sympathy. Critical judgment lay in the act of reiterating the vision. Whatever failed to arouse the participation of the listener or the seer manifested itself as artistically dumb.

These aspects of critical activity as formulated by Croce were referred to in speaking of the absolutely predominant influence of Crocean philosophy during the decades of the Fascist dictatorship. Criticism had to deal with purely literary or artistic facts—beauty, lyrical achievements—apart from thought, political involvement, and moral experience. All these were extra-artistic elements, *allotria,* as Croce called them. The task of the critic was entirely separated from politics. There could be a kind of co-existence; the regime had nothing to fear. The critic's search was for pure lyrics. The title of one of Croce's books was *Poesia e non poesia (Poetry and Non-Poetry)*, with the implication that the author's aim had been to isolate poetry from spurious and consistently negligible matters. In his book on Dante (*La poesia di Dante,* 1921) the critic also made a selection of pieces which according to his taste were not spoiled by intellectualism, religious purposes, or allegorical constructions. These other questions, relating to the thought or the evolution of the poet, were, of course, not studied. In another volume on Manzoni, moving from the assumption that his *Promessi Sposi (The Betrothed)* had been dictated by some edifying purpose of showing the influence of Divine Providence upon humble people, the critic did not hesitate to conclude that the novel (probably the greatest novel in all the literature of the last century) was only a work of moral teaching, not of art. No thought was given to verifying the correctness of the assumption (in fact, it was entirely false); the religious convictions and the aesthetic ideals of the author, which both most definitely excluded any edifying intention or belief in divine help in matters of this world, were not studied.

Croce's followers were not so rigid in the application of the system. They tried to avoid sharp distinctions and, among other accomplishments, managed to demonstrate that in the *Divine Comedy* there was no clear-cut separation between the tares of intellectualism and the grain of poetry. The approach to the work of art remained unchanged. However, the stringency of the judgments of the master gave place to a tendency to rephrase the work of poetry in order to manifest the vision of the poet and the feelings expressed. Criticism became increasingly a matter of evocation or inspiration: poetry added to poetry. The critic had to recreate in his own words, in prose, the magic of the artist, through an act of sympathy or, one would say, of absorption. There were many proofs of subtle auscultation and able phrasing; but, of course, there was no assurance that what the critic tried to reveal was really what the poet had put into his work, nor was there any attempt to present the evidence on which the interpretation was based. It was a subjective, exclusively personal, emotional approach.

The results of a great amount of such intuitive criticism were inevitably poor. The language was too subtle, almost esoteric. Very little of this production was accessible to foreign readers or appealed to translators. The critic who, significantly not only because of his subject matter, was best known outside Italy was M. Praz, an essayist well versed in English literature, with a strong liking for fine erudition and historical details very distant from the intuitionism of Croce's school. It may also be found that the most important works of the period between the wars were those of the few critics who reacted against Croce's influence. G. Toffanin wrote a *Storia dell'Umanesimo* (Napoli, 1933; *History of Humanism,* English translation, 1953), which, with the correlated work of E. Gilson on the Middle Ages and the *Waning of the Middle Ages,* represents the most important contribution to the definition of the humanism of the fifteenth and sixteenth centuries. At a time when the nineteenth-century Burckhardt's concept of humanism as an aspect of the development of secularism and a premise both of practical naturalism and the rejection of Christian transcendentalism was still universally accepted, Toffanin's work demonstrated that the study of classical authors (*studia humanitatis*) and the movement which thenceforth was called humanism were based on the absolute persuasion that those *studia* provided the most valid aid to the formation of the Christian conscience and to the rejection of dialecticism, naturalism, and incredulity prevailing in the "schools" and in the culture of the late Middle Ages. As J. H. Randall, Jr., H. Haydin, and P. Kristeller, among others, have later clearly recognized, "virtue and good works became more significant factors in the angelication of man." A new Christian vision was formed, free from the fears and the spiritual conflicts of medieval civilization, more confident, able to recognize the importance of nature and human values in the process of salvation: it was something very distant from the revival of paganism and the advent of naturalism of which traditionalistic critics used to speak.

The clarification brought about by Toffanin's work was very important. It did not reflect only upon Italian literature, but upon the basic relations between humanism, the Reformation, the English and French Renaissance, and the Counter Reformation. But the value of the work of Toffanin, who, with his *Cinquecento* gave a very illuminating example of literary history, was scarcely realized. Furthermore, the work was wrongly presented as an attempt to give a Christian or a Catholic interpretation of the whole Renaissance, although Toffanin had very well distinguished the humanistic current from the mainly secular trends to which personalities such as Leonardo, Pomponazzi, Pulci, and Machiavelli belonged.

Other valuable contributions, independent of Croce's influence, were the studies by A. Galletti on Manzoni's intellectual and religious world, the research on Dante's thought made by B. Nardi, and some extremely penetrating monographs by Concetto Marchesi on Latin authors.

Among studies more directly connected with Croce's method, one could mention the essays by M. Fubini on Alfieri and Foscolo and the work of L. Russo on Verga. We do not know how many others there were. In general, critics did not go beyond expressing again and again their impressions of poetical texts. The critic who in the late thirties accomplished this kind of work with great but hardly bearable verbal abundance was F. Flora, the author of a *Storia della letteratura italiana* in five or six large volumes which the publishing house of Mondadori was able to give very wide distribution. However, one would doubt that the work has been really read. Other critics, like N. Sapegno, the author of a *Compendio di letteratura italiana* (1947), were not so verbose, but the method did not change.

Since criticism consisted mainly in utterances of impressions with an almost complete disregard for the effort of providing new elements of judgment, it is no wonder, therefore, that there was little novelty or progress. The interpretations given by F. De Sanctis a century ago in a literary situation pervaded with romantic emotionalism, patriotism, and secular prejudices remained unchanged. Dante, among others, was still presented as a poet of hatred and love, of earthly impulses completely at variance with the true, absolutely consistent Christian or Catholic spirit of the *Divine Comedy*.

Yet there were certainly valid elements in Croce's system which may explain its exceptionally long and vast influence on Italian culture and that abroad. Not only did Croce give a clear, definite, and, above all, very consistent answer to problems of aesthetics, but, despite the hinted shortcomings of the criticism originating from his teaching, he certainly helped to form a pattern of criticism free from many false and yet widely diffused approaches to the world of art. If compared with the clarity and solidity of Croce's system, theories like those proffered by Cleanth Brooks, Kenneth Burke, and Richard P. Blackmur—which are really a kind of oversophistication with terribly private philosophical or pseudophilosophical terms—would appear no more than magnificent expressions of disordered minds. In the proper field of practical criticism Croce's system has, among other achievements, represented a solid protection against many confusions between psychology and criticism. As we have said, art in Croce's view is a creative primary act, a cognitive performance. Its value depends on previous sentimental or psychological impulses no more than a scientific demonstration can be evaluated on the basis of personal motives and feelings. The insurgence of personal emotions may be taken into account to explain why the poet failed, how the work was prejudiced by external elements; but the critic has to deal with what was successful, the new creation, to see whether it is consistent, pure. It is as great a mistake to take the work of art as a document of the author's life as to believe that poetry manifests his real feelings or is worthy because of the degree of sincerity with which it expresses them. What Petrarch's poetry says is not necessarily what the poet experienced; and at any rate it is what he *formed,* not just his feelings, that counts. Such terrible confusions of social and individual manifestations with poetical creation as can be found in Kenneth Burke or I. A. Richards are absolutely and consistently avoided in Croce's aesthetics. No less firm and valid is Croce's conclusion about the vanity of all attempts to recognize the sense and value of the work of art by more or less extensive research on the historical situation and the social milieu within which a work was created. Consistently, criticism based on the study of "influences" is discarded: the work of art and the mind of the artist are always unpredictable; they may turn out to be completely different from the developments that the critic has traced.

On the same grounds, Italian criticism based on Croce's system has been able to avoid the pitfalls of a moral appreciation of poetry as well as formalistic, archetypal approaches, the entanglements of Aristotelianism and an erudite play with structure and texture, ironies and tensions, which so often becloud the field of criticism. Aristotle may offer a useful tool to penetrate ancient tragedy, provided that the critic is aware (as unfortunately very few are) that Aristotle's is a very unilateral vision of Greek tragedy.

Despite the sterility to which we have pointed, there may be some justification for the somehow characteristic self-pride with which Italian critics have always regarded foreign doctrines of criticism and their generally constant allegiance to Croce's methodology.

The essential aspect of Italian culture, we should add, the one which most clearly differentiates it from American culture, is a strong feeling of affiliation with one or more dominant systems. It seems that Italy is a land of deep collective commitments. It is not without reason that Italy has, without any form of constraint, the largest Communist party in Europe, including Russia. Criticism itself is linked to vast political currents: it may be Marxist, Christian, or liberal. There is no place for isolated, free-lance thinkers. In Italy a political party in a kind of religion, a faith which affects one's way of thinking in all fields, not only in politics; it implies cultural attitudes, a vision, the acceptance of ideals and philosophical programs, and solidarity with other writers, critics, publishers, and even modes of life.

This situation obviously has negative as well as valid aspects. Personal perspectives are unlikely. There is always a strong tendency to move along established patterns with limited possibilities of differentiated approaches. On the other hand, critics base their research on a body of established theories, a fact which certainly helps them to avoid futile adventures, misdirections, and fragmentation of thought.

This accounts, of course, for the very limited changes that, despite many elements to the contrary, have taken place in Italian criticism since the war. Admittedly there were many efforts or at least many appeals for a renewal of the literary atmosphere which, it was felt, in past decades because of the Fascist domination, had been too secluded from the concrete problems of society. Literature had to be *militante, engagé*. Poets seemed to renounce hermeticism, which was now considered the consequence of a regime which had brought about the isolation of the intellectual and the lack of open, cordial communication between the writer and his audience, or a way of escaping the watchful control of political authority. Both explanations were probably false. Hermeticism is just one aspect of the modern aesthetic sensibility; it stems from the same source as abstract art, irrationalism, surrealism. But from the war, the Resistance, the common sufferings, arose the need of a literature expressing the new sentiments of participation and solidarity, the collective aspiration to a purified world. Quasimodo published poems which voiced the common anguish of the time of the Resistance, and, characteristically, it was Carlo Bo, a very intelligent representative of hermetic criticism, who wrote the preface for the collection of these poems.

Bo, together with O. Macri, M. Luzi, and, somewhat apart, G. Contini, M. Apollonio, and S. Solmi, had developed before the war a kind of criticism quite distinct from Croce's. It was characterized by subtle allusions, by attention to modes of expression and meters, by familiarity with the techniques of artistic creation, and by the use of hermetic language. After the war, with a deeply felt dissatisfaction with the sterility of Crocean intuitionism and a strong sense of revolt against the literature of the past, these critics seemed to acquire remarkable authority. But they failed to form a group, to find the support of a political party, and to develop a consistent system able to supplant, in a cultural situation mostly connected with the work and the influence of university professors, the still dominant Crocean aesthetics. G. Contini founded a review, *Paragone,* devoted half to art criticism, half to literature. It is still being published, with a rather generic program, a good deal of sophistication and avant-gardism, and a remarkable poverty of ideas. We should add that in the field of art criticism as well as classical scholarship, Croce's system was the only one which provided a solid basis for the activity of critics who generally did not have sufficient philosophical preparation or simply did not attempt to build a new system capable of competing with Croce's. Apart from any other consideration, only through adherence to the established method was it possible or, at least, less difficult to attain university positions. The judges in the state competitions were almost invariably L. Russo, M. Fubini, A. Schiaffini, W. Bosco, F. Flora, A. Momigliano, N. Sapegno, and G. Citanna. Through this established pattern such critics as G. Getto, W. Binni, L. Caretti, V. Branca, R. Spongano, C. Muscetta, M. Sansone, and others obtained university status. Besides, the chairs in Italy are not more than a couple of dozen in all.

To be precise, there was a vast, consistent effort, on the part of the Communists, to constitute a new pattern of criticism that could represent a complete break with the past and conform to the principles of Marxism. The culture inspired by Croce was seen as the product of the world of conservatism, capitalist and fascist as well (capitalism and fascism were, of course, synonymous). It was recalled that Croce at the beginning had supported the Fascist movement and had voted in the Italian senate for the attribution of dictatorial powers to Mussolini. The authors now looked to were Lukáks and Banfi, a Communist philosopher who under Fascism had developed a consistent aesthetics opposed to Croce's and in some ways conforming to the Marxist ideology. The notebooks of A. Gramsci, the leader of pre-Fascist Communism who was a man of very high moral and intellectual stature and who died in Mussolini's prison, gave many suggestions for a new direction in criticism and culture in general. In reviews such as *Società, Politecmico,* and *Rinascita* a vast debate took place for many years. But the movement did not succeed in creating a new organic system of criticism. N. Sapegno, C. Muscetta, G. Trombatore, and C. Salinari, the representatives of Communist culture, had a mentality previously formed on Croce's doctrines. L. Russo, who joined the cultural movement if not the Communist party (he was not able to put entirely aside his previous allegiance to Croce's liberalism) and edited a review which attained great authority, did not modify his critical methods. He only brought forth strong new tones of anticlericalism and secularism, a political rather than a cultural opposition to the ruling Demo-Christian party.

Substantially the efforts of the critics we have just mentioned consisted in trying to form a new culture without abandoning their previous Crocean mentality or showing any rejection of past tendencies. Croce, after all, was still a very useful tool in the battle against the new enemy: the Christian or the Demo-Christian ideology. The degree of confusion in all this was rather high. One may have an idea of the effort toward self-justification, the influence of political motives, and the unmistakable deception of the reader if he reads *Cronache di filosofia italiana (1900–1943),* (1953), by E. Garin, a professor at the University of Florence. The magic word which seemed to link Marxism and Croce was "historicism." There has been a very extensive use of it in the last decade or two.

In criticism, the absolute emphasis was, of course, on history, in opposition to Croce's monadistic, intuitionist approach. Sapegno, who has been the leading figure of Marxist criticism since World War II, has insisted on many occasions on the necessity of correcting Croce's methodology by returning to De Sanctis and "overcoming, without destroying it, that exclusive attention to the strictly aesthetic aspect of the work of art, which is the glory and the limit of our Crocean education, to reach a wider, historical consideration, where, furthermore, even the aesthetic side of the literary product will receive as much rich and substantial light as less exclusive attention" (*L'approdo letterario,* 1958). Clearly the critic did not reject the Crocean heritage and even repeated the customary patriotic claim that "in no other place has aesthetic speculation reached such a high level of philosophical rigor as in Italy." But substantially Sapegno's appeal did not go beyond the conviction that a work of art is always connected to literary as well as political and social factors and has to be studied and evaluated in the light of these. In other cases Communist critics made more rigid applications of vulgarized forms of Marxism, considering the works of art as "products" of a particular economic structure and attributing exclusive importance in their criticism to the progressive or reactionary elements, with a more or less complete disregard for true artistic values.

Sapegno in general did not follow the trend. But undoubtedly he has failed to realize that a work of art is not just a document or an aesthetic manifestation of the history of a society or a country. The critic is not a historian of civilization who traces the genesis of a work of art in the political and social tendencies of its time and establishes how, in turn, the work contributed to the general process of history. This may be an important task. But it has nothing to do with the proper function of a critic. For the historian of civilization, a very poor work from the artistic point of view, say *Le roman de la rose,* may have greater importance than a genuinely artistic production.

But the true, the only problem for the critic is to *evaluate* the object which appears to be a work of art. He does not have to say how the work was born; nor does he have to ascertain the style of such a production. His task consists in revealing the greatness of what has been accomplished, the artistic intensity, the depth, the consistency of the *form* which has been realized. It is the measuring which counts. Croce thought that once we have gathered all the elements which may clarify the sense of the work, we have only to listen to the voice of the poet. Our inner, personal response will be the only criterion. Sapegno's and other Marxist critics' positions, despite the great emphasis on the study of the historical premises and the social and political situation from which the work of art originated, remain the same as Croce's. These critics try to escape the basically subjective judgment which was the essence of Croce's criticism, but only to evaluate the work of art in relation to the evolution of society and the class struggle.

In this writer's view, as has often been expressed, a poem or a piece of sculpture belongs to general history: it is first of all a moment in the evolution of the world of art and, within this, in the history of the lyric or of sculpture. It cannot be measured against the process of political, social, or moral life— which are obviously heterogenous—nor does it have value in itself: it has value for what its author has accomplished in relation to the course of poetry and art. Man, when expressing himself, always creates some kind of poetry. The critic has to consider the weight or the impact of a particular artistic production. Each artist brings about a new approach to reality, a new, more effective, more impressive language. First of all he carries art to a new level of taste, of penetration, of truth. Of course, the *Iliad, Oedipus Rex,* and *Divine Comedy* still speak to our senses and our minds. But this happens only because spiritually, at least to some degree, according to our own historical sensibilities often out of a conscious process, we place ourselves at the moment in which these poems were written and appreciate their answers to our inner needs. We mirror ourselves in them.

The critic's task is always two-fold: he has to place himself *at that point*, so that he reacts with his own deepest emotion to the suggestion emanating from the poetry. At the same time he has to be on his own level and trace the historical process, detecting what is valuable and what is unsuccessful. His achievement will be manifested in his ability to give each work the place and the relief which are proper to it. Criticism can only be the history of art.

An interesting step toward a criticism consisting not only of the expression of personal feelings but also of the study of *poetica*, i.e., the conceptions and the literary orientation of the poet, was made by W. Binni. It seemed to lead to a more exact realization of the historical links between the work of art and the development of literary, aesthetic ideals. In a largely diffused dissatisfaction with Crocean impressionism, many were attracted by the proposal. Unfortunately, when Binni spoke of *poetica,* he referred almost exclusively to the personal feelings of the poet, rather than to his ideas. Accordingly, the critic traced the development of a new *poetica* characterized by the heroic acceptance of destiny in the late years of Leopardi's life (*La nuova poetica leopardiana,* 1947) and emphasized, in Ariosto, an alleged *poetica* of harmony and music which was not really the concept that Ariosto had of poetry but was what the critic believed to be the essence of his poem (*Metodo e poesia di L. Ariosto,* Messina, 1947).

No attempt was made by the critic to investigate the origin and the evolution of Leopardi's idea of the lyric, from which originated his poems, the first and certainly one of the highest and purest examples of the modern lyric form. In the case of Ariosto, Binni was completely unable to perceive the extremely fine texture of classical and modern taste, idealism and realism, and above all the omnipresent, apparently skeptical but deeply moral humor which make *Orlando Furioso* the greatest literary expression of the Renaissance.

Substantially, Binni's review, *La Rassegna della letteratura italiana,* can be regarded as the organ and the most evident proof of the lasting, prevailing Crocean trend in Italian criticism. The review is probably the most widely read by the new generation, and it does not differ markedly from *Il Giornale storico della letteratura italiana,* whose editor is M. Fubini, the most faithful representative of the idealistic tradition, or from *Letteratura moderna,* a review founded by F. Flora. Nor is there any difference, on the other hand, between these reviews and *Lettere italiane,* a review edited by G. Getto and V. Branca, two professedly Catholic critics.

As a matter of fact, after many attempts in various directions and despite the strong political divisions of which we have spoken, Italian criticism seems again firmly established in its pre-war positions. The reviews which at the time of the Resistance expressed deep aspirations to a literary as well as a moral renewal, *Mercurio, Nuova Europa,* and *Politecnico,* are no longer published. Marxists and Christians as well, Getto or Caretti, Branca or Salinari, or Sansone, follow the same method. Critics who have, or had, more personal approaches to a work of art—G. De Robertis, who made subtle technical analyses of many texts but in general failed to reach a complete, organic vision of the authors he examined; A. Pagliaro, who has given us many but often very doubtful examples of semantic study; and G. Contini, who has worked mostly on the study of variants and codices, i.e., in technical philology, with great mastery but very often with poor historical perspective—seem to represent tendencies concomitant with the basic one. There has been no opposition to Croce's system or to the politics of culture made by the representative of idealistic culture.

However, because of the need to give literary activity a more solid basis than the personal intuition of the critic and to provide something more concretely measurable in the state competitions for university appointments, gradually new importance has been given to textual criticism: not as a substitute for the old aesthetic criticism but as an addition to it. Young scholars have endeavored to find texts to be edited, have re-edited others, and have undoubtedly reached a high level of use of the scientific method. Among those who have the most authority in this field are L. Caretti, E. Raimondi, and A. Chiari. One can only doubt whether the time and the work spent to give a new critical text of *Il mondo creato* by Tasso or *Fiammietta* by Boccaccio will yield any useful new hint for the study of those poets. It is, in most cases, only a question of career.

In other cases, erudite research has been looked upon with new favor, without its implying any departure from the Crocean method. Croce himself often stressed the value of research preparatory for aesthetic judgment, and gave many examples of biographical and bibliographical study. G. Billanovich, with his extensive studies on Petrarch's and Boccaccio's minor works (*Lo scrittoio del Petrarca*, I, Roma, 1947; *Restauri boccacceschi*, Roma, 1945), C. Martellotti, F. Maggini, A. Schiaffini, and C. Segre have provided a large amount of interesting information in the fields of biography, the textual tradition, and the history of language. *Boccaccio medievale* (1956), by V. Branca, is also a manifestation of this erudite trend which has been largely appreciated in recent times as a complementary aspect of aesthetic judgment. The new words, at a certain moment, were *philology* and *criticism*. There was the illusion that from the combination of erudite research and Crocean critical intuition, finally a new, more complete method would result. But they were in most cases only two different things juxtaposed: actually there was no *history* of art, no historical judgment. There were many biographical facts, textual reconstructions, more or less interesting details, and then, added to these, there was the expression of personal feelings. History, of course, is not the accumulation of information; it is the formulation of a rigorous process which by itself shows the succeeding, more or less high values. Branca's book falls short just because of this inability to ascertain a true historical development and recognize Boccaccio's place within it. It shows some of the many links between the *Decameron* and the tendencies to moral *exampla* in medieval aesthetics; it also traces the diffusion of Boccaccio's novellas among the tradesmen and the other people of the growing middle class; but it substantially overlooks the basic medieval paganism, both popular and courtly, in the novellas, the characteristic atmosphere of the "waning of the Middle Ages" with which they are pervaded, and the detachment from moral, real experience which constitutes the essence of the novella genre. A mixture of useless erudition (very often second-hand) and aesethetic evaluation, a kind of Dantesque encyclopedia which inevitably has resulted in the acceptance of all the nineteenth-century commonplaces in this field, is the large commentary by N. Sapegno on the *Divine Comedy*. It also might be noted, as a characteristic of this trend toward erudite research which does not become history, that the essentially external studies on Petrarch by E. Wilking, including his recent, very dull biography of the poet, have been much acclaimed while the very important studies on Dante by C. S. Singleton and the intelligent interpretation of the *Purgatorio* by F. Fergusson have been almost completely ignored.

This writer has made an insistent effort, in the review *Delta* (which, however, has been published desultorily) and in his book *Arte, realtà e storia* (Napoli, 1952) to expose the basic shortcomings of the Crocean method and to give a new, rigorous, historical orientation to critical activity. It is the central concept of Croce's aesthetics that first of all needs to be revised. "Intuition" for the Neapolitan philosopher came to mean a kind of private creative imagination without reference to any existing reality. The vision of the artist had in itself its full value, regardless of the degree of truth that it included. This prevented one from considering the history of art as one of the aspects of man's perennial effort to grasp reality and reduced all artistic creations to isolated dreams deprived of any connection with each other and of any value for the world of knowledge. Furthermore, for Croce, intuition was already the full artistic production. Finding the words, placing the colors, shaping the piece of sculpture was only a secondary practical task aimed at providing some kind of record of the creative work. In the rather strange conception of the philosopher, if we have really a definite vision in our mind, we are able *ipso facto* to manifest it in words and colors. Croce completely failed to realize that the actual work is always the result of a difficult process of adaptation of the inner intuition to the chosen medium. The matter through which the artist tries to express himself always imposes limits, suggests new ideas, and operates on the previous image. It is only the final result that counts. Intuition is only the beginning; it has to assume a body, to become flesh. It is the final, physical composition that the critic judges, not the idea which existed in the imagination of the poet. It is now a historical reality—a novel, a painting, a poem—which takes its place along with other novels, paintings, and poems and thus is able to influence other poets.

Croce ignored the creative *making* of a poem and completely disregarded the historical process in which every work of poetry participates. There are no genres or differentiated arts in Croce's aesthetics: intuition is the same for all artists. On the other hand, according to Croce—this is also a great failure of his system which post-Crocean critics have failed to recognize and avoid— language is simply the creation of individuals; as such, it does not have history. Croce ignored the basic fact that every expression becomes an entity in the world, a means that others will use and recreate. There is always a process to which every creative act belongs: a word or a work of art is always a concrete fact which influences other persons and inspires them. We do not create anew, we use and transform. There would not be communication if every poet invented his own language. There are history, tradition, process.

Strangely enough, with all the claims for historicism made by Croce and his followers, the historical essence of language and of art in general has been completely ignored. There is no continuity in this consideration of the world of art and of language, of genres.

In some monographs on Manzoni (Napoli, 1951) and on Dante (1958 and 1962) this writer has tried to approach these authors from a historical viewpoint, reaching conclusions entirely different from the accepted ones. But these have scarcely affected the trend of criticism in Italy. Mention is made of them here only to show the resistance in the actual cultural situation to any serious modification of the accepted pattern.

Things, however, seem to have worked differently with regard to stylistic criticism. At a certain point stylistic analysis seemed to become fashionable. The names of Spitzer, Auerbach, Hatzfeld, and Alonzo were repeatedly mentioned. But the pheonomenon did not last; there was no real penetration. The traditional Crocean emphasis on language and poetry as the creation of individuals maintained its basic strength against those abstract definitions of "classic," "gothic," and "romantic" given by Wolfflin and other German historians of art, forming fixed categories with which each artist should be contrasted. Croce even denied the meaning of such categories as romanticism and classicism. Without going so far, Italian critics could understand that there is no classicism or romanticism apart from authors and their individual works; the only way to use the words is in tracing the history of the current, with primary accent on individual works.

In fact, stylistic analysis was accepted only as the study of individual styles, and there was no doubt, on the other hand, that style can be understood and defined only in the light of the inspiration of the work. The study of style by itself—it was clearly realized—in its external elements of words, images, and colors could only amount to a kind of sterile description or useless statistics of words. The problem remained that of reliving the work of art. Stylistic analysis was accepted by Italian critics only insofar as it could be integrated in their system. Sapegno stressed the fact that for Damaso Alonzo "style is the individualizing aspect of the work of art." Fubini insisted that new suggestions could be accepted from the study of style, provided that they did not imply any departure from "principles which it was not possible to renounce." The only approaches to the study of style that he could allow were those which were already in De Sanctis, in Carducci, the nineteenth-century poet who was also a critic of very fine sensibility for the forms and the technical elements of art, or in Parodi.

As a result, there has been no remarkable wave of stylistic analysis in Italian criticism. A volume of Spitzer's essays was published in Italy some years ago, but his manner of criticism was too casual and his system of comparing distant literary facts with no historical connection between them was too hazardous and arbitrary to help the formation of a consistent system of criticism and to satisfy persons accustomed to a rigorous methodology. At the margins of the official, academic world, numerous manifestations of stylistic analysis have appeared. One may find some in the *Lecturae Dantis* collected by G. Getto for the publishing house Sansoni. But essentially they remain ambitious school exercises with an evident excess of hermeneutics and great, gratuitous ostentation of sensibility. As such these analyses show some of the characteristic short-comings of the method: mainly the tendency to read a text without any historical knowledge of the spiritual world of the author and to study words and stylistic themes without an organic perception of the sentiments expressed in the work. The result is almost constantly a kind of mechanical classification of words and of psychological guessing. Lacking the vast, previous knowledge of the world of the poets and of literary history that can be found in Spitzer or Hatzfeld, stylistic analysis may be only a fruitless computing of words or (as is too often the case in American colleges) an encouragement to mental laziness and ignorance.

In Italy the stylistic approach might have helped to correct the monadistic study of the work of art which is the gravest weakness of Italian criticism. After all, style is something which develops; it is not just the creation of individuals. In order to know the style of an author, one should see what really changes in his work in relation to the style of his epoch. First of all the critic should know the conceptions, the artistic ideals of the author. But analysis has been restricted to single authors or single works, without historical perspectives.

There have been interesting discussions concerning the problem of literary stylistics in connection with the work of G. Devoto (*Studi di stilistica,* 1950; *Nuovi studi stilistica,* 1962) and other historians of language, such as E. Nencioni and B. Terracini. They originated from the effort to find a justification for a history of language, which had been substantially denied by Croce. Devoto stated that, while admitting the Crocean concept of the individual creation of language, there remained the possibility of tracing the history of language as an "institution." Theoretically the assumption was very weak, for Devoto did not refute Croce's premises; but it led gradually to a belief that a history of literary language and of style could be made up, allowing for both continuity and creation. Devoto lacked the necessary rigor to establish a new philosophy of language, nor did he realize that a history of style cannot exist apart from a study of the personalities of the poets and from the history of a particular art or genre. But probably all the discussion was responsible for the eventual appearance, after fifty years of Crocean literary dictatorship, of the first history of the Italian language, by B. Migliorini (1958).

A philosophical revision of idealistic aesthetics did not fail to materialize. After the war there were works by L. Payreson, L. Stefanini, A. Carlini, and A. Guzzo which tried to give new systematic solutions to the problems of art. It would be scarcely useful and quite difficult to say now in a short space how successful these efforts were. The fact is that, unlike the linguistic and stylistic critics who, from Spitzer to Devoto, lacked the philosophical preparation to justify and establish their methods, the philosophers now mentioned were unable to attain any considerable influence. There were no developments. Only from the work of A. Banfi and of some of his disciples, like Morpurgo-Tagliabue and G. Dorfles, there developed, not without inside contradictions, a new current of criticism, especially of the arts. Connected with the movement is the constant activity of L. Anceschi, who has linked these philosophical experiences with the study and the assimilation of Eliot's criticism and the experience of hermetic poetry. Anceschi is the editor of the review *Il Verri* and has made good contributions to the study of the Baroque. Also originally linked with Banfi's philosophy is the work of E. Paci, who is the editor of *Aut-Aut* and has become the exponent of an active movement of phenomenology, the most promising in Italian culture in the fields both of philosophy and of practical criticism. The thought of Merleau-Ponty seems to be gaining rather large influence, and it is certainly the most apt in the development of a new criticism.

For the sake of a new criticism, of course, the Crocean effort toward the recreation of the work of art, the Marxist emphasis on history, and the stylistic approach will not have been in vain. But there is the need to go beyond these defective and unilateral considerations toward a more direct and conscious discovery and evaluation—not only description—of works of art as moments in an artistic, historical process. The problem, of course, is not that of putting together some different approaches in a kind of eclectic combination. History is a unifying rigorous system of evaluation. One may only be a good or a bad historian. Many young forces are developing. It is to be hoped that their advocates will be able to resist the pressures of career, of economic exigencies, and of political interests, which are very strong in Italy, in fact, almost irresistible.

THE CATHOLIC UNIVERSITY OF AMERICA

ALLAN RODWAY

Crosscurrents in Contemporary English Criticism

S o MUCH criticism has been produced in the last forty years that the presence of numerous crosscurrents need occasion no surprise. What does require explanation, perhaps, is the fact that they have all been contained within one great tide, the movement that has come to be known as the New Criticism. Walter J. Ong has recently defined it as:

> The criticism you get when an academic community supplies an audience for vernacular literature large enough and mature enough and intellectually sophisticated enough to make possible intelligent, and often subtly contrived, talk about literary performance. The New Criticism is, in other words, simply a type of criticism which matures with the emergence of the vernacular full blown on the academic scene. . . . Even if you disagree with the New Criticism there is no point in looking back to a conjectural Old Criticism which previously performed the offices of the New. There was no Old Criticism. There were no academic offices for it to perform.[1]

This account allows for the variety within the movement and explains its predominance in the last half-century—the first period in which the study of vernacular literature has been regarded as culturally more central than the study of classical texts, the first period, too, of relatively widespread university education.

That the writer is American in no way diminishes the relevance of his account to the English scene; for, apart from a proportionate difference in quantity, the New Criticism of the two countries has been remarkably similar. Not unnaturally, since all varieties have stemmed from work done in the decade after World War I by T. S. Eliot, an anglicized American, and I. A. Richards, an americanized Englishman. Nevertheless, a closer look at the English scene reveals sharper significances than Ong's larger perspective could.

Two main points stand out: that the modern movement in criticism started in England and that it seems to have been more passionate there than in the States. The earlier start is probably due partly to a greater accessibility to French symbolist ideas (though they had to be imported by expatriate Americans) and partly to a greater involvement in the Great War, which brought about a violent reaction to traditionalism. The matter of passionate commitment seems to have been due partly to the deeprootedness of the tradition reacted against and partly to the interconnectedness of the comparatively small literary world in England. Both facts contributed to the fiercer nature of modern English criticism; the desire for change was greater and harder to achieve, and hostilities in a small world could be focused on personalities. (The divisions in the next section are categories rather than groups; the members were relatively few and might appear in more than one category—and when they did, they often took with them the hostility they had attracted in their first role.)

The state of criticism belonging to the old order is indicated by the fact that the Georgians were considered dangerous poetic revolutionaries determined to "surprise and even to puzzle at all costs," forgetting (as Arthur Waugh put it, in the *Quarterly Review* of October 1914) that "the first essence of poetry is beauty." This is the period of graceful impressionism, of new Chairs of English occupied by classical products of an old tradition, trained more in editing than in criticism and not at all in criticism of a living language. The feeling it engendered in the new generation of academics is well captured in Q. D. Leavis's retrospective essay *The Discipline of Letters, A Sociological Note*, which appeared in *Scrutiny* and was provoked by the publication of *The Letters* of G. S. Gordon, who followed Raleigh, the first Merton Professor of English at Oxford.

> The discipline of letters, he proclaims, is . . . twofold. On the one hand, linguistic-philological studies as an end in themselves. On the other, scholarship— the ideal of perfect editing, that is, a frivolous one which is hostile to any real standards in literature, since any text long enough dead is equally meet to be edited; the credit consists in producing the perfect index, etc., to a piece of writing not necessarily worth publishing in the first place. . . . It would be hard to justify a claim that a university school of English, as described by Raleigh, Gordon, Mr. C. S. Lewis, is of value to the community or the individual. . . .[2]
> We noticed, in summarizing this later inaugural lecture, how his position had changed from the complacent insolence of *The Discipline of Letters*. Now he would like to be on both sides at once, and though he cannot conceal his hatred of all that Eliot stood for he makes a great show of openmindedness. . . . This was a cunning move, obviously more serviceable than the last-ditch foaming-at-the-mouth attitude. It kept pace with the quiet ratting that was occurring at this time on the Hopkins controversy. . . .[3]

Not for her the snide urbanities of *The Sacred Wood*, whose author was outside the academic ring! But the criterion adopted by Eliot—also, of course, the editor of the significantly named *Criterion*—was undoubtedly that summed up by Mrs. Leavis:

> . . . . for the literary critic and the educationalist will insist that the question they must put to academic authority remains what it always was: are we or are we not to be allowed to apply real standards, to work with real values instead of currency-counters?[4]

The effect of the new criticism on the first recipients—at any rate, of its theoretical side—is recalled by Christopher Isherwood, with a touch of irony for his youthful enthusiasm:

> For both of us, the great event that term was the series of lectures on modern poetry given by Mr. I. A. Richards. . . . The substance of these lectures has since become famous through Mr. Richards's books. But, to us, he was infinitely more than a brilliant new literary critic: he was our guide, our evangelist, who revealed to us, in a succession of astounding lightning flashes the entire expanse of the Modern World. Up to this moment, we had been a pair of romantic conservatives, devil-worshippers, votaries of "Beauty" and "Vice," Manicheans, would-be Kropotkin anarchists, who refused to read T. S. Eliot (because of his vogue with the Poshocracy) or the newspapers or Freud. Now, in a moment, all was changed. Poets, ordered Mr. Richards, were to reflect aspects of the World-Picture. Poetry wasn't a holy flame, a firebird from the moon; it was a group of interrelated stimuli acting upon the ocular nerves, the semi-circular canals, the brain, the solar plexus, the digestive and sexual organs. It did you medically demonstrable good, like a dose of strychnine or salts. We became behaviourists, materialists, atheists. In our conversation, we substituted the word "emotive" for the word beautiful; we learnt to condemn inferior work as a "failure in communication" or, more crushing still, as "a private poem." We talked excitedly about "the phantom aesthetic state."[5]

Some years later (1929) Richards's *Practical Criticism* revolutionized English studies at Cambridge and has since affected such studies at all the newer, and some of the older, provincial universities.

Certainly, then, it is true of academic England that "there was no old *criticism*." It is also true, in Ong's general sense, that "New Criticism" is now predominant. But Oxford, traditionally the home of lost causes, has never radically altered its hostility to real criticism, despite the efforts of the less reactionary dons; and London, together with some of the older provincial universities, still inclines to the old combination of deep, dull, objective philology and superficial, bright, subjective criticism. Meanwhile, the New Criticism, by a natural evolutionary process, has gradually lost its attack and become self-critical, or perhaps it is more nearly true to say, it has turned its passion to internecine warfare and thus given the coelacanths an outside chance of making a comeback. Certainly there are signs of it in *The Literary Critics* (Baltimore, 1962), by George Watson, an Oxford product now established as a fifth columnist in Cambridge. The book could hardly have come about without the preliminary theorising of New Critics on criticism, yet in its misrepresentation and misunderstanding of modern criticism it seems to bring the wheel full circle, back to Gordonism.

The divisions within the modern movement in criticism, then, are likely to prove as important, for good or ill, as its tidal unity has proved. For good, if they lead to greater wariness about the many critical fallacies theory has pointed out, to increased care for proper critical procedures, and to a clearer awareness of the difference between strictly literary criticism and metacriticism. For ill, if they cause criticism to be discredited and thus lead to a revival of the old academicism.

Both the divisions and the unity, obviously, were inherent in the movement from the start. It began with *The Sacred Wood* (1920), a work of descriptive criticism, using illustrative quotation, and yet, for all its descriptiveness, inventing a new past; with I. A. Richards's lectures, later published as *The Principles of Literary Criticism* (1924), a work of general theory; and with his Cambridge experiments, published as *Practical Criticism* (1928), a work of pedagogical criticism. The differences are obvious; nor are they diminished if we add *The Calendar of Letters* (1925–27, forerunner of *Scrutiny,* 1932–53) and Pound's *Make It New* (1934), a collection of essays written between 1912 and 1931, whose title and tone are perhaps more significant than the content. What they have in common, less obviously, is a certain detachment and a new determination to stick close to the facts and effects of the text. The word "determination" suggests the seriousness of the attempt, the abandonment of elegant connoisseurship; the word "facts"—difficult as it is in a context of literary fictions—the desire to make criticism as objective as possible, to abandon subjective impressionism.

Concentration on the text, however, led to the discovery of the many-sidedness of a literary work—a rather paradoxical thing to "have in common," since naturally some critics concentrated on exploring one side, some another. Concentration on the reader's response, of course (in the *Principles*), led back to concentration on the text, and this in turn led to the desire for some sort of "objectivity," since *Practical Criticism* made evident the need to establish standards of correctness of response, as well as pedagogical methods of encouraging right readings, as against misreadings. Demonstrating the rightness of right readings was evidently less easy than spotting the wrongness of wrong ones.

Objectivity was required by other critics for several other reasons: to show that criticism could be as much of a "discipline" as philology or the Anglo-Saxon grind; to show that one really had abandoned subjective impressionism; to show that in education one opinion was not as good as another and taste not a matter of knowing the chic things to say; and finally to show the comparability of arts subjects with the sciences by providing a neutral basis for progress. The chief difficulty of attaining the desired objectivity lay in the immaterial nature of literary works. Obviously, their material existence is insignificant—mere paper and squiggles; their significant existence is immaterial. In short, they do not really exist; they take place (when read). Equally obviously, in the light of *Practical Criticism,* what does take place in reading is usually not what ought to take place. And this raises the key questions: What are the limits of variation in a "correct" reading? And how can criticism help to steer readers, reasonably, into those confines and away from eccentric, private readings?

Both questions involve enormous difficulties and complexities which are still engaging the attention of theorists on both sides of the Atlantic, but now seem on the verge of solution. Inevitably, however, the easier ways were tried first —looking before and after, rather than at the work itself. After all, the work's effects on social groups or even on individuals are objectively there to be examined; so are its causes in the writer's period or his life, at least if you can get enough documentary evidence together. Moreover this sort of work seems

scientific. Indeed it often is scientific, and that is why, as theorists in rival categories were to point out, it is not strictly literary criticism but metacriticism:
a specialised form of sociology or psychology, history, biography or anthropology. And the real difficulties of assessing what interpretations the nature of
the language properly allows and what the right response is, have been bypassed.
At any rate, almost bypassed, for in fact biography, history, philology, anthropology, sociology, psychology, and all the apparatus of scholarship may give
the critic valuable tips, by indicating what to expect and what not to. It is *relying*
on any of these extraliterary disciplines to answer the key literary questions
that leads to the numerous misconceptions we group as subdivisions under the
inclusive heading of the Intentionalist and Affective Fallacies.

In England, the partially abortive attempts of New Critics to put criticism
both on the map and on a sounder footing can be categorised, for diagnostic
convenience, as follows: moralistic criticism, psychological criticism, sociological
criticism, symbolic criticism, and, most recently and most hopefully, stylistic
criticism. These are by no means exclusive categories: moral criticism shades
off into the sociological on the one hand, through its concern with environ-
mental health, and into the psychological on the other, through its concern with
individual quality. Again, D. W. Harding, as a psychologist and a *Scrutineer,*
features in two categories. The Empson of *Seven Types of Ambiguity* (1930)
and *The Structure of Complex Words* (1951) is a stylistic critic; the Empson of
Some Versions of Pastoral (1935), a psychological one; and the Empson of *Milton's God* (1962), a moralist. Furthermore, Orwell, as an anti-Marxist, and
Caudwell, as a Marxist, naturally both come within the sociological category.
But, bearing such *caveats* in mind, we can briefly note under these headings the
virtues and limitations of what has been on the whole, for all its rancors and
theoretical failings, by far the most vital English criticism of this or any other
century.

Moralistic criticism: René Wellek has recently, and rightly, said:

> The impulses from Eliot and Richards were most effectively combined, in
> England at least, in the work of Frank Raymond Leavis (born 1895) and his
> disciples grouped around the magazine *Scrutiny* (1932–53). Leavis is a man of
> strong convictions and harsh polemical manners. He has in recent years sharply
> underlined his disagreements with the later development of Eliot [towards the
> subordination of literary to theological criticism] and Richards [towards purely
> linguistic and pedagogic studies]. . . . Leavis's concern with the text is often
> deceptive: he quickly leaves the verbal surface in order to define the peculiar
> emotions which an author conveys. He becomes a social and moral critic who,
> however, insists on the continuity of language and ethics, on the morality of
> form.[6]

The effectiveness of the combination of influences referred to is evidenced by
the fact that moralistic critics far outnumber those of any other category, and
Leavis has been easily the most influential critic of the century in England.
What Wellek might perhaps have stressed more is the fact that the *Scrutineers*
have generally been sufficiently scrupulous in their close attention to the text
to avoid the charge of naive moralism (i.e., judging crudely in terms of para-
phrasable content); they have focused rather on the quality of life revealed by

style. This is, however, a difficult poise to sustain, particularly under attack. One wonders if, for instance, it has been sustained in Leavis's John-the-Baptist championship of Lawrence or even in L. C. Knights's recent work on Shakespeare. Furthermore, such an approach, even at its best, must lead to a literary undervaluing of certain works. True, morality is being carefully associated with literary merit. But what about the purely literary merits of works not, in the critic's view, tending towards even so broad a concept of morality as the "life-enhancing"? Frivolous works, say, or pornographic ones? Yet such works may be dull, mediocre, or brilliant creations of their kind; and not to consider this is to be narrow in one's literary-critical outlook. At some point, in short, even the most subtle and enlightened moralism confuses essential differences, a confusion which has been increased in this case by Leavis's refusal to interest himself in theory and the consequent readiness of *Scrutineers* not only to move from description to evaluation a little too quickly, but also to be tempted into allowing unconscious, preliminary evaluations to affect the descriptions.

Psychological criticism: More obviously metacriticism—a form of psychology —than moralistic writing, this category of work nevertheless owes much to Richards's perfectly correct perception that an artscript exists significantly only as a response in the reader, though Graves's *Meaning of Dreams* (1924) and *Poetic Unreason* (1925) are first in the field. Richards's own development of his insight was immensely influential, but rather for its scientific tone, its astringency (poetry as mere pseudo-statement!) than for giving a working theory. The *Principles,* in fact, turned out not to be scientific (no one has measured an isolated esthetic impulse, let alone compared sets of them) and also not to be critical, since anything producing a harmonious balance of multiple impulses must count as good. But Richards also described the psychology of the artist and linked it with a theory of value—the artist being the man with a wider area of experience readily available—and this in turn was linked with a social ambition to improve society through literary culture, to train sensibilities so that more people would be more like artists, and fewer people bait for commercial stock-responses. This aspect of Richards's work, of course, leads on to Leavis and the moralists in one direction; in another, though, it combined with the scientific tone to lead to a revival of Coleridge's interest in the psychology of the creative process. D. W. Harding, once a *Scrutineer* and now a Professor of Psychology, has recently published a most interesting collection of essays of this kind, under the title *Experience in Words.* It is significant, however, that the least literary-critical essays, those dealing psychologically with preverbal experience and feelings of "social" kinship with dead authors, "speaking" to us through their works, are the most completely satisfying. The others, inevitably, tend towards the intentionalist or affective fallacies when they are literary-critical, towards metacriticism when they are psychological. F. L. Lucas's *Literature and Psychology* (1951) covered more relationships—social, biographical, sexual, and so on—but rather surrounded literature than took its citadel. Empson, as always, was dazzlingly brilliant in the Freudian analyses of *Some Versions of Pastoral* (1935), but nevertheless was necessarily open to the objection that the literary quality of a work is irrelevant to its suitability for such analyses and is rarely illuminated by it.

Romantic criticism tends to be inspirational and intuitive, but in so far as it concerns itself with the discovery of Jungian oppositions and integrations or Adlerian desires, it is closely allied to psychological criticism and is therefore open to the same objections. Maud Bodkin's *Archetypal Patterns* (1934) was one of the most important examples; and it did undoubtedly help to explain how certain works move us, though they are not realistic or even obviously applicable to real life in any way. But the "how" of such works must be very general and superficial, for *Macbeth* is as archetypal in comic strip as in blank verse; so the demonstration of archetypes has nothing to do with specifically literary quality.

G. Wilson Knight, Lord of the Symbol-hunters, has been less psychological than mystical in his romanticism, somewhat associating himself thereby with J. Middleton Murry, while Herbert Read links up rather with Miss Bodkin. Nevertheless, since Knight's symbols are always of an archetypal kind (Life and Death, Time and Eternity, Sex and Spirit, Light and Dark), his criticism ultimately runs into the same dead-end; and in fact he has, quite logically, claimed greatness for an amazing number of second-rate works, such as Byron's dramas and Eastern tales, on the ground that they reveal "Eternity." Other objections are that in his view translations must be equivalent to the originals; that no writer can protect himself, since anything, however naturalistically tested, that such a critic approves of can be made symbolical, given sufficient ingenuity; and that categories so general leave practically nothing a work is *not* about, and are thus uninformative. Admittedly, Wilson Knight's first book, *The Wheel of Fire* (1930), did give a new direction to Shakespeare studies, turning attention from "character" and "plot" to "theme" and "image-pattern," but the increasingly erratic quality of his later books clearly reveals the uncontrolled element in his critical theory. Perhaps one should rather say "interpretative" theory, as the introduction to *The Wheel of Fire* claims to be interpretative but not critical. Criticism, it allows to be equal with interpretation but different (at the same time always associating the word "criticism" with pejoratives). However, this simply seems an excuse for doing criticism without the usual safeguards against eccentricity of interpretation.

Sociological criticism ranges from Empson's minute analyses of the implications of Gray's "Elegy" (in *Some Versions of Pastoral,* called *English Pastoral Poetry* in the United States) to Christopher Caudwell's heady Marxist mixture of brilliance and nonsense, in the form of general ideas, in *Illusion and Reality* (1937), of which a non-Marxist socialist critic, Raymond Williams, has aptly written:

> Christopher Caudwell remains the best-known of these English Marxist critics, but his influence is curious. His theories and outlines have been widely learned, although in fact he has little to say, of actual literature, that is even interesting. It is not only that it is difficult to have confidence in the literary qualifications of anyone who can give his account of the development of medieval into Elizabethan drama, or who can make his paraphrase of the 'sleep' line from

Macbeth, but that for the most part his discussion is not even specific enough to be wrong. On the other hand, he is immensely prolific of ideas, over an unusually wide field of interest.[7]

Caudwell and other Marxist critics, however, can be contrasted with Arnold Kettle, a communist whose training in the Literature-Life-and-Thought complex of the Cambridge English Tripos is more evident in his criticism than communism is. In this way there is a direct line from Leavis (an anti-communist) to the communist critics. However, communist criticism in England has never been important or influential. Much more vital are critics like Raymond Williams, Richard Hoggart (*Uses of Literacy*, 1957) and George Orwell, all of whom have used literature, with stimulating and valuable results, as a means to an end: the metacritical extension of our insights into social culture, particularly as it is affected by the mass-media. Like Leavis, but in a different direction, they pass rather rapidly from close attention to the text to a more general concern. In between, come former *Scrutineers*, like the L. C. Knights of *Drama and Society in the Age of Jonson* (1937) or *Poetry, Politics, and the English Tradition* (1954), or non-Leavisite products of Cambridge and those provincial universities that set literature firmly in its age and ethos, who differ from older historical critics only in their closer focus on the verbal surface of the text.

Stylistic criticism springs from the combination of this belief in the primary importance of the words on the page and a knowledge of the fallacies lurking in reliance on other approaches. The historicist, personalist, romantic, biographical, or intentionalist and affective fallacies all somewhat discredit the non-stylistic modes of criticism, particularly in so far as any one is taken as a sole touchstone of merit. If one assumes the assessment of specifically literary facts and qualities to be the critic's chief job—while not denying him the right to push out into surrounding fields in which he is an amateur, providing he acknowledges what he is doing—then it seems to follow that close attention to language should be his first concern. From the beginning, of course, such attention had been given by Empson and Richards. But this was almost entirely a matter of the semantics of ambiguity and overtone. What is new is the development—recognised at Nottingham by a course called *Critical Linguists*—of adding to this semantic interest a concern with syntax, musical effects, and matters open to philosophical linguistic analysis.

Empson's brilliant *Structure of Complex Words* (1951), an analysis of the operation of key words in a larger structure, was first in the field. Donald Davie's *Articulate Energy* (1955) provided a theoretical argument for investigating the "poetry" of syntax, and incidentally put a bomb under the established modernist dogma, first stated by Richards, that creative literature should *be* not *say*, which led to the cult of the image, the omission of grammatical filling, and the consequent typical obscurity of modernism. This point was reinforced by Graham Hough in *Images and Experience* (1960); and finally Mrs. Nowottny, in *The Language Poets Use* (1963), demonstrated the strictly literary illumination to be derived from a critical practice which took the linguistic facts, especially those of syntax, to be the primary but not exclusive concern of a modern critic.

Undoubtedly, this approach, too, has its dangers. Already a linguistic fallacy seems due for exposure: the belief that certain syntactical structures must entail parallels of sense or suggestion. They may, but since structures in English are finite (and in practice rather limited) while possibilities of meaning are infinite, it is obvious that such a method must be used carefully. There is, in short, no substitute for sense in criticism, no automatic method. Nevertheless, the sheer commonsense of the basic idea of this approach—that verbal artefacts are most profitably approached through their use of language, rather than through the mind or the society that produced them or through the minds and groups that they affect—seems sufficient to warrant the feeling that this is now the growing point of a maturing New Criticism.

UNIVERSITY OF NOTTINGHAM

NOTES

1. *The Barbarian Within* (New York, 1962), p. 205.
2. *Scrutiny*, XII (Winter 1943), pp. 13, 23.
3. *Ibid.*, p. 20.
4. *Ibid.*, p. 22.
5. *Lions and Shadows* (London, 1953), pp. 121–122.
6. *Concepts of Criticism* (New Haven, 1963), p. 358.
7. *Culture and Society* (Baltimore, 1961), p. 269.

II

Literary Movements

There is no question that literary movements are positive historical developments about which an inexhaustible supply of evidence is available. Movements are sometimes designated by a term representing a specific chronological period during which these characteristics show greatest vitality and sometimes by a term referring to prevailing esthetic and psychological characteristics. For example, the interest in the classics, humanism, and art characteristic of the fifteenth and sixteenth centuries is called the Renaissance, and the revolt against dogmatism in literature, authority in politics, and conformity in behavior breaking out at the end of the eighteenth century is called Romanticism. Philip P. Wiener has pointed out that historians of ideas must distinguish between names which "they give to past periods, e.g. the Middle Ages or Red Decade, from the names consciously used during the period, e.g. Renaissance, Enlightenment, Depression" (*J.H.I.*, XXII [1961], 542). In the eighteenth century, for example, English poets considered themselves as belonging to a new Augustan Age, but the terms classical and classicism were not used to describe the age until the nineteenth century. Although designations of periods such as Renaissance or Enlightenment appear to be static, and designations of movements such as Romanticism or Naturalism appear to be fluid, these nuances are purely linguistic. Both designations refer to measurable characteristics apparent during a specific chronological period. At the same time it is correct to refer to romantic or naturalistic tendencies in any chronological period, but to the Renaissance or the

Enlightenment merely in reference to particular centuries. The latter two movements are closely related to political, philosophical, and social changes; whereas others such as Symbolism or Realism are more closely related to painting, music, and other arts.

Some periods or movements such as the Middle Ages and the Renaissance embraced all of Europe during a particular chronological span and affected all phases of life; whereas others such as the Baroque or the Enlightenment influenced only certain cultures and in varying degrees. A danger to which comparatists are especially prone is that of "homogenizing." Literary historians, like historians of ideas, sometimes assume that since a certain intellectual climate exists in two or three countries in a certain period, the same condition must inevitably exist in neighboring areas. This assumption, which is by no means always warranted, explains the embarrassed lack of success of scholars looking for extensive signs of the Baroque in England or of the Enlightenment in Spain. One of the most widely debated of all movements is that of Romanticism. The first of the following articles demonstrates that the concept means many things to many people, that its characteristics changed from country to country, and that it did not exist simultaneously in all the areas which it reached. The second article points out and corrects another danger of viewing by movements — that of attributing to single authors a wide range of characteristics supposedly typical of a certain movement, but which may not exist at all in the work of the author in question.

LILIAN R. FURST

Romanticism

in Historical Perspective

ABSTRACT

This article gives a chronological survey of the emergence of the Romantic movements in England, France, and Germany. The spread of new ideas is traced from country to country in the successive waves of Romantic writing between 1750 and 1830. The principal aim is to ascertain the correct sequence and historical perspective; for by recognizing that Romanticism was not a simultaneous outburst, but rather a series of distinct upsurges, a sounder basis is established for the exploration of the maze of similarities and differences linking the Romantic movements in Europe. [L. R. F.]

No subject in the whole field of comparative literary studies has provoked as much critical writing as Romanticism. And rightly so, for none indeed so insistently demands, and so richly rewards, a broad approach embracing several literatures. But all the attempts to discern the salient features of European Romanticism, all the arguments as to its fundamental unity or otherwise, and all the tentative definitions seem to be based on the assumption that simultaneous outbursts of Romanticism occurred in various countries about the beginning of the nineteenth century. This was simply not the case: the spread of Romanticism is characterized by curious time lags and unexpected spurts. In fact the movement's external history sheds so much light on its inner nature that a chronological survey, though apparently an elementary exercise in literary history, is a necessary and potentially illuminating preliminary to any further discussion. To establish the correct sequence and perspective not only obviates some, at least, of the more common misapprehensions but also creates a sounder base from which to explore the maze of Romantic movements in Europe.

"Une crise de la conscience européenne": [1] this is the succinct and telling phrase chosen by van Tieghem to describe the Romantic movement in Europe. The claim that it was far more than just another literary movement is not based primarily on the sheer extent, the expanse of Romanticism, though it is in fact true that no other literary movement has ever evoked such a wide response throughout Europe. The real significance of Romanticism as a *"crise de la conscience européenne"* lies not in its mere quantity, but in the *quality* of the changes it implied. For Romanticism brought not just a greater freedom and a new technique; these were only the outer manifestations of a complete and deep-seated reorientation, not to say revolution, in the manners of thought, perception, and consequently of expression too. The nature of this revolution has recently been outlined in vivid terms by Isaiah Berlin who defined it as a "shift of consciousness" that "cracked the backbone of European thought." [2] That backbone had been the belief in the possibility of a rational comprehension of the universe. When the rationalistic approach was applied to the arts as well as to the emergent physical sciences, it resulted in those rigid pronouncements on the immutable 'rules' of literature that were the bane of Neoclassicism. This dogmatism was first cautiously questioned and then vehemently rejected in the course of the eighteenth century, and finally the old standards were ousted by the Romantics' new criteria and values. In place of the Neoclassical ideals of rationalism, traditionalism, and formal harmony, the Romantics emphasized individualism, imagination, and emotion as their guiding principles. Hence the old 'rules' of 'good taste,' regularity, and conformity gave way to the unbridled creative urge of the original genius, and the ideal of a smooth beauty was scorned in favour of a dynamic outpouring of feeling. A new mode of imaginative perception gave birth to a whole new vocabulary and new forms of artistic expression: this is the essence of that *"crise de la conscience européenne"* which lies at the heart of the Romantic revolution, and this is also perhaps as near an approximation to a definition of Romanticism as is possible. It may not have the neatness of a snappy catchphrase (such as 'the return to nature' or 'the cult of the extinct'), but it is

sufficiently comprehensive and sufficiently plain to serve as a viable working basis.

This reorientation occurred in varying degrees throughout Europe in the latter part of the eighteenth and the early years of the nineteenth centuries. In this sense Romanticism can rightly be regarded as a European phenomenon that can be appreciated in all its implications only by means of a comparative study. Many of the Romantics themselves were well aware of the supranational character of the movement: the brothers Schlegel consciously cherished the notion of a specifically European Romantic literature as part of their striving for an all-embracing 'universal poetry,' and both Coleridge and Novalis hoped for an eventual European reintegration. Perhaps these cosmopolitan tendencies of the Romantics have encouraged critics to seek out the common denominators of the Romantic movements and to overemphasize the similarities between the literatures of various countries. The 'family likeness' which certainly meets the eye can be traced back to the communal ancestry of Romanticism throughout Europe, which springs from one and the same momentous spiritual and intellectual reorientation.

To delve into the origins of this revolution is beyond the scope of this study. The first unmistakable signs of impending change manifested themselves before the middle of the eighteenth century, and in this earliest phase—say 1740 to 1770—it is England that was to the fore. As early as 1742, Young, inspired by personal grief at the death of his daughter and of a friend, published his *Night Thoughts,* which were followed in 1745 by Akenside's *Pleasures of Imagination.* Historically these two works have much in common in that they stand midway between the conventional moralism of the age and a fresh outlook which admits imagination to respectability in poetic practice. Imagination, according to Akenside, "diffuses its enchantment" and makes the soul "to that harmonious movement from without / Responsive": [3] no very startling claim as yet, but at least a first glimmer of a recognition of the powers of the imagination. The personal melancholy and the funereal cult of the *Night Thoughts* were reiterated in Hervey's *Meditations Among the Tombs* (1746) and Gray's *Elegy Written in a Country Churchyard* (1751) with their awareness of the fleetingness and pathos of human life, their preference for darkness, solitude, the evocation of solemn, somber scenes. The slightly moralizing sensibility of the period is as apparent in these poems as in the novels of Richardson and his imitators. This sensibility was deeply affected by Macpherson's *Fingal* (1762) which, together with Percy's *Reliques* (1765), laid the foundations for the subsequent popularity of supposedly naive folk-poetry, the natural utterances of primitive, spontaneous genius. Macpherson's concoctions, purporting to be a transcription from the ancient bard Ossian, made a particularly strong impression throughout Europe with their highly-coloured intrigues, their gloomy Northern setting, their whole outlandishness, and, above all, their rhythmic prose, which seemed so much more poetic than the poetry of the early eighteenth century:

Star of descending night! fair is thy light in the west! thou liftest thy unshorn head from thy cloud: thy steps are stately on thy hill. What dost thou behold in the plain? The stormy winds are laid. The murmur of the torrent comes from afar. Roaring waves climb the distant rock. The flies of evening are on their feeble wings; the hum of their course is on the field. What dost thou behold, fair light? But thou dost smile and depart. The waves come with joy around thee: they bathe thy lovely hair. Farewell, thou silent beam! Let the light of Ossian's soul arise! [4]

Alongside Ossian, the other decisive document of English pre-Romanticism, Young's *Conjectures on Original Composition* (1759), was of far-reaching import as the herald of the new aesthetics. Some of Young's ideas were, it is true, already current in England among his contemporaries, notably in the discourses of Burke, Thomas and Joseph Warton, and William Sharpe. But never before had these ideas been stated as cogently as in the *Conjectures;* by his clear-sighted distinctions between imitation and originality, the ancients and the moderns, learning and genius, the observation of rules and the energy of the inspired enthusiast, Young was crucial in precipitating the reorientation away from the old accepted notions. Here for the first time, the superiority of the new ideals was proclaimed beyond a shadow of doubt: "An Original may be said to be of a vegetable nature; it rises spontaneously from the vital root of genius; it grows, it is not made: Imitations are often a sort of manufacture, wrought by those mechanics, art and labour, out of pre-existent materials not their own." [5] Or again, take the contrast between a "genius" and a "good understanding": "A genius differs from a good understanding, as a magician from a good architect; that raises his structure by means invisible; this by skilful use of common tools. Hence genius has ever been supposed to partake of something divine." [6] These two brief examples alone suffice to illustrate the incisive quality of Young's thinking. Many of the key concepts of Romanticism are already contained in the *Conjectures*, in the prominence given to such words as "original," "genius," "grows," "magician," "divine." There is thus some justification for the contention that "this vast romantic movement was the European reverberation of English eighteenth century romanticism, like the thunder of Alpine re-echoing to a pistol-shot." [7] Many of the essential elements of Romanticism were indeed present in England toward the middle of the eighteenth century: some recognition of the role of the imagination, the emphasis on the original composition of the genius, the cult of sensibility, the vague religious feeling, the melancholy reverie, the interest in 'natural' poetry, the discovery of external nature. But it would be premature to call this anything other than pre-Romanticism, for these were merely trends and beginnings with the stress on the natural—no doubt in reaction against the artificial overrefinement of Neoclassicism—whereas the dominant factor in Romanticism proper was the transfiguring imagination, whose true significance was not yet appreciated.

While this reorientation was progressing rapidly in England, France and Germany were far behind during this initial phase. France was still suffering from the backwash of its glorious Neoclassical age, which continued to overshadow creative writing and to a large extent to stifle innovation. A spirit of enlightenment does pervade at least the early criticism of Diderot, such as the prefaces to his plays *Le fils naturel* (1757) and *Le père de famille* (1758), where he advocates a greater realism; but after this advance towards emotionalism he was, in his later works, to return to the assumptions of the Neoclassical creed. Only Rousseau broke really new ground: his disgust with the social order of the time, based on ownership of land and goods, led him to idealize the primitive state of mankind and to call for the famous return to nature. Important though this was, it was by no means Rousseau's sole contribution to pre-Romanticism; his assimilation of external nature to man's moods in *Les rêveries du promeneur solitaire* and *La nouvelle Héloïse,* his musical prose style, and his spotlight on his ego in his autobiographical writings all plainly foreshadow certain later developments. Rousseau, however, was not understood, at least not in France, until later; meanwhile his most immediate effect was in Germany through the intermediary of Herder, an enthusiastic disciple of Rousseau's, who transmitted his admiration for Rousseau to the young adherents of the *Sturm und Drang* movement.

In the mid-eighteenth century Germany was in the literary field the most backward of the major European countries; politically disunited and economically disrupted by internal strife, Germany had in the latter half of the seventeenth and the early years of the eighteenth century virtually been lying fallow. A new era began to dawn in the 1730's with the notorious quarrel between the doctrinal rationalist Gottsched and the somewhat less narrow-minded Swiss critics Bodmer and Breitinger, who realized that poetry could not be made according to a set recipe—like a cake—as Gottsched had assumed. Bodmer in 1740 published his *Kritische Abhandlung von dem Wunderbaren in der Poesie* ("Discourse Concerning the Wondrous Element in Poetry"), the title of which already indicates the progression towards a more fruitful conception of art. The Enlightenment found its most vigorous and wise exponent in Lessing, who savagely attacked the 'frenchified' (*"französierend"* he contemptuously calls it in the seventeenth *Literaturbrief*) mode of writing favoured by Gottsched. He pleaded instead that German writers should model themselves on the freer products of the English, whose spirit was more akin to their own. Lessing was not the first to turn his gaze towards England; Bodmer and Breitinger had earlier championed and translated Milton, and Klopstock's *Messias* (1748) is patently indebted to *Paradise Lost*. Although Lessing was thus not the first to point towards England, nevertheless his position in Germany was as crucial as, and in some respects comparable to, that of Young in England. For it was Lessing who in his *Literaturbriefe* (1759) and *Hamburgische Dramaturgie* (1767) presented a reasoned and compelling case for the decisive reorientation not only from France to England but also from imitation to original creation, extolling Shakespeare as the supreme creative genius. Herder in his rhapsodic appraisal of Shakespeare and also of Ossian furthered the cult of genius, stimulated no doubt by the German translation of Young's *Conjectures* which appeared in 1760. The vital impetus therefore reached Germany from England, the fountainhead of European pre-Romanticism.

In the second phase, between about 1770 and 1790, this position was reversed, for the ascendancy which had been England's now passed to Germany. Both England and France were in no haste to accept new notions, perhaps because the native literary tradition was firmly established; in France it tended to exercise a retarding influence—the great 'battle' of *Hernani* took place only in the year 1830—while in England the lack of resistance to innovations paradoxically led to their comparatively slow infiltration. Germany, on the contrary, was thirsting for a fresh start after its long period of inertia. So Germany's very backwardness proved in fact an advantage when the young writers of the *Sturm und Drang* movement, for lack of a strong native tradition, eagerly seized on the stimuli from abroad, and it was they who popularized and propagated the new attitudes throughout Europe.

The essence of the *Sturm und Drang*, whose name was derived from Klinger's drama of 1776, lay in rebellion against finite restriction in any shape or form—literary, political, or social. This self-assertive rebelliousness was more than the adolescent defiance of a few gifted young men; it arose directly out of the proud conviction of the limitless rights and powers of the divinely-inspired genius. Thus the theories formulated a few years earlier by Young were activated by the *Sturm und Drang* and found living examples in the youthful Goethe and Schiller. All the favourite ideas of the *Sturm und Drang* pivoted on the figure of the truly great, exceptional man; it was his personal experiences and emotions which were to be transformed into art through the creative power of his unbridled imagination. No wonder that the *Sturm und Drang* is often and aptly termed the *Geniezeit* ("Period of Genius"). Incoherent and supremely arrogant though it was, the credo of the *Sturm und Drang* foreshadowed very many of the basic concepts of Romanticism: the belief in the autonomy of the divinely inspired genius, the release of the imagination from the bondage of 'good taste,' the primacy of spontaneous and intuitive feeling, the complete freedom of artistic expression, and, finally, the notion of organic growth and development, from which arose both an interest in the past, particularly the Middle Ages, and a new pantheistic vision of nature as part of a unified cosmos. Nor were these ideas to remain mere theories any longer; in the early works of Goethe and Schiller the new mode of perception and expression burst upon a startled Europe. And how immeasurable is the gulf that separates Goethe's dynamic nature poetry from the pretty lyrics of the preceding generation! Consider the formal, pedestrian description by Brockes in his "Betrachtungen des Mondscheins in einer angenehmen Frühlingsnacht" in the 1721 collection *Irdisches Vergnügen in Gott* (note the clumsy titles):

> Kaum hatte sich die Nacht zu zeigen angefangen,
> Die nach der Hitze Last der Kühlung Lust verhiess,
> Als sich ein neuer Tag dem Schein nach sehen liess:
> Der volle Mond war aus dem grauen Duft,
> Der nach des Tages schwüler Luft
> Mit Purpur untermischt den Horizont bedeckte
> Wie rötlich Gold nur eben aufgegangen,
> Aus dessen wandelbarem Kreise,
> Der alles in der Nacht mit Licht und Schimmer füllt,
> Mehr Anmut noch als Licht und Schimmer quillt.[8]

Compare these mundane lines with the intensely imaginative, mysteriously intuitive perception of the same scene in Goethe's bewitching "An den Mond":

> Füllest wieder Busch und Tal
> Still mit Nebelglanz,
> Lösest endlich auch einmal
> Meine Seele ganz;
> Breitest über mein Gefild
> Lindernd deinen Blick,
> Wie des Freundes Auge mild
> Über mein Geschick.[9]

In the face of these two texts, further verbal comment on the revolution wrought by the *Sturm und Drang* becomes superfluous. It was at this time too, in the early 1770's, that the great Romantic prototypes were delineated in the melancholy hero Werther and the insatiable seeker Faust, figures that were to haunt Europe. The impact of *Werther* is already notorious; Goethe became the idol of Europe. The success of Schiller's *Die Räuber* was even more immediate and widespread: in England as well as in France, Schiller was acclaimed with such wild enthusiasm as to trigger a veritable mania for the German theatre, admittedly excessive and short lived. Nevertheless, Goethe and Schiller remained in the eyes of both the English and the French the typical representatives of German Romanticism, and strange though this misconception may at first seem, it is in fact not without some justification. For in the *Sturm und Drang*, the culmination of pre-Romanticism, the first significant breakthrough was achieved, and in this Goethe and Schiller were largely instrumental. With the publication of Kant's three major works, the *Kritik der reinen Vernunft* in 1781, the *Kritik der praktischen Vernunft* in 1788, and the *Kritik der Urteilskraft* in 1790, the mortal blows were struck at the old rationalist system. F. Schlegel was justified in his proud claim that the springs of the new age were rising in Germany. To suggest, however, that Romanticism should really be called "Germanticism" on account of its essentially Germanic roots and spirit [10] is an exaggeration, not to say a distortion in view of its early sources in England, although it is not without some element of (albeit poetic) truth, and the high incidence of German words used in connection with Romanticism (*Sehnsucht, Weltschmerz, europamüde, Dies- und Jenseitigkeit*) in itself indicates Romanticism's deep entrenchment in Germany.

Thenceforth the overall picture of European Romanticism becomes increasingly complex as the new creed slowly spread from country to country. For a time yet Germany was to remain in the ascendancy, so that this third phase was again largely overshadowed by Germany. This was her most glorious age, for the 1790's witness not only the elaboration of Romanticism but also the heyday of her Neoclassical period. These were the momentous years of the Goethe-Schiller friendship when the former wrote *Reineke Fuchs* (1794), *Römische Elegien* (1795), *Wilhelm Meisters Lehrjahre* (1795), *Venezianische Epigramme* (1797), *Hermann und Dorothea* (1798), and many of his best-known ballads, while Schiller's work included *Über Anmut und Würde* (1793), *Über naive und sentimentalische Dichtung* (1795), *Briefe über die ästhetische Erziehung des Menschen* (1795), *Das Ideal und das Leben* (1795), *Wallenstein* (1798-99), *Das Lied von der Glocke* (1799) and other ballads, as well as the *Xenien* (1796) on which the two friends collaborated. In order to realize fully the extent to which Romantic and Neoclassical strains were contemporaneous in Germany—a fact that is often forgotten or overlooked—it is perhaps worth enumerating briefly some of the other works which appeared during this period: in 1794, Fichte's *Wissenschaftslehre;* in 1797, the great ballad-year of Goethe and Schiller, Schelling's *Ideen zu einer Philosophie der Natur,* Tieck's *Volksmärchen,* Wackenroder's *Herzensergiessungen eines kunstliebenden Klosterbruders,* A. W. Schlegel's first translations from Shakespeare; in 1798, the journal of the Jena Romantic group, the *Athenäum;* in 1799, Schleiermacher's *Reden über die Religion* and F. Schlegel's *Lucinde;* and the new century opened with Novalis' *Hymnen an die Nacht.* In these works the writers of the Jena Romantic group expounded their own *Weltanschauung*

which was in many essential points a development of the earlier
ideas of the *Sturm und Drang,* although these had never been
fashioned into a coherent aesthetic system. Like their predecessors,
the Jena group founded their whole system on the unquestioned
primacy of the subjective imagination of the original creative
genius, a doctrine which had been strengthened by the powerful
support of Fichte's philosophy, so that this subjective imagination
now became literally the alpha and omega of the universe. The
notion of organic growth and development and the consequent
interest in history and in living nature, the arrogation of complete
artistic freedom as the birthright of the autonomous divine genius,
the trust in spontaneous emotion and instinct: all these were
inherited from the *Sturm und Drang,* although German Romanticism was not a mere continuation of the earlier movement and
there were vital shifts of emphasis and mood which reveal the
distinct character of the Jena school. The later group was more
complex than the relatively straightforward rebels of the *Sturm und
Drang* who sought to live and create solely according to the dictates
of feeling, while the Romantic strives also for knowledge, consciousness, a mastery of those feelings which in turn produced a certain
self-detachment, the key to that curious Romantic concept of irony.
As its name implies, the *Sturm und Drang* had been youthful,
forward-looking, vigorous, and realistic in its rebellion against an
irksome reality, whereas with the Jena school an introvert, transcendental longing came to the fore as the Romantic looked beyond
this world in his quest for an intangible, unattainable ideal in a
dream sphere of his own creation. To the revolutionary naturalism
of Rousseau and the melancholy pietism of English pre-Romanticism was now added the transcendentalism of the German philosophers, for the Jena Romantic group, speculative rather than creative
by nature, was responsible for the major body of German Romantic
philosophy and it was at this point that German Romanticism
assumed its characteristic hue. An all-embracing expansiveness,
coloured by a pervasive mysticism, is its hallmark, so that it is a
way of living and perceiving rather·than merely of writing which
was expounded in the theories of the brothers Schlegel, Schelling,
Schleiermacher, and Wackenroder. The spread in scope and breadth
is vast. As poetry turns into *"eine progressive Universalpoesie,"* [11]
it tends not only to mingle the various genres and media but also
more and more to lose its specific meaning and to become confused

and amalgamated with philosophy, religion, history, philology, science, and politics. This cosmic extension of the meaning of poetry was to be of the utmost importance for the whole of the nineteenth century and beyond too.

So rapidly had the European balance changed that in these years it was the turn of England and France to be comparatively backward. In France, the Revolution blotted all else from men's minds and the Reign of Terror virtually silenced creative writing for a time. As Mme. de Staël reported: "Les Français, depuis vingt années, sont tellement préoccupés par les événements politiques, que toutes leurs études en littérature ont été suspendues." [12] Or again: "Depuis quelque temps on ne lit guère en France que des mémoires ou des romans; et ce n'est pas tout à fait par frivolité qu'on est devenu moins capable de lectures plus sérieuses, c'est parce que les événements de la Révolution ont accoutumé à ne mettre de prix qu'à la connaissance des faits et des hommes." [13] From the welter of arguments as to whether the Revolution impeded the advance of Romanticism or fostered it by breaking down the old authoritarian order in the social sphere, only one fact emerges with any certainty: namely, the dearth of creative writing during the Revolutionary period. Hence that curious hiatus in French literary development in the years 1790 to 1820. The few works which did appear were mainly in the Rousseauistic tradition, such as the exotic novels of Bernardin de Saint-Pierre whose *Paul et Virginie* (1787) and *La chaumière indienne* (1791) both illustrate the so-called return to nature. Chateaubriand's *Atala* (1801) and *René* (1805) are also indebted to the ideas of Rousseau, and none of these, no more than the *Génie du Christianisme* (1802), was regarded by contemporaries as a serious menace to the Neoclassical tradition which still reigned unchallenged. French Romanticism, when it did finally assert itself, was to be above all a revolt against this firmly entrenched and ossified Neoclassicism and it is significant that the earliest glimmerings of the new orientation first insinuated themselves into the stronghold of Neoclassicism in prose, the genre least subject to the dictates and rules of the Neoclassical creed.

There were no such hindrances to overcome in England, which was gradually awakening to the new tendencies. In Blake's *Songs of Innocence* (1787) and *Songs of Experience* (1794), imagery was used in a manner totally different from its eighteenth-century decorative function, and this was a vital breakthrough of the new type of poetic expression. The mid-1790's also witnessed the growing popularity of tales of horror with Mrs. Radcliffe's *Mysteries of Udolpho* in 1794 and *The Monk* by Lewis in 1796. It was in 1798, the year of the *Lyrical Ballads,* that Wordsworth accompanied Coleridge to Germany. Ironically, England was now to receive its stimulus from Germany, from ideas which had in fact originated on her shores and had been elaborated abroad while they were more or less ignored at home. That homecoming began in the 1790's with the spread of knowledge about German literature which had previously been dismissed, in spite of the success of *Werther,* as revolutionary, sensationalist, extravagantly sentimental, and not quite respectable. The term 'German Novel,' for instance, was for long a self-explanatory expression of opprobrium, a stigma stemming from the many worthless *Schauerromane,* stories that send a shudder down the reader's spine, which had been translated into English to satisfy the thirst for horror stories. A number of original English Gothic novels of dubious quality were at that time passed off as renderings from German, thus bringing German literature into further disrepute. Gradually a truer picture was to emerge, dating from Henry Mackenzie's paper on German drama read before the Royal Society of Edinburgh in 1788 and published in 1790. Here Schiller was mentioned for the first time in Britain in a startling eulogy of *Die Räuber,* the tremendous appeal of which lay in the novelty of its subject, the atmosphere of horror, and the unbridled expression of emotional crises. It made a vehement impression on Coleridge when he read it in 1794, arousing the curiosity about German literature that was to take him and Wordsworth to Germany in 1798.

While France was in the throes of the Revolution, and England was only gradually assimilating the new tendencies, Germany still remained the home of Romanticism. The Heidelberg group of 1805-1815 differed from the earlier, more closely-knit Jena circle in that it was far less philosophically inclined. Forsaking the metaphysical speculations of the Jena theorists, the Heidelberg poets created many of the works for which German Romanticism earned its fame abroad, such as the tales of Hoffmann, Chamisso, Fouqué, the poems of Uhland, Körner, Brentano, Arnim. More extrovert than their immediate predecessors, these Heidelberg poets exploited the Jena theories for practical creative purposes. Their demand for a spontaneous expression of emotion led to a glorious blossoming of lyric poetry; the probing of the irrational aspects of life—the so-called nocturnal sides of nature—was now precipitated into a host of supernatural and fantastic stories, such as those of Tieck and Hoffmann; and finally the interest in history, formerly part of a composite belief in organic growth and development, now also assumed more specific forms either in scholarly research into the past, as exemplified by the philological enquiries of the brothers Grimm, or in the newly emergent national consciousness and pride which evoked, under the threat of the Napoleonic wars, lyric cycles with such titles as the *Geharnischte Sonette* ("Sonnets in Armour") by Rückert (1814), Körner's *Leyer und Schwert* ("Lyre and Sword") of the same year, and Arndt's *Lieder für Teutsche* ("Songs for Germans"). This was the climate which fostered Arnim's and Brentano's *Des Knaben Wunderhorn* (1806-1808) and like collections of folktales in Görres' *Die teutschen Volksbücher* (1807) and Grimm's *Märchen* (1812). In these patriotic nationalistic endeavours the writers of the Heidelberg group foreshadowed the more directly political and social aims of the *Jung-Deutschland* movement of the mid-nineteenth century. It is at this point that the time lag in European Romanticism is at its most blatant; for while Romanticism has hardly stirred in France as yet and is only about to unfold fully in England, in Germany it is already past its zenith and moving steadily towards the more sober social preoccupations of the subsequent period. In the face of these discrepancies alone, who would dare to envisage European Romanticism as one unified and consistent entity?

In this interregnum there appeared a work that was of extraordinary importance in the history of Romanticism in Europe: Mme de Staël's *De l'Allemagne*. During her exile from France, Mme de Staël travelled fairly extensively in Germany, where she met, among others, Goethe, Schiller, and A. W. Schlegel, who became her son's tutor. In contrast to his volatile and inventive brother Friedrich, August Wilhelm Schlegel was the most perceptive and orderly of the Jena group, so that his elegantly clear formulations of German Romantic thought were more comprehensible and accessible to foreigners than the perhaps profounder, transcendental thinking of Friedrich Schlegel, Schelling, or Schleiermacher; and with the translations of his *Vorlesungen über dramatische Kunst und Literatur* into French in 1813 and into English in 1815, A. W. Schlegel truly became the *"Herold oder Dolmetscher"* [14] of Romantic thought. In A. W. Schlegel, Mme de Staël thus met a man well able to fan her enthusiasm for Germany. The external history of *De l'Allemagne*—the hindrances to publication, the role of political considerations, etc.—are irrelevant in the present context except in so far as this opposition in itself indicates the French reluctance, indeed fear, to import foreign ideas which seemed an insult and a menace to French cultural dominance. In spite, or perhaps partly because, of the violent resistance to its publication, *De l'Allemagne* became the standard source of knowledge on Germany, and beyond that a manifesto of the new cosmopolitanism and a decisive step in the renewal of French literature after its long subservience to the tenets of an emasculated Neoclassicism. In this work Mme de Staël sought to delineate the concept of a poetry different from the great native tradition of France, for she fully realized the need for a transfusion of new blood. In introducing contemporary German writing to France, she constantly contrasted its originality, vitality, and imagination with the sterile rigidity, *"le genre maniéré,"* [15] of moribund French Neoclassicism. Much valid criticism can be levelled against Mme de Staël: she saw Germany in the literary as well as in the social and moral sense as the country of *Hermann und Dorothea,* thereby nurturing the strangely persistent French picture of Germany as *"une région fabuleuse, où les hommes gazouillent et chantent comme les oiseaux."* [16] Moreover, she had little acquaintance with the work of the Jena group (there is, for instance, no mention whatsoever of Novalis) and regarded Goethe, Schiller, Bürger, and Tieck as the representative German Romantic poets; nor had she much head for abstract philosophy and no more than a superficial comprehension of Romanticism, distinguishing between Classical and Romantic poetry as *"celle qui a précédé l'établissement du christianisme et celle qui l'a suivi."* [17] All her judgments are formed from a plainly French standpoint so that she regards German and English literature as one entity, the literature of the Romantic North, as against the Classical literature of France and Southern Europe. Nevertheless, in spite of her undeniable weaknesses and failings, Mme de Staël was an astute, perspicacious arbiter, whose observations are often acute and who grasped the essence of the new orientation of German literature. In some respects Mme de Staël's position is reminiscent of that of Lessing: though more emotional and fanciful in manner than the sensible exponent of the Enlightenment, basically she advocates the same emancipation from the traditional rules in favour of a poetry fathered by the enthusiasm of genius. In fact, *De l'Allemagne* presents an admirable survey of the *Sturm und Drang* phase of German literature, that is, of pre-Romanticism rather than of the Romantic groups themselves. This is a crucial factor for the comprehension of European Romanticism since the opinions expressed by Mme de Staël and, perhaps even more important, her omissions, for long not only determined the French (and to a lesser extent the English) view of German literature but also shaped the course and nature of the French Romantic movement. So the preference for Schiller, the conception of Goethe as *"le chef de l'école mélancolique,"* [18] the appraisal of *Faust* as the supreme Romantic masterpiece, the emphasis on the picturesque element in poetry, and the belief that German literature is characterized primarily by 'fantasy' and 'liberty': all these curious notions stem from *De l'Allemagne*. And Mme de Staël's view of German literature was persistent as well as potent; until after 1830 the French continued to believe that German literature consisted solely of Goethe, Schiller, Bürger, Tieck, and Jean Paul. No good history of German literature was available in French; and while a few works, notably *Werther, Faust, Die Räuber,* and later, the dramas of Werner were read with respect and devotion, poets such as Novalis, Brentano, and Arnim were virtually unknown to the French Romantic poets, very few of whom, incidentally, had any knowledge of German. The belief that French Romanticism was directly influenced by German Romanticism, one of the principal and most common misapprehensions about the history of Romanticism in Europe, is therefore contravened by the undeniable evidence of chronological fact. The true relationship is rather between the German *Sturm und Drang* and French Romanticism. Once this correct historical perspective is established, the striking differences between the faces of Romanticism in Germany and France become somewhat less puzzling.

De l'Allemagne, which was originally published in England, also served in some degree as a mediator between Germany and England. In the early years of the nineteenth century, because of the political situation—the opposition to Napoleon—the English tended to turn more to Germany than to France, and many links were forged between the two lands through both travelers and translations.[19] These links were remarkable rather for their large number than for their depth, there being little to suggest any very decisive significance. As in France, so in England actual knowledge about Germany was fairly scant; the Carlylean image of a land of poets and thinkers succeeded the earlier one of a realm of the picturesque and fantastic. As for German literature, it was again the *Sturm und Drang* which made the only real impression through the early works of Goethe and Schiller and the dramas of Kotzebue, whose popularity turned into an absolute furor. The writings of the Jena group, on the other hand, gained little or no hearing until well into the nineteenth century; Carlyle was the first to write about Novalis in 1829, and even then Novalis was interpreted as a disciple of Kant and Fichte without any appreciation of his poetry. In her relationship with her European neighbours, England showed that same sturdy independence that characterizes her own Romantic movement. England had indeed no need to be instructed in Romantic thought and feeling by other nations, for in Shakespeare, Milton, Young, Macpherson, Percy, and Richardson she exported far more than she imported in Schiller, Goethe, and Rousseau.

The great flowering of English Romanticism occurred about the middle of the second decade of the nineteenth century when for some ten years England became the focus of European Romanticism. By then the Romantic impetus had slackened in Germany and was gradually being diluted by the beginnings of the sober realism of the mid-nineteenth century. Meanwhile France, apparently still stunned by the consequences of the Revolution, was taking stock in social and political affairs with thinkers such as Saint-Simon, Cousin, and Thierry, while artistic creativity was relegated to the background. England with a galaxy of fine poets in Blake, Wordsworth, Coleridge, Shelley, Keats, and Byron assumed the primacy which had been Germany's. Not that there was ever a Romantic 'school' in England as there had been in Germany; there was no conscious homogeneous program and there were few manifestos or literary discussions compared with those in Germany and with the violent controversies that were to sway France. Wordsworth's famous *Preface to the "Lyrical Ballads"* was conceived chiefly to counter criticism and to forestall further attacks. The second generation of English Romantic poets was even less concerned than the first with questions of poetic technique; Keats indeed was outspoken in his rejection of abstract theorizing, which he branded as "the whims of an Egotist." In a letter to J. H. Reynolds (February 3, 1818) he wrote: "Every man has his speculations, but every man does not brood and peacock over them till he makes a false coinage and deceives himself. . . . Poetry should be great and unobtrusive, a thing which enters into one's soul, and does not startle it or amaze it with itself, but with its subject.—How beautiful are the retired flowers! how would they lose their beauty were they to throng into the highway crying out, 'admire me I am a violet!—dote upon me I am a primrose!' " [20] Informal in character, "a warm intuitive muddle," as it has rightly been called,[21] English Romanticism remained less systematic, less dogmatic, less self-conscious than its Continental counterparts, of an independent approach consonant with the innate individualism of the Briton. Although Jeffrey, the most vehement opponent of the Lake Poets, accused them in the *Edinburgh Review* of 1802 of being "dissenters from the established systems in poetry," who had borrowed their doctrines from the Germans and from "the great apostle of Geneva," this charge was far from true. For the Romantic movement in England was above all of evolutionary, not revolutionary, origin; a sense of belonging to and restoring the native tradition distinguishes the Romantic poets in England, where there was no incisive break in continuity as in Germany and France. The English pre-Romantics and Romantics looked back with approval on Shakespeare and the pre-Restoration poets, nor did the Augustans rouse opposition comparable to the rebelliousness of the German *Stürmer und Dränger* or the French onslaught on their tyrannical literary establishment. In contrast to the necessity imposed on the French and Germans to find some way out of a kind of cul-de-sac, the English were cast in a historically more fortunate position. Whereas the Germans and the French Romantics had to follow and in some way outdo their glorious immediate predecessors, the English Romantics were strongly conscious of representing a new beginning and upsurge, not a reaction as in France or an overrefinement as in Germany. From this, perhaps, English Romanticism derives its special quality of freshness, freedom, flexibility, and grace.

With the deaths of Keats in 1821, Shelley in 1822, and Byron in 1824, the period of English ascendancy came to an abrupt and untimely end. Now it was the turn of France in the 1820's and 1830's. But how different was the face and spirit of Romanticism in France from what it had been in England! Whereas the English Romantic movement had evolved slowly and organically out of the native tradition, French Romanticism was essentially a revolt against the native tradition, an ousting of the firmly rooted Neoclassical attitudes and forms by alien lines of thought and feeling. Hence the violence and bitterness of the quarrels attendant on the emergence of Romanticism in France, hence also the stubbornness and vehemence of the opposition. For this was far more than a literary debate; all manner of political and national considerations were implicated in the complex web of this *"querelle nationale."* [22] The Revolution, though it had halted literary development for many years, can also be evaluated as an indirectly positive factor, for with the fall of the absolute monarchy the Neoclassical dogmatism that had been associated with it was severely undermined: *"à société nouvelle, littérature nouvelle"* became the popular slogan. Moreover, the revolutionary era with its free spectacle of the guillotine created a new theatre audience avid for rapid action, melodrama, and sharp contrasts. On the other hand, Napoleon's Empire tended to have a reactionary effect not only through its strict censorship but also through its revival of Neoclassical taste as exemplified by Corneille's heroic characters who were regarded as the apotheosis of martial glory. Romanticism was therefore feared as a tendency associated with revolution, violence, and foreign domination, a threat to the national heritage of Greco-Latin origin. Even in 1825 *Le Globe* still reported that: "On se sert aujourd'hui en France du mot 'romantique' pour désigner toute composition contraire au système suivi en France depuis Louis XIV." [23] This fear of the Romantic as tantamount to the revolutionary explains, in part at least, Constant's extraordinarily cautious attitude in his preface to *Wallstein,* where he compared the German and French dramatic systems. He deliberately avoided the word 'romantic' altogether and repeatedly stressed his support of the native tradition, which was to be strengthened and refreshed, not ousted by innovations from abroad. A similar revival of the French heritage was advocated in Sainte-Beuve's *Tableau de la poésie au seizième siècle* (1827) which was of vital importance in the history of Romanticism in France; here Sainte-Beuve rehabilitated the hitherto neglected French poets of the sixteenth century, thereby pointing to the existence of a native tradition anterior to and different from the Neoclassical one.

Considering the strength of this Neoclassical canon of clarity, harmony, and 'good taste,' as well as the complexity of the political and social background, it is little wonder that the new Romantic orientation was so slow to infiltrate into France. The French

Romantics had begun to emerge as a shadowy force in opposition to the Neoclassicists towards the middle of the 1810's, stimulated by *De l'Allemagne* and also by the translation in 1813 of A. W. Schlegel's *Vorlesungen über dramatische Kunst und Literatur*. During the years 1814-1822 an outburst of anglomania swept through France following the isolation during the Napoleonic wars; lively interest was focused on the 'conqueror,' on the workings of the constitutional monarchy and parliamentary government, the industrial revolution, new economic doctrines, and, of course, new writing, although unfortunately there was no outstanding personality to do for England what Mme de Staël had done for Germany. Nevertheless the technique of the *'Lakistes,'* their use of imagery, the music and innovations of their verse, and their note of mystery aroused curiosity. In fact, Scott, Byron, and Shakespeare as well as Goethe and Schiller were already known in France, but their real vogue came only about 1820 onward, when Byron in particular became the object of an idolatrous enthusiasm. This growing appreciation of English and German poets coincided with the formation of a number of Romantic groups centered either on a literary journal such as the *Muse française* (1823-4) or the famous *Le Globe* (1824-32), or in the French tradition on a salon such as that of Deschamps (1820), the *Société des bonnes-lettres* (1821), Charles Nodier (1823), and finally the *Cénacle* of Hugo and Sainte-Beuve (1827). The French Romantics were thus unlike the English, and more like the Germans, in their preference for groups, and the dates of these various groups and journals help to site the real breakthrough of Romanticism in France. Opposition was, however, far from silenced by the early 1820's; the traditionalists continued to attack Romanticism as an alien, dangerous element, branding it as a *"romantisme bâtard,"* to quote the phrase coined in 1824 by Auger, the director of the Académie Française, in spite of the efforts of the movement's defenders, such as Charles Nodier, who sought to distinguish between *le frénétique* (vampirism, mere sensationalism) and the genuinely *romantique*.

Long after Romanticism had become more or less acceptable in lyric poetry through the works of Lamartine, Hugo, and Vigny in the years 1822-26, the final and most acrimonious battle was fought in the field of drama, the *"dernière fortresse,"* the *"bastille littéraire"* [24] of the Neoclassical tradition. Several earlier attempts to storm this bastion had failed; a performance in 1809 of Lemercier's

Christophe Colomb, subtitled a *"comédie shakespearienne,"* proved an utter fiasco, and in his rendering of Schiller's *Wallenstein* trilogy, which dates from the same year, Constant cautiously felt the need to respect the rules of our drama, as he put it, by reducing the number of acts to five and the characters to twelve. In the winter of 1827-28 a company of English actors made a deep impression in Paris, and it was during that winter, when enthusiasm for Shakespeare was at its zenith, that Hugo wrote *Cromwell* with its epoch-making preface. Not that Hugo's ideas in themselves were of startling originality; sensational though it was in its historical context, Hugo's attack on the three unities is in fact very reminiscent of Lessing's arguments in the *Hamburgische Dramaturgie.* Indeed the whole tone and spirit of the polemics in France in the 1820's recalls the mood of the German *Sturm und Drang* of the 1770's. Thus *Le Globe* defines its doctrine as *"la liberté," "l'imitation directe de la nature," "l'originalité,"* [25] while the concept *"romantique"* is equated with *"vie, activité, mouvement en avant,"* [26] that is, in terms which clearly echo the dynamism of the *Sturm und Drang.* There is, therefore, ample justification for Goethe's perspicacious comment: "Was die Franzosen bei ihrer jetzigen literarischen Richtung für etwas Neues halten, ist im Grunde weiter nichts als der Widerschein desjenigen, was die deutsche Literatur seit fünfzig Jahren gewollt und geworden." [27] Goethe's estimate of fifty years as the time lag between Germany and France is well judged, for it was only with the noisy victory of *Hernani* in 1830 that French drama achieved the freedom attained in Germany in the 1770's by *Götz von Berlichingen* and *Die Räuber.* Moreover, while the French Romantics were related to the German *Stürmer und Dränger,* the true heirs of the German Romanticism of 1800-1815 were undoubtedly the French Symbolist poets of the latter half of the nineteenth century. Baudelaire, Mallarmé, and Rimbaud subscribed to a new conception of art and the artist, a conception which was closely akin to the theories of the German Jena Romantic group: poetic experience was envisaged as essentially different from ordinary experience, a magic form of intuitive spiritual activity, a mysterious expansion into the transcendental in which the visionary poet adventured into a dream-realm to explore the hidden sources and 'correspondences' of life.

The battle for *Hernani* in 1830 marks the last great milestone in the Romantic conquest of Europe. Although Romanticism was to reign in France for some ten more years, other currents were increasingly in evidence. By the mid-1830's Hugo was already advancing a more utilitarian conception of art, urging the artist to an awareness of his serious duty to further the progress of mankind. In this change of outlook, Hugo was anticipating a trend characteristic of the mid-nineteenth century throughout Europe. In England and Germany the springs of Romanticism had dried up much earlier than in that late-starter France, and in both countries by the mid-1830's only a diluted, rather sentimentalized form of Romanticism survived alongside some witty satire directed against Romantic attitudes, satire like Peacock's *Crotchet Castle* (1831), Carlyle's *Sartor Resartus* (1833-34), Heine's *Romantische Schule* (1833), and Immermann's *Die Epigonen* (1836) with its significant title, as well as his comic *Münchhausen* (1839). Romanticism was increasingly out of tune with the spirit of the age as the century advanced; the new sober mood and materialistic aims of the industrial era had little sympathy for obscure flights of individual imagination and no use whatsoever for an art that 'bakes no bread' to quote a pertinent American proverb. The artist was called to cease his selfish exploration of his private realm, to come out of his ivory tower, and to assume his share of social responsibility. The disciplined objectivity of Realism came to replace—at least for a time—the autonomous imagination of Romanticism.

This chronological survey should dispel a number of common misconceptions regarding Romanticism. Foremost among these is the misapprehension that 'European Romanticism is a clearly defined entity, a unified school which manifested itself in several countries simultaneously and shared certain ideals and predilections. Almost equally prevalent and mistaken is the belief that the origins of Romanticism are to be found in Germany and that both the English and the French Romantic poets were directly and decisively influenced by the German theories. Such notions are more than gross oversimplifications; they are false premises that can only breed further error. A historical analysis of the course of Romanticism in Europe reveals a far more complicated picture, for the Romantic manner of perception and expression appeared in various literatures at different times and in different guises. Its emergence is an uneven, straggling process of long duration, punctuated by curious time lags as the ascendancy passed from one land to another. Moreover, since the spread of new ideas was largely dependent on the chance reports of travelers in an age when communications were still relatively poor and further disrupted by war, information on contemporary developments even in neighboring countries was often so scant and belated that many assumptions of influence must be discounted. The outstanding example of such slow and fragmentary infiltration of ideas is to be found in *De l'Allemagne:* though written by a perspicacious and widely-traveled critic, it contains in 1810 very few of the ideas of the Jena Romantics which were to reach France only some half a century later.

The outer history of European Romanticism—its successive waves, its new upsurge in one country after another—suggests both the vehemence of its impetus and the complexity of its nature. Though part of that fundamental reorientation of values that took place throughout Europe at the turn of the eighteenth to the nineteenth century, it was not a single but a multiple movement; indeed it comprised a whole series of movements from the *Sturm und Drang* onward, each separate and distinct in character, yet all involved in a profound *"crise de la conscience"* as individualistic, imaginative, subjective attitudes replaced the old rationalistic approach. The timing and form of this crisis differed from land to land because it was in each case determined by the literary background as well as by social and political factors. Hence the bewildering variety of the faces and products of Romanticism: it is not just a matter of genre, with the English excelling at lyric poetry, the French concentrating on drama in their battle against the stronghold of the Neoclassical theatre, while the transcendental yearnings of the Germans find their most appropriate vehicle in the *Märchen*-like narrative. This in itself is only a sympton of far deeper divergences. German Romanticism, for instance, is not only the most radical and thoroughgoing, embracing all the arts and philosophy, politics, religion, science, and history, but also distinguished from its English and French counterparts at first by a strong bias towards the metaphysical and later by its patriotic colouring. French Romanticism resembles the German brand in its preference for organization in groups and in its dynamic thrust; on the other hand, it differs from the German movement (and is herein closer to the English) in remaining almost entirely in the domain of art, and it is characterized above all by its violent revolt against the stifling dominance of the native Neoclassical tradition. In contrast, English Romanticism is the freshest and freest, the least self-conscious and codified

CHRONOLOGY

	ENGLAND	GERMANY	FRANCE
1726- 1730	Thomson: *Seasons*		
1740		Bodmer: *Kritische Abhandlung von dem Wunderbaren in der Poesie*	
1742	Young: *Night Thoughts*		
1745	Akenside: *Pleasures of Imagination*		
1747	Richardson: *Clarissa Harlowe*		
1750	Gray: *Elegy in a Country Churchyard*		
1754			Condillac: *Traité des sensations*
1755			
1758			Diderot: *Discours sur la poésie dramatique*
1759	Young: *Conjectures on Original Composition*	Lessing: *Literaturbriefe*	
1760	MacPherson: *Fragments*	Translation	
1761			Rousseau: *La nouvelle Héloïse*
1762	MacPherson: *Fingal*, translation from Ossian	Translation	
1764		Herder: *Fragmente über die neuere deutsche Literatur*	
1765	Percy: *Reliques*		
1766			
1767			
1769		Lessing: *Hamburgische Dramaturgie*	
1770		Herder: *Journal meiner Reise*	
1773		*Von deutscher Art und Kunst* Goethe: *Götz von Berlichingen*	
1774		Goethe: *Werther*	
1775		First translation of Shakespeare	

	ENGLAND	GERMANY	FRANCE
1776			Rousseau: *Rêveries du promeneur solitaire*
1778		Klinger: *Sturm und Drang* Herder: *Stimmen der Völker*	Rousseau: *Confessions*
1781		Schiller: *Die Räuber* Kant: *Kritik der reinen Vernunft*	B. de St. Pierre: *Paul et Virginie*
1787	Blake: *Songs of Innocence*	Kant: *Kritik der praktischen Vernunft*	
1788		Kant: *Kritik der Urteilskraft*	
1790	Paine: *Rights of Man*		
1791			B. de St. Pierre: *La chaumière indienne*
1792			Rouget de Lisle: *La Marseillaise*
1793	Wordsworth: *An Evening Walk* : *Descriptive Sketches*	Fichte: *Wissenschaftslehre* Schiller: *Uber naive und sentimental-* *ische Dichtung*	
1794	Blake: *Songs of Experience*		
1796	Coleridge: *The Aeolian Harp*		
1797		A. W. Schlegel: Translation of Shake- speare Schelling: *Ideen zu einer Philosophie* *der Natur* Tieck: *Volksmärchen* Wackenroder: *Herzensergiessungen eines* *kunstliebenden Klosterbruders* *Athenäum*	

1798	Wordsworth: *Lyrical Ballads*
	Coleridge: *The Ancient Mariner*
	   : *Frost at Midnight*
	   : *Fears in Solitude*
	   : *The Nightingale*		

1799		Schleiermacher: *Reden über die Re-* *ligion* F. Schlegel: *Lucinde*	La Harpe: *Cours de littérature ancienne* *et moderne*

1800	Wordsworth: *Michael* / : *Ruth*	Novalis: *Hymnen an die Nacht*	Mme. de Staël: *De la littérature*
1801			Chateaubriand: *Atala*
1802	Coleridge: *Dejection*	Novalis: *Heinrich von Ofterdingen*	Chateaubriand: *Génie du Christianisme*
1804			Chateaubriand: *René*
1805	Wordsworth: *Prelude*	Arnim u. Brentano: *Des Knaben Wunderhorn* (-1808)	
1806			
1807		Fichte: *Reden an die deutsche Nation*	
1809		Görres: *Die teutschen Volksbücher* A. W. Schlegel: *Über dramatische Kunst und Literatur*	Lemercier: *Christophe Colomb* De Villers: *Sur l'état actuel de la littérature ancienne et de l'histoire en Allemagne* Constant: *Wallstein* Mme. de Staël: *De l'Allemagne*
1810	Byron: *Childe Harold*		
1812	Shelley: *Queen Mab*	Grimm: *Märchen* Arndt: *Lieder für Teutsche* Rückert: *Geharnische Sonette* Körner: *Leyer und Schwert* Chamisso: *Peter Schlemihl*	
1813	Wordsworth: *The Excursion*		
1814	Byron: *The Corsair* / : *Lara* / : *Bride of Abydos* Scott: *Waverley*		
1815	Wordsworth: *Poems*	Hoffman: *Elixiere des Teufels* Uhland: *Gedichte* Tieck: *Phantasus*	
1816	Byron: *Siege of Corinth* / : *Prisoner of Chillon* Coleridge: *Kubla Khan* / : *Christabel*		
1817	Shelley: *Alastor* Byron: *Manfred* Keats: *Poems* Coleridge: *Sibylline Leaves* / : *Biographia Literaria*	Hoffmann: *Nachtstücke*	

	ENGLAND	GERMANY	FRANCE
1818	Keats: Endymion Hazlitt: Lectures on the English Poets Peacock: Nightmare Abbey (-1824)	Hoffmann: Die Serapionsbrüder : Klein Zaches Schopenhauer: Die Welt als Wille und Vorstellung	Lamartine: Méditations poétiques
1819	Byron: Don Juan (-1824) : Mazeppa Keats: Eve of St. Agnes Shelley: The Cenci		Conservateur littéraire Lebrun: Maria Stuart Société des bonnes-lettres
1820	Keats: Hyperion : Lamia Shelley: Prometheus Unbound		
1821	Byron: Cain : Sardanapalus Shelley: Adonais : Epipsychidion : Defence of Poetry De Quincey: Confessions of an English Opium Eater	Hoffmann: Kater Murr	Vigny: Poèmes Hugo: Odes Lamartine: Nouvelles méditations poétiques Stendhal: Racine et Shakespeare Hugo: Han d'Islande Muse française Mercure du XIXᵉ siècle
1822	Shelley: Hellas Byron: Vision of Judgement	Hoffmann: Meister Floh Heine: Gedichte	Vigny: Eloa Hugo: Odes nouvelles Le Globe
1823	Carlyle: Life of Schiller		
1824	Byron: The Island Shelley: Posthumous Poems : Triumph of Life	Mörike: Gedichte	
1825	Hazlitt: Spirit of the Age	Tieck & Schlegel: Shakespeare Translations (-1833)	
1826	Coleridge: Aids to Reflection	Eichendorff: Taugenichts Heine: Harzreise Kerner: Gedichte Hölderlin: Gedichte Tieck: Aufruhr in den Cevennen	Hugo: Odes et ballades Vigny: Poèmes : Cinq mars

1827		Heine: *Buch der Lieder* *: Reisebilder*	Hugo: *Cromwell*
1828	Carlyle: *Goethe*		Sainte-Beuve: *Tableau historique* Vigny: *Othello* : *Poèmes* Deschamps: *Préface des etudes françaises et étrangères* Hugo: *Les Orientales*
1829	Carlyle: *Novalis*		
1830			Hugo: *Hernani* Lamartine: *Harmonies poétiques* Gautier: *Poésies* Musset: *Contes d'Espagne et d'Italie*
1831	Peacock: *Crotchet Castle*		Hugo: *Notre Dame de Paris* : *Feuilles d'automne*
1832		Lenau: *Gedichte*	Hugo: *Le roi s'amuse* Vigny: *Stello* Musset: *Les caprices de Marianne/Rolla*
1833	Carlyle: *Sartor Resartus*		Musset: *On ne badine pas* : *Lorenzaccio* : *Fantasia*
1834			
1835			Vigny: *Chatterton/Servitude et grandeur militaires* Hugo: *Chants du crépuscule* Musset: *La Nuit de mai* : *La Nuit de décembre*
1836		Immermann: *Die Epigonen*	Musset: *La Nuit d'août* : *Il ne faut jurer de rien* : *Confession d'un enfant du siècle* : *Lettres de Dupuis et Cotonnet*
1837		Eichendorff: *Gedichte*	Lamartine: *Jocelyn* Musset: *La Nuit d'octobre* Hugo: *Les voix intérieures*
1838		Mörike: *Gedichte* Lenau: *Gedichte*	Hugo: *Ruy Blas* Lamartine: *La chute d'un ange* Musset: *L'espoir en Dieu*
1839			Lamartine: *Recueillements poétiques*

because it evolved not against, but organically out of, the native tradition.

In view of the confusion surrounding the term and the concept of Romanticism, there is surely a strong case for an honest recognition of these differences—of the fact that there have been a number of Romantic movements in Europe. It is only in the light of the correct historical perspective that a new approach can then be made to the Romantic movements in England, France, and Germany in an attempt to appreciate the particular character of each and at the same time to understand their interrelationship.

LILIAN R. FURST · *University of Manchester, England*

NOTES

1. P. van Tieghem, *Le Romantisme dans la littérature européenne* (Paris, 1948), p. 247.
2. I. Berlin, "Some Sources of Romanticism," six lectures delivered in Washington, broadcast B.B.C. "Third Programme," August-September 1966.
3. M. Akenside, *Pleasures of Imagination,* Bk. I, 1. 120.
4. J. Macpherson,, *The Poems of Ossian,* I (London, 1784), 205.
5. E. Young, *Conjectures on Original Composition* (Manchester, England, 1918), p. 7.
6. Young, *Conjectures,* p. 13.
7. L. Abercrombie, *Romanticism* (London, 1926), p. 28, footnote.
8. Brockes, "Considerations on the moonlight of a pleasant spring evening," *Earthly Joy in God,* reprinted in *Deutsche Literatur in Entwicklungsreihen: Das Weltbild der deutschen Aufklärung* (Leipzig, 1930), p. 245:

> Hardly had the night begun to appear
> Which promised the joy of cool after the burden of the day's heat,
> When a new day seemed to dawn:
> Out of the grey mist covering the horizon with crimson streaks
> After the sultry atmosphere of the day
> The full moon had just risen with a reddish gold shine,
> And from its changing circle,
> Which fills the night with shimmering light,
> More grace flower than shimmering light.

9. Goethe, "To the Moon":

> Once more you fill the bushes and the valley
> Silently with a misty radiance,
> At last too you release
> My soul completely;
> Over my fields you spread
> Your gaze soothingly,
> Like the gentle eye of a friend
> Watching my destiny.

10. F. Strich, "Europe and the Romantic movement," *German Life and Letters,* II (1948-9), 87.

11. F. Schlegel, *Kritische Schriften,* ed. W. Rasch (Munich, 1956), p. 37: "a progressive universal poetry."

12. Mme de Staël, *De l'Allemagne* (Oxford, 1906), p. 1: "For the past twenty years the French have been so preoccupied with political happenings that all literary matters have been in abeyance."

13. Staël, *De l'Allemagne,* p. 171: "For some time people in France have been reading hardly anything other than memoirs and novels; it is not entirely out of frivolity that people have become less equal to serious reading, but because the happenings of the Revolution have accustomed them to attach importance solely to knowledge of events and men."

14. F. F. Schirmer, *Kleine Schriften* (Tubingen, 1950), p. 173: "herald or interpreter."

15. Staël, *De l'Allemagne,* p. 178: "the mannered style of writing."

16. X. Marmier, preface to a translation of Schiller's poems (1854), p. vi: "a fairy-tale land, where men warble and sing like birds."

17. Staël, *De l'Allemagne,* p. 33: "that which preceded Christianity and that which followed it."

18. Nodier, *Débats,* April 19, 1817: "the head of the school of melancholy."

19. F. W. Stokoe, *German Influence in the English Romantic Period,* Appendix V, pp. 180-87, lists German works translated into English 1789–1803.

20. Keats, *Letters* (Oxford, 1934), p. 72.

21. H. N. Fairchild, "The Romantic movement in England," PMLA, LV (1940), 24.

22. Nodier, *Débats,* January 6, 1816: "national controversy."

23. Duvicquet, *Le Globe,* December 6, 1825: "the word 'romantic' is used in France nowadays to denote any work contrary to the system current in France since Louis XIV."

24. Desmarais, *Le Globe,* October 29, 1825: "the final bastion, the literary Bastille."

25. Anon., *Le Globe,* October 29, 1825: "freedom," "imitation only from nature," "originality."

26. Duvergier de Hauranne, *Le Globe,* March 24, 1825: "life, activity, surging forwards."

27. Goethe, as reported by Eckermann, *Gespräche mit Goethe* (1955), p. 673, 6th March, 1830: "What the French now regard as a new tendency in their literature is basically nothing but a reflection of what German literature has sought and achieved during the last fifty years."

HASKELL M. BLOCK

The Alleged Parallel of Metaphysical and Symbolist Poetry

A T ITS BEST, the comparative approach to literature is concerned not only with questions of historical relationship, but with the interpretation and illumination of works of art, in themselves as well as in their interrelations. As a way of defining literary values, comparison moves hand in hand with analysis. Yet, comparison, by its very nature, implies contrast: differences as well as similarities. It is now a commonplace that comparative studies cannot be limited to strictly causal relationships. From the standpoint of theme, attitude, art form, or tradition, works widely separated in time and place may illuminate one another in vital and significant ways. This is not to say, however, that any work may be fruitfully compared with any other. The test of any comparison lies, I believe, in the degree to which our understanding and appreciation of the literature at hand is thereby enhanced. The natural tendency to magnify similarities and minimize differences may in fact result in serious falsification of literary history and critical judgment. Consideration of such falsifications may serve to point to some of the dangers in this approach and to ways in which they might be overcome.

The alleged parallel of metaphysical and symbolist poetry offers to my mind a classic example of gratuitous and arbitrary comparison. I would not deny for a moment the enormous and fruitful impact of the rediscovery of Donne and his contemporaries on English and American poetry in the twentieth century, and it is easy to appreciate at least some of the motives underlying the claim that metaphysical and symbolist poetry are essentially similar and indeed identical. Before proceeding to direct examination of this view, it might be well to consider briefly how it came to develop.

The history of the parallel has been described in some detail, although incompletely, by Joseph E. Duncan in *The Revival of Metaphysical Poetry*.[1] To the best of my knowledge, the first statement of this relationship appears in an essay of Edmund Gosse, "The Poetry of John Donne," first published in *The New Review* in September, 1893, and reprinted the following year in *The Jacobean Poets*.[2] In explaining what he considers as Donne's revolution in English versification, Gosse declares: "To see what he aimed at doing, we have, I believe, to turn to what has been attempted in our own time by Mr. Robert Bridges, in some of his early experiments, and by the Symbolists in France."[3] 1893 is indeed an early date for this *rapprochement* and it is no surprise that Gosse does not elaborate; from the context, it is clear that he has in mind Donne's mixed cadences and irregularities of accent rather than the themes, images, or attitudes in his poetry. Nevertheless, this brief suggestion provides the germ of one of the most consequential poetic theories of our time. Gosse did not hesitate to restate his view somewhat more extensively a few years later, in the second volume of his *Life and Letters of John Donne,* where he declares of the poet:

> He desired greatly to develop the orchestral possibilities of English verse, and I have remarked that the irregular lyrics of Mr. Robert Bridges and the endless experiments of the Symbolists in France are likely to be far more fruitful to us in trying to understand Donne's object, than any conventional repetition of the accepted rules of prosody.[4]

We should note in passing that Gosse did not exactly admire these "endless experiments" of the symbolists. For while he was one of the first critics to call the attention of the English public to Mallarmé's poetry, it can hardly be said that he did the French poet a service.[5]

The next significant assertion of the parallel is probably that of Herbert J. C. Grierson in his chapter on Donne in the fourth volume of the *Cambridge History of English Literature* (1910).[6] Grierson's essay is one of the pioneer scholarly discussions of Donne's poetic technique. Commenting on Donne's ingenuity and love of artifice, he declares that the poet is "one of those who, like Baudelaire, are 'naturally artificial; for them simplicity would be affectation.'"[7] Perhaps in this slight and offhand remark lies the origin of T. S. Eliot's famous pronouncement.

It was apropos of Grierson's anthology, *Metaphysical Lyrics and Poems of the Seventeenth Century,* that Eliot wrote his essay of 1921, "The Metaphysical Poets."[8] We should recognize that Eliot is no happier here with the phrase, "metaphysical poetry," than are most twentieth-century critics, yet he accepts the term in large measure in the sense in which it is used by Samuel Johnson in his essay on Cowley. For Eliot, the characteristic metaphysical device is "the elaboration (contrasted with the condensation) of a figure of speech to the farthest stage to which ingenuity can carry it." Donne's "brief words and sudden contrasts," his "telescoping of images and multiplied association," issue, in his best poetry, in "a direct sensuous apprehension of thought, or a re-creation of thought into feeling." I need not here take up the question of the "dissociation of sensibility" and the broad historical and cultural assumptions underlying Eliot's view of Donne. More to our purpose are his citations from Corbière and Laforgue, both of whom, we are told, "are nearer to the 'school of Donne' than any modern English poet." To this pair of French poets Eliot was soon afterwards to add Baudelaire, akin to Donne in his mastery of surprise, in his "unity and order";[9] and then, in an essay of 1926, Mallarmé.

It is noteworthy that Eliot describes his brief "Note sur Mallarmé et Poe," published in *La Nouvelle revue française,* as a contribution to comparative literature. Explaining that he does not propose to decipher the enigmas of .Mallarmé's poetry or to analyze his syntax or metrics, Eliot declares:

> Mais il y a un autre aspect du "problème" que je puis peut-être traiter avec plus de compétence, et qui n'est pas négligeable: ce qu'on pourrait appeler l'aspect de littérature comparée—je ne veux pas dire une vaine étude des origines et des influences, mais la définition du type du poète, établie par une comparaison avec d'autres manifestations de ce type dans d'autres langues et à d'autres époques.[10]

This classification of families of poets may very well have been set forth in the Clark Lectures delivered by Eliot at Trinity College, Cambridge, also in 1926. Eliot steadfastly maintained the privacy of these lectures, and they remain unpublished.[11] We have some notion, all the same, of Eliot's approach to his subject from the brief comments of Mario Praz, who states that Eliot spoke of three metaphysical periods in European poetry: medieval, baroque, and modern, with Jules Laforgue as the chief representative of the modern period.[12] It is this same formulation that we find in Eliot's remarks on Mallarmé.[13]

Mallarmé for Eliot in 1926 is part of a family of poets that includes Cavalcanti, Donne, and Poe, all of whom exemplify "le poète métaphysique." That is, they all make use of metaphysical speculation to refine and enlarge their power of sensibility and emotion. On the one hand, Eliot separates "la *poésie métaphysique*" from "la poésie philosophique." The latter is represented by Dante and Lucretius in a complete and systematic sense, or by Baudelaire on a simpler and more fragmentary scale. On the other hand, Eliot distinguishes the expansion of sensibility of the metaphysical poet from that of the *halluciné,* as in Rimbaud or Blake. "Il y a un fort peu de *l'halluciné,*" Eliot declares, "chez Mallarmé." Hence, for the poet of *Hérodiade,* the world beyond the limits of the normal and everyday is simply an extension of the real world, "aggrandi et continué." In both Mallarmé and Donne, Eliot declares, "nous sommes dans un monde où tout le matériel, toutes les données, nous sont parfaitement familières." The work of both poets, he insists, is rooted in common, elemental reality.

The essay of 1926 marks Eliot's fullest published statement of the metaphysical-symbolist parallel. His re-examination of the French symbolist tradition in his essay of 1948, "From Poe to Valéry," makes no attempt to establish the slightest analogy or affinity between Donne and Baudelaire or Mallarmé. Evidently by the end of the 1920's he had decided that his definition of "metaphysical" in the abstract, of what all "metaphysical" poets had in common, was "too general to be useful."[14] It is also apparent that as his interest in Dante and in Baudelaire developed, his interest in Donne declined.[15]

In his essay of 1921 on Andrew Marvell, Eliot did not hesitate to group Baudelaire with Donne and Laforgue, as poets who "may be considered the inventor of an attitude, a system of feeling or of morals."[16] By 1930, in large part under the impact of Charles Du Bos, his view of Baudelaire had developed considerably. In *The Criterion* in January of that year, he declared, "any adequate criticism of Baudelaire must inevitably lead the critic outside of literary criticism."[17] This is certainly the case in Eliot's famous essay on Baudelaire, a pronouncement of central importance for the understanding of Eliot's own development as both poet and critic; however, as a critique of Baudelaire, it is to my mind one-sided, partial, and essentially wrong.[18] René Galand in his perceptive study of the impact of Baudelaire on Eliot has rightly asked: "Is the Baudelaire whom Eliot sees the real one?" The same may be asked of the "metaphysical" Baudelaire described in Eliot's essays ten years earlier.

The parallel of metaphysical and symbolist poetry is as much the creation of Eliot's followers as of Eliot himself. By 1931 Eliot was ready to qualify his position sharply, and in his essay, "Donne in Our Time," he declared:

> . . . It is impossible for us or for anyone else ever to disentangle how much was genuine affinity, genuine appreciation, and how much was just a *reading into* poets like Donne our own sensibility, how much was "subjective." [19]

Yet, what for Eliot was literary strategy, soon became literary history; hypothesis came to be asserted as fact.

George Williamson opens his discussion of *The Donne Tradition* (1930) by insisting on a parallel between Donne and Baudelaire in their common obsession with death: "Especially in this morbidity, Donne reminds us of Baudelaire, for his own poems brought to the dying Elizabethan age the sharper flavor of *Les Fleurs du Mal.*" Both poets, according to Williamson, are poets of decadence, both express a desire to escape from this world, "and both wrote poetry which surprises, shocks, and baffles expectation."[20] Mr. Williamson insists that Baudelaire's "Le Goût du néant" helps us to understand Donne better, in view of their common pursuit of the strange and the perverse, their common fascination with ugliness and with death. Readers of Eliot's essays of 1921 and 1923 will recognize at once the source of the comparison. In *The Donne Tradition,* Eliot's suggestion is enlarged to the plane of generalization: Donne's imagery "can in fact be regarded as an early adventure into the field since exploited by the Symbolists." In both poets, Williamson insists, symbols function in the same way, whereby the emotion is "merged with the idea and both bound up with the scene which provokes them."[21] Donne's modernity, therefore, links him not only with Browning, Meredith, and Eliot, but with Baudelaire, Mallarmé, and Valéry in their common indirectness and intellectuality.[22]

Williamson's elaboration of Eliot's views has been shared by others. In his essay on "Donne's Relation to the Poetry of His Time," Mario Praz restates the definition of metaphysical poetry as the fusion of thought and feeling, and finds it "singularly akin" to Baudelaire's envelopment of philosophical thought in concrete sensation.[23] Praz, however, is concerned with an analogy in technique rather than with a broad statement of historical parallelism, and his remarks are not expanded.

By far the most extreme assertion of the identity of metaphysical and symbolist poetry may be found in Cleanth Brooks's *Modern Poetry and the Tradition* (1939). For Brooks, there is no essential difference between a definition of metaphysical poetry and of all poetry,[24] and the parallel between metaphysical and symbolist poetry is proof of this essential continuity. He finds that the "subtlety of the figurative language of the symbolist poets is analogous to that of the metaphysicals—and for the same reasons."[25] Brooks does not support this view by analyses of particular poems, metaphysical or symbolist, but it is characteristic of his flat identification that he can write of "symbolist-metaphysical poetry" as if the two terms were interchangeable.[26] Evidently for Mr. Brooks, a "symbolist poet" is any poet who uses images and symbols in a complex and subtle way.[27]

It might be well to examine this view of symbolist poetry more carefully. Brooks's view of the symbolists is based essentially on Edmund Wilson's *Axel's Castle*. In particular, Brooks accepts at face value Wilson's distinction between two modes of symbolist poetry: the "conversational-ironic" and the "serious-aesthetic,"[28] a distinction, as we shall see, of doubtful validity. In this way, however, it is possible for Brooks to include Corbière and Laforgue among the symbolists. He insists most strongly on the metaphysical parallel for the "conversational-ironic" poets, but he does not hesitate to extend it to all poets in the symbolist tradition. Thus, W. B. Yeats demonstrates "the ultimate identity of metaphysical and symbolist poetry."[29] In *The Well Wrought Urn*, Brooks qualifies this view of Yeats considerably,[30] but in *Modern Poetry and the Tradition* he seems to hold that any poet who employs symbols or who describes feeling in an ironic or paradoxical way is perforce a symbolist. It would be better to speak of *symbolic* poetry in this broad, generalized sense if confusion is to be avoided, and perhaps this is what Brooks meant. It is difficult to escape the conclusion that his easy coalescence of metaphysical and symbolist poetry is arbitrary and extreme.

More recently as well, scholars investigating the impact of metaphysical poetry in our time have on occasion followed the example of Eliot, Williamson, and Brooks. Sona Raiziss in *The Metaphysical Passion* (1952) insists on the "strong resemblance between the symbolists and the English metaphysicals,"[31] and extends similarities in technique into an all-embracing formulation.[32] Thus, Eliot's "Gerontion" is described as a "symbolist-metaphysical poem."[33] For Sona Raiziss, as for Cleanth Brooks, the great glory of the symbolists seems to be their emulation of the metaphysicals. Joseph E. Duncan, in his recent study, follows this approach in writing of "the metaphysical poetry" of Yeats and Eliot,[34] although he is acutely aware of the limitations of the parallel—of the basic differences which offset incidental similarities.[35]

Even at the very outset, the parallelism did not go unchallenged. In a brief review of *The Donne Tradition* in 1931, Charles J. Sisson aptly remarked:

> I do not think that the study of Baudelaire is likely to help one to understand Donne. There is a profound difference between the men in the very real zest of Donne. The *Goût du Néant*, I feel, is something that would have been almost meaningless to him. . . .[36]

Similarly, it was with such views in mind that Merritt Y. Hughes in his essay, "Kidnapping Donne," argued against the tendency to make Donne's wit "a master key to literary history."[37] Sisson and Hughes intimated what later critics came to assert: that the dissonance, complex intellectuality, and bizarre figurative language of the metaphysical poets offer little direct illumination of the art of the symbolists.

Perhaps the sharpest distinction between metaphysical and symbolist poetry was drawn by Allen Tate in his essay, "Tension in Poetry" (1938). Following the view of John Crowe Ransom, he declares that "in metaphysical poetry the logical order is explicit; it must be coherent; the imagery by which it is sensuously embodied must have at least the appearance of logical determinism."[38] As a rationalist, the metaphysical poet "begins at or near the extensive or denoting end of the line."[39] The symbolist poet—which for Tate includes the romantic—proceeds in an exactly opposite manner: beginning with intensive and connotative or richly associative experience and moving toward the opposite end of the scale. Tate's distinction is unduly schematic, and his categories are so broad as to make virtually every modern poet a symbolist. He adds, however, that these approaches, while exclusive of one another, are not exhaustive. His refusal to accept the common parallelism and to explain one group of poets by means of the other marks a significant departure from the traditional formula in modern criticism.[40]

The last twenty years have witnessed a noticeable coolness in the celebration of the metaphysical poets by contemporary critics,[41] and at the same time, fewer instances of rash parallelism. Frank Kermode in *The Romantic Image* contends that what he calls Eliot's "Symbolist historiography" has seriously distorted our understanding of Donne and Milton, and, indeed, of the whole course of literary history.[42] To my mind, Mr. Kermode is quite right in his view that "Donne is, to say the least, of doubtful value to the Symbolist theory," despite the tendency of Eliot and his followers to confound the two.

Attempts at redefining the character of metaphysical poetry have also worked to the disadvantage of the Eliot position. Leonard Unger has pointed out that while Donne occasionally uses a device or technique similar to that of the symbolists, such as implied metaphor,[43] figurative language in Donne is frequently explicit, marking a direct connection between the image or symbol and what it represents. Unger's analysis suggests that the common definitions of metaphysical poetry will not fit any particular poem when it is subjected to a close reading. The usual distinguishing qualities of metaphysical poetry—elaboration of conceits, irony, paradox, rich interplay of figurative language, dislocation of context, and the like, are all approximations rather than absolutes. Mr. Unger has shown convincingly that like romantic or symbolist, metaphysical is an approximate term; nonetheless, it is here to stay and we should try to use it with what precision we can.

An altogether different approach to the definition of metaphysical poetry has been suggested by Joseph A. Mazzeo, who sees a poetic of correspondences as the key to the essential character of early seventeenth-century poetry.[44] Mazzeo is undoubtedly right in relating the poetics of Tesauro or Pallavicino to metaphysical figurative language, and his attack on the emblem theory of metaphysical poetry is convincing.[45] Nevertheless, Tesauro's "Imprese eroiche e Simboli figurati" point to fixed and concrete values, more denotative than suggestive. Mazzeo leaps to an identification of Renaissance and Baudelairean correspondences,[46] but it should be observed that for the poets and theoreticians of the seventeenth century, correspondences aim at order and clarity rather than at vagueness and mystery, or at suggestiveness as an end in itself. As Joseph H. Summers has declared apropos of "The Poem as Hieroglyph" in the works of George Herbert, "the meaning was precise and clear even if complex and subtle."[47]

This central difference is borne out by studies of the language of metaphysical poetry. Josephine Miles has called our attention to Donne's reliance on active verbs which serve to give body to intellectual argument, and she sees a sharp difference between the modern "substantival emphasis" and the metaphysical "active predication."[48] Donne's technique is essentially one of logical relation developed through a process of intellectual analysis at once vigorous and striking. It is a technique that, at its best, has contributed to the making of some of the finest poems in the English language, but it is remote indeed from the characteristic manner of the symbolist poets.

The symbolist movement extended approximately from 1850 to 1920, beginning in France and spreading throughout Western literature. Just as it would be incorrect to describe every European writer between 1800 and 1830 as a romantic, so it is equally wrong to hold that every French poet in the later nineteenth century was a symbolist. As a distinct literary period and style, the symbolist movement rests not on mere chronology but on assumptions and techniques that define the works of its adherents and link them in a common tradition. Essentially, symbolist poetry is an art of suggestion, evocation, musicality, and mystery. Mallarmé's definition of poetry as *"l'expression par le langage humain ramené à son rythme essentiel, du sens mystérieux des aspects de l'existence: ...,"*[49] may serve as a key to the poetics of the movement. Increasingly, especially in France, Mallarmé has come to be viewed as the central figure and most typical exponent of symbolist poetry. Emile Verhaeren could write, as early as 1887, "A cette heure, il n'est qu'un vrai maître symboliste en France: Stéphane Mallarmé."[50] Similarly, in his masterful study of the poet, Albert Thibaudet declared, "nul mieux que Mallarmé, par la nature de son génie et par le sens de son art, ne fut authentiquement un symboliste."[51] The existence of the symbolist movement, historically and aesthetically, is in no way dependent on the manifesto of 1886. The main line of symbolist poetics and poetry moves from Baudelaire to Mallarmé to Valéry. To be sure, there were other important symbolists: Villiers de l'Isle-Adam, Verlaine, Verhaeren, the young Maeterlinck, the young Claudel, the early André Gide, all within limits are a part of the symbolist movement. We may add lesser but no less characteristic figures: Régnier, Dujardin, Rodenbach, Mockel, Van Lerberghe, and others of kindred spirit. Despite marked individual differences, all of these writers shared Mallarmé's conviction that the object of the poet is to seize "les rapports, entre temps, rare ou multipliés; d'après quelque état intérieur."[52] Poetry is the expression or revelation of an "état d'âme."[53] In its evocation of dream, vision, and analogy it moves inward, toward the abstraction and solitude of inner life. Suggestiveness and musicality are the essential properties of the magic and mystery of poetic utterance, itself an embodiment of the mystery and wonder of the universe.

If we consider the poetry of Jules Laforgue from this standpoint, we can understand why Warren Ramsey has declared that Laforgue takes his place among the "initiators of the Symbolist movement, rather than with the true Symbolists."[54] Clearly, the unusual rhythmic and musical properties of symbolist poetry are absent in the work of Laforgue. Ramsey further asks if we may properly insist on a resemblance "between Laforgue's psychological notation and the conceit, the fancifully elaborated image of the English Metaphysicals?" And he suggests that "offhand, there would seem to be little in common between the associationist, enthusiastic poet that was Laforgue and the imposer of rational design that was Donne."[55] Similarly, Martin Turnell has argued vigorously that Laforgue's psychological association is altogether different in organization from the intellectual coherence of the metaphysical conceit. "This difference," Turnell writes, "between Laforgue and the Metaphysical Poets is so vital that I must be forgiven for underlining it."[56]

The case of Rimbaud is analogous. Rimbaud was seized on by the young symbolists in 1886, largely owing to the efforts of Verlaine, yet his position as a symbolist poet is questionable, to say the least, if more than chronology is involved. André Dinar in *La Croisade symboliste* remarks, "Je confesse mon embarras devant le cas Rimbaud dans l'affaire du symbolisme."[57] At this distance and in view of post-symbolist literary developments, it is difficult indeed to group Rimbaud's poetry with that of Mallarmé and his followers. There are genuine and significant affinities in poetic theory, rising in large part out of Rimbaud's interest in magic and occultism, but these are overshadowed by the poetics of *dérèglement,* as well as by Rimbaud's turbulent and explosive poetic style. Rimbaud is no more a symbolist than he is a metaphysical poet.[58]

Nevertheless, English and American critics, ever since Arthur Symons' *The Symbolist Movement in Literature,* have not hesitated to regard Rimbaud and Laforgue among the symbolist poets. Paul Verlaine's account of Tristan Corbière in *Les Poètes maudits* may have had something to do with his inclusion in this group, yet Corbière is even farther from the center of the symbolist movement than either Rimbaud or Laforgue. One is obliged to conclude that what Edmund Wilson has called the "conversational-ironic" mode of symbolism does not deal with symbolist poetry at all.

The parallel between metaphysical and symbolist poetry rests not only on a casual reordering of literary history, but also on a radical elimination of the profound differences between the works of the principal metaphysical and symbolist poets. Assuredly, Donne was not a symbolist and Mallarmé was not a metaphysical. A brief comparison of two poems distinctly related in subject-matter may serve to support this view.

Donne's "The Dreame" is one of the better known poems of the *Songs and Sonets,* part of a group of poems concerned with the joy of passionate experience. As such, however, it is relatively subdued. It is not nearly as ingenious a love poem as "The Good-Morrow" or "The Extasie," and it lacks such singular imagery as the comparison of the poet's beloved to the foot of a compass or to a hemisphere. Joan Bennett considers the poem unusual among Donne's love poems in its concentration on a single object.[59] In this sense, the poem is perhaps not wholly representative of Donne's art, yet it embodies many of his characteristic attitudes and devices.

Pierre Legouis has pointed out that the poem is a dramatic lyric, wherein a single character expresses himself freely, and with the responses of his partner implied in the development of the poem.[60] This development mediates between the planes of past and present, dream and reality. While the poet was lying asleep, dreaming of the love of his beloved, she entered his room, waking him, and giving rise to the experience recreated in the poem. Dream and reality are thus inextricably bound together, as Donne suggests in the declaration, "It was a theame/ . . . much too strong for phantasie," that is, too vivid and overpowering to remain merely within the province of the imagination. The beloved is at once dream and reality, for in her presence she embodies the poet's vision. In his commentary, Grierson has called our attention to the abstract character of line seven: "Thou art so truth," in preference to the less metaphysical emendation: "Thou art so true."[61] The truth of the beloved is opposed to the falsity of dreams or fables or anything unreal. The conclusion of the first stanza issues, appropriately, in the poet's injunction: "Enter these armes." On the purely physical plane, the experience of the poem is at this point complete.

The subtlety of argument traditionally associated with Donne finds expression in the second stanza, wherein he provides an ingenious supernatural explanation of his beloved's entry into his room. She is like an angel in her loveliness, but her power to read his thoughts surpasses even that of angels. Grierson sees an analogy here to "the subtleties of scholastic theology," but Donne's avoidance of the profane is wholly for secular and private ends, even if set forth in religious terms. Louis L. Martz has described the effect as "witty blasphemy," wherein the poet deifies his mistress "by attributing her arrival in his bedroom to her Godlike power of reading his mind."[62] If angels lack this power, God does not.[63] For the poet, then, the beloved is like God.

The final stanza returns to the plane of physical passion, now viewed as a completed experience, and in the light of the celebration of the beloved in the preceding lines. The poet's assertion of the purity and spirituality of their love may be read as an appeal for its prolongation. The physical and spiritual are here fused; the poet is a torch, ready to be kindled or extinguished. With the departure of his love, he will return to the plane of dream, now inseparable from lived reality.

Mario Praz has pointed out the continental affiliations of the love-dream, wherein the poet experiences in a vision what he longs for in reality. Praz finds in Donne's poem a freshness lacking in earlier, similar poems, in that "The Dreame" is not simply "a rhetorical complaint to an absent beauty,"[64] but a passionate expression of the presence of the beloved, actually before the poet's eyes. It is out of the vividness of this experience that the simplicity and directness of the language arises. Of course, we cannot be sure that Donne actually had this experience. J. B. Leishman remarks that while he finds the poem dramatically convincing, "I think it is more likely to have been all dream than, as it professes to be, half dream and half fact."[65] This may be so, but the reality of the poem is insistent enough. As Leishman goes on to indicate, the diction "is precise and almost scientific."[66] The language may not be "strictly denotative," but it is indeed largely so, sharply restricted in association, vivid, concrete, and immediate.

Mallarmé's "Apparition" is also about the poet's dream of his beloved. It is described by Mallarmé's editors as probably his best known poem.[67] Its relative clarity of syntax and imagery makes it far more readily accessible than the poems of Mallarmé's later style, and in this sense, perhaps it is not altogether typical. As in the case of Donne, it is probably impossible to find a single poem that would embody all of the salient qualities of Mallarmé's art.

"Apparition" is an early poem, yet Mallarmé kept it for twenty years before releasing it for publication, possibly because of its unusual personal and sentimental quality. Just as Donne's poem may describe an experience with Ann More, so Mallarmé's may deal with an episode in his love for Marie Gherard. This is not of primary importance. There is, indeed, the likelihood that Mallarmé wrote the poem at the behest of Henri Cazalis, in homage to his friend's beloved.[68] In a letter of July 1862, the poet declares of a poem promised to his friend: "Je ne veux pas faire cela d'inspiration: la turbulence du lyrisme serait indigne de cette chaste apparition que tu aimes."[69] Quite unlike Donne's "The Dreame," "Apparition" is not a turbulent poem at all; it is chaste, subdued, remote from the plane of sensory experience.

The use of the imperfect tense throughout the poem is a principal source of this remoteness. Whereas Donne's poem moves from present action to past recollection and then back again to the present, Mallarmé locates the experience of his poem wholly in the past, and indeed, in three distinct phases of the past. First, there is the poet's solitary recollection of his beloved, which dominates the opening lines; then, there is the physical relation between the poet and his love, existing in a still more remote past; and finally, there is the evocation of the poet's childhood rising out of the dream-vision of his love. From the opening line, the atmosphere is one of melancholy: "s'attristait" is reinforced by "pleurs," "mourantes," and "sanglots," all suggesting a sense of pain and loss. The gap between the past and present is absolute. We should also note Mallarmé's use of synaesthetic metaphor, as in "blancs sanglots," and the rich connotative implications of "l'azur des corolles," pointing, I believe, to the loss of the poet's identity with the realm of the absolute. The dream takes place on the anniversary of the beloved's first kiss; the capitalization of "Rêve" testifies to its absolute centrality in the poem.[70] Dedicated to the total assimilation of the Dream, knowingly intoxicated by it, the poet identifies his dream-vision with his beloved, who reappeared as if in answer to the poet's self-abandonment to the allure of her image. We know that this reappearance in lines 11-12 is fictive, the result of the intensity of the poet's dream; it is described in language that heightens the contrast between the pervading sadness and the gaiety and beauty of the beloved. The final lines of the poem move from the plane of imagined reality to that of magic and supernatural revelation, whereby the image of the fairy, enchanting the sleep and, by implication, the destiny of the poet in his childhood, merges with the apparition of the loved one.

Even so casual a reading of "The Dreame" and "Apparition" will suggest not only a basic difference in the poets' attitudes toward love and the beloved, but more important for our purposes, antithetical renderings of the relation of dream to reality. For Donne, the two are continuous; for Mallarmé, they are not. Donne's dream leads outward, toward shared, physical experience; Mallarmé's leads inward, toward private and inner, spiritual experience. Hence, the relative concreteness and particularity of diction in Donne as opposed to the indefinite and suggestive language that dominates the poem of Mallarmé. Donne's poem issues in a return to active participation in love; Mallarmé's recedes to the point of outer remoteness from any physical relationship. Despite its relative accessibility, already in "Apparition" we may sense Mallarmé moving markedly away from his early, Baudelairean idiom, toward the technique he was to formulate in his revolutionary poetics: *"Peindre, non la chose, mais l'effet qu'elle produit."*[71] The conceptualization of the concrete that was to develop in Mallarmé's later work from this doctrine of effects carries us far indeed from the witty intellectuality of Donne.

We may return with justifiable scepticism to T. S. Eliot's declaration in 1926, that in both Mallarmé and Donne "nous sommes dans un monde où tout le matériel, toutes les données nous sont parfaitement familières."[72] Mallarmé's sense of what Eliot describes as the real world is vastly different from that of Donne. It is true that Donne uses symbols in his poetry, and we know that Mallarmé was profoundly interested in metaphysics, yet it would be reprehensible to call Donne a symbolist poet or Mallarmé a metaphysical poet if these terms have any meaning at all. Perhaps the history of the alleged parallel of metaphysical and symbolist poetry should inspire a reasonable caution in our use of such generalizations, even when speaking of their most illustrious and most typical representatives. Perhaps especially so. As Jean Cocteau has well remarked, apropos of Mallarmé: "Les grands poètes resistent par quelqu' endroit solide aux étiquettes qu'on leur impose."[73]

Comparison implies contrast; incidental similarity is not the same as basic identity. As part of the poetic strategy of certain poets of our time, the parallel we have considered may be altogether justifiable. Particularly in the United States, the impact of metaphysical upon modern poetry has been immense.[74] In retrospect, the parallel may charitably be viewed as an awkward attempt in the 1920's to justify the attractiveness and apparent modernity of the seventeenth-century poets.[75] However, from the standpoint of scholarship and criticism, the parallel offers an instructive lesson in the comparative study of literature.[76] Comparison must move hand in hand with analysis; it cannot be divorced from the aesthetic qualities of works of art in their uniqueness and radical particularity. As Mallarmé reminds us in a plea which comparatists fail to heed at their peril:

Le poëte puise en son Individualité, secrète et antérieure, plus que dans les circonstances même exaltant celle-ci, admirables, issues de loin ou simplement du dehors.[77]

BROOKLYN COLLEGE OF THE
CITY UNIVERSITY OF NEW YORK

NOTES

1. Joseph E. Duncan, *The Revival of Metaphysical Poetry* (Minneapolis, 1959), pp. 124-126.

2. See *The New Review*, IX (September 1893), 236-247. The essay was reprinted in *Living Age* (November 18, 1893), pp. 429-436.

3. Gosse, "The Poetry of John Donne," *The New Review*, IX (September 1893), 244.

4. Gosse, *Life and Letters of John Donne* (London, 1899), II, 334.

5. See Bruce A. Morrissette, "Early English and American Critics of French Symbolism," in *Studies in Honor of Frederick W. Shipley* (St. Louis, 1942), pp. 164-165; and Ruth Z. Temple, *The Critic's Alchemy* (New York, 1953), pp. 201-218.

6. Joseph E. Duncan, *op. cit.*, p. 124 and n. 29, finds a suggestion of the parallel in an anonymous article in *The Quarterly Review*, CXCII (July 1900), 239-240. I am unable to share his view. Frank Kermode has claimed in *Romantic Image* (London, 1957), p. 149, that "Arthur· Symons in fact developed the parallel to a considerable extent." Mr. Kermode offers no evidence for this view and I find no support for it in *The Symbolist Movement in Literature* or in Symons' essay, "John Donne," *Fortnightly Review*, n.s. LXXII (1899), 734-745. Symons was certainly capable of drawing the parallel or of extending the views of Gosse, but one may wonder if he actually did so.

7. Herbert J. C. Grierson, "John Donne," in A. W. Ward and A. R. Waller (eds.), *The Cambridge History of English Literature* (Cambridge, Eng., 1910), IV, 249.

8. First published in *The Times Literary Supplement*, No. 1,031 (October 20, 1921), pp. 669-670.

9. T. S. Eliot, "John Donne," *The Nation and the Athenaeum*, (June 9, 1923), p. 332.

10. T. S. Eliot, "Note sur Mallarmé et Poe," *Nouvelle Revue Française*, XXVII (1926), 524.

11. See E. P. Bollier, "T. S. Eliot and John Donne: A Problem in Criticism," *Tulane Studies in English*, IX (1959), 111, n. 23. For Eliot's definition of metaphysical poetry in the Clark Lectures, see Edward J. H. Greene, *T. S. Eliot et la France* (Paris, 1951), p. 88.

12. Mario Praz, "Donne's Relation to the Poetry of His Time," in Theodore Spencer (ed.), *A Garland for John Donne* (Cambridge, 1931), pp. 58-59. Also see Mario Praz, "The Critical Importance of the Revived Interest in Seventeenth-Century Metaphysical Poetry," in C. L. Wrenn and G. Bullough (eds.), *English Studies Today* (Oxford, 1951), p. 163.

13. It is interesting to note that Spanish critics have similarly insisted on a parallel between baroque and symbolist poetry. Thus, Guillermo de Torre declares that "Mallarmé es fundamentalmente un barroco," and sees between Góngora and Mallarmé "secretas armonías y paralelismos a la distancia!" *Las metamorfosis de proteo* (Buenos Aires, 1956), pp. 188, 190. This view leads to a further parallelism of the baroque and the avant-garde that was an important part of the literary strategy of the 1920's in Spain. For an account of the history of the Góngora-Mallarmé parallel, see Alfonso Reyes, "De Góngora y de Mallarmé," *Obras completas* (México, 1958), VII, 158-162.

14. Bollier, p. 112.

15. Duncan, p. 146.

16. T. S. Eliot, *Selected Essays* (London, 1946), p. 292.

17. Cited by René Galand, "T. S. Eliot and the Impact of Baudelaire," *Yale French Studies*, No. 6 (1950), pp. 32-33.

18. Cf. Granville Hicks, "T. S. Eliot's Baudelaire," *Nation* (January 7, 1931), p. 20. Hicks argues that "Eliot's conception of Baudelaire underestimates the poet's significance, and is, in its way, quite as narrow as Symons's." I am grateful to Professor William T. Bandy for this reference.

19. Eliot, "Donne in Our Time," in Theodore Spencer (ed.), *op. cit.*, p. 6.

20. George Williamson, *The Donne Tradition* (Cambridge, 1930), p. 4.

21. *Ibid.*, pp. 242-243.

22. *Ibid.*, p. 246.

23. Praz, "Donne's Relation to the Poetry of His Time," in Spencer (ed.), p. 58. For a similar view, see Martin Turnell, *Baudelaire* (New York, 1953), pp. 290-296.

24. Cleanth Brooks, *Modern Poetry and the Tradition* (Chapel Hill, N.C., 1939), p. 39.

25. *Ibid.*, p. 59.

26. *Ibid.*, p. 237.

27. Brooks, "Shakespeare as a Symbolist Poet," *Yale Review*, n. s. XXXIV (1945), 642-665.

28. Cf. Edmund Wilson, *Axel's Castle* (New York, 1950), p. 96.

29. Brooks, *Modern Poetry and the Tradition*, p. 64.

30. Brooks, *The Well Wrought Urn* (New York, 1959), p. 250.

31. Sona Raiziss, *The Metaphysical Passion* (Philadelphia, 1952), p. 51.

32. *Ibid.*, pp. 30, 111, 179.

33. *Ibid.*, p. 179.

34. Duncan, p. 129.

35. *Ibid.*, p. 219, n. 36.

36. Charles J. Sisson, review of Williamson, *The Donne Tradition*, in *The Modern Language Review*, XXVI (1931), 233.

37. Merritt Y. Hughes, "Kidnapping Donne," in University of California. Department of English, *Essays in Criticism*, 2nd series (1934), pp. 61-89. IV (1934), 67.

38. Allen Tate, *On the Limits of Poetry* (New York, 1948), p. 79.

39. *Ibid.*, p. 86.

40. It is important to note the similar reservations of John Crowe Ransom in "Eliot and the Metaphysicals," *Accent*, I (1940-41), 152.

41. Duncan, p. 181.

42. Kermode, p. 146. A similar stress on the contrast between metaphysical and symbolist styles is convincingly set forth by F. M. Kuna, "T. S. Eliot's Dissociation of Sensibility and the Critics of Metaphysical Poetry," *Essays in Criticism*, XIII (1963), 241-252.

43. Leonard Unger, "Donne's Poetry and Modern Criticism," in his *The Man in the Name* (Minneapolis, 1956), p. 55.

44. See Joseph A. Mazzeo, "Metaphysical Poetry and the Poetic of Correspondence," *Journal of the History of Ideas*, XIV (1953), 221-234.

45. Mazzeo, "A Critique of Some Modern Theories of Metaphysical Poetry," *Modern Philology*, L (1952), 88-96.

46. Mazzeo, "Metaphysical Poetry and the Poetic of Correspondence," *Journal of the History of Ideas*, XIV (1953), 232.

47. Joseph H. Summers, *George Herbert* (London, 1954), p. 145.

48. Josephine Miles, "The Language of the Donne Tradition," *Kenyon Review*, XIII (1951), 46.

49. Letter of June 27, 1884, reprinted in Mallarmé, *Correspondance, 1871-1885* (Paris, 1965), p. 266.

50. Cf. Emile Verhaeren, *Impressions,* troisième série (Paris, 1928), p. 115.

51. Albert Thibaudet, *La Poésie de Stéphane Mallarmé* (Paris, 1926), p. 93.

52. Mallarmé, *Œuvres complètes* (Paris, 1956), p. 647.

53. *Ibid.*, p. 869.

54. Warren Ramsey, *Jules Laforgue and the Ironic Inheritance* (New York, 1953), p. 5. The contrasts between Laforgue and the symbolists are emphasized by Marie-Jeanne Durry, *Jules Laforgue* (Paris, 1952), pp. 98-101.

55. Ramsey, p. 203.

56. G. M. Turnell, "The Poetry of Jules Laforgue," *Scrutiny*, V (1936), 143.

57. André Dinar, *La Croisade symboliste* (Paris, 1943), p. 60.

58. For a spirited attack on the view of Rimbaud as a symbolist poet, see R. Etiemble, *Le Mythe de Rimbaud: Structure du mythe* (Paris, 1952), pp. 63-104. M. Etiemble gratuitously extends his strictures to include symbolist poetry as well; his generalizations here are of very limited value, but his view of Rimbaud's relation to the symbolists is, I believe, essentially correct.

59. Joan Bennett, *Four Metaphysical Poets* (Cambridge, 1953), p. 19.

60. Pierre Legouis, *Donne the Craftsman* (Paris, 1928), pp. 75-77.

61. *The Poems of John Donne*, ed. Herbert J. C. Grierson (Oxford, 1912), II, 33.

62. Louis L. Martz, *The Poetry of Meditation* (New Haven, 1954), p. 213. Pierre Legouis has cogently described the poet's entreaty as part of a dramatic action wherein "metaphysical subtleties reveal themselves as amorous blandishments." *Op. cit.*, p. 76.

63. Cf. Grierson, *op. cit.*, II, 34-35.

64. Praz, "Donne's Relation to the Poetry of His Time," in Spencer (ed.), p. 55.

65. J. B. Leishman, *The Monarch of Wit* (London, 1951), p. 183.

66. *Ibid.*, p. 224.

67. Mallarmé, *Œuvres complètes*, p. 1412.

68. *Ibid.*, pp. 1412-1413. Cf. Lawrence Joseph, "Mallarmé et son amie anglaise," *Revue d'histoire littéraire de la France*, LXV (1965), 457-478.

69. Mallarmé, *Correspondance, 1862-1871* (Paris, 1959), p. 36.

70. For a different view, see Jean-Pierre Richard, *L'Univers imaginaire de Mallarmé* (Paris, 1961), p. 123.

71. Mallarmé, *Correspondance, 1862-1871*, p. 137.

72. Eliot, "Note sur Mallarmé et Poe," *Nouvelle Revue Francaise*, XXVII (1926), p. 526.

73. Jean Cocteau, "Discours sur Mallarmé," *Fontaine*, IV, No. 21 (mai 1942), 90.

74. For an able summary of the impact of metaphysical techniques on modern American poetry, see William Van O'Connor, *Sense and Sensibility in Modern Poetry* (Chicago, 1948), pp. 81-92.

75. Cf. Arnold Stein, "Donne and the 1920's: A Problem in Historical Consciousness," *Journal of English Literary History*, XVII (1960), 16-29.

76. Frederick J. Hoffman has argued that the modern attachment to the metaphysicals is an expression of the cult of the object and the "reductive strategies of modern criticism." See *The Mortal No* (Princeton, 1964), p. 357.

77. Mallarmé, *Œuvres complètes*, p. 876.

APPENDIX

THE DREAME

Deare love, for nothing lesse then thee
Would I have broke this happy dreame,
    It was a theame
For reason, much too strong for phantasie,
Therefore thou wakd'st me wisely; yet
My Dreame thou brok'st not, but continued'st it,
Thou art so truth, that thoughts of thee suffice,
To make dreames truths; and fables histories;
Enter these armes, for since thou thoughtst it best,
Not to dreame all my dreame, let's act the rest.

As lightning, or a Tapers light,
Thine eyes, and not thy noise wak'd mee;
    Yet I thought thee
(For thou lovest truth) an Angell, at first sight,
But when I saw thou sawest my heart,
And knew'st my thoughts, beyond an Angels art,
When thou knew'st what I dreamt, when thou knew'st when
Excesse of joy would wake me, and cam'st then,
I must confesse, it could not chuse but bee
Prophane, to thinke thee any thing but thee.

Comming and staying show'd thee, thee,
But rising makes me doubt, that now,
    Thou art not thou.
That love is weake, where feare's as strong as hee;
'Tis not all spirit, pure, and brave,
If mixture it of *Feare, Shame, Honor,* have.
Perchance as torches which must ready bee,
Men light and put out, so thou deal'st with mee,
Thou cam'st to kindle, goest to come; Then I
Will dreame that hope againe, but else would die.

The Poems of John Donne, edited by
Herbert J. C. Grierson (Oxford, 1912), I, 37-38.

APPARITION

La lune s'attristait. Des séraphins en pleurs
Rêvant, l'archet aux doigts, dans le calme des fleurs
Vaporeuses, tiraient de mourantes violes
De blancs sanglots glissant sur l'azur des corolles.
—C'était le jour béni de ton premier baiser.
Ma songerie aimant à me martyriser
S'enivrait savamment du parfum de tristesse
Que même sans regret et sans déboire laisse
La cueillaison d'un Rêve au cœur qui l'a cueilli.

J'errais donc, l'œil rivé sur le pavé vieilli
Quand avec du soleil aux cheveux, dans la rue
Et dans le soir, tu m'es en riant apparue
Et j'ai cru voir la fée au chapeau de clarté
Qui jadis sur mes beaux sommeils d'enfant gâté
Passait, laissant toujours de ses mains mal fermées
Neiger de blancs bouquets d'étoiles parfumées.

Stéphane Mallarmé, *Œuvres complètes*
(Paris, 1956), texte établi et annoté
par Henri Mondor et G. Jean-Aubry, p. 30.

III

Literary Themes

The subject of themes is one of the most controversial in comparative literature. We speak of the Faust theme, the Don Juan theme, or the theme of death, but also of the Faust *legend* or the *idea* of death. Themes, in other words, are so various and multiform that they may embrace mythology on one extreme and intellectual history on the other. The subject is further complicated by the use of two other terms, *types* and *motifs,* which are sometimes considered as synonyms for themes and sometimes as completely different.

The major group of themes is that consisting of personalities whose traits or behavior have established literary traditions. The origins of these personalities may be mythological or classical (Prometheus, Amphytrion), Biblical (David, the wandering Jew), Arthurian (Galahad, Tristram), historical (Július Caesar, Jeanne d'Arc) or literary (Don Juan, Hamlet). These personalities are also called types by some critics, but it would seem more logical to reserve the latter designation for character abstractions, social or historical, such as the soldier (either braggart or valiant), the deceived husband, wife, or lover; the farmer, bureaucrat, or proletarian; or the indolent servant and the alienated man.

Another possibility is to depersonalize these categories into social situations and consider the ravages or ironies of war; the eternal triangle, or the battle of the sexes; the pleasures or sorrows of life in the city or the farm; and man adjusted or maladjusted to his environment. These subjects could be classified as motifs or *Stoffgeschichte.* As one critic has pointed out, the motif of obstructed love has produced at least two separate literary themes — those of Tristan and Isolde and of Romeo and Juliet.

The concept of *Stoffgeschichte* opens to literary study an almost endless vista of concepts, situations, and natural elements. Various critics have considered as legitimate themes such materials as time, space, ocean, mountains, night, animals, cowboys, death, sacrifice, as well as such intellectual concepts as the sublime, the beautiful, primitivism, and progress.

The thematic approach to literature is particularly applicable to the method of *rapprochement* rather than to that of tracing sources and influences. Let us take an example already discussed in *Comparative Literature Studies*: Two modern masterpieces, Thomas Mann's *Der Zauberberg*, 1924, and Katherine Anne Porter's *Pale Horse, Pale Rider*, 1939, use the theme of illness to portray "the problem of intellectual and spiritual breakup before and during World War I" (John O. McCormick, "Notes on a Comparative American Literary History," V [1968], 176).

One of the major weaknesses of thematics is that it is likely to overlook the most significant features of a great work while concentrating on a theme which is of minor importance to it. A study of suicide, for example, would find little in *Hamlet* but the drowning of Ophelia. The thematic critic is in danger of missing the forest by hunting for leaves of a certain shape or color. Also in thematology each work which embodies a particular theme is considered as merely one link in a chain — the minor works are given as much attention as the masterpieces. Another danger is in emphasizing the banal or the obvious. An example is the theme of time. It is obvious that most works of fiction have a chronological plot and consequently that each author must take the element of time into consideration. A student who seeks to read psychological or cosmic significance into every reference to a clock or calendar runs the risk of overinterpreting. Some critics even treat with disdain the study of great personalities. There is some truth in the affirmation that Faust and Don Juan are the only great and enduring protagonists, and even they, through overexposure, are in danger of becoming uninteresting.

Another serious objection is that an examination of the complete history of a particular theme is little but an exercise in bibliography or erudition which contributes little to our understanding or pleasure. After we have read the ten or twelve most important works devoted to Don Juan, for example, we have no real interest in the two or three hundred minor ones, which are merely weak echoes of the masterpieces.

The opponents of thematology also affirm that treating the history of parricide, eating, or love-making as they appear in literary works is not literature, but social science or the history of human behavior. This view is based on a prior assumption that the material of literature is not necessarily human behavior — or that literature and life must remain separated. Other scholars, however, point to the close inter-relations between literature, psychology, sociology, and religion, and argue that each of these disciplines may shed light on the others.

It is also alleged against the study of themes that the portrayal of a series of writers who use any particular theme shows no consequential sequence from one to another. In other words, the last author to use a theme is not necessarily acquainted with the ones immediately pre-ceding him or even with a majority of all other works in the series. Finally, it is charged that the knowledge of how one author deals with a given theme gives no insight into the manner in which it will be treated by another. A study of the Don Juan theme in its prototype *El Burlador de Sevilla,* for example, gives no indication of the artistry of Molière in his *Dom Juan.* The answer to this is that the purpose of comparative literature is to reveal differences as well as similarities — and that a better understanding of either play may result from a consideration of the two together.

One of the most popular themes in modern horror films, that of Dracula, is generally considered to be of recent origin. Grigore Nandris in the following essay traces the theme back to a historical personage of the fifteenth century and reveals the development of two independent literary traditions, one in Eastern Europe, the other in Western. Frederick W. Dillistone in the second essay takes the ancient and universally significant theme of the fall of man and analyzes its psycho-logical implications in modern literature.

GRIGORE NANDRIS

The Historical Dracula: The Theme of His Legend in the Western and in the Eastern Literatures of Europe

A Fantastic Attempt of Dracula to Conquer England

The History and Legend of the Hero, and the Origin of His Name

The Background of the Theme in Folklore

The Psychological Significance of the Dracula Theme in the West

The Historical Significance of the Dracula Theme in the East

Conclusion

A Fantastic Attempt of Dracula to Conquer England

IN HIS HAUNTED CASTLE in the eastern Carpathians, Dracula, Count of Bistritza, prepares a strategic invasion and conquest of England.[1] He has appointed agents along his route of invasion—in Budapest, in Varna—who will ship the necessary material and transport the goods; and other agents—in London, Newcastle, Durham, Harwich, Dover, Exeter—who will buy houses and prepare strategic places necessary for the fulfillment of his plan. He does not allow any agent to know anything about the others. He works through a solicitors' firm in Lincoln's Inn, which buys for him estates on a strategic line from Exeter to Whitby on the Yorkshire coast.

In this castle in the forests of Transylvania within the recesses of the Borgo Pass, the Count lives a mysterious, nocturnal life in the company of ghosts and sorceresses. In an atmosphere of magic, horror, and terror, carefully recounted by the author Bram Stoker, a young English secretary from the London firm of solicitors leaves England to prepare, under the pretext of business, the Count's affairs for the expedition. Travelling by way of Munich, Vienna, Budapest, and Cluj, he arrives on May 3 in Bistritz and continues his journey in the evening of May 4, the eve of St. George's Day, an ominous night in the annual cycle of Rumanian folklore.

Travelling by stagecoach, he takes the road over the mountain pass leading to Dorna in Bukovina. Everywhere he encounters the horrified looks and blessings of the superstitious local people. In the darkness of night he changes the stagecoach for a calèche pulled by black horses and driven by a mysterious, bearded personage whose face is hidden by his wide-brimmed hat. Intensifying the atmosphere of mystery, snow begins to fall at midnight; dogs howl, and wolves surround the carriage. A blue flame appears and disappears in the night, and after a night which recalls Bürger's Lenore: "Denn die Toten reiten schnell!", the mysterious driver vanishes and the young English secretary arrives at a ruined castle in the depths of a forest. Here he becomes a prisoner of the Count, whom he sees only during the night, for Dracula disappears by day.

In his attempt to escape from this dreadful prison on the edge of a terrible precipice surrounded by inpenetrable valleys, the secretary explores the caves and the recesses of the castle—a fortress haunted by many strange things which drive him to the verge of insanity. To escape the nocturnal visits of the Count, he decides to spend the night in the former women's quarters of the castle. Instead of finding peace, he finds that the night turns into a Walpurgis-like nightmare. He becomes the object of attraction of three beautiful female ghosts and of Dracula who shouts to them: "How dare you touch him? This man belongs to me!" The scornful reply from a fair girl-vampire is: "You yourself never loved; you never loved!" [2] And all of them burst into soulless laughter.

From his castle in the forests of the Borgo Pass the Count of Bistritza sets off toward the North Sea, sailing from Varna on the Black Sea and taking with him six trunks of Transylvanian soil on which he will spend the daylight hours in various places on his planned battlefield. The attacks will take place at night; his brain-power is limitless and his physical strength invincible, for when he rests on his native soil he is neither alive nor dead, but *Un-dead*.

The campaign of terror starts with his arrival at Whitby from where he extends his field of operation concentrically, establishing fortresses from the North Sea to Exeter. He transports his trunks of Transylvanian soil to the interior of this area and establishes his headquarters in Piccadilly and in the Thames Estuary. The final purpose of his strategy is the transformation of the whole population into vampires. This transformation will extend even over the fauna, for "operation vampire" begins with a wolf in a zoo and continues with an inmate in a lunatic asylum and a woman. The vampire sucks the blood from the victim's throat and transforms him into a vampire which acquires eternal *Un-deadliness* and creates other vampires. The transformation into a vampire is based on the principle *attraction:repulsion,* and no remedy exists for those who fall under the spell of a vampire.

However, a group of heroes—a lord, a lawyer and his wife, a psychiatrist, and a citizen of London—led by a Dutch professor-specialist begins the fight to protect and liberate the population of London from the dreadful terror which paralyzes the whole country. If they do not succeed in cutting off the head and in piercing the heart of the vampire Dracula—in daylight and while he is separated from his trunks of soil—England will become a country of vampires. Because vampires like to be vampires, the danger is great. The weapons of attack used by the valiant group are: garlic, the Cross, and Communion wafers. But their fight against a supernatural power of terror is frustrated by the unlimited intelligence and strength of the monster, who "was in his time a most wonderful man: soldier, statesman and alchemist— the last of which represented the highest development of the scientific knowledge of his time."

When, in the end, Dracula is chased from his other hiding places by the alchemy-science (garlic) of the Dutch professor, and is cornered in his house in Piccadilly, the monster succeeds in escaping and in leaving the country for his castle in the forests of the Borgo Pass. He proffers a last scornful threat to his pursuers: "You think you have left me without a resting place, but I have more. My revenge is just beginning. I will spread it over centuries, and time is on my side. The girls that you all love are mine already; and through them you and others shall yet be mine—my creatures, to do my bidding and to be my jackals when I want to feed."

He now has to be pursued to his castle in the eastern Carpathians and killed according to the local ritual. Dracula flees by sea towards Varna; the pursuing heroes take the land-route and search for him in Varna, in Bucharest, and in Galatz. Here two of them try to engage the enemy from a motor-vessel on the Sereth and Bistritza rivers; two take the train to Veresti in southern Bukovina, and from there go on horseback through the mountains; the other two reach the Tihutsa Pass in the Borgo Valley in a cart.

Here, in the wild forest near his castle, the enemy is engaged before sunset. His allies and defenders, gypsies and Slovaks, hurry from the castle to save their master, and put up a fierce resistance around the trunk in which the monster lies on his native earth. At the end of the battle the head of the vampire is gashed, his heart is pierced. England is saved, losing only a single man in the battle. Protected by a snowstorm, the gypsies and the Slovaks flee into the forest; the victorious heroes return to London.

This Dracula story was one of the greatest successes in the English horror literature of our century. Some critics maintain that it is the best seller after the Bible. The sense and the psychological meaning of Bram Stoker's *Dracula* have been and are still much discussed; the book has been published in numerous editions; it has been dramatized; it has been filmed. As far as I know, however, there has been no examination of the historical background of Dracula, nor of how his name came to signify a vampire, and even to acquire the connotation of an evil man in the English of some African students. I once heard in London: "I will call you a Dracula!" shouted one African student to another. Quite possibly from Bram Stoker's book the word has entered the language of some African tribe.

The History and Legend of the Hero, and the Origin of His Name

The history of the Dracula theme in the European literatures is a typical example of the interplay of history, imagination, psychology, and the creative ability of a writer who tries to transform rough material into a literary work. The historical personage who appears in the rôle of the hero in three literary cycles as Dracula is Vlad V, called the Empaler, who ruled in the years 1456–1462, and again in 1476, as Prince of Walachia (southern Rumania). There are several princes called Vlad and some historians, e.g., N. Iorga, consider the Empaler as being the third not the fifth Vlad, short Rumanian form for the Slavonic Vladislav.[3]

One has usually assumed that *Dracula,* the nickname of this prince, represents the Rumanian word for 'devil' *dracul,* from the Latin *draco, dracu-illu-,* without accounting for the ending *-a* in English, German, and Russian which does not exist in Rumanian.[4] Moreover, with regard to the content, it has to be noted that in Rumanian folklore the devil is never confused with a vampire and fulfills a quite different function in the folk-mythology.[5] There is no association in Rumanian folklore between the Dracula story and the vampire mythology, as Striedfer assumes, due to a misreading of a passage of my article "Rumanian Folklore," published in *The Aryan Path* (April 1954), pp. 164–169.[6]

The Dracula story did not penetrate into the Rumanian vampire tradition. It was Bram Stoker who transformed Dracula into a vampire. Dracula (in this form) does not appear in Rumanian history except in external documents issued by Vlad V. His father, Vlad III, has the epithet *Dracul,* a homonym of the Rumanian *dracul* 'devil.' Vlad V has in Rumanian history the epithet

Tsepesh 'Empaler.' In the Rumanian folklore-tradition *dracul* 'the devil' and *strigoiul* 'the vampire' are two different mythological figures and are never confused.[7] *Dracul* is a taboo word and it is hardly conceivable that rulers who built churches and fought against the infidels would be called "devils." The meaning of *Dracul* as an epithet is that of a member of the Order of the Dragon. I explained the form and content of this false etymology elsewhere.[8] The ending *-a* in this form is the Slavonic morpheme defining the genitive of the *-o-* declension. As to the content of the word, it is important to emphasize two historical facts. The historical Dracula never used this epithet in his signature on internal documents, and he is not known in Rumanian history or tradition by this nickname.[9] In the later tradition he acquired the nickname *Tsepesh* (*Ţepeş*) 'the Empaler.'

His father, Vlad III, along with the young Polish King Vladyslav and John Hunyadi, the Protector of the Hungarian Kingdom, fought at Varna (1444) against the Turks. Vlad III appears in Rumanian history with the epithet of *Dracul* (not Dracula). This ruling Prince of Walachia was crowned in 1431 at Nuremberg by the Emperor Sigismund of Luxemburg. On this occasion the Emperor of the Western Roman Empire, Sigismund, granted to Vlad III the Order of the Dragon, i.e., Vlad became Sigismund's vassal with the obligation to fight for what that Order represented. This feudal title confirmed to Vlad III the possession of the territories in Transylvania round the castles of Amlaş and Făgăraş.[10]

The Order of the Dragon had been founded by Sigismund on December 12, 1418. Its badge was a cross, below which hung a dragon. It was created to defend the Church of Rome against the Hussites. Alphons V of Aragon (1435–1437) established the Order in his kingdom, but after the death of the founders it disappeared in Germany and in Aragon. John Hunyadi, by his original name Iancu of Huniedoara in Transylvania, was Protector and Governor of Hungary. He was the father of the Hungarian king Matthias Corvinus (1458–1490), and belonged to the Rumanian gentry of Transylvania. His father was Voicu, the Son of Serb, and his mother was from the Mărgineanu family. John Hunyadi was Prince (*Voivode*) of Transylvania, Ruler (*Ban*) of Severin, and after the battle at Varna he became Protector of the Hungarian Kingdom. On his way back from Varna, he was captured and imprisoned for a short time by his rival, Vlad III, the father of Vlad V Dracula. Later he captured Vlad III and murdered him and his son Mircea. In the dynastic struggle for the throne of Walachia, the same John Hunyadi aided Vlad V Dracula, another son of Vlad III, in seizing power. Vlad V proved to be more than worthy of the task of defending his country and central Europe against the menacing power of the Ottoman Empire.

The Rumanian chronicles are rather reticent about his heroic deeds. He was overshadowed by his contemporary, Stefan of Moldavia, and survived for posterity as an epitome of tyrannic cruelty. However, historically Vlad Dracula was far less cruel than other rulers of the Renaissance period like Richard III (1483–1485), Mahomet II (1451–1481), Cesare Borgia (ca. 1476–

1507), or Ivan IV (1533-1584), though he had better reasons of state for his procedure. The Rumanian chronicles mention briefly some of the punishments inflicted by this prince, telling us that he seized on Easter Day his boyars, their wives, and sons dressed in their Sunday best, and because they had done some wrong, forced them until their clothes were in rags to build a fortress. It is, however, a historical fact that he inflicted his policy on the large masses of the peasantry, whom he needed in order to confront the Turkish armies. He also had to curb the abuses and intrigues of his powerful vassals.

The foreign sources for the history of this period hail him as a hero of Christianity. The Byzantine chronicler Laonic Chalcocondiles praises Vlad Dracula, who defeated in 1461 on the Danube an Ottoman invading army of 250,000 men. A traveller describes the joy of the people of Rhodes, who greeted Vlad's victory over the Turks by ringing the bells in all the churches of the island.[11] After the great campaign of 1462, Vlad Dracula lost his throne. The Turks installed as ruler in Walachia his brother Radu the Handsome, who had been brought up in Constantinople and became a depraved tool of the Ottoman Empire.

Vlad Dracula lost the favor of Matthias Corvinus through the intrigues of the Saxon merchants of Transylvania whom he had forbidden to establish their trade monopoly in Walachia, and when they supported other pretenders to his throne while he was defending the independence of his country against the Turks, he punished them severely by empaling many of them and burning their towns and villages. Inside his country he lost the loyalty and allegiance of his feudal noblemen whose quarrels he subdued brutally. The exhaustion of the country by the scorched earth strategy of his campaigns estranged the loyalty of the peasant masses, and their expectation of being rewarded with lands confiscated from the unfaithful feudal lords was not realized, for Vlad Dracula had promised that nobody should be poor in his country, and that all should be rich. Moreover, the revenge of the Transylvanian Saxons created for him a "bad press" in the West and caused his imprisonment in Buda by order of Matthias Corvinus (1458-1490). It is of interest to mention that under this king the Szeklers (Săcui), who had been settled in the eastern corner of Transylvania as frontier guards, revolted in 1461, 1463, and 1465 against the abuses of the king and tried to reduce his authority.

The vampire Dracula, as reconstructed by Bram Stoker, can be identified with the historical personality of Vlad V of Walachia, who epitomizes the struggle of his nation for freedom and independence through the ages. Dracula has in Bram Stoker's story the title Count of Bistritza, historically a title of John Hunyadi, sometimes called Count of the Szeklers. The Count of Bistritza presents himself to his secretary who has arrived from London as a noble boyar, of the family of the Hospodars, who fought against the invaders and created civilizations in their countries. *Boyar* is a term applicable only to the noblemen and the rulers of the Rumanian countries of Moldavia and Walachia. "I am a *boyar*," Count Dracula says to Jonathan Harker, the

English lawyer who became his prisoner in the haunted castle in the
Carpathians, ". . . and there shall be to you many strange things . . . ."

> He then explained to me that it is commonly believed that on a certain night
> of the year . . . when all evil spirits are supposed to have unchecked sway—a
> blue flame is seen over any place where treasure has been concealed . . . for
> this was the ground fought over for centuries by the Walachian, the Saxon, and
> the Turk. In olden days there were stirring times, when the Austrians and the
> Hungarians came up in hordes, and the patriots went out to meet them—men
> and women, the aged and the children too—and waited their coming on the
> rock above the passes, that they might sweep destruction on them with their
> artificial avalanches. When the invader was triumphant he found but little, for
> whatever there was had been sheltered in the friendly soil.

This passage echoes history and legend. The destruction of the invader
in the Carpathian passes by throwing rocks and arrows upon him is depicted
in a miniature of the *Chronicon Pictum* representing the flight of King Charles
Robert after his defeat by Basarab, the ruler of Walachia (1330). The superstition concerning flames marking the places of hidden treasure is an element of
Rumanian folklore.

Count Dracula sometimes calls his ancestors Szekelys (Szeklers). The
Szeklers are a Hungarian dialect-speaking population settled in the late Middle
Ages in the eastern mountainous corner of Transylvania as frontier guards,
just as at a later date Rumanians were settled by the Hapsburgs as guards
on the northern borders of Transylvania and in the Banat. The historical
and ethnographic difficulty in establishing Dracula's genealogy by Bram
Stoker is due to the fact that Szeklers were often allies of the Rumanian
ruling princes of Moldavia and Walachia, and also because they often fought
in fierce revolts against the Hungarian king and the ruling class of Transylvania. Anyhow, historical and ethnographic accuracy is not the concern of
the author of this horror story. The Count of Bistritza exposes in rhetorical
tirades the deeds of his ancestors to his London secretary: "Here in the
whirlpool of European races, the Ugric tribes bore down from Iceland the
fighting spirit which Thor and Wodin gave them . . ." (an echo of the
invasion of Transylvania by Germanic tribes—Goths, Gepids, Vandals, Ther-
vingii, Victoalii, Taifalii, Lombards). And Count Dracula continues: "Here,
too, when they came, they found the Huns, whose warlike fury had swept
the earth like a living flame till the dying peoples held that in their veins
ran the blood of those old witches who, expelled from Scythia, had mated
with the devils in the desert." The vampire Count Dracula of Bistritza held
up his arm and declaimed:

> Is it a wonder that we were a conquering race; that we were proud; that when
> the Magyar, the Lombard, the Avar, the Bulgar, or the Turk poured his thou-
> sands on our frontiers, we drove them back? Is it strange that when Arpad and
> his legions swept through the Hungarian fatherland he found us here when
> he reached the frontier? And when the Hungarian flood swept eastward, the
> Szekelys were claimed as kindred by the victorious Magyars, and to us for
> centuries was trusted the guarding of the frontier of Turkey-land? . . . When
> the flags of the Wallach and the Magyar went down beneath the Crescent, who

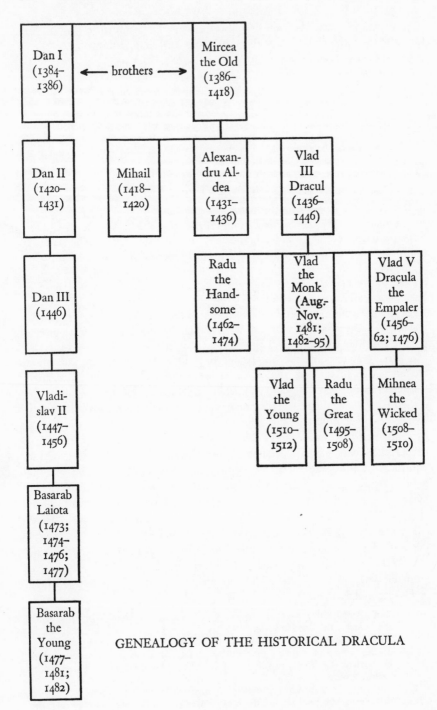

GENEALOGY OF THE HISTORICAL DRACULA

was it but one of my own race who as Voivode crossed the Danube and beat the Turk on his own ground? This was a Dracula indeed!

These tirades refer to the Germanic and the Mongolian invasions, they recall later fighting and resistance to the Ottoman power. The "Voivode," who "beat the Turk on his own ground," is evidently John Hunyadi, the son of Rumanian parents, and the Dracula ancestors he alludes to are Vlad III Dracul, who fought at Varna (1444), and Vlad V Dracula, his son, who defeated the Turks on the Danube (1461).

The author of *Dracula* takes liberties with history and ethnography, but his aim was not to write an historical work. On the whole he gathered his information in the British Museum, where Dracula's London secretary Jonathan Harker tells us he collected his information about the region he was about to visit:

> I had visited the British Museum, and made search among the books and maps in the library regarding Transylvania. . . . I find that the district he named (i.e. Dracula in his letter addressed to his solicitors in Lincoln's Inn) is in the extreme east of the country, just on the border of three states, Transylvania, Moldavia, and Bukovina, in the midst of the Carpathian mountains, one of the wildest and least known portions of Europe. I was not able to light on any map or work giving the exact locality of the Castle Dracula. . . (because such a castle does not exist) . . . but I found that Bistritz, the post town named by Count Dracula, is a fairly well known place.

He finds information even on some habits of the local Rumanian population: "I had for breakfast more paprika, and a sort of porridge of maize flour which they said was mamaliga and egg-plant stuffed with forcemeat, a very excellent dish, which they call impletata, . . ." probably a contamination of two Rumanian culinary terms: *umplute* 'stuffed,' and *împletite* 'plaited.'

In speaking of things and people, and especially of battles, Count Dracula speaks as if his house and name are his own pride, that their glory is his glory, that their fate is his fate. Whenever he speaks of his house he always says *we,* and speaks almost in the plural, as a king speaks. "Again, when after the battle of Mohacs, we threw off the Hungarian yoke, we of the Dracula blood were among their leaders, for our spirit would not brook that we were not free . . . the Szekelys—and Dracula as their hearts' blood, their brains and their swords—can boast a record that mushroom growths like the Hapsburgs and the Romanoffs can never reach."

So the history explained by Count Dracula to his London prisoner continues. It confounds events and personalities, but through the mist of this confused imagination the historical allusions reflect real events and personalities. In the battle of Mohács (1526) Hungary lost her independence, whereas Transylvania continued to enjoy a certain political freedom, like the other two Rumanian countries Moldavia and Walachia.

The physiognomic features of Count Dracula, interpreted in the tradition of studies by Lavater and by Herder of the eighteenth century, may have borne little resemblance to the available portraits of Vlad the Empaler (Dracula) as represented by woodcuts in German incunabula, or to his portrait in the

Castle of Ambras in the Tyrol, adapted by Bram Stoker to suit his literary purposes.

> His face was a strong—a very strong—aquiline, with high bridge of the thin nose and peculiarly arched nostrils; with lofty domed forehead, and hair growing scantily round the temple, but profusely elsewhere. His eyebrows were very massive, almost meeting over the nose, and with bushy hair that seemed to curl in its own profusion. The mouth, so far as I could see it under the heavy moustache, was fixed and rather cruel-looking, with peculiarly sharp white teeth; these protruded over the lips, whose remarkable ruddiness showed astonishing vitality in a man of his years. For the rest, his ears were pale and at the tops extremely pointed; the chin was broad and strong and the cheeks firm though thin. The general effect was one of extraordinary pallor.

It is not the purpose of this essay to try to ascertain the sources used by Bram Stoker for the historical background of his story. That is neither relevant to his literary work nor possible to achieve satisfactorily. His haphazard reading was without scholarly pretension. Considering that he places the castle of his hero in Transylvania, it is probable that he used Sebastian Münster's *Cosmographia,* in which not only the name Dracula and his legend appear, but also portrayals from a German incunabulum of the cruelties attributed to him. Some engravings in the editions of Basel (1544 and 1628) illustrate the episodes of Vlad the Empaler's cruelties and present his portrait. We are told that King Matthias "Draculam in Transylvaniae montes Vaivodam cepit." In fact, Vlad Dracula went to his kinsman and feudal ally in the struggle against the Ottoman power, seeking asylum and help after his defeat. Like his father, Vlad Dracula had always fought on the side of the Christian emperor of the West against the foe of Christianity.

Bram Stoker fused the historical information and confounded it in such a way that it is not possible to unravel the various sources. The blending of the history of the three Rumanian principalities—Transylvania, Moldavia, and Walachia—brings to our memory such extensive studies as the eighteenth-century amateurish product by Sulzer,[12] full of real and imaginary information about the whole Carpathian region of eastern Europe. The Austrian author confesses on the title page that he took liberties with history. The study is a kind of official justification for the annexation of Bukovina by the Hapsburgs only four years before the appearance of the book (1777). The maps at the end of the first volume could have been helpful for the study of the region.

More direct information about his subject could have been found in a later study by Engel[13] in which we find reproduced a German incunabulum of 1477 about Dracula, illustrated with a woodcut portrait. This guesswork could be greatly extended, but it would show only the existence of a rich literature indirectly connected with Bram Stoker's subject.

The Background of the Theme in Folklore

Elements of local folklore have been obviously used in building up the background of the story of Dracula. However, it is difficult to distinguish

between the local folklore elements and the general ones. Due to the fundamental attitude of the human mind towards the visible and the invisible
world of mystery, folklore elements, identical in form and in meaning, without genetic relationship to each other, appear in widely separated areas.
On the other hand, folklore themes are transmitted, like any other form
of civilization, from one community to another, with or without some
changes and adaptations. Themes circulate so easily that often it is hardly
possible to determine their center of dispersion.

According to the author's statement, attributed to Count Dracula's secretary, the folklore material was collected in the British Museum. "In the
population of Transylvania there are four distinct nationalities: Saxon in
the South and mixed with them the Wallachs, who are the descendants of
the Dacians; Magyars in the West, and Szekeleys in the East and North.
I read that every known superstition in the world is gathered into the horse
shoe of the Carpathians, as if the centre of some sort of imaginative whirlpool; if so my stay may be very interesting."

In fact, all folklore elements displayed in the Dracula story are to be
found in Rumanian folklore; most of them also appear in the folklores of
other European nations. In Bram Stoker's story the folklore is distorted
and confounded by the same studio-technique that we tried to analyze in the
preceding section, when we discussed the historical background of Dracula.
Concerning the name *Dracula,* as I have already observed, it is to be dissociated from the Rumanian *dracul* 'devil', because in Rumanian folklore the
vampire is not identified with the devil.[14] So, even if the forms are identical,
the contents are different. On the other hand, the word *vampir* 'vampire'
exists in Rumanian only as a neologism. As to the attributes ascribed to
Dracula by his English author, they correspond to those attributed to three
or four mythical personages of Rumanian folklore, namely to Balaur, Zmeu,
Strigoi, and Făt Frumos. The last two words are of Latin origin: *strigoi* is the
Latin *striga*+the suffix *-oneus.* The same word appears in the Albanian
štrgë 'witch', *štrigan* 'wizard'; in the Slovene *štriga* 'witch', *štrigan* 'vampire,
blood-sucker'.[15] Făt Frumos, the Prince Charming of Rumanian fairy tales,
is the Latin *fetu-* 'boy' and *formosu-* 'handsome.' In fairy tales this hero
fights against evil and defeats Zmeu a powerful personification of a human
and a supernatural creature. This word in Rumanian is of Slavonic origin.
The common Slavonic *zmiji* translates in Old Church Slavonic texts *Ostromir,
Suprasliensis,* the Greek *ofis, drakōn* 'serpent'. This Slavonic word is etymolo-
gically related to *zemlja* 'earth', and contains the idea of 'crawling on the
earth'.[16] In Rumanian the word *zmeu* does not have this connotation but
designates a mythological personage with limitless physical strength, of
demonic origin, fighting with Făt Frumos, the embodiment of moral power.
The physiognomic characteristics of Zmeu are not well defined. He appears
as a combination of human and super-animalistic attributes. He flies to his
castle, where he keeps imprisoned the fair-haired Ileana sought by Făt
Frumos. His mother is The Mother of the Forest, a wicked, satanic creature
who helps Zmeu in his undertakings. The other meaning of *zmeu* in

A PORTRAIT OF VLAD V DRACULA (1456–1462; 1476)

This is a drawn reproduction of a woodcut in a German incunabulum of the fifteenth or sixteenth century. The incunabulum is in the Széchényi Collection of the Magyar Nemzeti Museum in Budapest.

Plate 1

"THE FANTASTIC SERPENT"

This marble carving of the second or third century A.D. was recently excavated at Constanta (the ancient Tomis) in Rumania. It now reposes in the Regional Museum of Archeology in Constanta-Dobruja.

Plate 2

DRACO, THE BATTLE-STANDARD OF THE DACIANS

This drawing by Domenico Ghirlandajo (1449–1498) depicts the Dacian banner situated on the the wall of a Dacian fortress and blown by the wind. Ghirlandajo used representations of Draco on Trajan's Column and in the Codex Escurialensis as his sources. (See Note 20.)

Plate 3

CARNYX, A TYPE OF TRUMPET, AND DRACO, THE BATTLE-STANDARD,
TOGETHER WITH OTHER MILITARY EQUIPMENT OF THE DACIANS

This eighteenth-century engraving by Pirandesi is based on representations on Trajan's Column. It is noteworthy that the trumpet depicts
the head of an animal. (See Note 20.)

Plate 4

Rumanian, 'kite', is a metaphorical development of the first. In connection with this word it is interesting to remark that in Serbian it appears as an epithet of a ruler—Zmaj Despot—of the same period as Dracula and Matthias Corvinus. Whether the Serbian epithet is a loan-translation of the Dracula or an independent creation is outside the scope of this study.[17]

For *vampire* the Slavs had a word, which does not exist as a loan word in Rumanian, and the Russian form of which is *upyr*. It is defined by Dal as "the corpse of a wicked sorcerer or of a witch, which wanders about at night disguised as a wolf or as an owl and kills humans and animals. In order to appease him one must find his tomb and pierce his body with a pale." This Slavonic word is considered by some philologists as the prototype of the German *Vampir*.[18] All Dracula's attributes, except his limitless strength, are present in this concept of the vampire.

The etymology of the fourth mythological element which contributes to Dracula's definition, the word *balaur,* is not clear. Most probably it is an autochthonous word of Thracian origin. Its meaning is 'dragon, monster-serpent' of a great size, usually with several heads, recalling the monster Cerberus of classical mythology and St. George's dragon. The word appears to be related to the Albanian *bole* 'giant serpent', *bulár* 'sea-serpent'. In Serbian (Montenegro, Ragusa) the word appears in various forms: *blavor, blavur, glavor,* etc., having the connotation of 'sea-serpent'. The Indo-European root, which it represents, seems to be the same as that represented by the Latin *bēlua* 'serpent', Old Indian *bhalam* 'shininess, glittering'; *bhati* 'it shines, it burns'; Lithuanian *belúoti* 'to glitter'. The geographical area covered by these representatives of the Indo-European root (*bhel-* 'to shine') supports a hypothetical Thracian origin of the Rumanian word. This mythological personage of Rumanian folklore is a chthonic deity and is respected as a totem, in the form of a serpent or a dragon. The Dacians, a branch of the Thracians, had as their battle-standard a head of an animal, usually identified as a wolf. When the wind blew through the open mouth into a long bag forming the body of a serpent, it became inflated, as it appears on Trajan's Column. This animal has been identified as a wolf, but it seems rather to be a serpent, a dragon. An important support for the latter identification appears in the recently discovered "monster" in the excavations at Constanţa, the ancient Tomis. The monster is a serpent with a human-like head and piercing eyes.[19] (See Plate 2.) An attempt has been made to identify this monster with a deity associated with the cult of Aesculapius. However, there is a striking similarity between this monster and the *Draco* of the Dacian battle-standard, as represented on Trajan's Column in a drawing by Domenico Ghirlandajo (1449–1498), or in an engraving of the eighteenth century by Piranesi—both reproduced in a recent publication.[20] (See Plates 3 and 4.)

Dracula incorporates from this folklore the "undeadness" of Strigoi, the supermanly strength and wickedness of Zmeu, the mystery of Balaur and the power of attraction of Făt Frumos. No one can imagine that Bram Stoker studied the folklore and mythology of that "horseshoe of the Carpathians" to obtain this picture of his Dracula. It is pure chance that the folkloric background conveys to the reader who is acquainted with that folklore this picture of Dracula. However, Bram Stoker might have been acquainted with such folklore sources as the German study by W. Schmidt,[21] or the English study by E. Gerard.[22] To his reading on folklore the current press of his time could have added its contribution. The memories of Londoners at the time of *Dracula's* gestation were haunted by the horror of the undetected murders of women by the criminal sex maniac, Jack the Ripper of the 1880's. Echoes of the sensation caused by some vampire stories of that time in eastern Europe could have reached the West through the press. Towards the end of the nineteenth century there was related a vampire case from Luzheni, a village in the Pruth Valley of Bukovina. A dead man who had committed suicide and was red in the face when buried, was exhumed by the villagers in the night and thrown into a river in order that they might avert the danger of a threatening storm.[23] Other vampire cases have been recorded by folklorists.[24]

When we consider the context of events contemporaneous with the genesis of this literary product, we realize that there were happenings close-at-hand and of much excitement to capture the imagination of Bram Stoker who transposed them, symbolically transfigured, in his literary work. Perhaps it is not too imaginative to bring in the fact that when *Dracula* was written the minds of Londoners were preoccupied with the trial of Oscar Wilde —a trial regarded as a conflict between Victorian bourgeois notions and the Bohemian conception of art for art's sake, and as an ideological crisis at the end of the Victorian period. The Bohemians considered themselves as above the laws governing common mortals and as having unlimited freedom to pursue their artistic talents. It may be purely accidental, but it is interesting to recall the resemblance between the scene of the dancing harlots in front of the Old Bailey at Oscar Wilde's condemnation and that of the vampire-women with their sarcastic remarks and debauched gestures in the haunted castle of the Count of Bistritza on the night when the London lawyer became aware of his dreadful master's intentions. The Bohemians find their counterpart in the gypsies and in the Slovaks of the forest who are the helpers and servants of Count Dracula.

As for the attributes of vampires, here is a description of them as popularly imagined:

> Vampires are only men who in their lives were wizards, committed suicide, were hanged or were betrayed in love. When they die, they are recognized as vampires by the striking red color of their faces. They find no rest in their graves; they leave their coffins before midnight and wander about. They suck the blood of young children and young girls; sometimes strangle them. When the cock crows for the first time after midnight, the vampire must return to his grave (which can be recognized by the collapsed earth or by a hole in the tomb). Vampires are able to bring on storms and hail-stones. . . . The vampire should be put face downwards in his coffin and a pale stuck through his heart; then he will be unable to leave his tomb.[25]

Bram Stoker adds horrible details to this gruesome picture:

> Here lay the Count, but looking as if youth had been half renewed . . . the cheeks were fuller, and the white skin seemed ruby-red underneath; the mouth was redder than ever, for on the lips were drops of fresh blood, which trickled

from the corner of the mouth and ran over the chin and neck. . . . This was the being I was helping to transfer to London (said the secretary), where, perhaps, for centuries to come, he might, among its teeming millions, satiate his lust for blood, and create a new and ever widening circle of semi-demons to batten on the helpless.

An entirely different conception of a vampire is presented by N. Gogol in his story *Vey* (*The Vampire*) based on Ukrainian folklore. It is a female vampire, a witch, a kind of horrible nightmare, which tortures the young man who betrayed her in life. The folkloric background in the Dracula story would by no means be exhausted by quoting a few other striking elements, like the fateful date of St. George's Eve, May 4, when the London secretary leaves Bistritz to reach Dracula's castle. This anniversary has now been appointed by the Church, but old superstitions still linger and recall the Walpurgis Night, May 1. In *Dracula* these superstitions are lumped together with those of St. Andrew's Eve.

The journey of Dracula at night from Bistritz to his haunted castle, the wolves which pursue the mysterious coach, the blue flames which appear and disappear in the forest, contain elements which feature the local folklore. "On the eve of the Feast of St. George, who is celebrated as the patron of spring and as helper in the fight against wild beasts, people used to place green turf on the doorposts, on the hedges and on the roofs of their houses. In each sod they stuck a green willow twig to protect them against evil spirits and witches. For the same purpose, in some villages people kindle fires on bridges, round the settlement or in marshy fields and let them burn for several hours." [26]

"On the Eve of St. Andrew (November 29, Old Style) the doorposts and window-frames of the houses, of all barns and stables are rubbed with garlic, because the smell of garlic keeps away not only evil spirits like *strigele, strigoii, moroii,* but protects the inhabitants against the wolves which used to prowl about the villages at that time of year." [27] The garlic and the Cross added by the Church are general weapons to fight vampires and evil spirits. That blue flames burn at certain dates over hidden treasures in the earth is commonly believed in that part of Europe. The Count of Bistritza explains to his prisoner-secretary the mysterious signs he saw on his journey to the castle: "He then explained to me that it is commonly believed that on a certain night of the year—last night, in fact the 4th May (St. George's Eve) —when all evil spirits are supposed to have unchecked sway, a blue flame is seen over any place where treasure has been concealed. . . . In the region through which you came last night there can be but little doubt that treasures had been hidden, for it was the ground fought over for centuries by the Wallachian, the Saxon and the Turk."

The unearthing in Rumania of some really famous treasures like the gold Gothic Treasure of Pietroasa, now in the National Museum in Bucharest; or the Silver Treasure of Conceşti in northern Rumania, now in the Hermitage in Leningrad; or the Germanic gold treasure of St. Nicholas the Great in Transylvania, now in Budapest, might have become known to the author of

Dracula through the press and have excited his imagination. The past with its medieval superstitions were mingled with this concoction of studio-mystery. That the brain-power of the monster vampire is unlimited and survives physical death; that he is not dead but *Un-dead;* recall the Mephisto-phelic power in Faust. Mephistopheles was in life a most wonderful man, soldier, statesman, and alchemist. Such characteristics echo the medieval striving for supernatural power and wealth.

Into this folkloric background fantasy is introduced by a description of the mysterious landscape of Transylvania, awakening, it seems, a distant recollection of the local version of the German legend of the Pied Piper of Hamelin who brought his victims to the surface here, through one of the caves. "With this one [Dracula], all the forces of nature that are occult and deep and strong must have worked together in some wondrous way. The very place where he has been alive, *Un-dead,* for all these centuries, is full of strangeness of the geological and chemical world. There are deep caverns and fissures that reach none know whither. There have been volcanoes, some of whose openings still send out waters of strange properties and gases that kill or make to vivify."

In conclusion: The folkloric background of *Dracula* is built up by elements available in the geographical region of his origin. These elements are used haphazardly and are distorted in the same way as the historical ones, in order to suit the author's intention of creating an exotic atmosphere of horror.

The material was collected in the then available literature about folklore in eastern Europe. It would be a rather farfetched assumption to state that Bram Stoker had in mind, as well, the Thraco-Phrygian Bacchanalia which penetrated from the Lower Danube into Roman mythology.

The Psychological Significance of the Dracula Theme in the West

There is hardly another literary theme which has attracted and fascinated the reader's curiosity more permanently than the Dracula theme. The still enigmatic best seller by Bram Stoker (1897) is, however, chronologically the last literary product which popularized the name of this personage in the litera-tures of the West and of the East. This theme has not inspired great works of art, of the kind of Goethe's Faust, but the literary works based on it have captivated the imagination of the European reader for centuries, in the form of chronicles, stories, plays, poems, films, and radio productions. A sensational film *Dracula,* of very doubtful artistic value, produced soon after World War I, did not fail to excite the curiosity of, and to provoke a comment by, André Gide.[28]

In the last century, literary criticism, with the help of psychoanalysis and of history, explored from various points of view the meaning of the Dracula theme. A rich bibliography in English, German, Rumanian, Russian, and Hungarian testifies to this interest.[29] Less attention has been paid to this subject from the point of view of comparative literature. In spite of this rich bibliography and of all attempts to explain the psychological and the historical background, and the artistic intentions of the various literary products based on this theme, the relationship between three main literary groupings in which the historical personality of Dracula appears—the migration of the theme, the psychological interpretation, and the historical significance of the theme—remains unclarified.

If a comparison is indulged in, there is some similarity between the Dracula story and Marlowe's *The Tragical History of Doctor Faustus,* as to their place in literary history, as to their content based on the magic conceptions and superstitions of their periods and places. Dracula is a kind of Faustus without the medieval religious conflict, if we allow a distance between the two themes equal to that between Goethe's *Faust* and Bram Stoker's *Dracula.* These themes attracted the curiosity of writers, of literary critics, of historians, of psychologists. All the approaches to explain the Dracula theme illustrate the interplay of literary history, literary criticism, and of history itself in the study of a literary work if one is not satisfied to establish only its intrinsic aesthetic literary value. The study of the general context, historical, cultural, and social, provides a better understanding of the literary work. With regard to the Dracula theme, so far the identification of the historical personage has been established with certainty; his name has been philologically explained,[30] and the texts in which it appears have been, more or less fully, described.

The theme of Dracula appears in Western literature, in German incunabula representing a kind of medieval newsletter. This material has constituted, since the second half of the nineteenth century, the subject for research by many scholars, and scholarly interest in the subject has not diminished until our times. One of the first scholars to study the German incunabula from a philological and historical point of view was I. Bogdan of the University of Bucharest. He records, quoting K. M. Kertbeny,[31] six editions of a pamphlet printed against Vlad V Dracula of Walachia.[32]

According to Kertbeny, the oldest incunabulum was printed in Bamberg, in 1491, by Hans Sporer. This imprint appeared in Transylvania in the Old Saxon dialect. Bogdan shows, however, that the language of the text is *plattdeutsch (niederdeutsch)* and could not have been printed in Transylvania, because it has been sufficiently proved that the first book was printed in Transylvania only in 1529. The 1491 incunabulum contains four leaves without pagination, signature, or catchwords. Its title is *Ein wünderliche und erschröck enliche hystori von einem grossen wüttrich genant Dracole wayda, der do sogar unkristenliche matter hat angelegt, die manschen als mit spissen, auch dy leut zu tod geslyffen,* etc. The British Museum copy does not contain the name of the printer. It was reproduced by Hubay Ilona.[33] On the first page this incunabulum presents a woodcut portrait of Vlad Dracula the Empaler. It is a simplified form of another woodcut from the incunabulum of the Magyar Nemzeti Museum in Budapest (originally belonging to the Libarary of F. Széchényi) and reproduced by I. Bogdan. (See Plate 1.) This Budapest incunabulum, assumed by some authors to have been printed before 1477, is most probably that published first by Engel[34] in the original version and by Kertbeny in modern German translation. A recent description of an incunabulum is given in Hungarian, with an English and a French summary, by Hubay Ilona. It was printed in Lübeck and conjecturally is dated 1485. In Hubay's article the woodcut portrait is compared with the woodcut of the Bamberg edition. The title of this portrait is: "Van eyneme bosen tyrane ghenomet Dracole Wyda. Nach der bort unses heren Ihesu Christi MCCCCLVI yaer hefft desse Dracole wyda vele schrecklike wunderlike dink ghedan unde bedrenen in Walechyan unde ok in Ungaren." After this title follows an analytical table of contents under four items.

This incunabulum printed by Bartolomaeus Gothan in Lübeck ends the story of Dracula with his imprisonment in Buda and his release in 1476. Gothan moved from Magdeburg to Lübeck in 1484. About 1486 he went over to Sweden, where he printed Swedish publications on his printing press at Stockholm. There is no known copy of the first edition of this incunabulum. Hubay assumes that it was first printed in Augsburg, Leipzig, or Nuremberg, and that Gothan translated it into Low German for the benefit of the Hanseatic towns. Bogdan, like Engel,[35] assumes that this edition was printed after 1477; Karadja, in a more recent study of all editions of incunabula known so far, dates this edition with probability as an imprint of 1480. The Rumanian philologist, philosopher, and romantic writer, B. P. Hasdeu, attempted a psychological study of the portrait of Dracula printed in this incunabulum.[36]

A third such medieval newsletter is dated ca. 1488, and was printed by Peter Wagner, in Nuremberg, without date. There exist several copies of this incunabulum, in Munich (Bayrische Staatsbibliothek); in Solothurn (Kantonsbibliothek); in Stuttgart (Landesbibliothek); in Wernigerode (Fürstliche Bibliothek); and in Bucharest (Biblioteca Academiei Române). The title of this incunabulum reproduced by Bogdan is *Dracole Wayda,* and the story begins: "Nach Christi unseres Herren gepurt MCCCCLVI jar hate Dracole Wayda vil erschreckenlicher und wunderbarlicher ding gethon als hernach geschriben stat."

A fourth incunabulum on Dracula has the title *Hie facht sich an gar ain graussenlichen erschroken ystoren . . . Dracole Wayde.* This version was printed by Christoph Schnaitter in Augsburg in 1494. There are two copies of this version in Munich (Bayrische Staatsbibliothek); one in Solothurn (Kantonsbibliothek); and one in Zwickau (Stadtbibliothek). The portrait of Vlad Dracula was replaced in this version by a woodcut representing the Crucifixion.

A fifth incunabulum is known to have been printed in Strasbourg in 1500 on six leaves. The first and sixth leaf have blank versos. This version was printed by Matthias Hupfuff and several copies are known; in Berlin (Staatsbibliothek), Colmar (Stadtbibliothek), Copenhagen (Royal Library), and in Mainz (Library of the Episcopal Seminary). The text was reproduced by Karadja.[37] The portrait is replaced by a woodcut representing Vlad Dracula the Empaler at a table in a forest of empaled corpses. In the foreground of the scene a hangman is cutting corpses before boiling them in a cauldron. This drawing corresponds to that of the Sbornik No. 358 in the Rumjancev Museum, and mentioned by Bogdan.[38] The title of the Strasbourg incunabulum is: *Hie*

*facht sich an gar ein graussemsliche und erschröckenliche hystorien von dem
wilden wütrich Dracole weyde. Wie er die leüt gespist hat und gepraten und
mit den haubtern yn einen kessel gesotten.*

A remark on this incunabulum made by Karadja [89] indicates that it belonged
to the library of the humanist Hartmann Schedel, where recently (after World
War I) was found the manuscript of the German chronicle of Stefan the
Great of Moldavia (1457–1504), the contemporary of Vlad Dracula.

Finally, a sixth incunabulum is that of Nuremberg, published, according to
Karadja, by Ambrosius Huber, on six leaves in 1499. Bogdan mentions an
imprint in 8vo of 1521, and attributes it to Jobst Gutknecht. The title begins:
Von dem Dracole Wayda, dem grossen Tyrannen. The text, however, is
identical with that of the Lübeck version of 1480 (1485). Bogdan knows two
copies, one in the Library of the Rumanian Academy. It is possible that we have
to deal with reprints of the same version under different titles.

In fact, the number of the Dracula incunabula has not yet definitively been
determined, and their chronology is only conjecturally established. Bogdan [40]
knew six texts, Karadja recorded ten texts,[41] and J. Striedter [42] adds two further
texts. According to Striedter, the oldest incunabulum was printed by Marcus
Ayrer in 1488 in Nuremberg; it is dated and belongs to the Landesbibliothek
in Weimar. The next text is that printed in Nuremberg by Peter Wagner and
assigned by Karadja to the year 1488.[43] Striedter does not accept the date of
1485 attributed to the Lübeck incunabulum of the National Museum in Budapest. The importance of Striedter's conclusion is that the Dracula story was
printed in Germany not before the oldest Russian manuscript on Dracula, but
only two years after the date of the oldest Russian manuscript, so the story
could not have been transported to Russia and have served as a prototype for
the first historical novel in Russian literature.

These incunabula are not the only sources of information on Dracula in the
literature of the West. In the monastery of St. Gall and in that of Lambach
exist two manuscripts of the fifteenth century written in the Alemanic dialect.
The original was probably written by a Saxon of Braşov because the author
shows great knowledge of the local topography; the dialect was linguistically
adapted for the benefit of other German readers. The content of these manuscripts agrees nearly word for word with that of the incunabula. This version
is the source for the Latin *Chronica regum Romanorum* by Th. Eberndorfer
and for *Commentarii Rerum memorabilium* by Pius Secundus.[44]

The Dracula theme did not inspire any great writer of western Europe.
Michael Beheim, a wandering minstrel of Wiener-Neustadt, who wrote a poem
on this theme at the court of Frederic III, affirms that he got his information
from a monk Jakob, who fled to the West to escape Dracula's cruelties. A
manuscript of Beheim's poem is in the Library of the University of Heidelberg.
The poem was published by G. C. Conduratu.[45]

It is hardly imaginable that the English author of *Dracula* used any of these
western sources for his vampire story. It is possible, however, that Bram Stoker
had known of Sebastian Münster's *Cosmographia,* of which an English edition
appeared in London in 1558, under the title: *A treatise on the New India*

. . . . by S. Münster, translated by Richard Eden. In 1574 another edition appeared in London: *A brief collection of Strange and Memorable things gathered out of the "Cosmography" of Sebastian Münster.*

Already in the Basel edition of the *Cosmographia* of 1544, we find the name of Dracula mentioned on page 554 in the chapter "Von der Siebenbürg Regierung." There it is related that while Matthias Corvinus was reigning in Hungary, in Walachia reigned "der streng ja tyrannisch man Dracula," whom Matthias then held for ten years in prison. "Man lisst wunderbarlich ding von seiner tyrannischen Gerechtikeit."

Münster's *Cosmographia* in several of its editions enumerates episodes of Dracula's cruelties: (1) the nailing of the caps on the heads of the Turkish ambassadors, (2) the empaling of the Turks and Dracula's feast with his friends in the forest of the hanging corpses, (3) the feasting of the beggars and then their being burned in a house, (4) the skinning of the foot-soles of the Turks on which salt was then spread and goats set to lick them, and (5) the ordering of the Florentine merchant to leave his purse with gold overnight in the street to show him that nobody would touch it. In the 1550 edition an engraving of Dracula appears, representing him in a long-sleeved overcoat, wearing long socks to his knees, a sword, and a beret with a feather.

His cruelty is not condemned in the *Cosmographia,* because it was directed toward the attainment of justice, against the Turks, and against the disorders in his country. The episodes are not intended to disgrace Dracula as do the incunabula newsletters written by Transylvanian Saxons as propaganda against him. The Rumanian prince, who was fighting fiercely to keep the invaders away from the Danube, had to undertake punitive expeditions across the Carpathians into Transylvania against the Saxon and the Rumanian settlements, which supported his rivals to the throne of Walachia. The Saxons had a grudge against him because he had curtailed their trade monopolies and their economic privileges in Walachia.

The Historical Significance of the Dracula Theme in the East

A different function was fulfilled by the Dracula story in the literature of Russia, where it was very popular, as indicated by the great number of versions available in Slavo-Russian. Dracula's legend served in Moscow the cause of Ivan III, who united the Rus-lands by ruthlessly destroying the apanage system and by centralizing their administration under his autocracy. This process came formally to an end at the enslavement of the democratic republic of Novgorod by the dictated treaty of 1471, in which Ivan III formulated the right to freedom of the Novgorodians in the clause: "You are free, and you can do what you like, provided that you do as I like." Having granted this Magna Carta of freedom, Ivan III ordered in 1495 the closure of all offices of the Hanseatic League. An impenetrable iron curtain fell down, separating East from West. The outward order of the new freedom was made complete by his grandson, Ivan IV the Terrible, who added to the religious mania of his grandfather a pathological sadism exceeding everything thought of by Oriental tyrants to inspire fear and horror in their subjects.

The Russian texts, compared with the German ones, are more elaborate. Their popularity was enhanced by the religious element in the epilogue. Moreover, the relationship between the Russian and the German texts does not appear to be a close one. The Russian *Povest' o mut'anskom* [*muntjanskom*] *vojevode Drakule* includes among its seventeen episodes, followed by an epilogue, six episodes present in the German incunabula. However, the Russian text is more extensive and its political tendencies appear in the epilogue, in which Dracula is condemned because he adopted the Roman Catholic heresy while he was harbored at Matthias Corvinus' court in Buda. This confessional feature is perhaps significant for the origin and the purpose of the Russian text. This text was meant to—or in any case it did—help the political efforts of Prince Stefan of Moldavia (1457–1504) to win over to his anti-Turkish League Ivan III, the Grand Duke of Moscow, and to undermine Ivan's confidence in Stefan's southern neighbor and rival, Vlad Dracula of Walachia, as well as in the Western rulers—the Emperor, the Pope, the Venetian Doge—who looked passively on at Stefan's struggle against the spreading of the Ottoman Empire. Stefan was related by marriage to Ivan III, whose cousin Eudokia, a princess of Kiev, was his wife. Moreover, Stefan and Eudokia's daughter Elena was married to Ivan III's son, Ivan the Young, and their son, Dmitri Ivanovitch, was proclaimed heir apparent to the Grand Duchy of Moscow (1483). However, the astute Ivan III, who felt safe against the Turks in his distant capital, preferred to let others fight his wars while he gathered the Rus-lands. Being sure of Stefan's loyalty he could have supported Vlad Dracula, who was a valiant fighter against the Turks before his confinement in Buda at the court of Matthias Corvinus, another of Stefan's rivals having close diplomatic relations with Ivan III. The heresy of Vlad Dracula would have shaken the confidence of Ivan, who was a fanatical Orthodox, in Vlad, Stefan's rival. Ivan III would have preferred that Vlad Dracula fight the Turks on the Danube, and so curtail Stefan's growing power.

The importance of the confessional element in this struggle for power and in the court intrigues is strikingly illustrated by the fate of Ivan III's heir apparent, his grandson Dmitri, who—after having led his grandfather's armies in battles—fell into disgrace in 1502, and was thrown, together with his mother Elena, the daughter of Stefan of Moldavia, into the dungeons of the Kremlin, from which they never reappeared.

Vasilij Ivanovitch, a son of Ivan's second marriage with Sophia Paleologue, a pretended niece of the last Paleologue, and sent with great pomp to Ivan III by the Vatican, was proclaimed heir apparent. Sophia had been imprisoned by Ivan III; her son Vasilij had betrayed his father several times and fled to his enemies. In spite of these incidents, the court intrigues of Sophia succeeded in obtaining Dmitri and his mother's disgrace, which perhaps suited Ivan's political strategy. The formal reasons given for the disgrace was that Dmitri was too independent, and that Elena had embraced a new religious sect, the Judaist, brought from the West. Nothing, in fact, supports this accusation, and the Judaist sect seems to have been a Hussitic influence, at that time very active in eastern Europe. One of Ivan III's counsellors, Ivan Volk Kurycin, was burned at the stake for the same confessional guilt.

The oldest text of Dracula's story (*Povest' o mut'ansjkom vojevode Drakule*) dates from 1490 and is known as Mss Kirilo-Beloozerski No. II/1088, because it was written by a monk, Efrosin, in the monastery of Beloozero. It is preserved in the Public Library at Leningrad. In the title, the attribute appears as *mutjanski* and *muntjanski*, i.e., Walachian. The second form preserves its Rumanian phoneticism, a derivation from *munte*, which appears in the Rumanian name of Walachia, i.e., *Țara Muntenească* 'the country in the mountains'. The first form adapted its spelling to the Serbian and Russian phoneticism.

There are known to be nineteen Slavo-Russian manuscripts containing the Dracula text. They cover the period between the fifteenth and the eighteenth centuries; most of them are from the sixteenth and seventeenth centuries. Interest in the Russian *Povest' o Drakule* was alive at an early date among scholars of Russian history, but its hero has not been connected with Bram Stoker's vampire. Its social-political function and the interpretation of its content differ from the function and interpretation of the Dracula stories in German literature, and also from the meaning of the English ghost story.

The Russian texts contain South Slavonic words like *poklisar* 'ambassador', *siromah* 'poor, orphan'—a word of Greek origin appearing in Serbian and in Slovene, and known in Slavo-Rumanian charters. *Kapa* 'hat, cap' also appears in South Slavonic, and words of Hungarian origin like *birev* 'administrative official' (Rumanian *birău*, Hungarian *biró*). The form *birev* hints at a Rumanian pronunciation, where the Hungarian *-ó* developed into *-ău* (cf. *Bakó, Bacău*). Two place-names appear in Hungarian form: *Bodon* for *Vidin*, and *Borodnskag* for *Varadin*. Also found are the words *dukat*, an Italian gold coin (*ducato*) which was used in Moldavia and in Hungary in the fifteenth century, and *milja* 'mile' (Latin *mille passūs*), a word also of western origin, although it was used in Russian as early as the fourteenth century in the descriptions of the pilgrimages to Jerusalem.

Karamzin, the Russian romantic historian, considers the *Povest'* as the first historical novel in Russian literature and the beginning of the profane western influence on this literature. For Karamzin the hero of the *Povest'* is most probably a mythological figure expressing the philosophical conception that the only remedy against all human evils is death.[46]

A critical survey of the studies on the Russian texts is given by A. Sedel'nikov.[47] I. Bogdan of the University of Bucharest knew, in 1896, seven texts and he published four of them. The content of all versions is nearly identical. According to Sedel'nikov, Bogdan did not make use of five other versions described by ninteenth-century bibliographers.[48] Sedel'nikov adds versions of the sixteenth and seventeenth centuries found in various Russian archives. The oldest version is considered to be the Kirilo-Beloozerski, whereas Bogdan thought that the Rumjancev text is the earliest. This text is dated ca. 1500. There are sixteen episodes and an epilogue.

The archetype of the Russian texts has not been traced, but Kirilo-Beloozerski seems to be near the prototype. Bogdan eliminates any connection between the

Russian versions and the German texts. According to Sedel'nikov, the arche-type was of foreign origin. Where that archetype was written, why and how it was introduced into Russia, are problems which have not yet been solved in spite of the various hypotheses advanced by scholars.

H. Raab, the German scholar, suggests that the *Povest'* was written by Ivan Volk Kurycin, who was a personal friend of Ghotan, an agent of the Russian diplomatic service.[49] Ivan Volk Kurycin was the brother of Fedor Kurycin, who headed a diplomatic mission sent by Ivan III to Hungary. Ghotan had literary interests and printed the German incunabulum of 1483. The text was introduced into Russia by the Hanseatic trade route, through Novgorod, like other western imprints translated about 1500 into Russian: *Lusidarios* and *Povest' o Troje*. Already P. A. Syrku looked for a German prototype of the Russian text.[50]

Lately, the German scholar J. Striedter submits the whole material, both German and Russian, to a critical study, making use of the whole bibliography and basing his research only on positive facts.[51] Striedter observes that the printed and handwritten German texts do not mention Dracula's death, which occurred in 1476, whereas the Russian texts contain this fact. Moreover, in the Russian versions it is pointed out that the author of the text or his source of information saw after the death of the Voivode of Muntenia (Walachia) some of his kin in Hungary. The whole construction of the Russian *Povest'* shows that there is no association between the Russian and the German sources. Only six items of the thirty-one in the oldest German text appear also in the Russian story.

Concerning the content and its interpretation, the difference between the Russian and the German sources is striking. In the German texts Dracula punishes thieves, overbearing diplomats, lazy women who neglect their obliga-tions, indolent men, Turks, and hypocrites. Dracula empales the coward monk who insincerely praises his wicked deeds and rewards the monk who condemns his cruelties. In the Russian text the critic of Dracula's cruelties is empaled and the hypocritical adulator is rewarded. The significance of this ethical inversion is emphasized by the Russian conception of autocracy according to which the ruler is always right because he derives his authority directly from God and has not to be judged by humans. The Russian text was a moral code for Ivan III, and even more for his grandson Ivan IV the Terrible. This text which supports and justifies the autocratic power of rulers is not unique in the Russian literature of that period. In October 1490 the Archbishop of Novgorod, Gena-dij Gonzov, sent Zosima, the Metropolitan of Moscow, a "western" message to be transmitted to Ivan III, who united by every means at his disposal the Russian feudal states and confiscated the church estates. In this message, warmly recommended because it came from the Frankish (*Frjazov-Catholics*), we read: "I have been told by the ambassador of the Spanish emperor, how the latter purged his country, and I send to you a record of those procedures. And you, my Lord, should speak insistently to the Grand Duke about those things, not only for the sake of his salvation but also for the honor of the ruler, the Grand Duke." [52]

This kind of literature should be studied against the background of the conflict between Church and state, represented in the Church by two currents:
one headed by the monk Nil Sorskij, who demanded the separation of the
Church from the state and the renunciation of earthly goods by the Church's
servants; the other headed by Iosif Volokolamskij, who defended the political
power of the state as protector of the Church and the autocrat-ruler as God's
representative at its head. God's representative is too powerful to be challenged,
but he is the distributor of earthly goods, and the representatives of the Church
being loyal to him will get their shares. This doctrine is fully applied by Ivan
IV when in all earnestness he writes to his chancellor Kurbskij who fled to
Sweden and condemned his ruler's unlawful procedures: "Your obligation is
to come back and to give me the opportunity to punish you," wrote Ivan IV
"and so to save your soul!" However, the skeptical exile Kurbskij hesitated to
accept the graceful invitation to salvation by being skinned and cooked on
charcoal, under the merciful eye of God's representative in Moscow, who after
the hot purification gave to his grilled victims a cooling bath in the frozen
river, before allowing them to die.

Some one hundred years after the earliest Russian Dracula text, a writer,
Peresvetov, produced a treatise on judgment by torture in order to justify the
morbid sadism of the mad Grand Duke of Moscow. According to this apologist
of sadism, the sovereign has to be cruel and to punish his subjects without pity
and without control. According to Peresvetov, the example to be followed is the
Sultan Mohamed. There exists a subtle distinction in the Old Russian Penal
Code between torture to death and torture without death.[53]

The Dracula story was first printed in Germany, at Nuremberg, in 1488. The
earliest known Russian text is dated 1490. So there are two years between
the two versions. However, a notice on the 1490 text mentions an older
manuscript dated 1486. So, the chronological argument alone is not conclusive. The German and the Russian versions must go back to a common
archetype, even if a common source has not been found for the texts known
thus far.

Regarding the author of the Russian *Povest'*, Striedter attributes the work to
Fedor Kurycin who headed the diplomatic mission to Matthias Corvinus in
Buda. Of the same opinion is J. S. Lurje.[54] Raab, as already mentioned, attributes the paternity of the Russian text to Ivan Volk Kurycin, the brother of
Fedor, both belonging secretly to the Judaist sect.[55] The objection to the
hypothesis, raised by Petukhov,[56] that a Judaist (Hussite) sectarian could not
have produced a work against the heretics and in defence of Orthodoxy is put
aside by Striedter, who remarks that Ivan Volk Kurycin wrote a pamphlet,
Merilo pravednoje (The right measure), in which he justifies judgment by
torture. The principle of the right and of the obligation of the ruler to punish
with cruelty without any consideration for the person did not contradict the
conception of the Judaist sect.[57]

Sedel'nikov rejects Fedor Kurycin's authorship on the ground that in 1486
Kurycin had not yet arrived in Moscow. On his way back from his mission in
Hungary Kurycin had to wait at the court of Stefan of Moldavia, Ivan III's

relative, while his sovereign was corresponding with Mengli Girey, the Khan of the Crimean Tartars, to obtain from him a safe-conduct because the Khan's territory lay along the only way of communication between central Europe and Moscow. After the conquest of the territories from Novgorod southwards, Ivan III blocked himself off from the West from Lithuania and the Baltic to the Black Sea, where in addition the Turks occupied the Moldavian harbor Chilia. Even Stefan of Moldavia could not get news from his daughter Elena, the wife of Ivan the Young, son of Ivan III, except through his friend, the Khan Mengli Girey. Up to his death, in 1504, Stefan was not able to verify the rumor passed to him by his other friend, the Jagellon King Alexander of Lithuania, as to the fate of his daughter and of his grandson, who had disappeared in the dungeons of the Kremlin.

In June 1484, the Grand Duke wrote that he had received information about Fedor Kurycin who was on his way back, accompanied by a messenger from King Matthias and by craftsmen from the West. Kurycin was waiting in Suceava, the capital of Stefan of Moldavia, for a safe-conduct. He reached Moscow in 1484 via Akkerman at the mouth of the Dniester on the Black Sea, and the Crimea.[58] So he would have had about two years in which to write the earliest Russian text of the *Povest'*. A monk could have brought the text to the monastery of Beloozero and copied it there, for according to a notice on that text: "In the year 6994 (i.e., 1486) February 13 first written, then in the year 6998 (i.e., 1490) January 28 the second time copied, I the sinful Efrosin." The Beloozero text contains two toponymics whose phonetical forms seem to indicate that the text was not written in Russia: *Vardanskog* (Varadinum-Wardei), *Bordonskog* in the Rumjancev text lacks the expected pleophonic development; *muntjanskoj* (Walachian-Muntenia) preserves the original *n* of the Rumanian form. (Rumjancev has *mutjanskoj*.)

In the epilogue of the Beloozero text appear some confused references to Rumanian history. One reads: "And he (Dracula) married, he took a princely (*vojevodskuju*) wife, and after that he lived a short time and was murdered by Stefan of Walachia." (Walachia has been incorrectly used for Moldavia. The Russian chronicles often confuse the names of the two Rumanian principalities.) Vlad Dracula fell in the battle against the Turks who supported the accession to the throne of Walachia of their puppet Basarab Laiotă. The marriage to a wife (woman) of a voivode (*ponjal vojevodskuju ženu*) might refer to the marriage of Stefan of Moldavia, who defeated Dracula's brother, Radu the Handsome of Walachia, captured his wife and daughter and married the captive daughter; unless it means that Dracula married a relative of Matthias Corvinus in Hungary. It is true that the date of the event is not correct, but the date of the epilogue in the Beloozero text might not be contemporary with the text. The scribe was careful to record facts connected with Dracula, and also careful to note that Stefan of Moldavia was related to the Grand Duke of Moscow. The same epilogue condemns Dracula for having embraced Roman Catholicism. This condemnation expresses the confessional atmosphere in Moscow after the attempt to force the union of the Byzantine Church with Rome in the Council at Florence and Ferrara. It aims—as already noticed—also to estrange Ivan III's sympathy for Dracula, the rival of Stefan of Moldavia and the tool in the hands of Matthias Corvinus. In later Russian texts of the *Povest'* the *Vojevoda Drakula* becomes the *car groznyj* 'The Terrible Czar.'

The defense of Orthodoxy against Roman Catholicism, known to be a paramount concern of Ivan III, as well as the references to the history of Rumania, especially of Moldavia, appearing in the epilogue of the Beloozero text, seems to point to Moldavia as the place of origin of the *Povest'*. The language used in the Church and in the administration of the country was a South Slavonic form developed from the language of the Cyrillo-Methodian translations, showing East Slavonic influences and local features. The chanceries of Moldavia were very well organized and the Greco-Slavonic culture reached a high standard. Texts of a higher standard than the *Povest'* were produced in the Moldavia of Stefan the Great. Advancing this hypothesis, one should also bear in mind that Stefan had feudal possessions in Transylvania and the commercial as well as the cultural relations with this province could account for the Hungarian forms. Whether the text was composed by Kurycin at the court of Stefan in Suceava or by a scribe of the Moldavian chancery cannot be established. Anyhow, it was meant to help Stefan's policy in the East, just as his German chronicle informed the West about his deeds. In Russia the text was copied in various centers. In the monastery of Volokolamsk, the center of the autocratic ideology of the ruler, where Iosif Volockij (Volokolamskij), the head of this movement lived, a strong Rumanian influence was apparent in the calligraphy as well as in the ornamentation of manuscripts. The copyist of a chronicle found in the library of this monastery was nicknamed Dracula.

As to the way by which the *Povest'* reached Russia, Sedel'nikov suggests that it would not be too speculative to think of the occasion of the wedding of Elena, the daughter of Stefan of Moldavia with the son of Ivan III on January 6, 1482, Old Style; or of another Moldavian mission to Moscow. The purpose of this propaganda activity was to win over to his Christian league his very astute Moscow kinsman, who being protected against the Ottoman invasion by the distance and by the armies of other countries, preferred, as the Russian chronicles point out, to fight his battles for gathering the Rus-lands sitting at home in front of the fire to going out to the battlefield, as did Stefan. It is true that in the West Stefan found the same lack of response to his appeals, from the Pope, from the Jagellons ruling in Warsaw, Prague, and Vienna; and from the Venetian ruler.

In view of this effort of Stefan to inform the West and the East about his country and his enemies, and to unite the Christian powers in a league against the common danger, one is inclined to see in the *Povest'* another instrument of information and propaganda for Stefan's aims in the context of that historical period.

In Russia, however, the *Povest'* acquired a political function in the service of the despotic theocracy. Its literary influence was rather without importance. It entered the popular epic literature in works like *Bova, Peter Zlatyje-Ključi, Eruslan Lazarevič Vasilij Zlatovlasij, Devgenievo Dejanie, Akir Premudryj,* and *Prenje Života so Smertju.*[59] In the seventeenth century its tradition comes to an end, though as late as 1833 the *Povest'* is echoed in the story *Ivan Ivanič Syn Nemčin*,[60] whose connection with folklore is doubtful.

Confessional and political jealousies, commercial cupidity, court intrigues, and local rivalries wrecked Stefan's plan for a Christian league, for the sake of which he tolerated humiliation from the vain king of Poland at Colomea (1485) to whom he was paying homage. For this reason, too, he sacrificed his daughter, whom he married to the son of Ivan III of Moscow; he abstained from any unfriendly gesture against a Christian state; and tried to settle the differences between those states by persuasion. In 1497 his country was invaded by the Poles whom he defeated. In 1499 he concluded a treaty of permanent peace with his old friend the Lithuanian Jagellon Alexander. The Pope covered him with high praise; to chroniclers he was "the hero of Christ"; but the Turks were at his doorstep and no help was in sight from anywhere. In his pathetic appeal to the West he gave the warning: "I shall be defeated but afterwards the same will happen to you!" And history confirmed his warning. After Mohács (1526), Hungary was conquered and transformed into a Turkish province; the Turks reached Vienna and were later defeated due to their overstretched lines of communication and the carelessness of the Ottomans whose power was declining.

Stefan refused to have Moldavia become a province of the Jagellons, who had concluded a treaty with the Turks. His feudal relationship with Poland was a danger for him. He dissolved this relationship and avenged his humiliation at Colomea by invading Poland in 1502. After having convinced himself that his Christian league was a self-deceiving fiction, he bought his independence from the Turks by choosing to pay tribute.

The Russian *Povest'* contains an episode which does not appear in the German incunabula, but is developed in Bram Stoker's *Dracula*. The *Povest'* relates that while Vlad Dracula was imprisoned by King Matthias in Buda, he would catch mice and buy birds in the market in order to torture them by empaling them, by cutting their heads, by plucking their feathers, and then letting them free. Such an incident is found at the beginning of Bram Stoker's horror story when the vampire arrives in England. Dracula's power is exercized on a patient in the lunatic asylum, who catches flies and spiders in order to devour them in the belief that their life will strengthen his own vitality.

The nineteen Russian texts known so far originated in various places in Ruthenia and Russia and cover the period from the fifteenth to the beginning of the eighteenth century. This time span indicates that the *Povest'* was a popular text in eastern Europe because its content was agreeable to the political and social climate in Russia.

The Russian manuscripts have no portraits of Dracula; in the seventeenth-century *Dvinskaia Letopis'* (Moscow, 1889) is reproduced a Dutch engraving with the caption: "Wreedheid van den Groot—vorst in Moskovien." The engraving represents the nailing of the caps on the heads of the Turkish ambassadors. The same scene appears in Münster's *Cosmographia* and is described by the English traveller Collins as a deed done by Ivan the Terrible, who angrily asked the English ambassador Jeronim Baus whether he knew how the French ambassador was punished who appeared in front of him with his head covered, just as Baus did. The best available portrait of Vlad Dracula is a late one preserved in the collection of the castle of Ambras (Ambros) in the Tyrol. Another portrait is in the Royal Collection of Sweden.

This research on the Dracula theme was limited to English, German, and Russion literature. Echoes of this theme are bound to be found in other literatures as well, not to mention the translations of Bram Stoker's *Dracula*. Monsieur E. Turdeanu of Paris drew my attention to an article by the late Felician Brânzeu of Constantinople on Vlad Dracula in Turkish literature.[61]

Conclusion

Bram Stoker's *Dracula* is known all over the English-speaking world. In the changing moods of literary criticism, this historical theme has been invested with various meanings and it still attracts and puzzles the literary critics. It fascinates large masses of readers, while its vitality and its large circulation are hardly justified by its intrinsic literary value. *Dracula* has overshadowed all vampire and ghost-stories. In contrast to Mary Shelley's *Frankenstein* (1818), which is built on individual psychology and represents the romantic conclusion of the alchemic dreams of the Middle Ages and the Faustian search for the conquest of eternity, *Dracula* is constructed on mass psychology in the nineteenth-century period of romantic historicism and folklore. It foreshadows the twentieth-century attempt of psychoanalysis to dissect the human soul and to penetrate into its arcana by a secret door opened with a magic key.

A turbid, undefined undertone runs like a subterranean stream through Bram Stoker's *Dracula*. Innocent human desires and dark underground instincts are blended and fused by folklore-vampirism. Frankenstein's magic was changed into morbid psychism. Potentialities of contemporary scientism replaced the magic conception. A reaction against materialistic scepticism, an attack on contemporary literature (the novel) and on Victorian prudery, the personal relations of Bram Stoker with Irving—all these and other concepts have been invoked by the literary critics in their attempts to reveal the real meaning of the Dracula theme which is considered to hide a cryptical psychological problem. From a formal point of view the material used to build it up—historical, psychological, anthropological, folkloric—is amateurishly confused and results in a literary product with all the features of a hybrid makeshift.

The psychological elements on which Dracula's power over his victims is based are those of horrifying repulsion and irresistible attraction. Once a victim's blood was mixed with that of the vampire the person became irremediably lost and created other victims by bloodmixture. The only defense against vampirism is that recommended by folklore and accepted by science: garlic, to which Bram Stoker adds also the Host. The only cure is the piercing of the vampire's heart with a stake, during the day, when the vampire is powerless, according to folk superstition.

The vampire superstition is remarkably well-suited to a psychoanalytical explanation, as summed up in Freud's dictum: "Morbid dread always signifies repressed sexual wishes." Vampirism is a kind of twilight borderland where religious and psycho-pathological motives intermingle. Ambivalence is the key-note. The vampire Count, centuries old, is a father-figure of enormous potency. He is planning, from his ancestral lair in the Carpathians, a raid on England to set up a contemporary vampire empire.

There is little information available about Bram Stoker's life (1847–1912), but his relationship with Irving might throw some sublimated shadows of his personal experience for the understanding of *Dracula*. Bram Stoker reminisced about the first impression of Irving on him. The fascinating power of Irving on Bram Stoker increased during the forty years that followed after the first impression left on Stoker by Irving acting in the play *Captain Absolute*.

Bram Stoker studied at Trinity College, Dublin University, and for ten years he was a civil servant, a journalist, and a teacher. In a description of Irving's role as Eugene Aram, Bram Stoker gives, as it were, a foretaste of his Dracula: "The awful horror . . . of the Blood avenging sprite," with "eyes as inflexible as Fate," "eloquent hands slowly moving, outspread fanlike," "from his sin there was no refuge." Though Bram Stoker was athletic, he became hysterical at that performance. This happened on December 3, 1876. "From that hour began a friendship as profound, as close, as lasting as can be between two men," wrote Bram Stoker in his *Personal Reminiscences of Henry Irving*. In 1878 Bram Stoker resigned his civil service post and became Irving's acting-manager of the Lyceum Theatre in London. Perhaps it is opportune to remember that on such sublimated friendship was also based the Oxford Movement in the Church of England.

Dracula as a character has always attracted the press, the film industry, the broadcasters, who continue to make the worst use of his macabre cruelties. In 1916 the book reached its eleventh edition in England; it was dramatized in 1933.[62] The inflated legend has transformed the character Dracula into an embodiment of human cruelty as awe-inspiring as Ivan the Terrible (1533–1584) of Moscow, though of another kind of human perversity. The theme has been widely popularized, not because of its literary value, but in order to excite the morbid enjoyment of collective sadism lingering subconsciously in the individ-ual. The films found a profitable source of income in various variants produced with little understanding of the subject. However, not only the masses but also literary personalities of the stature of André Gide displayed an interest in these productions. In 1922 the Dracula theme was adapted in a German film, under the title *Nosferatu, the Vampire*. André Gide writes in his *Journals* (English translation) ". . . that Dracula is not well represented because he starts as an impetuous young man and changes quickly into a monster." Gide would have liked him to be presented as a charming, courteous Don Juan whose kiss would change slowly into a bite. He would have liked this monster to be presented as a horrible creature to all except the young woman for whom he would never lose his charm. Then, when the cock crowed he would disappear, to everybody's relief, and to the great regret of the woman.[63] Bram Stoker attempted to continue his horror story, which had captivated the reading public, by producing an unsuccessful sequel to *Dracula*.[64]

The theme of the Prince of Walachia, Vlad V Dracula, has undergone many metamorphoses in the literatures of western and eastern Europe in its adaptation to various periods of history. It entered America through the film industry. The success enjoyed during the last seven decades by this horror story—as a best seller, as a play, and as a film—has surprised the literary critics. It is, however, astonishing that literary historians have not shown any curiosity in its historical background. The present study is an attempt to reveal this.

LONDON, ENGLAND

NOTES

1. The subject of this theme was presented as a paper under the title, "The Dracula Theme in the European Literature of the West and of the East," at the Ninth Congress of the International Federation for Modern Languages and Literatures in New York, August 30, 1963. An abstract of the paper may be found in Leon Edel, Kenneth McKee, and William Gibson (eds.), *Literary History and Literary Criticism,* in *Acta of the Congresses of the International Federation for Modern Languages and Literatures* (New York, 1965), ix (1963), 295–296.

2. All quotations in the text are from Bram Stoker, *Dracula (A Tale),* 10th ed. (London, 1913). The first edition was published in London in 1897.

3. N. Iorga, *A History of Roumania* (London, 1925), p. 70. Forms in –a (*Dracul-a*) are found only in external documents, e.g., in a letter dated August 4, 1475, addressed to the burghers of Sibiu (Transylvania), Vlad V signs: "Dragwyla, Vaivoda partium Transalpinarum." In another letter to the same burghers he signs: "Nos Ladislaus Dragkwlya." In a letter of 1476 we read: "Ladislaus Dragulya salutem omnibus castellanis." (Cf. I. Bogdan, *Documentele . . . Ţării Româneşti cu Braşovul* [Bucureşti, 1905].)

4. M. Vasmer, *Russisches etymologisches Wörterbuch* (Heidelberg, 1953), p. 367.

5. S. Puşcariu, *Etymologisches Wörterbuch der rumänischen Sprache* (Heidelberg, 1905), pp. 47, 152.

6. By a misreading of my article "Rumanian Folklore," J. Striedter in his article "Die Erzählung vom walachischen Voivoden Drakula in der russischen und deutschen Überlieferung," *Zeitschrift für slawische Philologie,* XXXIX (1961), 412, assumes a direct association of the Dracula story with the vampire mythology. It must be noted that in that folklore the devil is never confused with the vampire, who has quite a different function in folk mythology.

7. Puşcariu, *op. cit.*

8. Grigore Nandriş, "A Philological Analysis of Dracula . . . ," a paper read at the Sixth International Congress of Onomastic Sciences, Munich, August 24–28, 1958. It was published in the *Slavonic and East European Review,* XXXVII (June 1959), 371–377.

9. A. Murgoci, "The Vampire in Rumania," *Folk-lore,* XXXVII (1926). A. Murgoci and Helen Murgoci, "The Devil in Rumanian Folklore," *Folk-lore,* XL (1929).

10. G. Beckmann, *Der Kampf Kaiser Sigmunds gegen die Weltmacht der Ottomanen 1392– 1437* (Gotha, 1907). —Révai, *Nagy Lexikona,* XV, 567. This second bibliographical citation was communicated to me by the late Masaryk Professor of London University, R. Betts.

11. William Wey, *The Itineraries of Wey* (London, 1857), p. 101. F. Pall, "Notes du pèlesin William Wey à propos des opérations militaires des Tures en 1462," *Revue Historique du Sud-Est Européen,* XXII (1945). Cf. Eric Tappe, *Documents Concerning Rumanian History 1427– 1601* (The Hague, 1964), p. 19.

12. Franz Joseph Sulzer, *Geschichte des Transalpinischen Daziens d.i. der Walachei, Moldau und Bessarabien in Zusammenhang mit der Geschichte ubrigen Daziens als ein Versuch einer allgemeinen dazischen Geschichte mit kritischer Freiheit entworfen,* 3 vols. (Wien, 1781–1782).

13. Johann Christian Engel, *Geschichte der Moldau und Walachei nebst der historischen und statistischer Literatur byder Länder* (Halle, 1804). This history of the Rumanians is the fourth volume (parts 1 and 2) of "a general history of the world."

14. Puşcariu, *op. cit.,* p. 47.

15. *Ibid.,* p. 152.

16. Vasmer, *op. cit.,* p. 455.

17. Vuk Karadzić, *Srpski Riječnik* (Belgrade, 1935), p. 221.

18. Vasmer, *op. cit.,* p. 186.

19. *Tezaurul de sculpturi dela Tomis* (Bucureşti, 1963). Studies by Canarache, A. Aricescu, V. Barbu, A. Rădulescu.

20. Romeo Ghircoiasiu, *Istoria muzicci româneşti* (Bucureşti, 1963), Plates 32, 48.

21. W. Schmidt, *Das Jahr und seine Tage in Meinung und Brauch der Rumänen* (Hermann-stadt, 1866).

22. E. Gerard, *The Land beyond the Forest* (Edinburgh, London, 1888).

23. E. Manasterski, *Die Ruthenen—oesterreichische Monarchie in Wort und Bild* (Wien, 1899), p. 263.

24. Puşcariu, *op. cit.*

25. Manasterski, *op. cit.*, p. 263.

26. *Ibid.*, p. 226.

27. Gerard, *op. cit.*

28. André Gide, *Journals*, trans. Justin O'Brien, III (London, 1948–55), p. 7.

29. I. Bogdan, *Vlad Ţepeş şi naraţiunile germane şi ruseşti asupra lui* (Bucureşti, 1896).

30. Nandris, *op. cit.*

31. C. Kertbeny, *Ungarn betreffende deutsche Erstlingsdrucke 1454–1600* (Budapest, 1880), pp. 9–10.

32a. Here are the German editions of the Dracula incunabula as presented in I. Bogdan's study, mentioned in Note 29. The incunabulum represented by the copy of the Széchényi Collection now in the Magyar Nemzeti Museum in Budapest under the mark M.H. 705. Date and place of print are not known. Conjecturally it is dated later than 1477, probably 1480. It was published by Engel in Halle in 1804 (cf. Note 13) in the original *plattdeutsch* recension and by Kertbeny (cf. Note 31) in modern German. The portrait of this incunabulum comprises Plate 1.

b. The copy has an identical text with the title *Dracole Wayda*, as mentioned by I. Bogdan, without date and place. In a footnote on page 87, however, Bogdan mentions a copy in the Sturdza Collection of the Rumanian Academy, with the title: *Von dem Dracole Wayda, dem grossen Tyrannen.* More recent studies refer to this imprint as having been published in Nuremberg by Peter Wagner (cf. Note 36).

c. The Bamberg edition of Hans Sporer, dated 1491, of which a copy was acquired by the British Museum in June 1846, is reproduced by photocopy in Hubay Ilona (cf. Note 33). The title of this incunabulum is: *Ein wünderliche und erschröckenliche hystori von einem grossen wüttrich genant Dracole wayda*, etc.

The British Museum copy belonged to the Frenchman Henri Ternaux, who probably wrote on one of the three blank pages the note: "Ce petit volume imprimé à Bamberg en 1491 contient l'histoire des cruautés de Vlad V Dracu, prince de Valachie, surnommé Cepelussu ou l'empaleur. Kogalnitschan l'historien de la Valachie ignorait l'existence de cette edition quoiqu'il en cite d'après Engel une traduction en bas-allemand."

d. The Augsburg edition printed by Christoph Schnaitter in 1494. The title begins: *Hie facht sich an gar ain graussenlichen erschrocken ystoren*, etc.

e. The Strasbourg edition, dated 1500, printed by Matthias Hupfuff, is extant in four copies in various German libraries (Berlin, Colmar, Mainz), and in Denmark (Copenhagen). The text was published in the original language by Karadja (cf. Note 36). It begins: *Hie facht sich an gar ein graussemsliche, und erschröckenliche hystorien von dem wilden wütrich Dracole weyde.*

f. The Nuremberg edition. Apparently there are two Nuremberg incunabula because I. Bogdan (cf. Note 29) cites one printed by Jobst Gutknecht, in 8vo; whereas C. J. Karadja (cf. Note 36) cites one printed in 1499 by Ambrosius Huber.

33. Hubay Ilona, *Egykorú úiságlap Drakula Vaydáról* (Budapest, 1948).

34. Engel, *op. cit.*

35. *Ibid.*

36. C. J. Karadja, "Incunabulele povestind despre cruzimile lui Vlad Ţepeş," *Inchinare lui N. Iorga* (Cluj, 1931), pp. 196–205.

37. *Ibid.*

38. Bogdan, *op. cit.*, p. 129.

39. Karadja, *op. cit.*

40. Bogdan, *op. cit.*

41. Karadja, *op. cit.*

42. J. Striedter, "Die Erzählung vom walachischen Voivoden Drakula in der russischen und deutschen Überlieferung," *Zeitschrift für slawische Philologie*, XXXIX (1961).

43. Karadja, *op. cit.*, p. 404.

44. Bogdan, *op. cit.*, pp. 398–427.

45. G. C. Conduratu, *Michael Beheims Gedicht über den Woiwoden Vlad II Drakul*, 1903. Diss.

46. N. M. Karamzin, *Istorija gosudarstva rossijskogo*, VII (Moskva, 1903), pp. 139, 230–231, note 411.

47. A. Sedel'nikov, "Literaturnaja istorija povesti o Drakule," *Izvestija po russkomu jazyku i slovesnosti,* II (Leningrad, 1929), 621–659.

48. *Ibid.,* p. 5.

49. H. Raab, "Zu einigen nierderdeutschen Quellen des altrussischen Schrifttums," *Zeitschrift fur Slawistik,* III (1958), 323–335.

50. *Ibid.*

51. Striedter, *op. cit.*

52. J. S. Lurje, *Povest' o mutjanskom vojevode Drakule. Russkije povesti XV-XVI vekov,* ed. M. O. Kripl (Moscow and Leningrad, 1958), pp. 420 ff.

53. A. A. Zimin, *I. S. Peresvetov i jego sovremenniki* (Moskva, 1958).

54. Lurje, *op. cit.*

55. Striedter, *op. cit.*

56. E. Petukhov, *Russkaja Literatura. Drevnij Period* (St. Petersburg, 1916).

57. Striedter, *op. cit.*

58. Bogdan, *op. cit.,* p. 418.

59. A. X. Vostokov, *Opisanije slavjanskikh rukopisej Rumjancevskogo Muzeja* (St. Petersburg, 1842), pp. 512 ff.

60. D. A. Rvinskij, *Russkije narodnyje kartiny,* V (St. Petersburg, 1887), p. 258.

61. Felician Brânzeu, "Vlad l'Empaleur dans la littérature turque," *Revista Isotorică Română,* XIII (1946), 68–71.

62. Hamilton Deane and John L. Balderston, *Dracula, the Vampire Play in Three Acts, Dramatized* . . . (New York, 1933).

63. Gide, *op. cit.*

64. Bram Stoker, *Dracula's Guest, and Other Weird Stories* (London, 1914).

FREDERICK W. DILLISTONE

The Fall: Christian Truth
and Literary Symbol

AT THE END OF JULY 1965 the regular Saturday commentary in the London
Times on the week's broadcasting was devoted to the first teach-in which
had been staged on television—an exercise described by the critic as the most
protracted and colossal bore in the history of British broadcasting. But some
of the phrases used in the commentary were intriguing. This was a kind of
"tribal conclave," similar to a Red Indian "pow-wow," to consider the basic
question "how to get Britain moving." Many walks of life were represented, but
"their total contribution to the problem set was disappointing. The spokesmen
of management and labour wrangled about their familiar differences, and
doled out the blame to each other. Most of the eloquence was at least 10 years
old and there was a woeful shortage of constructive comment about how to
get out of the hole we are in."

I have begun by referring to what may seem a trivial event and a lighthearted
commentary in order to draw attention to a ritual form and a verbal symbolism
which have characterized human life from the dawn of history. Men get together to consider what has gone wrong in their common life and to ask what
may be done to improve their present condition. And in the attempt to describe
this condition no picture comes more readily to the imagination than that of a
fall—a fall into a hole, a trap maybe devised by an enemy, or simply a natural
pit unforeseen because of overgrowth or darkness. Man has fallen. He is
immobilized. How can he get out of the pit? How can he get moving again?
The question of how he ever came to fall into the hole may be secondary, but
it may also be of great importance when it comes to the search for a way out,
for a reversal of the unhappy disaster.

This simple imagery is not, of course, the only scenery associated with the
drama of a fall. Man may fall from a tree, from a great rock, or even from a
tower of his own construction. This can be still more disastrous than the act of
stumbling into a pit. It can easily be inflated in the imagination until it becomes

a fall from the skies or from some celestial realm. Heights have exercised a strange fascination over the human psyche, and yet man has been quick to recognize that the greater his achievement in climbing to the heights, the more serious will be the hazard of falling to the depths. "Humpty-Dumpty had a great fall." From the most elementary nursery rhymes to the most complex dramas of sophisticated culture, the fall theme retains its popularity and its moving appeal.

What is true of life in general has certainly been true of the life of religion. Until comparatively recently, a coming-together to consider the ills afflicting a community would have felt bound to ask whether something had gone wrong in the relation between the seen and the unseen worlds, between the human and the Divine, between man and the supernatural forces which surround him on every side. Had man "fallen" out of favor through some trespass? Had he "fallen" into a condition of helplessness through the malevolent trickery of some evil spirit? Had he, through aspiring to some "higher" level of existence, exceeded his limits and been therefore cast down to something "lower" than he had known before? Such questions were incapable of what we should call "rational" answers. Answers, rather, were framed in terms of "myths, dreams and mysteries," to use the title of one of Mircea Eliade's books. There was no single myth of the Fall. But the stories which we in our Western civilization have inherited from Greece and Rome and Israel directly, as well as those which have come from Egypt and Babylonia and Persia indirectly, have had as one of the constantly recurring themes the hole into which man has fallen and the way in which he may get moving again.

Within the Christian tradition, which dominated Western culture at least until the beginning of the nineteenth century, the Biblical fall stories were those most widely known; and they provided a natural background for man's imaginative thinking. It is true that at the time of the Renaissance the Greek myths and tragedies began to make their impact upon limited circles of the intelligentsia. But any poet or painter or dramatist who wished to appeal to the general conscience of his contemporaries turned almost instinctively to the great themes which had been vividly portrayed to successive generations of Christendom through sculpture, through stained-glass, through mystery-plays, and above all through the simple recital of the Biblical stories themselves. Through the Bible an authoritative Divine revelation had been given to mankind. It was man's duty, whether he were statesman or poet or peasant, to pay heed to this revelation, both for the saving of his own soul and for the carrying out of the particular function he was called to fulfill in the life of the society to which he belonged.

Now, although there was constantly the need to consider what could have brought about the immediate ills of the community—defeat at the hands of an enemy, plague and sickness, drought and flood—there was a constant reminder, through the Church's living representatives and institutional forms, that there was an ultimate condition whose seriousness transcended all immediate ills, however unpleasant they might be. In the past there had been a Golden Age and a Garden of Blessedness. Man had enjoyed that high estate until the primordial disaster had overtaken him when, assailed by temptation, he had fallen into the sin of radical disobedience and had consequently been expelled from the paradise in which he might have lived forever. Yet even in that dark hour there had come the promise of a way out, and it was the church's task to proclaim that way as it had been inaugurated by the Divine Redeemer and continued through the sacramental system which brought life and healing to mankind.

This was the background myth of the human situation which maintained its hold on the Christian imagination for some 1600 years. Yet, strangely enough, there is no direct use of the imagery of *falling* in the foundation story of Genesis 3. There are a state of innocence, an invitation to pass beyond innocence to a knowledge of good and evil (though this advance had been forbidden by a Divine fiat), the fateful act of grasping the forbidden fruit, the loss of innocence, the involvement in toil and pain, and the expulsion from the garden of immortality. The obvious imagery is that of being shut out, excluded, repulsed rather than of falling or descending to a lower level. "The presumption of man and his exclusion from Paradise" is in a sense a more accurate title for the myth than simply "the fall of man." But somehow the language and imagery of "fallenness" came to prevail.

For this I suggest two or three possible explanations. First, there is the fact to which I have already drawn attention: that to fall is one of the commonest and most shattering experiences of life. A glance through a concordance reveals constant reference to "falling" in battle in the Old Testament. "How are the mighty fallen!" is repeated twice in the moving lament over Saul and Jonathan. It is always distressing to fall. To fall in death is the final disaster—and in later theology the sin of Adam and his death were inextricably interrelated. Again, in the Apocryphal Book of Wisdom a Greek word meaning literally a fall or a falling aside is used as a summary description of the defection of the first formed father of mankind; and this word was later taken up and used by St. Paul in his exceedingly important and influential commentary on Adam's transgression in the fifth chapter of the Epistle to the Romans.

But more significant still, it appears to me, is the vivid language of the prophets employed to denounce the tyrannous powers of their day. Nineveh, Tyre, and above all Babylon are seen as guilty of the fearful sin of *superbia,* of proudly exalting themselves in defiance of the living God. Yet their glory lies in ruins, and some of the most magnificent dirges in all literature are those in which the prophets look either back upon the fall which has already come to pass or upon the downfall which they regard as inevitable in the future. And in one oracle, perhaps the most influential of all, the prophet links the collapse of the Babylonian empire with the fall of the Prince of Evil from the bliss of heaven itself:

> How hath the oppressor ceased!
>   the golden city ceased!
> Hell from beneath is moved for thee
>   to meet thee at thy coming.

How art thou fallen from heaven,
    O Lucifer, son of the morning!
How art thou cut down to the ground,
    which didst weaken the nations!
For thou has said in thine heart,
    I will ascend into heaven;
I will exalt my throne above the stars of God;
    I will ascend above the heights of the clouds;
I will be like the most High.
Yet thou shalt be brought down to hell,
    to the sides of the pit.   (Isaiah 14:4 ff.)

Though the first reference to Lucifer may have been to an imaginative astral counterpart to Babylon, it was easy for later generations to read it as referring to Satan, the angel who had exalted himself against God and for this reason had been cast out of heaven. In an unusual but striking outcry Jesus is recorded as having said, "I beheld Satan as lightning fall from heaven"; and the theme recurs in the great visions of the Apocalypse, when Satan's final overthrow is envisaged. This I think is one of the great archetypal pictures which have become engraven upon the imagination of the West: the rebellious angel in heaven tries to exalt himself and instead falls headlong to earth; this same angel now in earth-bound disguise tempts man also to exalt himself that he may be "like God"; and man shares, though in a less dramatic way, the fate which overcame Satan himself. The total universe of man is now a "fallen" system, doomed to final destruction unless somehow a champion intervenes to rescue man from his prime adversary and to remove the incubus of his folly which weighs so heavily upon him. This is the picture of fallenness which Christendom accepted and made normative for both its theology and its culture.

Even the revolutionary changes brought about by the Reformation did not seriously affect the general view of the Fall. They may have resulted in a new emphasis in some sectors of Christendom on the heinousness of man's crime and the helplessness of his condition. They may, in Reformed circles through the new acquaintance with the text of the Bible, have led to a more widespread knowledge of the details of the Fall and a more literalistic interpretation of its place in human history. Certainly a major division arose between those who believed that the effects of the Fall had been undone for all men by the work of the Redeemer and that all could enjoy the benefits of His redemption by being incorporated into the Church which He founded and those who believed that God had from all eternity chosen certain men unto salvation and that only those who were joined to His Christ in faith and love would be rescued from the fallen world of darkness and given an inheritance amongst the sons of light. But whatever theories of grace and redemption and the church and the sacraments were entertained, the background picture of man's condition and the fundamental analysis of how he came to be in such a situation were common to all. Man was a fallen creature and in need of redemption to eternal life—this was the conviction of Augustinian and Pelagian, Calvinist and Arminian alike.

With this common conviction so securely held, the Fall theme could provide a natural background for literature as well as for theology. It is not necessarily elaborated: it is simply assumed. In Dante, for example, references to "Adam's evil brood," to "our first parent" confined to Limbo, to the tree pleasant to taste from whence "the appetite was warped to evil," to the nature which

> Created first was blameless, pure and good;
> But, through itself alone, was driven forth
> From Paradise, because it had eschewed
> The way of truth and life, to evil turned;

perhaps above all to Adam's own imagined confession:

> Not that I tasted of the tree, my son,
> Was in itself the cause of that exile
> But only my transgressing of the mark
> Assigned me:

all these reveal a general background of the human imagination to which the poet could appeal and be assured of immediate response. Even in Shakespeare, who is far more concerned with man in history, his possibilities, his achievements, his conflicts, his disasters, there is one moving passage which indicates that the imagery of a primal Fall was tacitly assumed—though it could be claimed that man has far greater power to deal with his own inheritance and to shape his own destiny than any Augustinian tradition would allow.

The passage to which I refer is at the conclusion of Act 3 in *King Henry VIII*. First Wolsey alone meditates on the state of man: tender leaves of hope, blossoms of honor, then the killing frost: "and then he falls as I do." Like little wanton boys that swim on bladders he has ventured far beyond his depth; his high-blown pride has broken under him:

> And when he falls, he falls like Lucifer,
> Never to hope again.

Now Cromwell enters, "amazedly," but Wolsey asks:

> What, amazed
> At my misfortunes? can thy spirit wonder
> A great man should decline? Nay, and you weep
> I am fallen indeed.

Cromwell gives news which makes Wolsey's future even darker, but the great man fallen will not allow him to stay by to assist or defend. He must seek the king and enlist in his service, yet not until he has heard a concluding charge wrung from his former master's bitter experience:

> Mark but my fall and that that ruin'd me.
> Cromwell, I charge thee, fling away ambition;
> By that sin fell the angels; how can man then
> The image of his Maker, hope to win by't?
> Be just and fear not,
> Let all the ends thou aim'st at be thy country's,
> Thy God's and truth's; then if thou fall'st, O Cromwell,
> Thou fall'st a blessed martyr! Serve the king.

As is clear, the mythology of Lucifer and his angels, of man created in the image of God and tempted to presume, is taken for granted, though far more is

included within the individual's responsibility than would have been allowed
by the Puritans of Shakespeare's own time. For them mankind in general was
in a state of complete fallenness: only the mercy of God could draw individuals
out of the pit. For Shakespeare, on the other hand, the primordial picture of
the Fall presented man with the warning not to exalt himself above measure
lest the same disaster should overtake him as had been the case with the Prince
of Darkness.

The translation of the Bible into the common tongue, the wider distribution
of books through the coming of the printing press, and the general advance of
the new learning resulted in a still more extended popular familiarity with the
great drama of the rebellion in Heaven, the fall of Lucifer, the creation of man
and his subsequent capitulation to the wiles of the fallen angel, and the still
greater redemption of man, the harrowing of hell, and the restoration of Paradise. Writers in many European countries saw the possibilities of expressing this
all-powerful theme through the media of epic poetry and tragic drama, and
their works still bear witness to the universality of interest which it evoked.
But it was the destiny of one outstanding Englishman to sum up, as it were,
in one great epic poem the assumptions of European culture in a prescientific,
precritical age. Deeply versed in the classics and natural philosophy, Milton had
virtually committed the Bible to heart. Because he also possessed an almost unparalleled genius for the composition of rhythms and cadences of language, no
other man could have been better qualified to construct the imaginative work
which was to magnify the wisdom of God and to expose the tragedy of angels
and of men. And it has I think been rightly claimed that Milton did more to
engrave the Fall drama upon the English imagination than did even the Bible
itself.

It would be superfluous to quote at length from Milton's great work. Within
the first fifty lines occurs one of the most magnificent passages in all literature.
Here is the age-long question—"What could possibly have caused mankind to
'fall off from their Creator'"? The answer is expressed in unforgettable words:

> The infernal Serpent, he it was whose guile
> Stirred up with envy and revenge deceived
> The mother of mankind, what time his pride
> Had cast him out from Heaven, with all his host
> Of rebel Angels, by whose aid, aspiring
> To set himself in glory above his peers,
> He trusted to have equalled the Most High,
> If he opposed, and, with ambitious aim
> Against the throne, and monarchy of God,
> Raised impious war in Heaven and battle proud,
> With vain attempt, Him the Almighty Power
> Hurled headlong flaming from the ethereal sky,
> With hideous ruin and combustion, down
> To bottomless perdition, there to dwell
> In adamantine chains and penal fire
> Who durst defy the Omnipotent to arms.

Milton rose to the heights in expressing the Fall in terms of the Ptolemaic
world-picture at the very time when that picture was being severely threatened

(and it seems clear that Milton felt the threat himself) by Copernicus and Galileo. He reached a similar eminence in describing the great Rebellion in terms of the Hebraic picture of absolute Divine sovereignty at the time when that picture was being threatened by new ideas of human freedom and responsibility (and this threat must also have been present to Milton's mind). The poem coincided with the end of a theocentric, theonomous universe. The question was what would happen to the imagery of the Fall as the new scientific and new libertarian notions gained increasing acceptance in Western culture.

It is almost exactly three hundred years since *Paradise Lost* was published. During that period enormous changes have taken place in the Western world, the most obvious of which has been the advance of science in theory and in practice. The whole temper has been empirical, and this has brought about a gradual loosening of all close ties with traditional theological disciplines. As science has grown in confidence, theology has adjusted its sights, re-examined its presuppositions, clutched eagerly at an alliance with historical research, and broadly speaking tried to retain its autonomy over whatever its rival might discover about the universe in which we live. Yet at one point the two disciplines were bound to confront and challenge each other. This point was the doctrine of man—his nature, his potentialities, his limitations, his destiny. What effect would the scientific investigation of man's past and the technological direction of his present capacities have upon the Christian doctrines of the Fall and Original Sin? What effect, if any, would the theological affirmation of man's createdness and necessary limitations have upon the progress of science?

It is already clear that this has been a very one-sided encounter. Science has marched triumphantly forward, little troubled by notions of a Fall or inherited sinfulness. Theology, on the other hand, has seemed constantly to be fighting rearguard actions or to be withdrawing from the conflict into some fastness of its own. By 1924 a position had been reached which was brilliantly summarized by N. P. Williams in his Bampton Lectures delivered at the University of Oxford and bearing the title "The Ideas of the Fall and Original Sin." "There was a time," he said, "when the scheme of orthodox dogma appeared to all as an unshakeable adamantine framework, resting upon the two pillars of the Fall and of Redemption. These two complementary conceptions—that of the great apostasy which defaced the image of God in man, and that of the great restoration through the Incarnation and the Atonement, which revived it—were universally taken for granted as the twin focal points which determined the eclipse of traditional theology: and the imagination of Christians loved to play around the parallelism of Adam and Christ—of the death-bringing Tree of Knowledge and the life-giving Tree of the Cross. But the days when this conviction reigned unchallenged were days when most men believed that they dwelt in a comparatively small, geocentric universe. Since then the world in which we live has expanded like a wizard's creation, at the touch of the magic wand of science. The imagination is staggered by the illimitable leagues of interstellar space and the uncounted aeons of geologic time.

"It is not too much to say," he continued, "that, whilst for professed and genuine Christians, the second great pillar of the Faith, the doctrine of Redemption, remains unshaken, founded upon direct experience of the redeeming love of God in Christ, even they have the uneasy feeling that the first pillar, the doctrine of the Fall, has been irretrievably undermined, and totters on its base, no longer capable of bearing its former share of the super-incumbent weight. There are indeed those who urge that it is now a source of weakness rather than of strength to the fabric which it supported for so long and should be razed to the ground."

But if this was the situation in the relationship of theology and science, what was the attitude of literature and the arts? They for their part could certainly not be indifferent to the doctrine of man. In fact their abiding concern has been to interpret the actions, the perceptions, the sensitivities, the anxieties of man through symbolic forms. Normally, as I have suggested, until Milton's time this was done against the background of the general assumption of a Fall and its legacy of evil to posterity. But if this assumption were to be doubted or denied, what would take its place?

It can be said at once that poetry and drama and the novel were almost as disinclined as theology was to accept the presuppositions and outlook of science. Yet at the same time they had no wish to be hampered by any kind of orthodox theology. So we see the emergence in the nineteenth century of various doctrines of man, doctrines described by Norman Nicholson in his book *Man and Literature* by such titles as "Liberal Man," "Natural Man," and "Imperfect Man." The study of history suggested a picture of a gradual ascent upon an inclined plane rather than a fall into a hole from which no ordinary escape was possible. Or it suggested a picture of conflicting elements on a lower plane, ultimately finding a creative synthesis on a higher, rather than of continuous fighting in a cockpit from which a limited number of combatants were snatched by the exercise of some supernatural fiat. There was a richly varied output of literature in the nineteenth century, and generalizations about it are highly dangerous. Obviously Browning was deeply concerned about the liberalistic and idealistic assumptions which were gaining credence in his time. Hawthorne and Melville had little doubt about the fallenness of man. Yet it can at least be said that the old assumptions were being questioned and modified even when they were not abandoned. There was no longer any single myth undergirding literature and poetry. Man's growing knowledge of his universe, his increasing power to organize his social environment, his developing ethical insights—these were themes which the sensitive artist tried to represent in word and action and pictorial form without necessarily setting them within any all-inclusive world-picture. Above all there was uncertainty about the existence of transcendent elements, whether of good or of evil, of wisdom or of irrationality, within the range of human experience. That there was room for improvement in man's condition few could doubt. But could this not be achieved by man himself, given time and patience and co-operation and fuller knowledge and a removal of the prejudices and dogmas and restrictions of the past?

"In or about December 1910," Virginia Woolf once wrote, *"human nature changed."* The question immediately arises: Why this particular date? Here Mr. Walter Allen, from whose recent book *Tradition and Dream* I have quoted this statement, comes to our aid. He points out that December 1910 was the date of the opening in London of the Post-Impressionist Exhibition: a wide public became aware of the paintings of Van Gogh, Gauguin, Cezanne, Matisse, Picasso. Dostoievsky's novels, which had been appearing in French translations, began to be made available in English in 1912. Twelve volumes of Frazer's *Golden Bough* were published between 1911 and 1915. Most important of all, both Freud and Jung had been lecturing in America in 1909; and by 1913 *The Interpretation of Dreams* could be read in England. So, Walter Allen concludes, the men of 1914—writers, critics, interpreters—"all break up the accepted realistic surface of things and emphasize, at the expense of the rational and mechanical, of the scientific in its simpler manifestations, the irrational, the unconscious, the mythical" (*Tradition and Dream,* p. 3). Yet had human nature really changed? Or had the Western view of human nature begun to change?

Let us look in another direction—to a recent poem by Philip Hobsbaum:

"The Beginning of a War"

That Sunday I was at classes, I remember,
But we didn't do much work. The teachers all
Were clustered in another room listening—
We clustered round the door, listening—
To tones which trembled as a life's work fell:
"That Note has not been received . . . War is declared."

War is declared, they said: the words seemed tame.
So many things had been declared of late.
We thought the teachers' faces were absurd
As solemnly they sent us home. The sun
Shone and the park was leafier than the street.
I went the long way round. A siren wailed.

My street had changed. No neighbours were in sight.
I found my mother rushing up and down.
She clutched me to her as I came and glanced
Rapidly up at the sky as we ran in.
The gestures, clear to her, were vague to me.
It seemed the threat was only in her head.

That innocence has gone, stately, primal.
Signs leap out at us from every page,
Rumble in the air over our heads, are breathed
In with the air we breathe, wake when we sleep—
We would call back our innocence again,
So troubled is the air after the fall.

Did a Fall, the second Fall, the ultimate Fall, take place in September 1939?

I take one more example. "On the 10th of September 1945," Edith Sitwell tells us, "nearly five weeks after the fall of the first atom bomb, my brother, Sir Osbert Sitwell, and I were in the train going to Brighton, where we were to give a reading. He pointed out to me a paragraph in *The Times,* a description by an eyewitness of the immediate effect of the atom bomb upon Hiroshima. That witness saw a totem pole of dust arise to the sun as a witness against the murder of mankind—a totem pole, the symbol of creation, the symbol of generation." And out of that experience the poem "The Shadow of Cain" took shape.

"The poem," she tells us, "is about the fission of the world into warring particles, destroying and self-destructive. It is about the gradual migration of mankind, after that Second Fall of Man that took the form of the separation of brother and brother, of Cain and Abel, of nation and nation, of the rich and the poor, the spiritual migration of these into the desert of the Cold, towards the final disaster, the first symbol of which fell on Hiroshima."

> The living blind and seeing dead together lie
> As if in love—There was no more hating then
> And no more love. Gone is the heart of Man.

Did human nature change at eighteen minutes past eight o'clock on the morning of Monday, the 6th of August 1945? Was this the inexorable outcome of the Second Fall which took place when Cain sought to obliterate Abel? Was Hiroshima the ultimate Fall, the death of the heart of Man?

1910, 1914, 1939, 1945. What is the significance of dates such as these? I have drawn attention to three remarkable attempts by modern writers to interpret the character of the age in which we are living. There is obviously no certainty, no precision here but rather agonizing questions: What has gone wrong? Where did things begin to go wrong? Has the final wrong-turning been taken? It would be easy to adduce other examples of this desperate anxiety: T. S. Eliot and *The Waste Land,* W. H. Auden and *For the Time Being,* Arthur Koestler and *Darkness at Noon,* George Orwell and *1984.* Man is sick, hollow, sterile; man is frantic, bewildered, lost; man is in bondage, enslaved by the fabrications of his own intelligence and imagination. Mr. C. S. Lewis deliberately chose as title for his Riddel Lectures "The Abolition of Man." Man as evolution has produced him, man as history has recorded him, man as Western civilization has disciplined him, this man has fallen, has been ruined, has been abolished. Can this be true? Has human nature really changed?

It is evident that this change of emphasis or direction in the world of letters has been motivated by two main factors: (a) the open recognition of irrational and unpredictable elements in human nature to which testimony has been borne so massively by modern psychological investigation and (b) the grim awareness of the violent and destructive elements in human nature to which similar testimony has been borne by twentieth-century world wars and concentration camps. Internal and external, psychological and historical factors, these combined have caused men to speak again in terms of fall and corruption, of human depravity and transcendental evil, in ways which echo the theological pronouncements of an earlier age. At the same time the two factors which I have mentioned have strongly affected theological discourse. There has been a marked tendency to turn from the literalistic and chronological to the psychological and existential, even to rehabilitate the mythical. If the traditional doctrines of the Fall and Original Sin and corporate guilt are to mean anything to the contemporary mind, they must, it is recognized, be expressed in the light of the new knowledge which has been made available to us by psychologists, social anthropologists, and existential thinkers.

Perhaps this new attitude can best be summarized by quoting a passage from a notable series of open lectures given at the University of Cambridge some fifteen years after Williams' lectures at Oxford. "The idea of a Fall from an original state of perfection," the lecturer, J. S. Whale, said, "is not a scientific statement about the dawn of history. The Fall is symbolism, necessary to the intellect, but inconceivable by the imagination. It involves no scientific description of absolute beginnings. Eden is on no map, and Adam's Fall fits into no historical calendar. Moses is not nearer to the Fall than we are because he lived three thousand years before our time. The Fall relates not to some datable aboriginal calamity in the historic past of humanity but to a dimension of human experience which is always present—namely, that we who have been created for fellowship with God repudiate it continually; and that the whole of mankind does this along with us. Paradise before the Fall . . . describes the quality rather than the history of 'man's first disobedience.' "

This brief statement received ample and learned expansion almost at the same time in Reinhold Niebuhr's Gifford Lectures and has been reinforced since by a man well-versed in depth psychology and existential philosophy—Paul Tillich. For him any ideas of an origin in time or of stages in time within which the Fall can be set are meaningless. The Fall is entirely concerned with what Tillich calls the transition from essence to existence, the passage from "the dreaming innocence of undecided potentialities" to self-actualization. This transition "is a universal quality of finite being. It is not an event of the past; for it ontologically precedes everything that happens in time and space. It sets the conditions of spatial and temporal existence. It is manifest in every individual person in the transition from dreaming innocence to actualization and guilt" (*Systematic Theology*, II, 36). In other words, the Fall story is a cosmic myth interpreting universal human existence and is in no way patient of a purely logical or historical analysis. Human freedom, responsibility, anxiety, and alienation all gain meaning in the light of the Fall myth, and the re-establishment of categories such as these opens the way to the reinterpretation of redemption, the second pillar identified by Williams as essential in the Christian structure of faith.

In the realm of literature, besides those attempts to identify certain events as critical turning-points in the development of human nature to which I have already referred, there have been imaginative reconstructions of the Fall story in existential and psychological terms. The most obvious example of the former is Albert Camus' *The Fall*, of the latter William Golding's *Free Fall*.

The central figure in *The Fall* is Jean-Baptiste Clamence, a name which is almost certainly linked with that of John the Baptist, the man whose cry in the wilderness defined the desolation of the human spirit in its estrangement from its true meaning and destiny. His story, told as a monologue, is of the passage from what Tillich calls "dreaming innocence" ("I was in perfect harmony with life. I blended with its entire being and avoided no part of its irony, its grandeur and its demands") to one of conscious despair ("Things kept slipping. Yes everything slipped past me"). The moment of crisis had come when a young woman had thrown herself from a bridge into the Seine (had "fallen"), but he, Clamence, had done nothing to help, had passed by on the other side. Henceforward he himself was not so much fallen as *continually falling*. There were no longer any securities. The self in which he had trusted had failed him. He acknowledged no standards of judgment save his own, and these had proved impermanent. So at every moment human existence is the experience of falling. The only relief that Clamence can find is to talk continuously, particularly by buttonholing others and by confessing to them his own cowardice in order to convict them of their own. But even with that relief, the haunting cry of the drowning woman may be heard at any moment—and then he falls—forever.

William Golding wrote *Free Fall* some five years after *Lord of the Flies,* a book in which, Angus Wilson has suggested, he solved the problem of expressing transcendent evil and good more successfully than has any other living English novelist. There the theme is essentially that of the transition from dreaming innocence to conscious freedom, responsibility, guilt. In *Free Fall* it is worked out in terms of the autobiography of an individual rather than in the form of a universal fable. An artist, Sammy Mountjoy, incarcerated in a Nazi prison camp, goes back over his past life trying to determine when exactly he *fell,* when, that is, he lost the buoyant sense of inner freedom and became aware of something not only holding him fast but dragging him down. He pursues a ruthless self-analysis, punctuated by moments of crisis when he asks:

> Is this the point I am looking for?
> No,
> Not here.

until at length he reaches the point of no return.

Golding will not allow that heredity—a fatherless bastard—or environment—a rural slum—is the necessary background of the Fall. Sammy is exposed to influences good and bad in his early years. There is nothing to suggest that the scales are unduly loaded on the side of evil. But a moment comes when he is confronted by a choice which has within it the potential of an ultimate. As he left school his headmaster spoke these words: "I'll tell you something which may be of value. I believe it to be true and powerful—therefore dangerous. If you want something enough you can always get it provided you are willing to make the appropriate sacrifice." Sammy knew what he wanted. He deliberately made the sacrifice. And the chain of events was set in motion which ended in stark and unrelieved tragedy not so much for Sammy himself but for the one he had wronged.

In his most recent book, *The Spire,* Golding returns again and again to the symbolism of falling. Dean Jocelyn is obsessed with the vision of the tower rising above his Cathedral. But the master-builder knows the plan is sheer folly: "I tell you—whatever else is uncertain in my mystery—this is certain, I know. I've seen a building fall." One after another of the characters falls. Yet this time the tragedy is not unrelieved, for the book ends with the vivid symbol of the appletree (the tree associated with the original Fall myth) standing and growing (the tree of redemption), glittering like a waterfall but an *upward* water-fall, breaking all the way to infinity in cascades of exultation.

To sum up: Theology and imaginative literature will always have this in common: each is concerned with the nature and experience and destiny of man. Neither has been prepared to accept (I am speaking of Western culture) an exclusively scientific view which would regard man as an object in nature to be observed, experimented with, manipulated, and conformed to some arbitrarily chosen standard. Any kind of consistent materialism, mechanism, or auto-matism leaves no room either for a theological or for an artistic interpretation of human existence. If, however, the extremes such as I have mentioned are rejected, how still will the theologian and the artist go about their task of constructing a modern doctrine of man?

On the theological side there are still those who cling to literalistic interpre-tations of the Biblical stories, to traditional formulations of Original Sin or to the belief in a Fall crisis which can somehow be located in history, even though this may be placed in some remote past. On the literary side there are still those who seek to interpret man in terms of nineteenth-century liberalism, or of twentieth-century eroticism, or of some general philosophy of existentialism or nihilism such as have been in vogue in this mid-twentieth century. Between these two groups a wide and seemingly impassable gulf is fixed.

On the other hand, there has been a powerful movement in theological circles towards a reinterpretation of the traditional doctrine of sin and the Fall by the aid of insights derived largely from the research of psychologists and social anthropologists. And the same may be said I think of those whose interests are primarily literary and artistic. They too have in many cases become aware of the importance of psychological insights and anthropological research for their own continuing task. Through both of these disciplines we have learned how significant a place is occupied in human experience by the myth and the symbol, the dream and the image, the parable and the ritual pattern. These may appear in different forms in the course of man's historical development, but certain archetypal symbols seem to be indestructible. One such, I have suggested, is the Fall; and for this reason it has renewed its appeal to theologian and artist alike.

From the psychological side the Fall has been seen to express a dimension of human existence which is powerfully present from the beginning to the end of life. The fear of falling is one of the earliest forms of anxiety in the human psyche, and it is never finally overcome. In a certain sense all life is a falling—a falling below and away from one's aspirations, one's ideals, one's hopes, one's intentions. Falling short is a reality even if the ideas of an aboriginal Fall and inherited guilt seem unimaginable and are virtually meaningless. From the side of social anthropology the Fall has been seen to express a crisis in social develop-ment which again constitutes part of the experience of any society wherever found. As I have shown, modern artists have made attempts to identify such crises in modern times—turning points in human affairs brought about by the onset of new knowledge bringing untold possibilities of good or evil. Even if the possibilities for good are kept in view, there cannot fail to be a sense of lost innocence, of a fall from a state which was easier to cope with and in which no such fearful possibilities threatened.

All this in no way constitutes a new dogmatism. Rather it is a new openness to interpret human existence not as a closed system—moral, logical, historical, or scientific—but as related to transcendent categories and values. If it is possible to speak imaginatively and convincingly of a fall or of falling, then a context of height or "aboveness" must be inferred. And if it is man himself who has *fallen* or is *falling,* the height or the "aboveness" is not a part of man's own self-contained existence. In other words, some recognition of transcendence, however this may be interpreted, is involved. Further than this it does not seem to me that we can at present go. But it is by paying attention to the symbols and myths and archetypes which have captured the interest both of theologians and of artists in our contemporary world that we may hope to make progress in constructing a doctrine of man which is true to the heights and depths of universal human experience.

ORIEL COLLEGE,
OXFORD

IV

Literary Forms

Formalist literary analysis is very closely related to genre studies — a type of extended *explication de texte* in which emphasis is deliberately placed on the work itself to the neglect of the biographical, historical, and intellectual background. *Explication de texte,* a close line-by-line or even word-by-word scrutiny of a specific passage, is a legitimate and highly useful branch of the comparative study of literature as long as the relation of the work to its milieu or to similar works is properly emphasized. But when analysis is limited exclusively to structural components and esthetic effects, the process can hardly be considered a part of comparative literature. This is not to say, however, that the comparatist may not himself undertake an examination of this kind as a preliminary step to a comparison or rapprochement. The distinction between the two purposes of analysis and comparison may perhaps seem clearer in an example emphasizing intellectual rather than esthetic elements. A close scrutiny of a passage from Sartre, valuable as it might be, could not in itself be called comparative literature. But if this passage after dissection were shown to incorporate the essential ideas of a passage or theme in a novel of Thomas Mann, the analysis and rapprochement, or the double analysis, would constitute comparative literature. The same principle would hold if purely esthetic rather than philosophical elements were being compared.

The word *genre* means a *kind* or *species.* Just as the natural scientists classify plants and animals into distinctive groups according to common characteristics, critics of art and literature group works of the imagination according to their style, form, and purpose. Although Aristotle clearly specified only two genres, epic and tragedy, later critics used his *Poetics* to build up the tradition of genres. During the neoclassical period of the seventeenth and eighteenth centuries, the traditional genres were observed with great seriousness. In other periods the classification was likely to be ignored or condemned as artificial. John Dennis in 1704 considered the greater or more sublime poetry (i.e. literature) to comprise epic, tragedy, and the pindaric ode; the lesser poetry to comprise comedy, satire, the Horatian ode, the elegiac, and the pastoral. During the course of the eighteenth century, many new genres of prose fiction came into being, and the presumably fixed boundaries of the poetic genres began to dissipate. In the modern world, the requirements for all genres have become increasingly fluid, and the novel at least can hardly be considered a genre at all. Genre studies would seem to be by definition formalistic in character, but the history of ideas is by no means excluded from them. In some ways, moreover, the study of genres may blend with the study of themes. The proletarian novel, for example, would represent a genre, the study of which would involve the history of ideas; whereas the proletarian as an individual in fiction would be a type; and the struggle of factory workers for subsistence would be a theme.

The study of genres may be made to seem most significant if each genre is compared to an extra-literary art such as painting, sculpture, symphony, or opera. In this perspective each genre seems to have its own artistic unity and character. The creator seems to look at the world and write as a narrator, a lyric poet, or a dramatist. This comparison appears plausible when genres are limited to the three major ones of fiction, poetry, and drama, but dubious when they are expanded to include such minor forms as the pastoral and the various conventions of satire or sonnet. Also in the modern world, as we have said, the novel has tended to lose its identity, and in the nineteenth century the opera had already blurred the distinction between lyric poetry and drama as well as that between music and drama.

In national literatures, studies of genres may be entirely descriptive and analytical, but in comparative literature genres in one national literature are compared to corresponding ones in other literatures, an aspect of our next category, literary relations.

The great reproach made against genre study is that it is mechanical and artificial, directed toward the superficial accoutrements of literature rather than toward its essence. But this is true only when the approach is rigidly formalistic. It is somewhat of a paradox that some ardent comparatists who argue strongly against the study of national literatures in isolation are willing at the same time to defend the study of a single work in isolation. The objection of stilted formalism cannot be raised against the three essays which follow since each uses the genre approach to reveal significant literary relations. The essay by Edwin M. Moseley shows how literary genres reflect timeless human values and suggests a parallel between religion and literature in the dual response to a personal and social end. The essay by François Jost not only presents a skillful analysis of the epistolary novel, but at the same time explains its evolution in three major literatures. The essay by John Gassner reveals the manner in which modern drama portrays historical and biographical themes of social significance.

EDWIN M. MOSELEY

Religion and the Literary Genres

THE RELIGIOUS ORIGINS OF THE DRAMA of every culture are accepted even though in the passing of time they are forgotten. One comprehends Greek tragedy more fully through some awareness of its original purpose as part of the Dionysian festival, but a neglected corollary is that we understand the religion of the Greeks with a natural and non-academic empathy because even now, some two thousand years later, the well produced Greek tragedy achieves its originally intended cathartic function. Its effectiveness as drama continues not simply because, to be redundant, its themes are universal and its representations or imitations of human behavior are valid, but because its form, its structure, its pattern of words and action reduce timelessness to the time the theater-goer, ancient Greek or modern American, can give to attending a performance.

I have written elsewhere that in this very containing of timelessness in time is the essence of art:

> Selection, the symbolic short cut, careful manipulation of structure allow us to live a lifetime in two hours in the theater or through thirty pages or a thousand in fiction. It is literally time and space that are shortened for us so that we suspend our disbelief and accept the eternal and the universal which endure beyond all time and space. In these terms, Greek tragedy is perhaps the epitome of art in that it juxtaposes the vastest of themes with the greatest limitations of time and space. There is something here subtly akin to the essential pun [at the center of much great literature]: timelessness is effectively proclaimed in a short time! At the beginning of the play, Oedipus seems to be on two feet. The attaining of his lofty position even from birth is traced for us in summary after summary: the very technique of the delved-out memory is essential to the central narrative. Before the day is done Oedipus has moved from innocence and pride to experience and humility. He leaves the stage virile and kingly in appearance, though aged now in spirit, and returns suddenly and shockingly a broken old man, the guise of the flesh compatible with the state of the soul. As if this were not enough, now old, he is for the first time truly young; now blind, he at last sees. All of this literally and artistically in less than an hour![1]

An irony that I did not pursue is that this supreme artist, this Sophocles, this Euripides, this Aeschylus, could and did accept without questioning something non-artistic, something non-intellectual, something non-literary: a ready-made, an appropriate, a faith-provoking ritual which celebrated each spring the resurrection of Dionysus after various associations with persecution and death and assured the audience of the spiritual rebirth of man made in the image of God. A literary tradition circumscribed by ritual for its form and by myth for its content is constraining by definition, but it frees the artist within the tradition to achieve the highest possible polish of his art without the random and non-economic distraction of the modern writer's passionately literal pursuit of realism. Maud Bodkin writes that "the nature of the ritual dance, as communication of a complete experience . . . makes it an illuminating prototype of the various differentiated modes of art."[2] She compares the dance with its "sequence of bodily attitudes so related that each, within the total rhythm, enhances the experience of the rest" to drama, music, visual art, and poetry with "the sensible object created by the arts—the spatial form seen, the sequence of sound, or of action sensuously imagined—that serves as a vehicle of a vision, intuition, or emotional understanding, of certain aspects of our common reality." The closeness of Greek drama to the ritual dance was an advantage denied writers in later cultures concerned with law, with exploration, with scientific discovery, with man's freedom on earth, with accumulation, with technocracy. Paradoxically, as dramatists have drifted farther away from the ritual at the source of their genre and willingly so as reflectors of their respective ages, they have remained consciously and unconsciously nostalgic for the artistic economy to which the Greeks were in a sense born. As a culture becomes more sophisticated and the religion becomes either more elaborate or less ritualistic, the neatness of the primitive ritual is lacking. Drama may still serve its religious function directly or implicitly, but the central "sensible object" may be obscured, for example, in scenes of comic relief and details for the achievement of psychological and social realism as ends in themselves.

Still, out of the subplots and the realistic details the critic or the playgoer in his retrospective quest for meaning may abstract the essentially religious pattern. Note the critics' application of what Herbert Weisinger calls "the myth and ritual approach to Shakespeare."[3] Theodore Spencer declares "birth, struggle, death, and revival" to be "not only the themes of the individual final plays" but also "the themes which describe the course of Shakespeare's work as a whole, from his earliest plays through *King Lear* to *The Tempest*." Tillyard describes the pattern of the last plays in a way significantly suggestive of Greek tragedy: a "general scheme of prosperity, destruction, and re-creation. The main character is a King. At the beginning he is in prosperity. He then does an evil or misguided deed. Great suffering follows, but during this suffering or at its height the seeds of something new to issue from it are germinating, usually in secret. In the end this new element assimilates and transforms the old evil. The King overcomes his evil instincts, joins himself to the new order by an act of forgiveness or repentance, and the play issues into a fairer prosperity than had first existed." And Knight finds the "habitual design of Shakespearean tragedy" to be "from normalcy and order, through violent conflict to a spiritualized music and then to the concluding ritual."

About these and a number of other comments recognizing patterns of myth and ritual in Shakespeare, Weisinger raises several questions. A predictable one paying homage to old-line scholarship is: but "there is no satisfactory way of explaining how Shakespeare got at it." The traditional scholar asks for proof of historical continuity from Greek drama to Roman drama to the medieval pattern of out-of-the-church, to the churchyard, to the town square, to the inn, to the theater constructed like an inn or for evidence of a specific influence such as Sophocles on Seneca on Kyd on Shakespeare; but even if proof of development or influence did exist, it would somehow be beside the point. Serious drama treats the fact and the mystery of life and death—that is, man's physical birth, his rise into manhood, his physical death, his spiritual rebirth—regardless of the particular moment, the particular tradition, the particular roots, literary or religious. Lord Raglan's fascinating study has defined the fundamental pattern of the hero in "genuine mythology, that is, mythology connected with ritual" and with "the imitation mythology" that grows out of them:[4] "(1) The hero's mother is a royal virgin; (2) His father is a king, and (3) Often a near relative of his mother, but (4) The circumstances of his conception are unusual, and (5) He is also reputed to be the son of a god. (6) At birth an attempt is made, usually by his father or his maternal grandfather, to kill him, but (7) He is spirited away, and (8) Reared by foster-parents in a far country. (9) We are told nothing of his childhood, but (10) On reaching manhood he returns or goes to his future kingdom. (11) After a victory over the king and/or a giant, dragon, or wild beast, (12) He marries a princess, often the daughter of his predecessor, and (13) Becomes king. (14) For a time he reigns uneventfully, and (15) Prescribes laws, but (16) Later he loses favour with the gods and/or his subjects, and (17) Is driven from the throne and city, after which (18) He meets with a mysterious death, (19) Often at the top of a hill. (20) His children, if any, do not succeed him. (21) His body is not buried, but nevertheless (22) He has one or more holy sepulchres." He might have pursued his study further from ritual to mythology to imitation mythology to conscious literature. This is simply another way of saying that the pattern of man is timeless, that great themes are archetypal, that effective literature is universal and enduring. If the pattern of Shakespearean tragedy or of the tragedy of any other time is reminiscent of the pattern of the hero in myth or more fundamentally of the structure of religious rituals which preceded even myth, the answer lies in the unchanging nature of man, of nature, of the universe, not in how the author "got at" the myth and the ritual which seem to lie beneath and to give order to the richness of his literal details. To be sure, the artistry lies in those details: the distinction of Greek tragedy from Shakespearean tragedy from whatever may pass for modern tragedy, but the significance is in the meanings that transcend the moment which determined the particular details and the particular traditions.

We are here emphasizing the essentially religious *content* of serious drama in every age: depictions of the physical rise of man, which is life, and of the physical fall of man, which is death, and assurance of the spiritual rise of man, which may suggest that man is greater than the physical forces which contain him, either by his very actions on earth or his rebirth into a life beyond earth. These depictions may be of a god, any of the great scapegoats for human frailty, whose story gives man a way of coping with life and with death (the ritual, the religious literature itself, such as the Bible). Or they may be of heroes part-god and part-man, who demonstrate the physical weakness and the physical strength of man but also the spiritual strength of the god-in-man (the center of classical tragedy and of the epic, the former one step away from the ritual in both form and content, the latter one step away in content but further, much further away in form). Or they may be of man, imagined or historical, whose inevitable pattern through life to death receives the consolation of the reminders in various ways that man is created in God's image, comes from him, and will return to him (the extension into modern tragedy, the development of the historical hero into the legendary hero, the elegy in verse and the eulogy in prose). Dionysus, Mithra, Christ may serve very well as examples of the great scapegoat gods; Oedipus, Beowulf, Arthur, as examples of the great tragic and epic heroes; Willy Loman, Becket, Edward King of Milton's "Lycidas," as examples of man saved by tragic treatment, by movement from history into legend, by elegiac transcendence.

What then of the religious form when the total rhythm of the dance which originally circumscribed the content has been submerged or forgotten? The rhythm of the dance may emerge in the strict pattern of the content, the highly stylized and selective nature of the action, the resultant economy of the unities of time, place, and action; or it may emerge in the rhythm of the verse, a matter of form in the most exact sense of the word. If we refer to audience or readers, who after all give life to any art form, we can say with Aristotle that tragedy is *cathartic*, or we can say more broadly that verse is essentially incantatory. The most effective religious art combines inseparably the structure of content and the structure of form; and as we have suggested above, the writer closest to ritual, the writer taking for granted the incantatory nature of verse, that is, the writer nearest to form in its essence, has a remarkable advantage in conveying his basically religious content.

Eliot's *Murder in the Cathedral* is a marvelous example of the intellectually achieved, though certainly sincerely felt, intertwining of ritual, verse, and content. A former student of mine has pointed out that the play is essentially a liturgical drama taking for its basic structure the form of the mass in the Roman Catholic Church: "The first and perhaps the most striking feature of the drama is its structure. It is written in what is actually two parts which are separated by an interlude: Part I, the return of the archbishop to England and his temptation; Part II, the murder of the archbishop. The Interlude which separates the two is written in the form of a Christmas sermon. . . . The mass itself is divided into parts as is the play. The first part of the mass is called the 'Mass of the Catechumens.' The second part of the mass is called the 'Mass of the Faithful' and it is in this part that the sacrifice of the mass is actually performed. These two parts are separated by what is not really a part of the mass but is often included, the sermon. These parts correspond directly, both in function and overall structure, with the divisions that Eliot uses in his drama. Both the Mass of the Catechumens and the sermon are preparations for the second, the part in which the victim is offered. It is with this in mind that Eliot places the actual murder in the corresponding part of the drama. One specific example that will demonstrate these observations more clearly is the last chant of the chorus, which Eliot uses as a sort of choir in his 'mass':

> Lord, have mercy upon us.
> Christ, have mercy upon us.
> Lord, have mercy upon us.

which in the liturgy of the Church has its specific correlative:

> Kyrie, eleison.
> Christe, eleison.
> Kyrie, eleison.

The structure of the drama is also based upon the two dominant facets of the life of Christ on earth: namely, his coming, advent; his 'going,' the crucifixion."[5]

Consider by contrast a second modern play, Robert Bolt's *A Man for All Seasons,* which treats Sir Thomas More, another clergyman who achieved martyrdom in the face of temporal pressures. The basically religious content is present; nothing distracts from the pivotal pattern of man's rise to temporal power, man's fall from temporal power, and man's transcendence beyond the temporal. The form to be sure is in the skillful structure of the content, in the author's adherence both to the tradition of English tragedy and the pattern of the sacrificial archetype. But do the absence of a containing ritual and the use of prose compatible with its psychological and social realism interfere with the achievement of the cathartic and incantatory function, that is, result in a play comparatively prosaic and mundane in both the literal and the metaphorical senses of the words?

I am not asking for verse drama, for literally poetic drama, if the religious function of tragedy is to be fully achieved. The poetry can lie in the concentration and suggestiveness that are the essence of poetry even if, indeed particularly if, they are achieved in prose. Arthur Miller's *Death of a Salesman* may be an excellent example of poetry achieved not through the rhythm of verse but by the rhythm of movement back and forth through the past and present of Willy Loman's career in Brooklyn, New York, and Boston, of the careers of his two sons and his neighbor, so much a part of Willy's consciousness, and of the perhaps imagined career of his brother, through time and through space, from one age to another, from coast to coast, from continent to continent, all without moving an iota of scenery and all within the short time spent in the theater. Stepping through walls and stepping through time free the stage from the confines of modern realism and move it back to Shakespeare, who changed scene after scene with a word, or Sophocles, who without changing a scene delved out the memory endlessly in one spot.

Critics argued at length as to whether Miller actually returned tragedy to the modern stage.[6] Miller made several pleas directly to the audience to accept the play as tragedy, one of the most moving through a speech of Linda, Willy's wife, who in effect pleads for the acceptance of what Ivor Brown called the "tragedy of the stool" instead of the "tragedy of the throne":

> I don't say he's a great man. Willy Loman never made a lot of money. His name was never in the paper. He's not the finest character that ever lived. But he's a human being, and a terrible thing is happening to him. So attention must be paid. He's not allowed to fall into his grave like an old dog. Attention, attention must finally be paid to such a person. . . . A small man can be just as exhausted as a great man.

No gods, no hero, only a small man, but a human being to whom attention must be paid—that is, to whom admiration of a sort must be added to the pity and the horror. If it is added, man, not a god yet somehow more than man, is effectively portrayed, and the religious function of a literally non-religious play is served.

The question of whether Miller achieved tragedy, which is religious in its origin and its point, or pathos, which may have the same origin but implicitly mocks the religious point, raises the larger question of the closeness of tragedy and comedy. Both reveal the ridiculousness of man, but tragedy nevertheless gives him a place, however small, in the vast scheme of things whereas comedy gives him his place, small to be sure, in the small scheme of things, and perhaps even this ironically or romantically. That is, in comedy we are not even asked to suspend disbelief. Wylie Sypher in his brilliant essay "The Meanings of Comedy"[7] reminds us that both tragedy and comedy derive from the same sacrifice and feast which were the ritualistic center of "some sort of fertility rite— Dionysiac and phallic." Following Cornford,[8] he describes the ceremony familiar to every culture, "the death or sacrifice of a hero-god (the old year), the rebirth of a hero-god (the new year), and a purging of evil by driving out a scapegoat (who may be either god or devil, hero or villain)," along with its variations, its peripheral actions, its extensions. Cornford and after him Sypher point out that the accompanying drama included a contest between the old and new kings, a slaying of the old, "a feast and marriage to commemorate the initiation, reincarnation, or resurrection of the slain god, and a final triumphal procession or *komos,* with songs of joy." The conclusion is interesting that tragedy kept only that part of the ritual portraying the suffering and death of the god or hero whereas comedy kept both sacrifice and feast, "retaining its double action of penance and revel." Again, we are talking primarily about content, but I find especially meaningful Sypher's point that comedy, attempting to balance its opposites, to attain unity out of a difficult dichotomy, "remains an 'improvisation' [Aristotle's word for the beginning of all Greek drama] with a loose structure and a precarious logic that can tolerate every kind of 'improbability.'" One might contrast rather the ritual of the sacrifice with its strict and predictable order which gave to tragedy both its content and its form with the revel of the feast, the disorder of which effused the entire comedy, even the part recalling the sacrifice, with an atmosphere of looseness. The corollary may be that form and reverence, formlessness and irreverence go together to make up the dramatic whole. The ritual dance, poetry, and tragedy have for the other side of the coin the revel, perhaps prose, and comedy.

Tragedy and poetry, comedy and prose as the two sides of the same coin are strikingly apparent in English drama, primarily of course Shakespeare's, in the sixteenth and seventeenth centuries. We are accustomed to saying that the low scenes, the scenes of comic relief, are in prose by contrast to the dignified, the majestic, the seriously moving, fundamentally the incantatory verse as if the prose said: here is what man is in this our world, vulgar, mocking, ridiculously imitative of the ideal, in contrast to the poetry's: here is the promise of man in spite of his involvement in the world, in spite of his excesses from which his god-like nature will ultimately save him. The prose scenes of Marlowe's *Dr. Faustus* in which the servant Wagner re-enacts almost precisely the verse scenes of Faustus' dealings with the devil are reminders of ritual in content but a denial in form and tone and hence a reversal of content. They are a kind of black mass presided over by a god of misrule—revel in effect, yes, but hardly in form, for the mockery of the ritual is too circumscribed, too strict. In all literatures the development of prose as a vehicle of expression, ironically since man supposedly *talks* in prose, is slower than the development of verse, reminding us once more of the ritualistic, the unsophisticated origins of drama, the incantatory nature of poetry. For reasons we shall pursue below, in Western literature the use of prose extensively did not develop until the Renaissances of the respective countries. Marlowe is literally Shakespeare's contemporary, but to move from Marlowe to Shakespeare is to cover practically an entire history of drama from the morality play to modern realism. Shakespeare can use prose to invert the poetic scenes, to mock his ritual, but at times he succeeds in freeing it from certain confines to give us a deep and awful look into the true nature of man, indeed into man's very non-public, subconscious self. Peter's vulgar prose remarks to the Nurse in juxtaposition to Romeo's high-flown and poetic wooing of Juliet is *public* enough because that is what we expect of the low-born, but Iago's prose plotting with Roderigo and, more frightening yet, Hamlet's obscure and prose bewilderment of Ophelia are *secret* scenes in which a god of misrule takes over, Iago an extensionally allegorized one (as if Shakespeare has separated every man into an Othello and a Iago) and Hamlet expressive of some other side of his princely public self (a mad side? a repressed side? a true side?). One can hardly say here the *improvisation* of the revel instead of the *form* of the sacrifice—*improvisation* rather than *form,* yes, but of revel only in the sense of frightening chaos, of repressed evil rearing its head to subsume public order. The realism achieved by the prose is much more than the realism of possible and probable action; it is the psychological realism of man's hidden and awful self for a moment without the assurance of salvation that the total drama, the containing ritual, the prevalent rhythm of the verse leave with the audience.

All that we have been saying about the relationship of formlessness and irreverence, further about the relationship of the revel, prose, and comedy, and finally about the relationship of comic improvisation to psychological realism, revealing the un-revel-like chaos within man, suggests the entire history of the novel from its random beginnings to its flowering in the Renaissance and indeed to its emergence as the dominant literary form in both quantity and quality in our time. Any attempt to place the precise beginning of the novel is difficult because the novel, defined loosely as a long prose narrative, is delimited neither as to form nor as to content. The literature of every culture contains prose tales of varying lengths, but these universally tend to be *outside* of the ritual-based literature which affirms man's tie to some god or other or even counter to the implications of such literature. Petronius' *Satyricon,* often referred to as an early example of a novel, is a medley of prose and verse describing through a series of loosely connected episodes the adventures of three rogues in southern Italy. The tone is unredeemed mockery; the content or butt of the tone is the materialism of an entire age found both in the aristocracy and the upstarts who threatened and imitated the aristocracy. Again, formlessness and irreverence characterize this work by a man who spent his time at Nero's loose court as a self-appointed Master of Revels, a kind of god of misrule in the flesh. The pastoral Greek romances of two centuries before Petronius, such as Longus' *Daphnis and Chloe,* are characterized by formlessness in that their narratives are far from being the necessary series of events that warrant the name of plot or attain the unity of emotional impact at which ritual aims. The idealistic presentation of characters in idyllic settings is far from irreverence but just as far from any imitation of human behavior that would achieve the cathartic function of serious or significantly comic literature. Actually, the improvisations presided over by a god of misrule are ironically stronger reminders of ritual celebrating God's order than pastoral fantasies and romantic adventures which have no relationship to man's confessed failures and man's painful redemption. One could continue a consideration of isolated examples of prose narratives that superficially point toward the novel, but the prose tale was not produced in any number until a large public was able to read without effort. This condition came to pass during the Renaissance, when printing resulted in mass production of books at prices within the public's reach. The technical development of printing, then, encouraged the emergence of the novel, but this very development both provoked and was provoked by an increased freedom of individuals, of which increased literacy was only one evidence.

Writing elsewhere on the development of the novel in quite a different connection, I have summarized: "An author's contribution to the development of the novel is his particular addition to the previously established ways of describing individual behavior. In this connection it is natural that the English prose tale had its beginning in the Renaissance, when attention to the individual in contrast to the social organism was becoming a characteristic attitude."[9]

Medieval man conceived of the universe as an organic whole with every part in its ordained place, serving its ordained function. Of society it was similarly believed that each "member," that is, class, whether the nobility, the merchants and artisans, or the serfs, was essential to the whole and therefore equal in the sight of God. Each individual was bound by divine law, reflected of course in natural and human law, to perform his duty within the class of his birth. A man might change his station within his class: the gradations of the guild system, from apprentice to journeyman to master, allowed for this possibility, and a nobleman could acquire more land, hence higher status. But to move from one class to another, to assume pretentiously the manners of the class above or to debase one's self by marrying into the class below, was sacrilegious as a defiance of God's will and treasonable as a denial of the stated and tacit mores which manifested His will. The metaphor of the organism and its necessary members was derived from the physical being of the human individual, for whom, paradoxically, the medieval climate of opinion had so little concern.

Attention to the individual was a conscious concept of the new humanism, which was as much a nostalgic as a progressive, intellectual movement; the individual was also the chief emphasis of the new bourgeois climate, which questioned and looked forward from the feudal milieu. The Renaissance as a revival of learning found its most zealous expression in the humanists. They approved of the translation of the classics, including the Bible, into the native tongues of the Western world, and they aimed at the creation of literature worthy of comparison with that of ancient Greece and Rome. Still, their motivation was more moral than aesthetic: they desired to arrive at ethical direction other than that laid down by the medieval Church and consequently at a new definition of the individual in relation to his society. But the humanists were not radical in their demands for social change: they worked for the purification rather than the destruction or replacement of existent institutions; they were in effect the liberals of their time, wanting to analyze the discrepancy between current myths and actual behavior and to eliminate pretense. They constantly asked the questions: what is *true* nobility, what is *pure* Christianity, what is *ideal* kingship? using the familiar concepts of feudal organization and objecting only to the refutation of words by acts. They attacked ignoble noblemen, unChristian Christians, and unruly rulers, but they approved of each group in the ideal. They described seriously or they ridiculed abuses: they wrote essays on morality, dramatized utopias, satirized corruption, and even recorded behavior realistically, often by way of pointing out moral lessons.

That humanistic criticism contributed to changes more drastic than the humanists intended is the familiar irony of the liberal position in every age. Wyclif, the English churchman of the fourteenth century, would still describe himself as an advocate of the true Church rather than an originator of European Protestantism. Sir Thomas More, preaching the sacrifice of the individual to the common good, consistently criticized abuses which were deviations from the feudal system and literally lost his head in defense of the medieval Church. Spenser lamented corruption at court but blamed it in part on change, and Shakespeare judged tragic heroes whose flaws were usually sins against the medieval values. Even Caxton, the first English printer, whose very trade helped to make literature available to the middle class, romantically yearned for the good old days before the disintegration of King Arthur's Round Table, dramatic symbol of the ideally functioning feudal system. It is, then, in spite of such conservative allegiances that the humanists contributed to a fresh conception of the individual so necessary for the development of the novel as we think of it.

The entire context of the novel's development was a questioning of established form in society, in religion, in government, that is, a kind of figurative formlessness, and the tone was repeatedly irreverence, intended or not. Significantly, the medieval climate of opinion which was being questioned had as its pivot faith and ritual whereas the modern climate which succeeded it took as its slogans *individual* responsibility, *individual* endeavor, *individual* revelation, the very denial of form becoming the theme of the content.

To put it simply, the long prose tales, the creation of which was encouraged by and the circulation of which was made possible by the invention of printing and the growth of literacy, were at first mockeries of feudalism and implicitly of the feudal rituals, social and/or religious, and of the keepers of the feudal rituals, the landed knights and the priests. The form they tended to take, paradoxically an inversion or a complete neglect of form, came soon to be known from its Spanish origins as the picaresque novel, a genre which has pervaded the development of the novel from its strong emergence in the Renaissance both on the Continent and in England until well into the nineteenth century and indeed in isolated but significant examples in our own time. The center of the usual picaresque story is the picaro or rogue, a fellow of low birth, often of uncertain origins, or at least in temporary low position. His lack of status in society allows him the advantage of having nothing to lose and therefore considerable freedom of insight and comment. Armed with this freedom from vested interests, he is exposed to the world and soon taught that professed morals and actual behavior have little to do with each other. Then with this additional weapon of knowledge gained from experience, he proceeds on adventures of his own. This picaresque pattern has the panoramic advantage as a vehicle of social comment because the picaro in his movements usually covers considerable territory, but it has the truly dramatic disadvantage of trying to cover so much literal space that attention is primarily to things external, to a journey through some defined world so very literally that any journey of learning for the central character is beside the point. It is everything that Aristotle's tragedy is not: the character at the center is self-consciously non-heroic; the development of character from physical birth through the stages of life to physical death and at least the promise of spiritual birth, the very point of most ritual, is a concept of man's nature precisely denied by the picaresque; and the unities of action, of time, and of place, which in a sense reflect the form of the original ritual and determine the form of the literature which derived from it, are flagrantly disregarded. The conspicuous characteristics of the picaresque are irreverence and formlessness. If the picaro seems to arrive at some moral re-evaluation from his experience, as we are *told* that he does at the end of such works as the Spanish *Lazarillo de Tormes* or *The Unfortunate Traveller* by the English writer Nashe, the learning does not dramatically develop out of his experience step by step; it is arbitrarily tacked on. The adventures may go on until the author chooses to stop or at least so long as anything in society remains to be mocked, and furthermore they may go on in any order the author wishes: that is, they lack the necessary order known as plot.

The picaresque is mock-heroic, or with specific reference to its anti-feudal origins mock-chivalric, and some examples are self-consciously mock-epic. Aristotle, comparing and contrasting tragedy and the epic as to length (essentially a matter of content) and meter (essentially a matter of form), criticized the writers of epics who neglected the very unity of action which he considered essential to effective drama. The same criticism could be made severalfold of such deliberate mock-epics as *Don Quixote* and *Tom Jones.* The communal epic and the effective literary epic contain and are contained by the recurrently emerging pattern of the hero which Lord Raglan found in his "genuine mythology . . . connected with ritual" (Aristotle refers to epic content as matter for a series of tragedies). One does not expect a precise repetition of the hero's pattern in ages less susceptible to what Aristotle called *the marvelous,* but since the hero's pattern is symbolically the pattern of every man's life, which in turn gives ritual its symbols, the narrative lacking the control of the original ritual, however far away, whether respectful or inverse and mocking, may deny emotional closure to its readers. Many of the famous eighteenth-century English novels, not only *Tom Jones* but also, say, *Moll Flanders, Roderick Random, A Sentimental Journey,* interest us historically and delight us part by part but admittedly lack the sustained and single impact of works in which nothing is wasted. The improvisation of the irreverent, then, continued to be encouraged by a society which mocked form in every fundamental context, including the religious, even when it paid attention to the superficial form of manners and dress.

There was of course another kind of narrative emphasizing not the individual's questioning of or rebellion against society, not, that is, negative in its tone, but extolling the positive values of the new individualism at the center of the bourgeois climate of opinion. According to this set of values, every man was endowed with the capacity for endeavor and obligated to use this capacity in the employment of resources about him. Each man had equal opportunity on God's earth to use his natural industry to reach the goal at which he aimed without fear of class restrictions. The bourgeois virtues of diligence, thrift, and morality, which came naturally to him, would protect him from seeking the vain goals which characterized the decadent feudal aristocracy. Economic success was considered evidence of man's thorough exercise of his natural virtues and hence a symbolic promise of the religious salvation which he had earned. These ways of thinking, condoning as just and natural the economic revolution of the middle class and the concomitant Protestant Reformation, gave the condemned *avarice* of the Middle Ages the admirable name of *ambition.* This social philosophy suggested the entire structure of a prose tale in which the central character journeyed through trial after trial, contest after contest, adventure after adventure, always with success until he ended with a climactic reaching of whatever earthly goal he had before him, his success of course proving his righteousness. Excellent examples are the tales of Deloney, Bunyan's *Pilgrim's Progress,* Defoe's *Robinson Crusoe,* and Richardson's *Pamela.* In contrast to the picaresque mockery, the tone is prevalently positive, but as in the pastoral romances of the Greeks, if irreverence is absent, so is the convincing imitation of human behavior that achieves catharsis; the reader cannot with any honesty identify with the optimistic experience described. Too, though the direction of the journey is, so to speak, upward in such success stories, the order of events toward the final goal is generally random. Again, the concept of character and the economy essential respectively to the content and form of ritual are lacking. The mockeries of the bourgeois climate, from much of Dickens and *Vanity Fair* to Lewis' *Babbitt* and Dreiser's *The Financier,* are in effect the picaresque novels of the modern age, with irreverence as their unifying intention and formlessness as a function of their attempt to cover society thoroughly.

At the end of the nineteenth century the irreverence was abetted by the new scientism in the center of which Darwin, Marx, and Freud were the gods, and the formlessness was abetted by the deterministic denial of "God's in his Heaven,/All's right with the world." As the humanists' brave new look at man in the Renaissance resulted in a redefinition of his nature and in experimentations in art to represent this nature, the determinists freed the characterization of man from both the romantic emphasis on his basic goodness and the bourgeois emphasis on his predestined capacity for success. By the beginning of our own century, however smothered in naturalistic details of social and psychological realism the novel had become, novelists were not afraid to treat man's failures and not afraid to seek ways to transcend them.

Whereas the irreverence of the picaresque story lies in its comprehensive mockery of social and personal values and the irreverence of the success story lies, dichotomously, in its refusal to admit the limitations of society or of man, the failure of both as significant literature was usually the absence of any journey of learning for a central character or a central intelligence to give meaning to the external journey about society or upward through it. One can of course point to earlier examples, but as novels continued to be produced in great number throughout the nineteenth century, authors gave increasingly greater attention to the development of central characters or to the maintenance of a central point of view. Steps in the extensional journey in society became subordinate to, dependent upon, or actually symbolic of steps in the intensional journey of the protagonist or the focus of narration. The journey of learning, then, subsumed the journey in time and space just as in Greek drama the unity of action subsumed the unities of time and place. For the last hundred years, in significant story-telling on the Continent, in England, and in America, though it may provide a particular author's special richness, movement through a setting has been secondary to the coming of age of the pivotal character, to his movement from innocence to experience, to—as we have said—his journey of learning. Examples are too abundant and too rich to discuss or even to list with any thoroughness here, but I have been thinking of such novels as Dickens' *Great Expectations* (a mockery of the bourgeois success story, yes, but a kind of rites of passage for Pip, the central character, as he moves from innocence to experience, from pride to humility), Twain's *Huckleberry Finn* (a truly picaresque journey baring in its movement down the river the pretenses of mankind in America and everywhere else at all times, but more than that, as an endless number of critics have pointed out, a ritual journey of the coming of age in any time), James' *The Ambassadors* (the journey of Strether, the middle-aged innocent, from the optimistic illusions of America to the awful truths of Europe, again from innocence to experience and perhaps self-understanding), Flaubert's

Madame Bovary, Joyce's *Portrait of the Artist as a Young Man,* Turgenev's *Fathers and Sons,* the early Hemingway, Fitzgerald's *The Great Gatsby,* Camus' *The Stranger,* and so on even unto Salinger's *The Catcher in the Rye.* The lessons learned in these journeys and the many other possible examples may vary; some may be negative and some may be positive in implication; but they are all achieved by a step-by-step, stage-by-stage, carefully structured look into the self on the part of the central character. Whether there is the seemingly irreverent discovery of no promised salvation for man or the universally reverent one of salvation out of suffering, in novels of the kind which I mention there has been a remarkable emergence of form, conscious or not on the authors' part. Rituals dramatize the cycle of man and of nature, and in the emergence of attention to man's development, authors have shown a striking awareness of ritual in a supposedly non-ritualistic age.

I am not neglecting, say, the despair of Hemingway's *The Sun Also Rises,* the disillusionment of Fitzgerald's *Tender Is the Night,* or the secular existentialism of Camus' *The Stranger,* for in these novels and in many others in our time the denial of God's order is most firmly dramatized by the inverted ritual, the mock sacrament, the correlative of the mythic quest unfulfilled. Nor am I neglecting in a consideration of form the impressionistic or stream-of-consciousness novel which may take advantage of the flexibility of prose to desert entirely the extensional journey for the intensional one, making the subconscious and unconscious levels of action even more important than the conscious ones. We have referred before to the Renaissance dramatists' adventurous use of prose to reveal the un-revel-like chaos within man, a kind of foreshadowing perhaps of the novel completely subjective in its technique. But interestingly enough, the novels accused of betraying the very genre by their disregard of ostensible action achieve their order implicitly from the timeless symbols, the archetypal shapes, the unchanging myths which persist in man's dreams and in the rituals which precede and transcend time. Joyce's *Ulysses* with the *Odyssey* for its paradigm and Faulkner's *The Sound and the Fury* with the story of the Passion Week for its paradigm are highly experimental in style, but myth and ritual give them a stronger order than does the syntax of a particular language.

Whatever the multiplicity of reasons, the novel in the last century has become a tighter form artistically and a more intense genre in its content. Is the tightening of content as well as of form simply a natural refinement of a genre after several centuries of extensive practice with it? Did a disillusionment with the values of the modern world lead to a gradual resurgence of belief in man's ennobling capacity for suffering, or at least to an unashamed lament for the passing of his heroic qualities? Or does the archetypal pattern of man, celebrated in ritual, by its very definition endure and by its very endurance recur, however the peculiar expressions of a particular age may seem to have obscured it? Has the novel in our time moved toward serving the communal religious function of ritual-based drama and achieved it, without help from the incantatory nature of verse, through an intensity of content and an economy of structure? The ritual dance is hardly just off stage as it was and occasionally is even now with significant drama, but nevertheless in the modern authors mentioned and in many others the action is "sensuously imagined" and conveyed with nothing wasted. Somehow form and reverence converge often indeed in a prose genre, the very beginnings of which were a denial of them.

The development of an effective literary form in our time is assuring aesthetically and—if one likes—spiritually. I have suggested before that the great religions and the great literature which dramatizes them evolve from a profound sense of personal and social end; and I wondered then, in recognition of the strength of the novel in our time, "what manner of end are we experiencing?" In his fine essay "The Spiritual Problem of Modern Man" Jung quotes Hölderlin's "Danger itself/Fosters the rescuing power."[10] With the public ritual of the communal drama no longer available, has the structured and intense novel come to the religious rescue with a private ritual offering personal drama, with a form, that is, to contain and convey reverence?

SKIDMORE COLLEGE

NOTES

1. Edwin M. Moseley, *Pseudonyms of Christ in the Modern Novel* (Pittsburgh, 1963).

2. Maud Bodkin, *Archetypal Patterns in Poetry* (New York, 1958).

3. Herbert Weisinger, "An Examination of the Myth and Ritual Approach to Shakespeare," in Henry A. Murray, ed., *Myth and Mythmaking* (New York, 1960).

4. Lord Raglan, *The Hero: A Study in Tradition, Myth, and Drama* (London, 1949).

5. William James, "History, Religion, and Literature: Eliot's 'Murder in the Cathedral,' " *The Wall* (Washington and Jefferson College), Winter, 1958-59.

6. Reviews of *Death of a Salesman* by Brooks Atkinson, Ivor Brown, John Mason Brown, Eleanor Clark, and Frederick Morgan, in Eric Bentley, ed., *The Play: A Critical Anthology* (New York, 1951).

7. In Wylie Sypher, ed., *Comedy* (Garden City, N.Y., 1956).

8. Francis M. Cornford, *The Origin of Attic Comedy* (London, 1914).

9. Edwin M. Moseley, "Introduction," in Robert Ashley and Edwin M. Moseley, eds., *Elizabethan Fiction* (New York, 1953).

10. C. G. Jung, "The Spiritual Problem of Modern Man," in *Modern Man in Search of a Soul* (New York, 1933).

FRANÇOIS JOST

Le Roman épistolaire et la technique narrative au XVIIIe siècle

L ES HISTORIENS DES LETTRES EUROPÉENNES se plaisent à redire qu'au siècle des lumières la mode était au roman épistolaire: ils appliquent la remarque surtout à l'Angleterre et à la France, puis à l'Allemagne post-werthérienne; moins aux autres littératures sujettes à des lois qui différaient souvent de celles des pays qu'on vient de nommer. Jusqu'à une date relativement récente, la critique ne s'est guère occupée de l'évolution des formes et il est à souhaiter que se multiplient les efforts entrepris dans ce domaine par un trop petit nombre de savants[1]. Elle cesserait d'emprunter le langage de la haute-couture lorsqu'elle parle de faits essentiels pour l'histoire de notre civilisation. Le phénomène littéraire, en effet, reflète le caractère fondamental d'une société donnée; expression esthétique, au moyen du verbe, de tout ce qui touche l'homme, la littérature concilie une substance et une forme. Cette forme ne saurait être une simple mode.

Des raisons profondes ont amené les auteurs de romances à transformer peu à peu leur genre. Mais le roman moderne, qui en est résulté, demeure l'héritier aussi de l'épopée et de la pastorale. Au cours du XVIIIe siècle, le roman cherche ses techniques et ses méthodes; tant qu'il n'aura point trouvé sa forme, il restera un genre méconnu et méprisé. En 1780 encore, Johann Carl Wezel, dans la préface de son *Herrmann und Ulrike,* doit constater ce fait: "Der Roman ist eine Dichtungsart, die am meisten verachtet und am meisten gelesen wird." C'est exactement ce que Laclos remarque, quatre ans plus tard dans une critique de *Cecilia,* roman de Fanny Burney: "De tous les genres d'ouvrages que produit la littérature, il en est peu moins estimés que celui des romans; mais il n'y en a aucun de plus généralement et de plus avidement lu." [2] Les tâtonnements des romanciers ne menèrent donc point, semble-t-il, à la prompte découverte d'une recette. Précisément, parce que très souvent ce ne fut qu'une simple recette qu'ils cherchaient: et le roman épistolaire, pour la foule des médiocres, en restait une.[3] Pour les génies, ce fut, dans le domaine, la trouvaille du siècle, dont les conséquences, pour l'évolution du roman, n'ont guère encore été étudiées.

Le *croyable* a de tout temps constitué la matière littéraire, et tout l'art de l'écrivain consiste à faire accepter—fort provisoirement, parfois—l'irréel comme réel le fictif comme vrai. Le lectur, avant tout, doit croire le dramaturge, le romancier, le poète lyrique, du moins le temps que dure la représentation, la lecture, le rêve. Avant l'avènement du réalisme, cette adhésion était d'autant plus spontanée que le public, dans l'oeuvre littéraire, voyait surtout un moyen d'évasion. L'enchantement se produisait en transférant d'emblée le spectateur ou le lecteur dans un monde merveilleux et lointain—éloignement dans le temps ou dans l'espace. L'exotisme, en littérature, m'apparaît comme un dernier soubresaut de la romance: une réaction de l'ancienne école. L'auteur de romans exotiques prenait avantage de l'ignorance du public ou de son impuissance à contrôler les événements relatés, les moeurs et les paysages dépeints. Dans tous les cas ce public acceptait certaines données, et cela tout naturellement. La pastorale, le conte, l'épopée, la romance, le récit de chevalerie—comme le roman exotique—échappaient à la censure de la raison raisonnante tels les articles du credo. Une logique interne liait les diverses parties de l'ouvrage. Un des motifs pour lesquels la séparation des genres a été si longtemps maintenue est que chacun d'eux supposant d'autres prémisses tout changement de ton risquait de rompre le charme: le lecteur perdait la foi. Le pouvoir d'illusion que toute oeuvre littéraire exerce tant qu'elle ressortira au domaine de l'art, s'adressait surtout au sentiment, à cette faculté d'appréhender spontanément les faits et les choses. Cependant, plus l'histoire approche de l'ère de l'*Aufklärung,* plus le public substitue à la notion de *croyable* celle de *vraisemblable.* Sous le règne du premier, le lecteur *oubliait* tout ce qui se passait au delà de l'enceinte circonscrite par le récit. Dès l'avènement du second, l'on *reconnaît* dans la trame sa propre destinée, telle qu'on la vit, telle qu'il aurait bien pu arriver qu'on la vécût: on identifie l'oeuvre avec son existence réelle, ou virtuelle.[4] Croyable, vraisemblable: il ne s'agit nullement ici d'une simple question de sémantique. Quoique les deux termes s'emploient souvent l'un pour l'autre, ils ne sont nullement synonymes. Le premier s'adresse à la puissance intuitive, le second cède aux tendances syllogistiques de l'esprit humain. *Truth-like, wahrscheinlich, vraisemblable,* supposent qu'une intelligence procède à la vérification: on arrive à la conclusion que tel fait narré dans le roman, ressemblant à la vérité, pourrait bien être vrai, doit l'être, l'est. Le pouvoir d'illusion ne repose plus sur une magie, il se fonde en la réalité: l'ère du réalisme fait irruption dans l'histoire littéraire.

Le vraisemblable: hantise de l'ère nouvelle.[5] Wieland, en 1776, publiant *Die Abderiten,* met en sous-titre: *Eine sehr wahrscheinliche Geschichte.* Mais il faut étudier surtout les deux premiers tiers du siècle, où presque tout roman est publié sous forme de document: un document, assume-t-on, exprime toujours la vérité. Prévost publie les *Mémoires* du chevalier des Grieux, Lesage, l'*Histoire de Gil Blas,* Marivaux, *La Vie de Marianne*—et on verra encore

Stendhal appeler *Le Rouge et le noir; Chronique de XIXᵉ siècle*.[6] A l'époque, le roman historique, au sens moderne du mot, avait, depuis vingt ans à peine, pris son plein essor, avec *Waverley*, avec *Ivanhoe*,[7] avec *I promessi sposi*— selon Scott "the best novel ever written"—qui sont en même temps quelques-uns des chefs-d'oeuvre du genre.[8] L'île britannique témoigne de ce même souci de la documentation qu'on vient de constater en France. Defoe publia *A Journal* sur l'année de la peste—oeuvre d'imagination prise d'abord pour un rapport authentique; le docteur Samuel Johnson[9] écrit une *History* de Rasselas, terme qui, avec celui de *Life*, revient dans le titre d'innombrables romans, dont on tenait à documenter l'historicité dès la couverture. L'habitude avait gagné les pays germaniques. Gellert présenta au public *Das Leben* de la comtesse suédoise de G***, et Sophie de Laroche *Die Geschichte* de Mlle de Sternheim. Tout, dans la technique même que l'on choisit, doit corroborer, chez le lecteur, l'impression d'un récit susceptible de vérification. On exhume et exhibe des parchemins, toujours l'auteur produit ou fait semblant de produire ses preuves.

La vérité historique repose sur des témoignages. Et voici que la première personne obtient droit de cité au Parnasse des romanciers, où elle ne s'était glissée jusque-là que fort occasionnellement: encore une caractéristique des premières oeuvres de l'âge moderne, de *Robinson Crusoe* au *Vicar of Wake-field*, de *Gil Blas* à *Manon Lescaut*, d'*Anton Reiser* à *Agathon* et à *Franz Sternbalds Wanderungen*. Le lecteur sent la présence du témoin, mieux, la présence du héros même, puisque c'est lui qui rapporte les événements et se porte garant de leur authenticité; à chaque page, il semble lui redire le vers de La Fontaine:

> J'étais là, telle chose m'advint.

Il est clair que c'était là un parti pris: l'élément autobiographique n'entrait souvent pas davantage dans le récit que s'il était narré à la troisième personne. Le but de la méthode, encore une fois, était de donner le change, de créer l'illusion, de commettre le mensonge artistique dont parlait déjà Platon. Le roman-expérience remplaçant le roman-imagination n'en demeure pas moins une oeuvre fictive. Ce qui disparaît, c'est l'omniscience de l'auteur; jusque-là tout romancier s'était senti libre de sonder les reins et de scruter le coeur des personnages, assumant ainsi les fonctions que l'on croit communément réservées au bon Dieu. Le lecteur d'un Ich-Roman[10] peut, à chaque ligne, non certes vérifier directement les faits, mais reviser les raisons qu'il a de croire l'écrivain: parle-t-il en témoin ou parle-t-il en poète? Que l'un se métamorphose en l'autre: c'est bien là le voeu du public. "Le duc de Nemours, à cette nouvelle, éprouva une douleur sensible." Cette phrase est de 1678, époque des conjectures sentimentales. L'auteur, non seulement devine, mais connaît d'une conaissance infaillible les mouvements secrets qui agitent les héros. "Whether cold, shame or the persuasions of Mr. Jones prevailed most with Mrs. Waters, I will not determine, but . . ."—voilà un passage typique, une sorte de tropos, dont on pourrait, dans *Tom Jones*, trouver une cinquantaine d'exemples. On voit l'abîme qui sépare deux époques et deux auteurs: Mme de La Fayette, pour la méthode, se rattache encore à l'ére de la romance, Fielding consacre la fortune du roman réaliste.

A l'avènement des "lumières" un changement profond s'opère dans l'esprit du lecteur; les incidents extraordinaires commencent à le lasser. En 1731, Marivaux justifie la publication de *La Vie de Marianne* en insistant, au début de son récit, sur le fait que cette *vie* est "particulière." Trente ans plus tard, Rousseau notera que les Âmes doivent l'être. Dans la seconde préface de *La Nouvelle Héloïse,* il oppose d'une part "événements rares" et "personnages communs," et de l'autre, "événements communs" et "personnages rares." Voilà qui marque une évolution essentielle. Merveilleuse, l'action ne pouvait ravir le lecteur que parce qu'il y *croyait.* Prouvée, elle le ravissait dès qu'il l'apprenait, dès qu'il la *savait.* En littérature, du *credo quia absurdum* on passait au *scio quia probatum.* A la fin de la lecture on avait, jusque-là l'habitude de se dire: *se non è vero, è ben trovato.* Maintenant on abrège, on transforme le mot: *è vero è non trovato.*

Si je reviens au chef-d'oeuvre de Fielding, c'est pour ajouter cette remarque. Dans son récit, l'auteur témoin peut revenir sans cesse à la première personne sans jamais avoir l'air d'un intrus, et en fait, le *I* et le *we* se retrouvent fort souvent dans *Tom Jones.* Mais l'auteur se plaît surtout à assumer les fonctions d'une sorte de cicérone. A maints endroits de l'histoire, il rappelle qu'il la contemple *"together* with the reader." Précisément, *reader* est un des mots qui reviennent le plus fréquemment sous la plume de Fielding. Mettez les neuf cents pages du roman dans un computeur électronique, la machine vous dira qu'elles font quelque deux cent vingt fois appel au lecteur, qui, de la sorte, cesse d'être tout simplement "bénévole," pour se changer en partenaire. *Reader* se substitue à la seconde personne, dont Fielding interroge l'opinion (sans certes jamais l'apprendre): il s'agit d'une sorte de consultation méthodique. Le roman ressemble à un monologue s'adressant à un antagoniste toujours présent: le public.[11]

Les avantages de l'Ich-Roman sont notoires. Le merveilleux même peut devenir vraisemblable grâce à l'autorité, non de l'auteur lui-même, mais de son témoignage direct. Toute la vie sentimentale des héros prend la couleur du réel: avantages dont jouissent à un degré supérieur, en principe, les trois variantes du genre: le dialogue, le journal et la confession; les deux dernières étaient promises à un succès croissant à partir du dernier tiers du siècle, à l'époque où naissait la première génération romantique. Mais les inconvénients d'un récit à la première personne ne sont pas moins réels. Le même personnage ne cesse d'être en scène, et cela, parfois, dans des oeuvres fort volumineuses. Ce personnage finit-il par trouver le *moi* haïssable, se faufile-t-il dans les coulisses et donne-t-il la parole à d'autres, qui racontent à leur tour leur histoire, celle-ci, alors, prend trop facilement le caractère d'un interlude, d'une digression, d'un hors-d'oeuvre: technique menant très vite aux plus pénibles invraissemblances. Prenons l'exemple de *Gil Blas.* Le premier chapitre du cinquième livre est intitulé "Histoire de don Raphaël." Il faut quelque soixante-dix pages à ce seigneur pour héberger sa biographie—presque la longueur d'*Adolphe.* Mais voici que se pose le problème du style direct, auquel Lesage tient absolu-

ment. Problème sans solution. Dans le récit de Raphaël, en style direct, rapporté
par Gil Blas, s'insère un autre récit, lui aussi en style direct, de la mère de
Raphaël, Lucinde. Mais elle encore, répète, en style direct, les paroles de son
amant, le duc de Medina Céli. Ainsi Lesage donne la parole à Gil Blas qui la
donne à Raphaël, qui la donne à Lucinde, qui la donne à Céli. Au septième livre
du chapitre septième, les propres mots de Phénie sont rapportés par Laure, dont
le discours est rapporté par Gil Blas. Au chapitre dix du livre quatrième, Gil
Blas cite Steinberg, qui cite Séraphine, qui cite le comte de Polan. Lesage, par
un emploi inconsidéré de la première personne tue ce sentiment de vraisemblance qu'un usage circonspect aurait dû aviver.

Mais d'autres dangers menacent l'Ich-Roman: la méthode ne permet pas
toujours le dénouement que réclamerait la trame. Si la fin est tragique, l'auteur
peut se sentir embarrassé: comment faire mourir un personnage à qui l'on a
confié la tâche de narrer l'histoire? Le romancier changera-t-il de méthode dans
le dernier chapitre et donnera-t-il la conclusion dans un épilogue? Ou imitera-t-il
l'auteur de *La Vie de Marianne* qui laissa à d'autres, à Mme Riccoboni par
exemple, le soin d'achever son histoire? Si l'intérêt du drame avait réclamé
non seulement la mort de Manon, mais encore celle du chevalier des Grieux, il
semble clair que Prévost aurait dû changer de technique; celle-ci, on ne saurait
trop le redire, demeure hautement fonction de la trame: la première personne
ne saurait donc être la panacée contre les faillites du génie.

La méthode épistolaire ne l'est pas non plus. Mais elle donne à l'écrivain tous
les avantages du roman personnel, et quelques autres par surcroît, tout en lui
laissant la possibilité d'en conjurer certains périls. Le *je* est toujours là, mais,
dans la plupart des types de roman épistolaire—on va les étudier plus loin—ce
je a plusieurs identités. L'histoire est narrée par plusieurs personnages paraissant
successivement sur la scène. L'issue tragique, en outre, est parfaitement possible
et l'auteur n'est point réduit, comme Walpole, à faire conter à des revenants les
détails de leur propre trépas. Ces deux avantages, essentiels aux préoccupations
de l'époque, ne sauraient cependant à eux seuls expliquer l'ampleur et la durée
d'un tel succès, ni surtout d'une telle influence sur l'évolution de la littérature.

*   *
*

Il n'est guère possible, dans le cadre d'un simple article, d'établir la fortune,
en territoire européen, ou même dans un seul pays, d'un genre littéraire donné.
Je considère donc certaines données comme acquises et ferai appel à l'érudition
de Daniel Mornet, dont l'étude sur "Les Enseignements des bibliothèques
privées"[12] me permet de tirer des conclusions certaines. Mornet, ayant procédé
au relevé des livres contenus dans trois cent quatre-vingt-douze bibliothèques
parisiennes constituées entre 1740 et 1760 (donc immédiatement avant la publication de *La Nouvelle Héloïse*), établit d'une part la liste des neuf romans
français qu'il a rencontrés le plus souvent et, de l'autre, celle des romans anglais
traduits ou adaptés, figurant également sur ces rayons. Voici ces listes:[13]

—*Lettres d'une Péruvienne* (Mme de Grafigny)   81****
—*Confessions du Comte de C**** (Duclos)   46****
—*Acajou et Zirphile* (Duclos)   42*

—*Mirza et Fatmé* (Saurin)   42*
—*Mémoires de Cécile* (de La Place)   35***
—*Histoire de Marguerite d'Anjou* (Prévost)   33*
—*Histoire des Passions* (Toussaint)   31**
—*Histoire de Mme de Luze* (Duclos)   30*
—*Les Malheurs de l'amour* (Mme de Tencin)   29***   369
—*Pamela* (Richardson)   78****
—*Tom Jones* (Henry Fielding)   77**
—*Clarissa* (Richardson)   69****
—*L'orpheline anglaise* (Mrs. Sarah Fielding)   46**
—*Sir Charles Grandison* (Richardson)   44****
—*Joseph Andrews* (Henry Fielding)   40**
—*Le Véritable ami ou la vie de David Simple*
    (Mrs. Sarah Fielding)   35**
—*L'étourdie ou l'histoire de Miss Betsy Tatless*
    (Mrs. Eliza Haywood)   26****[14]
—*Oronoko* (Mrs. Aphra Behn)   25**   440

                      Total   809

Tous les romans anglais sont à la première personne; l'on a affaire à des oeuvres épistolaires ou à des *Rahmenerzählungen,* ces deux espèces illustrant la méthode de Richardson et celle de Fielding. La rivalité de ces auteurs se voit donc aussi à travers leur influence en France. Au total, six romans sont par lettres, dans ces listes contenant dix-huit ouvrages: un tiers. Et sur un total de huit cent neuf romans, trois cent quarante-quatre sont épisto-laires: plus de deux cinquièmes. Voilà qui démontre un succès de librairie. Mais on ne sait ni si l'acheteur a lu l'ouvrage, ni, pour le cas où il est lui-même écrivain, s'il s'en est laissé influencer. Pourtant le calcul des probabilités nous permet d'assurer que le pourcentage des livres acquis simplement pour garnir les rayons de la bibliothèque demeure le même pour tous les romans, épisto-laires ou autres. Ainsi le rayonnement relatif est constant. La propagande pour les oeuvres littéraires, par ailleurs, se faisait en grande partie dans les salons: l'hôte devait être en mesure de dire son opinion sur les livres du jour—et l'invité de soutenir la conversation—surtout, par conséquent, sur ceux qui figurent dans ces listes. Celles-ci, du reste, sont fort instructives pour qui étudie l'histoire de l'anglomanie en France. Elles semblent aussi suggérer que l'Angleterre, pour l'essor du genre, a joué, avant la publication de *La Nouvelle Héloïse,* le rôle essentiel.

D'autre part la liste des ouvrages français montre un fait qui se vérifie encore durant la seconde moitié du XXᵉ siècle: la qualité de l'oeuvre ne se mesurant pas au chiffre de tirage, il arrive souvent que la médiocrité jouisse des faveurs du jour. Une sélection plus littéraire s'opère souvent lorsqu'on se décide de traduire. Cette première liste de Mornet ne contient que deux ou trois ouvrages connus aujourd'hui d'un amateur des lettres françaises, tandis qu'à peine un ou deux ouvrages de la seconde liste, celle des traductions, est ignoré de l'amateur des lettres anglaises. Si l'on voulait—conscient que toute liste de cette sorte comporte une part d'arbitraire—dresser l'inventaire des romans français qui, au cours de tout le siècle, ont marqué d'une manière significative l'évolution du genre, on pourrait, en limitant leur nombre à celui que donne Mornet, y faire figurer les dix-huit titres suivants:

1) 1713, Hamilton, *Les Mémoires du comte de Gramont.***[15]
2) 1715-1736, Lesage, *Histoire de Gil Blas de Santillane.****
3) 1721, Montesquieu, *Lettres persanes.*****
4) 1731-1739, Prévost, *Le Philosophe anglais ou histoire de M. Cleveland.****
5) 1731-1741, Marivaux, *La Vie de Marianne.*****
6) 1733, Prévost, *Manon Lescaut.**** [16]
7) 1735, Marivaux, *Le Paysan parvenu, ou Mémoires de M***.****
8) 1736-1738, Crébillon fils, *Les Égarements du coeur et de l'esprit.****
9) 1742, Duclos, *Les Confessions du comte de*** écrites par lui-même à un ami.*****
10) 1747, Mme de Grafigny, *Lettres d'une Péruvienne.*****
11) 1760, Diderot, *La Religeuse.*****
12) 1761, Rousseau, *La Nouvelle Héloïse.*****
13) 1755, Restif de la Bretonne, *Le Paysan perverti.*****
14) 1782, Laclos, *Les Liaisons dangereuses.*****
15) 1787, Bernardin de Saint-Pierre, *Paul et Virginie.***
16) 1791, Sade, *Justine ou les malheurs de la vertu.****
17) 1794-1797, Restif de la Bretonne, *Monsieur Nicolas.****
18) 1799, Mme Cottin, *Claire d'Albe.*****

Sans exception aucune, nous avons affaire aux divers types de narrations à la première personne—celle-ci ne jouant pas toujours, il est vrai, un rôle également important. Et dans les dix-huit oeuvres choisies pour représenter l'art du roman au XVIIIᵉ siècle français, il se trouve que la moitié d'entre elles sont écrites sous forme de lettres (No 3, 5, 9, 10, 11, 12, 13, 14, 18). On pourrait soutenir que dans l'ensemble leur valeur littéraire l'emporte sur celle de l'autre groupe.

En Allemagne, du reste, la situation n'est guère différente; le courant littéraire qui entraînait la France et l'Angleterre vers le réalisme était plus lent, plus calme dans les régions germaniques et ne s'accélérait qu'à partir du *Sturm und Drang*: ici, il faut donc tenir compte d'un décalage du temps. Parmi les romanciers allemands—ceux qui eurent le plus de succès et ceux qui possédaient le plus de génie—qui ont écrit entre 1770 et 1810, je ne vois guère que Novalis (auteur, du reste, d'un seul roman, lequel est tout autant un poème) qui se soit abstenu de contribuer à la fortune du genre. Des oeuvres comme *Lucinde*, comme *Der Jubelsenior* participent à un très haut degré à la technique épistolaire. Leur droit de figurer dans la liste ci-dessous serait parfaitement justifié. Mais limitons-nous au nombre que Mornet nous a suggéré pour nos comparaisons et donnons neuf exemples:

1) 1771, Sophie Laroche, *Geschichte des Fräulein von Sternheim.*
2) 1774, Goethe, *Die Leiden des jungen Werther.*
3) 1787, Hermes, *Für Töchter edler Herkunft.*[17]

4) 1787, Heinse, *Ardinghello und die glückseligen Inseln.*
5) 1789, Schiller, *Der Geisterseher.*
6) 1796, Tieck, *Geschichte des Herrn William Lovell.*
7) 1799, Hölderlin, *Hyperion oder der Eremit in Griechenland.*
8) 1800–1802, Wieland, *Aristipp und einige seiner Zeitgenossen.*[18]
9) 1802, Brentano, *Godwi oder das steinerne Bild der Mutter.*

A ces noms on pourrait ajouter ceux de Jacobi, de Knigge, de Musäus, de Miller, de Moritz, de Lafontaine, de Kotzebue, de Dorothea Veit (femme de Frédéric Schlegel), d'Achim von Arnim. Ils ont tous, à cette même époque, donné dans le genre avec plus ou moins de talent et de succès.

Les avantages que présente la technique épistolaire pour la présentation de l'histoire ne peuvent pas expliquer à eux seuls l'immense succès de cette catégorie d'oeuvres littéraires. Cette technique, en effet, comporte aussi des inconvénients graves dont il sera question lorsqu'on analysera les différents types de romans par lettres. Une des raisons du succès doit être cherchée dans le rôle que jouait dans la vie di l'homme du XVIIIe siècle la lettre réelle, celle que lui apportait le facteur. Le romancier exploitait l'impatience éprouvée par le lecteur, dans sa vie ordinaire, à recevoir du courrier, principale et parfois unique source d'information sur des événements ou des personnes. On était à une époque où les voyages étaient lents, les absences longues, les quotidiens, en France, inexistants:[19] d'une part, désir ou nécessité de déplacements, de l'autre, moyens inadéquats de les exécuter. De nos jours, où un billet d'avion ou quelques litres d'essence rapprochent en peu d'heures des êtres qui se cherchent, où le téléphone s'est en grande partie substitué à la lettre privée, où l'*ens* en soi *rationale* qu'est l'homme, ne se soucie que tous les douze mois de dresser l'état de ses amitiés, au moyen de cartes de nouvel an, le roman épistolaire s'éloigne du vraisemblable dans la mesure même qu'il s'en était rapproché au temps de Clarissa et de Julie.

Des raisons d'ordre psychologique ont donc grandement contribué à l'éclosion du genre. Mais il y a plus: la tradition des lettres fictives a été vivante à travers les siècles. Au lieu de formuler son enseignement dans un traité, l'auteur le présente souvent dans une ou plusieurs lettres adressées à des personnes réelles ou imaginaires. On peut suivre l'évolution de cette technique des *Epîtres aux Corinthiens* aux *Provinciales,* on peut en constater la permanence des *Letters to Dead Authors* à *Briefe an einen jungen Dichter.* Tradition millénaire encore que les *epistolae poeticae.* Et enfin il y a des correspondances réelles qui sont passées par de nombreuses éditions. Sainte Catherine de Sienne, Erasme, Cromwell, Madame de Sévigné: leurs lettres étaient lues par un large public.

Même l'homme ignorant son alphabet se voyait parfois contraint d'écrire une lettre. Dans les grandes villes, le métier d'épistolier pouvait être fort lucratif. Par ailleurs, des formulaires pourvoyaient les semi-lettrés d'épîtres-modèles. Richardson lui-même n'a-t-il pas au début de sa carrière de romancier composé un tel ouvrage? Le succès de ses *Familiar Letters on Important Occasions* (1741)[20] l'encouragea dans la voie où il était déjà entré: construire, au moyen de lettres, un roman. Non qu'à l'époque où parut sa *Pamela* (1740),[21] l'idée eût été entièrement neuve. Dans ses *Héroïdes,* Ovide nous montre la correspondance entre deux amoureux, et Alciphron, dans ses *Lettres,* qu'il suppose écrites par des pêcheurs, des paysans, des parasites et des courtisanes, aime à amorcer, sinon à développer une trame.[22] L'usage de la lettre incluse dans la romance n'a pas discontinué: forme la plus primitive d'un simple message, d'un signe indirect—tel le copeau di Tristan confié à l'eau et qui apprend à Yseult la présence de son ami—ou billets divers, lettres formelles jouant un rôle aussi bien pour le développement du récit que pour l'impression esthétique communiquée au lecteur. Les premiers romans épistolaires proprement dits restent ceux de Juan de Segura, *Processo de cartas de amores que entre dos amantes pasaron,* de 1548, et d'Alvise Pasqualigo, *Lettere amorose,* de 1563. Mais ni l'oeuvre espagnole, ni l'oeuvre italienne n'ont exercé en leur temps quelque action sur l'évolution de la méthode du roman. Puis, dans l'*Astrée,* on compte cent vingt-neuf lettres, dans *Polexandre,* de Gomberville, on en trouve vingt-deux, dans *Cléopâtre,* de La Calprenède, soixante et onze, et dans le *Grand Cyrus,* Mademoiselle de Scudéry en a inséré cent dix-sept. Enfin, les *Lettres à Babet,* de Boursault, publiées en 1669, la même année que les *Lettres portugaises* sont, à plusieurs égards, de véritables romans: les *Lettres d'Héloïse et d'Abélard* que Bussy-Rabutin avait traduites en 1687 furent · éditées dix ans plus tard, et bientôt allaient paraître les *Lettres persanes.*

Richardson pouvait lire la plupart de ces ouvrages dans des traductions anglaises. Mais il trouvait la tradition épistolaire dans la fiction de sa propre littérature. *A Post With a Packet of Mad Letters,* de Nicholas Breton, imprimé pour la première fois en 1603, connut de nombreuses éditions au cours du siècle. En 1683 Mrs. Aphra Behn publie ses *Love Letters Between a Nobleman and His Sister,* analyse fine, par endroit, du coeur féminin. Et il y avait déjà, en Angleterre, une série de recueils-types; on trouvait des variantes nombreuses sur le thème de l'Héloïse, la religieuse portugaise, l'espion turc, le facteur dévalisé; on installait un correspondant en ville, transportait l'autre à la campagne, et l'on avait ainsi une excellente occasion de célébrer, dans des lettres fort didactiques, les bienfaits du primitivisme et de dénoncer la corruption des capitales. Thèmes impossibles de nos jours, où l'on pourrait tout au plus inaugurer, avec quelque garantie de succès, des série comme *Indiscrétions à "Western Union"* ou l'*Écouteuse aux PTT.*

Il n'y a pas de doute: Richardson peut être considéré comme le père du roman d'analyse psychologique; pourtant, quant à la technique du roman épistolaire, on est tenté de redire à son propos ce que Madame de Staël avait écrit su Jean-Jacques: "Rousseau n'a rien inventé, mais il a tout enflammé." Comme tout grand homme, l'auteur de *Clarissa* est en partie l'ouvrage de son temps.

*   *
*

La technique épistolaire ne se justifie pleinement que si le signataire de la lettre est impliqué lui-même dans l'action relatée. Passez outre cette condition préliminaire; et le roman par lettres ne se distingue guère des *Rahmenerzählungen* que par des signes extérieurs tout conventionnels: des dates et des par-

aphes. Il cesse même d'être un Ich-Roman. Ceci dit, il faut s'empresser de distinguer les divers types de romans épistolaires; il est bien entendu qu'il ne s'agit
nullement ici de ranger les oeuvres selon leur contenu, leur ton ou leur dénouement, mais bien selon leur forme; la méthode et la structure employées—choisies
évidemment en fonction de la trame—vont seules être l'objet de mon analyse
et le critère de la classification.

Une distinction essentielle s'impose d'emblée: la lettre peut s'adresser à un
ami, qui devient ainsi le confident du héros. Mais ce héros peut également se
tourner vers son antagoniste; l'action peut se passer, comme sur des tréteaux,
entre des personnages en contact immédiat les uns avec les autres. Absence
physique pourtant: les apostrophes et les réparties, au lieu d'être déclamées sur
la scène, sont arrêtés dans des lettres. D'un côté, on a ainsi la lettre-confidence,
de l'autre, la lettre-drame—et je voudrais prendre ici le terme de drame dans
son sens étymologique: l'*action,* en effet, est mise tout entière dans cet échange
de lettres: elles la font progresser, elles en sont le ressort. Deux types fondamen-
talement différents: là, on parle *du* partenaire, ici, on parle *au* partenaire; d'une
part, attitude passive de la part de l'expéditeur et du destinataire, les missives
n'influençant en rien la trame, et, de l'autre, attitude essentiellement active,
chez l'expéditeur toujours, chez le destinataire s'il répond, puisque le but même
de la lettre et de la réponse éventuelle est de développer l'histoire, d'agir ou de
provoquer des réactions. Pour la commodité de cet exposé je distinguerai donc,
dans le genre épistolaire, entre méthode *passive* ou *statique,* et méthode *active,*
ou *cinétique,* ou *dynamique,* le lecteur sachant le sens précis j'attache à ces
termes.

Si la lettre n'influe en rien sur les événements, si son but est de les rapporter,
en quoi diffère-t-elle donc des mémoires et des confessions? Les lettres, dès
lors, sont-elles autre chose qu'autant de chapitres? Pour répondre à ces questions, il faut d'abord distinguer entre plusieurs types de romans statiques. Je les
appellerai type Marianne, type Werther, et type Clinker. Les deux premiers
types vont d'abord nous occuper. Ni *La Vie de Marianne* ni *Die Leiden des
jungen Werther* ne contiennent de correspondance entre les héros de l'histoire.
Valville et Charlotte [23] se taisent. Un des personnages principaux raconte son
récit—ici l'histoire de sa vie, là, l'histoire d'un amour—à un confident. Mais
voici la différence essentielle: Marivaux fait faire à son héroïne une biographie;
elle a cinquante ans; il s'agit de narrer un passé lointain. L'histoire est fournie
en onze livraisons—onze lettres qui ne portent ni date ni signature. A première
vue, elles ne forment guère que les diverses parties d'un Ich-Roman. Pourtant,
l'impression du lecteur est fort différente: il sent très vivement la présence de la
marquise, de l'amie recevant la confidence.[24] Non pas seulement parce que
Marianne s'adresse à elle au début de chaque lettre, mais que très souvent, en
cours de route, elle en appelle au style direct. Le ton de la conversation se mêle
au récit. "Et savez-vous pourquoi?" demande Marianne à telle occasion. "Atten-
dez pourtant, ne vous alarmez pas," ajoute-t-elle pour rassurer son amie (IIe
partie). On peut trouver dans le roman une bonne centaine de phrases analogues:
Marianne, on le voit, associe la marquise à ses aventures, à ses craintes, à ses
amours. Et le lecteur, évidemment, se substituant à la marquise, éprouve le

sentiment d'être lui-même le confident de l'héroïne. Une atmosphère d'intimité se dégage du livre, que l'on ne retrouve pas dans un simple récit à la première personne. Ces remarques valent pour les romans de Madame de Charrière, pour *La Religieuse* de Diderot, pour tant d'autres ouvrages de ce type. Mais qu'on ne s'y méprenne pas: Marivaux représente un sommet, et il s'en faut que tous les auteurs qui ont choisi (volontairement ou non) *La Vie de Marianne* pour modèle de leur roman en aient su profiter comme lui de tous les avantages que ce prototype peut offrir. Et parmi ces avantages il faut relever ceux de l'ordre linguistique: la narratrice peut se permettre toutes les familiarités du langage épistolaire.[25] Voici un exemple: Marianne veut présenter à son amie le supérieure du couvent où on l'avait conduite. "Je viens de vous dire qu'elle était âgée; mais on ne remarquait pas cela tout d'un coup. C'était de ces visages qui ont l'air plus anciens que vieux; on dirait que le temps les ménage, que les années ne s'y sont point appesanties, qu'elles n'y ont fait que glisser; aussi n'y ont-elles laissé que des rides douces et légères. Ajoutez à tout ce que je dis là je ne sais quel air de dignité ou de prudhomie monacale, et vous pourrez vous représenter l'abbesse en question, qui était grande et d'une propreté exquise."[26] Style badin et charmant que l'on retrouve à tant de pages—annonçant les confidences de soeur Sainte-Suzanne au marquis de Croismare—style, certes, qui prend, à d'autres phases de l'histoire, un caractère d'autant plus tragique, d'autant plus tendu que Marianne peut exprimer sans nulle contrainte les sentiments qu'elle *éprouvait*.

Ce sont les sentiments qu'il *éprouve* au moment même d'écrire sa lettre, que Werther communique au lecteur. La différence est notoire. Cette fois-ci, le romancier écrit avec sa vie présente, et non avec ses souvenirs. Et le verbe est au présent, tout au plus au passé immédiat. L'action que le héros vient d'accomplir et qu'il relate n'a pas encore porté ses fruits, ni même fait deviner sa dernière conséquence. Le roman de Goethe demeure, du point de vue de la technique, l'exemple classique de ce type.[27] Werther confie à Wilhelm l'histoire de son amour pour Charlotte, non pas en homme mûr se rappelant sa folle jeunesse:[28] Werther est dans le mêlée. "Die Unmittelbarkeit der ersten Aufwallung," voilà l'expression dont aime à se servir la critique d'alors. Cet aspect de la méthode est fort bien décrit dans la préface de *Clarissa*. "All the letters are written while the hearts of the writers must be supposed to be wholly engaged in their subjects . . . so that they abound not only with critical situations, but with what may be called *instantaneous* descriptions and reflexions." Cette même idée sera reprise dans le préface de *Sir Charles Grandison:* "The nature of familiar letters, as it were, to the *moment,* while the heart is agitated by hopes and fears, on events undecided, must plead an excuse for the bulk of a collection of this kind."[29] Wilhelm, comme la marquise amie de Marianne, est pris à témoin—et le lecteur cette fois encore s'identifie avec Wilhelm, un Wilhelm qui, du reste, ne demeure nullement impassible. Werther, à douze reprises, fait allusion à des réponses, et parfois il règle sa conduite d'après les conseils reçus. Du reste, la vraisemblance réclame ces réponses. On cesse de parler à qui ne prouve qu'il écoute. Et cette présence ne rend que plus poignante la plainte de l'amant malheureux. Certes, le confident, parfois, peut jouer dans un roman de ce type un rôle plus actif que celui de Wilhelm. Ses lettres peuvent être reproduites. C'est le cas des oeuvres de Richardson, du moins quand ce confident a nom Belford. *Clarissa,* du point de vue méthodique, est *Werther* sur un double plan: Charlotte qui aurait sa confidente, une Miss Howe. La trame, dans l'oeuvre anglaise, n'est pas développée, non plus dans l'oeuvre allemande, par la correspondance des héros qui se confronteraient directement. Parmi les cinq cent trente-sept lettres dont *Clarissa* se compose, on en trouve cinq en tout de Lovelace à sa victime (quatre au livre VI et une au livre VII), et une seule de la victime au bourreau (au livre VII).[30] En revanche, Clarissa écrit cent trente-deux lettres à sa confidente Miss Howe, qui répond cinquante et une fois, et Lovelace écrit cent soixante fois à Belfort, qui répond soixante-trois fois. On discerne le type Werther non seulement dans les nombreuses imitations de l'ouvrage goethéen, mais dans des romans d'un contenu tout à fait différent. *Una excursión a los indios ranqueles,* de l'Argentin Lucio V. Mansilla, malgré le rôle très effacé de l'interlocuteur, en demeure un exemple. Mais la variante la plus remarquable de ce type de la méthode statique peut être trouvé dans les *Mémoires de deux jeunes mariées.* Louise ouvre son coeur à Renée qui, à son tour, lui ouvre le sien. L'une des amies écrit une trentaine de lettres, l'autre une vingtaine. *Confidence réciproque,* tel serait le titre technique du roman de Balzac, *double confidence,* celui du roman de Richardson.

Le type Werther qui offre tous les avantages du type Marianne présente comme lui quelques traits du journal intime et de la confession; mais il transcende l'un et l'autre de ces genres. Dans un cas, le lecteur est un indiscret qui furète dans les tiroirs du héros, le "diaire" n'étant destiné, en soi, qu'à satisfaire un besoin secret d'effusions égoïstes ou qu'à se consoler par les paroles du vieil Enée: "Forsan et haec olim meminisse juvabit"; dans l'autre cas le protagoniste s'ouvrant de propos délibéré à un public travesti en confident, le lecteur cesse de jouir de sa situation privilégiée: il lit une confession publique. L'écrivain peut obvier à ces deux inconvénients en se décidant pour le genre épistolaire. Pourtant, le roman du type Werther court aussi certains des dangers du journal— dangers que seul le génie du romancier saurait conjurer. Les événements étant relatés au jour le jour, pour demeurer vraisemblables, ils ne sauraient refléter la logique de l'auteur; celui-ci n'est pas supposé connaître le dénouement de l'histoire: l'architecte travaille, apparamment, sans plan. Le type Marianne—et notamment l'oeuvre de Marivaux elle-même, quoique restée inachevée— présente souvent la même sorte d'anticipations que l'on trouve dans l'antiquité, ou dans les récits du moyen âge: méthode qui consiste à dire, à l'instar de l'auteur de *Tristan et Yseult:* "Ne vous inquiétez pas outre mesure, ami lecteur, le méchant nain aura bientôt sa punition." A propos de Mlle de Varthon, Marianne remarque: "Vous allez voir dans un instant ce que c'était que cette preuve qu'elle s'engageait à me donner" (VIIIᵉ partie). Un peu plus loin, parlant de Mme Dorsin, elle s'exprime ainsi: "Elle avait trouvé un ancien ami de la maison, un officier, homme de qualité, d'un certain âge, et qui dans un moment va se faire connaître lui-même." La méthode est commune à celle des mémoires. Parlant de Geneviève, le *paysan parvenu* note: "Comme on le verra par la suite, ma saillie lui fit dans le coeur une blessure sourde dont je ne negligeai pas de m'assurer" (Ière partie). Ici et là le regard de l'auteur embrasse toute la trame; ce récit rétrospectif prend un caractère essentiellement organique. Les événements, non seulement sont narrés en fonction des faits passés, mais aussi bien en fonction des faits à venir. Pourtant en vertu de quelle grâce intuitive le héros écrivant au présent peut-il prévoir l'avenir et y conformer les événements de son récit? Pourquoi ne relater que ce qui a trait au dénouement? Ici encore, il s'agit de créer l'illusion. Les imperceptibles insinuations d'une oeuvre finissent par créer une atmosphère, et ne se comprennent, par l'intellect, qu'à la fin du roman. A la seconde lecture de *Werther,* on a la certitude, après dix pages, que le héros se suicidera—à la première lecture, on l'appréhende. L'oeuvre est supérieure par son étonnante unité. Cette impression est complètement absente de *Clarissa.* Issue incertaine jusqu'à la catastrophe. Aussi, avant que Richardson publie les deux derniers volumes, l'accable-t-on de billets. Les dames de Londres lui crient en choeur: "Spare Clarissa!" Plusieurs solutions étaient encore plausibles. Du point de vue du réalisme, Richardson demeure supérieur à Goethe. Qui l'emporte du point de vue artistique? Les débats restent ouverts.

Le roman de la méthode statique présente une troisième variante, le type Clinker. Il offre les caractéristiques suivantes. Plusieurs personnnages écrivent une même histoire, relatent des actions qui se complètent ou se succèdent. L'essentiel: ils jugent d'un angle différent. Toute la méthode de Smollett tend à faire éprouver au lecteur ce plaisir rare et délicieux: l'opinion spontanée de divers témoins au sujet d'un même fait ou de faits analogues, ou encore de faits liés entre eux par la logique ou la chronologie. Opinions qui s'opposent, se heurtent ou s'harmonisent. C'est bien ici tout l'intérêt spécifique du type. Le flirt amorcé entre Lydia et Wilson, l'épisode de Bath, les incidents de Londres, l'accident du coche, les aventures d'Edimbourg, autant d'événements dont la valeur est singulièrement rehaussée par les doubles descriptions, les multiples narrations que l'on pourrait disposer en synopse. S'il y a des réponses (il n'y en a pas dans l'oeuvre de Smollett) elles ne peuvent, d'ordinaire, être que moins significatives encore que dans le type Werther.[31] Communication à sens unique; la liste des correspondances illustrera cet aspect de l'oeuvre:

Matthew Bramble au Docteur Lewis	28 lettres
Jery Melford à Watkin Phillips	28 lettres
Lydia Melford à Laetitia Willis	9 lettres
Lydia Melford à Mrs. Jermyn	2 lettres
Win Jenkins à Mary Jones	10 lettres
Tabitha Bramble à Mrs. Gwyllim	5 lettres
Wilson à Lydia Melford	1 lettre

Notons deux messages et un poème inclus dans ces lettres, et nous arrivons, pour tout le roman, à un total de quatre-vingt-six documents.[32] Le vieux Bramble, d'une culture ostentatoire mais d'un délicieux bon sens, assaisonne ses missives de latinismes et ses raisonnements de traits d'esprit. Son neveu, Jery Melford, ne montre guère moins de vivacité; il prouve abondamment qu'à Oxford les leçons sont données dans la langue de Cicéron et ses discours comme ceux de son oncle sont émaillés de citations d'auteurs classiques. Style alerte, jugements dénués de maturité, mais jamais tout à fait faux; plus la trame avance, plus il semble perdre ses allures de snob. Sa soeur Lydia a reçu l'éducation soigneuse des jeunes filles de bonne famille. Impulsive, sentimentale, optimiste, elle écrit une langue un peu coupée, et si des fautes lui échappent, elle a ses dix-sept ans pour excuse et sa grande spontanéité. Quant à Tabitha, la soeur de Matthew, elle compte neuf lustres. Vierge *de jure* et surtout *de facto,* elle pense qu'à son âge il serait opportun de trouver un mari: aussi considère-t-elle l'Ile britannique comme un terrain de chasse où réaliser ses ambitions matrimoniales. Elle n'a nullement conscience de son inculture; elle ne sait pas l'orthographe, son style est prétentieux, ses verdicts tranchants et erronnés: personne égoïste et grincheuse qu'on apprend d'ailleurs à connaître bien mieux par les relations des autres correspondants que par les siennes. Mary Jenkins, elle, n'est que la servante. Son langage? au moins divertissant. "O Molly!" s'écrie-t-elle. "What shall I say of London? All the towns that ever I beheld in my born-days, are no more than Welsh Barrows and crumlecks to this wonderful sitty!" [33] Vaniteuse, elle se fait couper les cheveux "by a French freezer," affectueuse, elle ne manque pas "the importunity" d'écrire à son amie qu'elle s'empresse de saluer "with true infection." Voilà nos épistoliers. On est tenté de donner raison à Buffon: le style est l'homme même. A lire les lettres des héros, on devine leur attitude en face des événements. C'est eux qui nous font connaître le véritable caractère des personnages dans *The Expedition of Humphry Clinker,* tel que leur style nous l'avait fait pressentir.

Les *Lettres persanes* sont du même type. Dans ces missives les héros ne s'affrontent guère: Usbek écrit une lettre à Roxane qui lui en envoie deux. L'intrigue, du reste est des plus minces et l'oeuvre peut à peine être comptée parmi les romans—pas plus d'ailleurs que quelques autres oeuvres mentionnées dans ces pages. Mais acceptons le genre tel qu'il est défini au début du XVIIIᵉ siècle. Qu'est-ce qui fait le fond de l'oeuvre de Montesquieu? Une critique, menée sur deux plans, des institutions et moeurs de Paris. Usbek et Rica se chargent de cette tâche: l'un écrit soixante-dix-sept lettres, l'autre, quarante-huit,[34] et l'on notera qu'ils ont tous deux leur ami personnel (Rhédi pour l'un, M.*** pour autre), mais aussi un confident commun, Ibben. Ces amis lointains ne répondent guère. Le fait que Rica, installé à Paris mande quinze lettres à Usbek parti pour la campagne n'altère point le caractère général de l'oeuvre qui est du type Clinker: même technique, de part et d'autre, qui cause au lecteur un plaisir analogue. Voici les principales correspondances:

Usbek à Rhédi (Venise)	29 lettres
Usbek à Ibben (Smyrne)	13 lettres
Rica à Ibben (Smyrne)	11 lettres
Rica à *** (s.l.)	18 lettres
Rica à Usbek (s.l.)	15 lettres

Ces quatre-vingt-six lettres—on a trouvé ce chiffre dans l'oeuvre de Smollett— donnent des jugements et des critiques à propos de faits et d'idées du même ordre. Leurs auteurs contribuent, à parts égales, à former chez le lecteur une opinion précise de Paris et de ses habitants, de la France et de ses institutions. Nous avons donc bien affaire au type du multiple témoignage, type éminemment propre à consolider chez le lecteur l'impression de vérité. Il faut rappeler ici que *The Citizen of the World,* publié quarante ans après l'oeuvre de Montesquieu et si proche de celle-ci par les idées et la trame, représente un autre type de roman épistolaire, le type Werther. Un seul témoignage est invoqué, celui de Lien Chi Altangi, philosophe chinois qui, installé à Londres, écrit de là quatre-vingt-douze lettres à son compatriote demeuré dans le pays, Fum Hoam, ainsi que onze lettres à son fils Hingpo. Il ne reçoit de ces deux correspondants que douze réponses en tout, qui ne font nullement avancer la trame et n'enlèvent aucunement au livre son caractère de roman-confidence. Certes, l'objet de cette confidence, pas plus que dans les *Lettres persanes,* n'est point, comme dans *Werther,* une tragédie intime, mais la comédie de Londres. Du reste, les romans satires sont presque toujours du type statique: la trame n'étant guère d'importance, on voit mal quel antagoniste les narrateurs pourraient affronter. Même pour *Les Lettres d'Amabed,* où pourtant l'action tient une place considérable, mais veulent essentiellement être une critique de la société, Voltaire se décide pour la méthode qui sera celle de Goethe. Trente et une lettres sont envoyées à Shastasid. Amabed ne se fait remplacer, dans cette correspondance, que sept fois, par sa femme Adate. On voit encore la même technique dans *Cartas Marruecas.*[35] Gazel, voyageur maure qui explore la presqu'île ibérique, censure les moeurs espagnoles du temps dans soixante-neuf lettres,[36] la plupart adressées à Ben-Beley. Dans sa préface, José de Cadalso se réclame de Montesquieu. Mais il est clair que l'architecture de l'ouvrage est celle de Voltaire et de Goldsmith. En revanche, celle de Smollett-Montesquieu est reprise dans *Julia de Roubigné* de Henry Mackenzie, dans *The Dodd Family Abroad* de Charles Lever, et encore dans les deux petits romans épistolaires de Henry James: *The Point of View* et *A Bundle of Letters.*

*   *

*

L'auteur optant pour le type statique le fait pour des raisons précises. J'ai déjà commenté sa spéculation d'artiste: le lecteur est appelé à se substituer au destinataire de ses lettres; il se sent le confident du héros, à qui, en retour, il prête toute son attention, sinon toute sa sympathie. Il ne s'agit pas de débattre une idée, de justifier un sentiment: la faire comprendre, le faire partager, voilà le but de l'épistolier.

Mais voici un écrivain plus agressif: il se décide pour la discussion, pour le combat. Non pas avec un ami choisi pour confident—la partie serait inégale [37]— mais avec l'antagoniste lui-même. Il est clair que l'effet produit sur le lecteur par un tel procédé est d'une autre nature. Les personnages principaux, loin de se plaindre ou de se vanter, s'affrontent. Le héros, cessant de parler *de* son antagoniste, parle *à* son antagoniste. La trame, au lieu de progresser *dans* les lettres, progresse *par* les lettres. C'est du choc produit par elles que jaillit l'étincelle enflammant les esprits et les coeurs: la méthode est cinétique, dynamique. Non que l'action demeure purement extérieure: il peut s'agir du développement d'une passion sourde, tout comme de l'intrigue la plus raffinée. Alors que pour le roman du type statique, comme on l'a vu, la réponse du confident n'a souvent point d'intérêt majeur, ici, elle est essentielle. Essentiel peut-être aussi est le fait de n'avoir point de réponse.

Le premier type de cette méthode cinétique est le *type portugais*. On aura compris que je désigne ainsi les romans composés selon la technique suivie dans les *Lettres de la religieuse portugaise,* publiées parfois avec le titre de *Lettres portugaises.* Le petit livre qu'on a attribué tour à tour à Mariana Alcoforado et au comte de Guilleragues, qu'on a pris tantôt pour une traduction et tantôt pour une oeuvre originellement composée en français, garde une place à part dans la littérature passionnelle du vieux continent.[38] Cri de l'amour trompé, de la femme abandonnée,[39] prête à souffrir plutôt que de renoncer à sa passion; cri sans écho et sans apaisement. Mariana cessera d'écrire, mais non pas d'aimer: la rupture sera éternelle, mais cette âme semble, en dernièr analyse, imperméable à la haine.[40] Correspondance unilatérale quoiqu'il soit fait allusion à une réponse du cavalier, réponse froide, évasive, propre à exacerber la souffrance de la nonne. Décor réaliste, d'ailleurs, mais auquel on ne prend guère garde. Doña Brites, la supérieure, ainsi que des religieuses, puis le frère de Mariana, un officier français enfin, apparaissent dans la correspondance qui ne se compose que de cinq lettres. Des événements historiques, des allusions à des faits vérifiables par le lecteur frappent l'oeuvre au coin de l'actualité, confèrent l'illusion de l'expérience vécue. L'illusion? Question toujours litigieuse.

La méthode est particulièrement propre à l'analyse d'une passion mise à sa plus rude épreuve. Technique bien différente de celle dont se sert le journal: ici, c'est le récit, là, le fait; ici, le hèros révèle, explique ses sentiments, là, ils brûlent, ils éclatent; ici, la passion est narrée, décrite, là, elle justifie son nom: elle est souffrance. Elle s'étale avec tous ses illogismes; flux et reflux de réminiscences et de rêves, de jugements et d'émotions, de questions et de réponses, de décisions et d'irrésolutions, de remords et de désespoirs. L'agencement même des cinq lettres[41] ne tend guère à développer une véritable trame. Il marque les phases d'un conflit intime qui culmine dans cette révélation: "J'ai éprouvé que vous m'étiez moins cher que ma passion" (lettre V). Méthode éminemment propre à prendre sur le vif les mouvements de l'âme.

La méthode, dans le principe, n'était pas nouvelle. On en peut trouver les éléments essentiels dans les *Confessions* de saint Augustin. Dieu, dans cette oeuvre, n'est pas le confident d'un récit autobiographique. Elles sont un acte d'adoration: longue prière de l'âme mystique, aux prises avec la grâce. C'est le ton du vocatif, dès le commencement: "Magnus es, Domine, et laudabilis valde"; et ce ton est maintenu dans tout l'ouvrage: "Tu, Deus misericordiarum." A chaque page, un appel, une prière.[42] Le héros s'adresse bel et bien à l'antagoniste qui, dans le livre même, ne répond point. L'ouvrage peut donc, quoique l'auteur n'ait point choisi la forme épistolaire, être rapproché, du point de vue de la méthode, du roman par lettres du type portugais. Chez saint Augustin, la confession a gardé son sens chrétien. Voyez Rousseau: il entre au confessionnal pour y faire davantage que son autobiographie: son apologie; ici, "self-justification," là, "justification" au sens théologique du terme. Le ton de la sincérité que l'on perçoit à toutes les pages des *Confessions* de Jean-Jacques

.explique le titre: mais elles demeurent sans pénitence . . . et, pour quelques critiques, sans absolution. Dans l'autre cas, il s'agit d'épanchements: les *Herzensergiessungen eines kunstliebenden Klosterbruders* prouvent que du temps de Wackenroder le genre jouissait de la faveur du public. On peut ici noter la différence entre deux autres sortes de romans. Dans la préface à son livre *Of Human Bondage,* l'auteur déclare que l'oeuvre "is not an autobiography, but an autobiographical novel; fact and fiction [on est dans l'ambiance *Dichtung und Wahrheit*] are inextricably mingled." Mais le genre ne dicte pas la personne à laquelle l'oeuvre doit être composée: Maugham écrit à la troisième personne, Goethe à la première.

La plupart des imitateurs des *Lettres portugaises,* tant en Angleterre qu'en France, en adoptèrent aussi la méthode architecturale. L'emploi n'en fut pas toujours très heureux. Crébillon fils, dans ses *Lettres de la marquise de M*** au comte de R**** (1732) transpose l'histoire de soeur Mariana du couvent au salon. Soixante-dix lettres adressées au héros dont les rares réponses ne sont connues du lecteur qu'à travers des allusions qu'y fait la maîtresse délaissée. Roman incolore n'est mentionné ici que pour rapprocher la technique de celle de ce chef-d'oeuvre que restent les *Lettres portugaises,* dans son texte originel, certes, mais aussi dans la traduction de Rainer Maria Rilke.

Ce roman peut encore être considéré comme le modèle des *Lettres d'une Péruvienne.* On peut comparer les deux ouvrages pour leur méthode surtout, la qualité de la composition, et pour leur retentissement. Les *Lettres péruviennes* ont toutes Zilia pour auteur; trente-six d'entre elles sont adressées au prince Aza, cinq au chevalier français Déterville. La trame, ici encore, a décidé du type. Aza infidèle ne répond pas. Reçoit-il même les missives déchirantes de celle qui l'aime? "Cette horrible pensée affaiblit mon courage, gémit Zilia, sans rompre le dessein que j'ai à continuer à t'écrire. Je conserve mon illusion pour te conserver la vie." La monotonie, ici, est rompue par l'intrigue Déterville, mais surtout par les descriptions des moeurs parisiennes.[43] Zilia, parfois, se révèle être un Usbek, un Rica féminin. Dès qu'elle met le pied sur le vieux continent, elle parle moins de son amour pour se tourner davantage vers le peuple de Paris et dans un français trop XVIIIe siècle pour être d'une Péruvienne qui apprend la langue en six mois. Le roman mêle donc deux éléments d'ordinaire si délicats à unir: le lyrisme et la satire. Il eût fallu un génie supérieur à celui de Madame de Graffigny pour le faire avec bonheur. Mais elle avait pour elle le goût du temps.

Avantage essentiel de la méthode épistolaire: à l'époque où les principes aristotéliciens continuent à perdre de leur vigueur, elle rendait enfin possible le mélange des genres. Les *Lettres péruviennes* (1747) nous montrent un exemple de mélange de tons. Dans les romans du type Laclos on verra ce qu'Auerbach appelle le nivellement des *Höhenlagen:* dans la même oeuvre, une Cécile et une Madame de Tourvel font de Valmont tour à tour un personnage comique et un personnage tragique. Mais revenons au type portugais. Le héros vit de souvenirs et d'espoirs, se nourrit de sa passion: dès que celle-ci s'affaiblit, la trame languit. Et le roman dynamique vient alors à manquer singulièrement de dynamisme. Le héros cesse de provoquer son partenaire, il reste sur le plan de l'exposé, lui communique des impressions, lui fait part de ses opinions, approuve ou condamne. De cinétique qu'elle était dans son principe, elle dégénère en la méthode statique: l'antagoniste devient confident.

C'est notamment le cas des *Lettres à une inconnue*. Ici, la trame est des plus insignifiante. Disons-le tout de suite: nous avons affaire à une oeuvre fort médiocre. Signée de Prosper Mérimée, elle mérite d'être notée malgré la fadeur insupportable de la plupart des trois cent trente-deux missives envoyées de tous les coins de l'Europe. Rhapsodie indigeste que la préface de Taine n'améliore point et qui se prolonge durant vingt-huit ans, ce roman sans action aucune, ni extérieure ni intérieure, fut pourtant traduit en anglais;[44] c'était la priver, avec une partie de cette aisance stylistique dont Mérimée possédait le secret, de sa seule utilité: les jeunes filles d'outre-Manche, le lisant en français, pourraient y prendre le ton épistolaire d'une certaine société cultivée ou snobe. Le lecteur s'aperçoit très vite qu'il s'agit d'une correspondance qui a réellement passé par un bureau de poste. Il y a un souci du concret, de l'actuel, du journalier qui ne se trouve guère dans une oeuvre de pure imagination. Richardson déjà était conscient de l'importance des dates; elles marquent, telles les pages d'un almanach, l'écoulement du temps. Voyez donc la précision de Mérimée: "Saint-Lupicien, le 15 août 1843, au soir, à 600 mètres au-dessus de la mer. Au milieu d'un océan de puces très agiles et très affamées." On tombe dans un bavardage insupportable qui nous fait regretter jusqu'aux langoureux épanchements de la tendre Clarissa. Mais revenons à la méthode. Dans le cas de Mérimée, elle conduit à la désintégration du genre épistolaire. Elle représente le point de fusion entre l'oeuvre d'imagination et une certaine correspondance réelle, celle qui consiste, non pas à dire quelque chose, mais tout simplement à jaser. La "Mariquita de mi alma," comme l'auteur aime à appeler la destinataire de ses missives, semblerait appelée à être l'âme mystérieuse du livre, le centre d'intérêt, le personnage absent qui conférerait à l'ouvrage son unité. Elle est moins qu'une ombre, une parfaite inconnue.[45] De tant de sujets amorcés aucun n'est traité; le ton seul confère au volume une certaine homogénéité.

Le type portugais est choisi parfois par des auteurs contemporains, tel Saul Bellow. *Herzog,* dont la technique mériterait hautement d'être étudiée dans le détail, est loin d'être un pur roman épistolaire. Outre les six billets que le protagoniste s'adresse à lui-même, l'oeuvre renferme cinquante-quatre lettres à des personnages qui ne répondront jamais;[46] quelques-uns d'entre eux pourraient alléguer une raison fort valable pour leur silence: ils sont morts. Messages à Heidegger,[47] à Teilhard de Chardin, au général Eisenhower, à Spinoza, à Nietzsche, à Nehru, à Martin Luther King, à Dieu même. Une phrase explique le choix de la méthode: "I've been writing letters helter-skelter in all directions," dit le héros. "More words. I go after reality with language. Perhaps I'd like to change it all into language to force Madeleine and Gersbach to have a *Conscience.*"[48] Une pensée analogue s'exprime dans *Briefwechsel zwischen zwei Zimmerwinkeln:* "Ich schreibe, weil so der Gedanke voller klingt und deutlicher vernommen wird—wie ein Laut in der Stille."[49] Un des buts du genre est clairement exprimé: quand le verbe s'incarne, il devient plus vrai. Il y a un sérieux, dans l'échange de lettres, qu'on ne sent pas toujours dans l'échange de paroles: verba volant, scripta manent. Et voilà bien le sentiment que produisent notamment les lettres imaginaires du roman de Bellow. Au lieu de s'interroger, par la méthode introspective, sur le sens de tel passage de livre, de telle politique d'un gouvernant, Herzog interpelle l'auteur, qu'il se nomme Rozanov, il aborde le "Governor," qu'il se nomme Stevenson. L'oeuvre prouve que le type portugais est susceptible d'usages fort divers, dont le meilleur sans doute demeure la révélation d'un état d'âme: par une plainte, par un cri.

Une lettre appelle une réponse: le genre de roman épistolaire le plus naturel serait donc celui dans lequel le protagoniste et l'antagoniste, au lieu de s'affronter dans un récit, s'affrontent par une correspondance réciproque. C'est le type Abélard. Il est clair que l'accent n'est pas nécessairement mis sur l'action extérieure, à laquelle, comme dans le roman du type portugais, l'auteur peut substituer une action intérieure: accords ou contrastes de pensées et de sentiments, souvenirs communs ou projets divergeants, discussions ou disputes, désirs ou renoncements. Cette classe de roman est essentiellement dialogue entre les deux principaux personnages: *Le Neveu de Rameau* qui consisterait en un échange de lettres. Il n'est nullement surprenant que le livre-type se fonde sur une correspondance réelle: la correspondance d'Abélard, en effect, comprend une autobiographie, malheureusement incomplète, cinq lettres à Héloïse, une à saint Bernard et cinq autres lettres.[50] Bussy-Robutin publia en français les lettres des deux amants en 1697 et, à Londres, après qu'on y avait vu paraître, en 1708, une traduction anglaise. L'oeuvre eut, sur le continent européen comme dans les Iles britanniques un succès comparable à celui des *Lettres portugaises:* à leur exemple, elle contribua à l'extraordinaire essor que le genre prit au cours du XVIIIᵉ siècle, essor qui se prolongea dans certains pays jusqu'au siècle suivant. Le type Abélard fut adopté notamment par Dostoïevsky pour l'oeuvre qui fonda sa renommée: *Bednye lyudi* (*Pauvres gens*) terminée en 1845. En tout cinquante-cinq lettres: trente et une de Makar Dievushkin à Barbara Dobrosolova, et vingt-quatre de celle-ci à celui-là. Ce n'est pas l'histoire d'une passion, mais d'une amitié. On pourrait se demander dans quelle mesure le romancier russe qui, en 1844, avait achevé la traduction d'*Eugénie Grandet,* s'est laissé influencer par les *Mémoires de deux jeunes mariées:* à première vue, il y a analogie de méthode. Mais il est clair que les deux épouses, quoique amies, ont chacune son propre antagoniste, le mari, et les lettres qu'elles s'écrivent portent un caractère de confidence; Makar et Barbara, au contraire, bien que n'ayant point de conflit dramatique et bruyant à liquider entre eux, font figure de héros principaux, non pas indépendamment l'un de l'autre, mais l'un en fonction de l'autre. Le premier joue dans la vie de la seconde un rôle éminemment actif: ils se révèlent l'un à l'autre, il est vrai,[51] mais ils vivent, dans le roman, l'un par l'autre: la trame est fonction des rapports qui les lient: méthode cinétique.

Elle est portée à sa perfection dans le roman du type Laclos. *Les Liaisons dangereuses*[52] s'opposent au type portugais et au type Abélard. Alors que le premier est essentiellement monologue, et le second dialogue, le type Laclos est ce que j'appellerais volontiers *polylogue.* C'est bien autour de la liaison Valmont-Merteuil que se groupent tous les événements: unité dans la diversité, telle est la principale caractéristique du roman, de tout roman de ce type. Pourtant, le vicomte et la marquise ont leurs intrigues propres; en fin de compte, cependant, tous les fils se réunissent à leur secrétaire, dans leurs lettres à eux. Celles-ci fusent dans toutes les directions: Mme de Merteuil est en rapport avec quatre correspondants, de même que Valmont et Mme de Volanges; la Présidente avec trois, ainsi que Cécile; Danceny avec cinq et Mme de Rosemonde avec deux. Ces personnages, que l'on peut considérer comme essentiels pour le développement de l'action, signent en tout cent soixante-huit lettres sur les cent soixante-quinze que renferme la roman. Valmont, Mme de Merteuil, la Présidente, Cécile, Danceny, Mme de Volanges, Mme de Rose-monde écrivent respectivement cinquant et une, vingt-sept, vingt-cinq, vingt-quatre, dix-neuf, treize et neuf lettres. Ces chiffres suggèrent au moins deux remarques. A supposer que les missives de Valmont et de Mme de Merteuil soient à peu près de la même longueur—et on peut dire qu'elles le sont—on serait tenté de croire que le rôle du premier dans la trame est deux fois plus important que celui de la seconde. Il n'en est rien. Ces rôles sont parfaitement équilibrés. Ces chiffres montrent tout simplement que la Marquise décide et que le Vicomte agit: ici, pouvoir exécutif, là, pouvoir législatif. Le nombre de lettres n'indique pas nécessairement l'importance du rôle que le signataire joue dans l'histoire. Seconde remarque: ces chiffres à eux seuls indiquent une action complexe, une bataille menée à la fois sur plusieurs fronts: caractéristique de ce type. *Les Liaisons dangereuses* représentent bien, du point de vue méthodo-logique, le modèle de son genre. Un drame se déroule entre le vicomte et la marquise; c'est le drame principal, qui donne le sens à l'oeuvre; mais d'autres drames se lient à celui-là, eux accessoires, joués entre Valmont et la Présidente, Danceny et Cécile, sans compter les interférences: Valmont se charge de Cécile, la marquise, de Danceny. Toutes ces actions sont simultanées et peuvent aisément l'être, grâce, précisément, à la méthode épistolaire. Le lecteur, tout naturellement, accepte un classement des lettres, celui que l'éditeur lui propose; le facteur les apporte dans cet ordre. Un problème capital de l'art du récit trouve ainsi sa solution: dire deux choses, plusieurs choses à la fois. L'action de *Tom Jones* est tout aussi imbriquée que celle des *Liaisons*. Mais Fielding ne saurait raconter simultanément les aventures de Mr. Jones et celles de Lady Sophia. Aussi éprouve-t-on très souvent l'impression d'une sorte de décalage entre les événements qui, pourtant, eurent lieu au même moment. A quel procédé, alors, Fielding a-t-il recours? Il invite tout simplement le lecteur à jeter un coup d'oeil en arrière. Regardons ces titres de chapitres: "Wherein the history goes back. . . ," "In which the history goes backward," "In which the history is obliged to look back." L'unité de l'ouvrage n'en souffre guère, ici, grâce à l'incomparable génie de l'auteur.[53] Son précurseur Lesage en revanche, ne nous présente qu'un roman épisodique. C'est qu'il n'a pas trouvé de méthode pour présenter en même temps plusieurs faits, n'a pas su les emboîter les uns dans les autres. Trop de personnages entrent en scène sans autre raison apparente que le hasard, et la quittent pour jamais après avoir amusé ou instruit le parterre. Le roman épistolaire du type des *Liaisons* résout ce problème de la narration simultanée, qui jusque-là semblait la quadrature du cercle; ici, le génie de Laclos est incomparable. Deux événements coïncident dans le temps, mais non dans l'espace; le roman épistolaire les rapproche de la façon la plus naturelle, le courrier distribué tous les jours arrivant des quatre coins du monde.

Laclos, pour sa méthode, eut son précurseur, Rousseau. Remarquons que *La Nouvelle Héloïse* contient exactement le même nombre de lettres que *Les Liaisons dangereuses:* soixante-neuf (plus trois fragments) de Saint-Preux, soixante et une de Julie, vingt-cinq de Claire, et neuf de Milord Edouard. Quatre personnages secondaires écrivent les huit lettres qui manquent pour arriver au total de cent soixante-quinze. On voit tout de suite que la méthode est entièrement différente de celle de Richardson, qui ne permet guère à ses héros de dire ce qu'ils pensent l'un de l'autre que dans des lettres à des tiers. Mais Jean-Jacques, lui, ne construit-il point son oeuvre selon le plan Abélard? Le titre même de l'oeuvre semble l'insinuer. Et, en fait, les trois quarts de toutes les lettres consistent en une prise de contact directe entre Julie et Saint-Preux. Pourtant, à y regarder de plus près, tant pour le développement des caractères, que pour les progrès de l'intrigue, celles de Claire et d'Edouard sont indispensables. Elles ne portent pas seulement un caractère de confidences. Il y a même superposées à l'histoire principale, des actions secondaires. Bref, le roman de Jean-Jacques contient déjà tous les éléments distinctifs dont se constituera celui de Laclos, et c'est bien parmi les oeuvres de ce type qu'il faut le classer. *La Nouvelle Héloïse* illustre fort bien, du reste, qu'un certain type peut se réaliser d'une façon plus ou moins parfaite: cette réalisation du type idéal n'a évidemment aucun rapport avec la perfection esthétique de l'oeuvre; la proportion d'éléments propres à tel ou tel type dont se compose l'oeuvre dépend hautement des intentions de l'auteur, de la nature de la trame, et une même action peut être narrée selon des méthodes différentes; mais ainsi le ton même du roman se nuancera et par là aussi l'effet produit chez le lecteur.[54]

Il n'est pas étonnant que Mme de Staël, cette fervente disciple de Jean-Jacques, se soit à son tour arrêtée, pour son premier roman, au type choisi par son maître, un type dont cependant elle n'épuise pas davantage que lui les nombreuses possibilités. Les quinze correspondants que Germaine mobilise pour sa *Delphine* écrivent en tout deux cent vingt-trois lettres—et l'héroïne, derrière laquelle évidemment se cache—très mal—l'auteur, signe à elle seule plus de la moitié d'entre elles.[55] Nombreuses sont celles qui portent un caractère purement confidentiel. (Soixante-deux lettres son adressées à sa belle-soeur, Mlle d'Albémar.) Mais Leonce en recoit dix-huit, et des plus importantes pour l'évolution de l'intrigue, et celui-ci en envoie vingt-cinq à sa partenaire, ainsi que seize à Barton, son ancien précepteur, par lesquelles, de nouveau, on a recours à la méthode passive. On le voit: dans ce roman les éléments propres au type Werther jouent un rôle plus continu, plus décisif que dans *La Nouvelle Héloïse*. D'ailleurs, dans bien des oeuvres du type dynamique, certaines lettres revêtent un caractère mixte. Et, pour revenir à Laclos, remarquons l'exemple de la lettre LXXXI. Elle est une des plus longues du livre et représente essentiellement une autobiographie de Madame de Merteuil. Pourtant toute la première page est la réponse à une lettre reçue, réponse qui amène la confidence. Dans l'oeuvre de Madame de Staël, des actions superposées se développent, partiellement, grâce à des lettres reçues et écrites par les agents du drame. *Delphine* participe au type Laclos.[56]

*   *

*

Le roman épistolaire intéresse-t-il toujours l'écrivain et le public? Infiniment moins que jadis. On pourrait, certes, dresser toute une liste d'oeuvres écrites dans le genre durant les cent dernières années. J'ai déjà mentionné Herzog; rappelons, de Wilder, *The Ides of March,* intégralement épistolaire; et l'on sait combien populaire a été *Daddy-Long-Legs,* de Jean Webster. Mais il ne faut pas oublier *Les Jeunes filles* de Montherlant; et pourquoi ne pas citer deux excellents livres: *Briefe, die ihn nicht erreichten,* d'Elisabeth von Heyking, et *Der letzte Sommer,* de Ricarda Huch? Et l'on peut aussi se souvenir d'un ouvrage qui garde sa place bien définie dans la littérature espagnole: *Pepita Jiménez,* de Valera. Comment peut-on encore être dans la tradition werthérienne un siècle après la publication du roman de Goethe? Voilà posé un problème d'évolution littéraire qui mériterait d'être étudié dans le cadre du comparatisme. Il est aussi d'autres romans dont la formule, quoique n'étant pas strictement épistolaire, semble dériver du roman par lettres: dans *Dracula* (1897), à côté de lettres, d'entrefilets de journaux il y a, comme éléments importants, des extraits de diaires de personnages différents, dont une partie phonographique— de Seward, parlé par Van Nelsing. Ces extraits, du point de vue technique, jouent le même rôle que des lettres missives envoyées à des confidents; et l'on pourrait rapprocher le roman de Stoker de celui, plus récent d'Auchincloss, *The Rector of Justin.* Dans *Ich an Dich* (1950), que je ne cite pas pour sa valeur littéraire, l'auteur, Dinah Nelken, raconte un flirt au moyen de tickets de chemin de fer, de billets de wagon-lit, de cartes de cinéma, de factures d'essence: souci d'une certaine documentation, mais qui n'était pas celle dont pouvait se préoccuper le XVIIIe siècle.[57] De nombreux romans contemporains, comme *Le Dîner en ville,* de Claude Mauriac, comme *Up the Down Staircase,* de Bel Kaufman, posent et résolvent des problèmes structuraux analogues à ceux qu'il y a deux cents ans s'étaient posés, qu'avaient résolus à leur manière les Richardson, les Rousseau et les Goethe.

Le roman par lettres proprement dit tend à disparaître sous le nombre effrayant des romans d'autres types, romans qui se multiplient année par année. Il est clair qu'à la longue le public trouverait le récit épistolaire lassant. Ce qui en est resté, c'est le goût du dialogue; mais il faut voir là aussi une influence du théâtre sur le genre narratif. Ce qui a survécu, encore, c'est l'habitude assez répandue d'insérer des lettres dans un roman écrit soit à la première, soit à la troisième personne. Dans *Vanity Fair* de Thackeray, par exemple, ces lettres prennent de l'importance, dans la première partie, pour le progrès de l'action; dans *Martin Rivas,* d'Alberto Blest Gana, des missives contribuent à hâter le dénouement. Ce rôle de la lettre est encore illustré par tels romans de Kierkegaard.[58] Genre mixte: au XVIIIe siècle et durant le premier quart du XIXe, les Allemands l'ont pratiqué, plus volontiers que d'autres nations, et avec succès. Ils avaient *Werther* pour exemple. Goethe fait intervenir l'éditeur à la dernière partie du second livre, où il le charge de narrer des faits essentiels pour le dénouement. Evidemment, le jeune homme "im blauen Rock mit gelber Weste" qui, baigné dans son sang, se mourait étendu sur le plancher de sa chambre, n'était plus guère en état de communiquer à Wilhelm ses impressions. Il fallait une intervention. Mais l'éditeur, à son tour, parle à la première personne une certaine unité de ton étant ainsi garantie.

Autre détail technique: un esprit nouveau, on le sait, souffle dans *Werther,* celui d'Ossian. Il était souhaitable et naturel de donner la parole au héros nordique. Le long texte de Macpherson, du point de vue de la méthode, est un interlude, mais jamais interlude n'a été plus significatif pour l'ensemble d'une oeuvre.[59] Du reste, *Das Leben der schwedischen Gräfin von G****, qui nous remet au temps des romans de Richardson—auteur que Gellert se plaît d'ailleurs à imiter—est également du genre mixte. Puis, la tradition sera continuée, par *Der Geisterseher* de Schiller, *Ardinghello* de Heinse, *Godwi* de Brentano, et en 1833 on verra encore *Das junge Europa,* de Heinrich Laube, appliquer la formule. On est tenté de dire que la littérature allemande représente surtout le type du roman semi-épistolaire. De même pourrait-on observer en France une tendance marquée vers le type cinétique,[60] alors que le type statique est représenté bien plus fréquemment en Angleterre. Ces constatations inviteraient à tirer quelque conclusion générale sur des tendances structurales dans ces trois littératures; pour ce faire, il faudrait de beaucoup élargir les prémisses que peut exposer un simple article.

D'autres remarques s'imposent au terme de cette étude. En la commençant, j'ai insisté sur les avantages que voyaient dans le roman épistolaire ses promoteurs. Il faut à présent mettre en relief les inconvénients inhérents au genre, lesquels ont déterminé le monde des romanciers à le negliger, sinon à l'abandonner. Et tout d'abord, il y a, de cette évolution, des raisons évidentes. Au XIXe siècle, quelques-unes des causes qui avaient favorisé l'éclosion du roman épistolaire s'avéraient parfaitement inopérants. Les quotidiens se multipliaient, et dès le second tiers du siècle on se mettait à construire, dans les îles britanniques tout comme sur le continent, un réseau de chemin de fer qui était destiné à rapprocher même les héros de romans. Une correspondance suivie, sur un thème donné, une action jouée dans une enveloppe dans bien des cas devenait hautement improbable. De plus, les conventions sociales perdaient de leur élégance. Il devenait ridicule de se passer des billets—à la manière des héros de Mademoiselle de Montpensier,[61] ou encore de quelques-uns des plus illustres hôtes de Coppet—de chambre à chambre, alors qu'on pouvait transmettre le message par un regard, par un mot de vive voix glissé au salon entre un compliment et un bon mot, placé, à la salle à manger, entre une tranche de williams et une bouchée de gruyère. Mais le déclin du genre a des causes bien plus sérieuses; elles me paraissent être au nombre de trois.

J'ai parlé de la théorie de Richardson. Il pensait que le sentiment de la vraisemblance et de l'immédiat était produit surtout par un texte composé "while the heart is agitated by hopes and fears." J'ai cité la satire de Fielding: or, l'histoire littéraire et le bon sens donnent raison à Fielding. Le *writing to the moment* est basé sur une psychologie toute conventionnelle. Quand le coeur du héros est encore agité, celui-ci ne prend pas encore la plume. Il ne se confie même pas à un ami, il se regarde d'abord lui-même: débat intérieur, auquel ne se mêlent ni date ni signature. La tendre Clarissa, aujourd'hui, nous apparaît comme une grande malade. On ne l'aime que si on oublie son intolérable scriptomanie, en d'autres termes, si on oublie que son histoire appartient au genre épistolaire. Le genre, décidément, n'était qu'un moyen pour atteindre une fin: conférer au roman la vraisemblance; l'on y arriva par les moyens les plus invraisemblables—aux yeux du lecteur contemporain. Songeons à l'exemple bien connu de la lettre écrite par Saint-Preux dans le cabinet de Julie, et nous comprendrons à quel point les auteurs de romans épistolaires pouvaient devenir les victimes de leur propre système. Les "instantaneous descriptions and reflections" étaient en elles-mêmes hautement vraisemblables, mais rendues "at the least appropriate moment." Ainsi ce que le fond gagnait en vraisemblance, la forme le faisait perdre incontinent.[62]

Le genre comporte un second désavantage fort grave. Il suppose que les auteurs des lettres soient éloignés les uns des autres. Or, ils sont souvent les héros principaux, notamment dans les romans du type Laclos. A-t-on assez remarqué que Valmont ne rencontre jamais la marquise au cours des quatre cents pages du roman?[63] Les personnages, à l'occasion, se plaignent de cette absence, que l'auteur doit prolonger artificiellement pour sauver la méthode. C'est ainsi que Benedikt écrit à Ardinghello: "Ich möchte mich lieber mit Dir einige Augenblicke mündlich unterhalten als in dem längsten, triftigsten Buchstabenwechsel." Et Ardinghello confesse à son ami: "Ich muss Cäcilien selbst sehen und sprechen, mit Briefen ist's nicht getan." L'antagoniste en présence du protagoniste peut, dans un simple récit à la troisième personne, conférer au lecteur un sentiment d'immédiateté supérieur à celui qu'il éprouve en lisant leurs messages, quelque directs qu'ils soient. Pour certaines trames, du reste, la méthode épistolaire n'est tout simplement pas appliquable—à moins de choisir la technique du type Marianne dont, par ailleurs, les avantages, pour bien des cas, demeurent douteux. Richardson pensait qu'une lettre communiquait un sentiment aussi spontané ou plus spontané peut-être que la conversation. Et l'étude, même de la société française du XVIIIe siècle, peut lui donner partiellement raison: l'emprise des conventions sur la conversation avait longtemps gardé un caractère tyrannique. Cependant, une lettre elle aussi exprime toujours un sentiment qui a passé—parfois fort rapidement il est vrai—par la partie raisonnante de notre être. Il faut le mettre dans une certaine forme, fût-elle négligée. D'autre part, la conversation, le dialogue, si formels dans les salons, perdaient peu à peu leur solemnité, et déjà vers 1750 s'étaient multipliés, en France comme ailleurs, les écrivains, qui, souvent issus des classes moyennes, refusaient d'accepter dans leur vie et dans leurs oeuvres le style aristocratique. Depuis *Le Neveu de Rameau*—qui devra longtemps rester inaccessible au public français—ils savaient rendre la conversation vivante et naturelle, alerte et directe. Si l'on avait à décider de quel côté se trouve généralement plus de spontanéité, dans la lettre ou dans le dialogue, je n'hésiterais pas, en songeant aux oeuvres du XIXe siècle, à répondre: dans le second.

Une troisième raison sérieuse, d'ordre technique, a contribué à discréditer le roman épistolaire. En 1776, Marmontel écrivait ces lignes: "Un récit qui ne serait qu'un enchaînement d'aventures, sans cette tendance commune qui les réunit en un point et les conduit à l'unité, ce récit serait un roman et ne serait pas un conte." [64] La question de l'unité, quoi qu'en pense l'auteur du *Nouveau Dictionnaire,* a toujours préoccupé, à des degrés divers, les meilleurs romanciers d'Europe.[65] Mais, et en cela Marmontel a raison, elle n'avait pas l'importance qu'elle a prise, dans les lettres occidentales, au début du XIXe siècle. Or, si l'on excepte le type Marianne, la méthode épistolaire devrait interdire à l'auteur de construire son roman—du moins d'une façon apparente —en fonction du dénouement qu'il ne saurait logiquement prévoir. Il ne connaît que le passé du héros, passé qu'il peut rappeler; il ignore l'avenir, dont il ne saurait tenir compte d'une façon visible dans le developpement du récit. La première qualité de ces romans—car ils entendent rester vraisemblables— devrait donc être l'héterogénéité. Mais l'écrivain habile s'entend, en ce point encore, à tromper le lecteur. Dans *Werther* on découvre vingt allusions à la fin tragique du héros: sorte de prophéties aussi vagues que celles de la bible et que l'on ne reconnaît comme telles qu'après les événements. Néanmoins, et notamment dans le roman de Goethe, elles créent une certaine atmosphère: cette atmosphère de pitié et de crainte où baigne la tragédie antique. D'autre part, l'orchestration harmonieuse de toutes les parties de la pièce demeure volontiers une exigence du roman contemporain: cette orchestration produit les effets esthétiques les plus sûrs. Or, plusieurs types de romans épistolaires insistent au contraire sur la variété des tons. Dans *Les Liaisons dangereuses* aussi bien que dans *The Expedition of Humphry Clinker* une certaine sorte d'unité est compromise ou délibérément absente. Tabitha et Jenkins, par exemple, confèrent à l'oeuvre de Smollett un charme qui n'est pas précisément le charme propre du roman, mais bien plutôt celui de la comédie, voire de la farce. Il est certain que la faveur dont jouit un genre donné dépend hautement, d'une part, de l'idéal littéraire du temps, et de l'autre, de l'évolution de la société elle-même, dont la littérature demeure, peut-être, de tous les arts, l'expression la plus complète, et surtout la plus immédiate: elle doit de plus en plus être envisagée aussi comme une branche de la sociologie et être étudiée dans cette perspective. Dans une telle étude, le roman épistolaire fournirait la matière d'un chapitre essentiel.

UNIVERSITY OF ILLINOIS

NOTES

1. Ce n'est pas le lieu de parler de cette trentaine d'excellents ouvrages écrits sur le problème depuis une quinzaine d'années. Quelques-uns d'entre eux consacrent un chapitre à mon sujet particulier, comme B. Romberg, *Studies in the Narrative Technique of the First-Person Novel,* traduit du suédois (Stockholm, 1962), chapitre sur *Clarissa;* et J. Rousset, *Forme et signification. Essai sur les structures littéraires de Corneille à Claudel* (Paris, 1962), chapitre sur le roman épistolaire.

2. Le compte rendu de Laclos fut publié dans le *Mercure de France.* Cf. *Oeuvres complètes,* éd. de la Pléiade, p. 523.

3. Plus d'un millier de romans épistolaires ont vu le jour en Europe entre 1740 et 1820: une vingtaine de chefs-d'oeuvres, une cinquantaine de livres qui restent classiques, quelque trois cents

ouvrages intéressant l'histoire littéraire . . . et le reste est littérature. Une étude sérieuse et complète sur le genre épistolaire devrait, je pense, inclure, en termes de commerce, un tiers de la production totale.

4. Il serait quelque peu simpliste de vouloir réduire l'évolution littéraire à l'antithèse que je viens de décrire: *realism versus escapism*. Il n'est de feuilleter *Mimesis*, d'Auerbach, par exemple, pour se rendre compte des nuances réalistes de certains textes anciens et médiévaux. L'opposition est surtout frappante lorsque'on considère le roman XVIIIe siècle comme l'héritier de la romance. Le problème du réalisme n'a, du reste, rien perdu de son actualité. Les arts, depuis la génération de Mallarmé, voguent vers un réalisme tout différent de celui que l'on vit prendre son essor aux XVIIIe siècle et dont l'école de Balzac s'était chargé de faire la fortune. *La deshumanizacion del arte,* de José Ortega y Gasset explique avec élégance et persuasion le phénomène suggéré par le titre. Le roman, de tous les arts et de tous les genres littéraires, est demeuré le plus près de l'homme—et l'on peut noter que le "nouveau roman" représente une sorte d'*infraréalisme*, étape que d'autres arts ont déjà derrière eux.

5. L'auteur est prêt à renoncer au vrai si le vraisemblable doit en profiter. Dans *Monsieur Nicolas*, par exemple (Restif de la Bretonne, *Monsieur Nicolas, ou le coeur humain dévoilé. Mémoires intimes de Restif de la Bretonne* [édition réimprimée sur celle de 1796, Paris, 1883], XIV, 111), l'auteur, dressant la liste des personnages de la *Paysanne pervertie*, note: "16) La Marquise: Il est tant de femmes comme elle dans sa condition, que son personnage est vrai, sans être vraisemblable."

6. La plupart des éditions omettent ce complément, que d'autres changent en *Chronique de 1830*. La gent érudite traite parfois fort librement ses victimes. Ainsi la critique anglaise, et à sa suite la critique internationale, ne cesse de parler de *Clarissa Harlowe*, titre que l'auteur, pour de fort bonnes raisons, s'est gardé de donner à son oeuvre. On peut penser que le premier pas vers une interprétation scientifique d'un ouvrage consisterait à lui rendre le titre que son auteur lui avait donné, titre qu'on peut couper, dans le cas de *Clarissa,* puisqu'il prend une page entière, mais non certes remanier. Pour en revenir à Stendhal, rappelons qu'il a rédigé des *Chroniques italiennes* et des *Mémoires* d'un touriste.

7. Cependant, du point de vue de la technique épistolaire, c'est *Redgauntlet* surtout qui mériterait d'être étudié.

8. En France, cent ans avant ces publications, on nommait "roman historique" des oeuvres dont le seul cadre relevait de l'histoire, mais dont les problèmes psychologiques étaient de pure invention. L'*Histoire de Marguerite d'Anjou, reine d'Angleterre* en est un exemple. Notons qu'à l'époque de Prévost, des femmes surtout se consacraient à ce genre—mais rarement, hélas, elles y excellaient. *Le Siège de Calais, Nouvelle historique,* de Madame de Tencin, offre quelque intérêt. P. M. Masson mentionne une quinzaine d'oeuvres "historiques" dans *Une Vie de femme au XVIIIe siècle, Mme de Tencin* (Paris, 1910), p. 160, note 1.

9. Comme le docteur Johnson, Wieland aimera à assimiler à l'histoire une oeuvre de pure fantaisie: *Geschichte des Prinzen Biribinker.*

10. Je n'emploie pas ce mot parce qu'il est plus commode que "Roman personnel" ou "roman à la première personne," mais parce qu'il traduit exactement ce que je veux dire: non seulement le *moi* raconte l'histoire, mais ce *moi* en est aussi le héros. Le Ich est sujet et objet, ce que l'expression allemande ambivalonte rend exactement. Cf. note suivante.

11. Mon but n'est pas d'analyser les différentes techniques de l'Ich-Roman proprement dit ni de la *Rahmenerzählung* et de ses variantes. L'un est autobiographique (biographie du héros s'identifiant parfois avec l'auteur), comme c'est le cas de *Robinson Crusoe,* l'autre est simplement biographique, tel *Tom Jones.* Dans le premier, le narrateur est héros, dans le second, il ne l'est point. Le *je* ne cesse d'être présent dans un cas, dans l'autre il ne surgit qu'accidentellement, lorsqu'il s'agit pour le narrateur d'insérer une remarque personnelle dans la série des événements racontés. *Der Heilige,* de Conrad-Ferdinand Meyer, représente le cas fort instructif d'une oeuvre participant aux deux types: l'arbalétrier qui mène le récit ne prend part à l'action qu'en tant que personnage secondaire: le roman n'est donc pas, en premier lieu, une autobiographie (Ich-Roman), puisque Thomas Becket, et non son serviteur, l'arbalétrier, occupe le centre du drame. D'autre part, le *je* n'apparaît pas seulement pour juger les actions du chancelier et du primat d'Angleterre, mais aussi pour conter celles du narrateur lui-même: le récit de *Tom Jones—mutatis mutandis*—mis dans la bouche du maître d'école Partridge. Dans la *Rahmenerzählung* qui nous intéresse ici, seul le cadre participe à l'Ich-Roman, ce Ich racontant l'histoire d'un tiers. De longs passages de l'oeuvre de Meyer sont à la troisième personne et confèrent au lecteur l'impression d'un Er-Roman. C'est encore le cas de *Paul et Virginie,* où le vieillard qui relate les événements y participe, quoique dans une mesure bien moindre que dans *Der Heilige.*

12. Dans *Revue d'histoire littéraire de la France,* XVII (1910), 449–496. On trouvera ci-après

une bibliographie succincte du roman épistolaire. L'ouvrage de G. F. Singer, *The Epistolary Novel* (Philadelphia, 1933), est intéressant en ce qu'il montre, avec une liste d'oeuvres fort longue (nécessairement incomplète, et, hélas, parfois fautive) l'importance du genre. Le titre n'est guère exact, puisqu'il traite surtout du roman épistolaire en Angleterre. Il faut aussi citer F. G. Black, *The Epistolary Novel in the late Eighteenth Century* (Eugene, Oregon, 1940), ainsi que Charles E. Kany, *The Beginnings of the Epistolary Novel in France, Italy and Spain*, University of California Publications in Modern Philology, Vol. XXI, no. 1 (Berkeley, Calif., 1937), pp. 1–158. On trouve dans tous les pays des travaux sur le sujet. Voici ceux que je pense être les principaux:

J. Brink, *De Roman in Brieven 1740–1840* (Amsterdam, 1889).

F. Böök, *Romanens och prosaberättelsens historie i Sverige intill 1809* (Stockholm, 1907).

F. C. Green, "Montesquieu the novelist and some imitations of the *Lettres Persanes*," *Modern Language Review*, XX (1925), 32–42.

M. Sommerfeld, "Romantheorie und Romantypus der deutschen Aufklärung," *Deutsche Vierteljahrsschrift für Literaturwissenschaft und Geistesgeschichte* (1926), 459–90.

V. V. Vinogradov, 'Skola sentimental' in *Evoljuciia russkogo naturalizma, Gogolj i Dostoevskij* (Leningrad, 1929).

S. Skwarczyńska, *Teoria lista* (Lwów, 1937).

C. P. Barbier, "Letters of an Italian Nun and an English Gentleman (1781), a Bibliographical Problem," *Revue de littérature comparée*, XXVIII (1954), 75–89.

K. R. Mandelkow, "Der deutsche Briefroman. Zum Problem der Polyperspektive im Epischen," *Neophilologus*, XLIV (1960), 200–208.

E. Th. Voss, *Erzählprobleme des Briefromans* (Bonn, 1960).

R. A. Day, *Told in Letters. Epistolary Fiction Before Richardson* (Ann Arbor, Michigan, 1966).

Outre les chapitres de Romberg et de Rousset déjà mentionnés, on lira les quelques notes instructives de A. Pizzorusso, "La concezione dell'arte narrativa nella seconda metà del seicento francese," dans *Studi mediolatini e volgari* (Bologne, 1955), pp. 125–134.

13. Les astérisques suivant les chiffres signifient:

* récit à la troisième personne (*Er-Roman*).

** histoire rapportée directement par une tierce personne (forme particulière de la *Rahmenerzählung*, dont le "cadre" seul est à la première personne).

*** la première personne raconte le roman dont elle est elle-même un des personnages principaux (*Ich-Roman*).

**** roman épistolaire dans ses différentes formes (*Briefroman*).

14. Mrs. Eliza Haywood, 1693?–1756, a été une des plus actives femmes de lettres, avec Mrs. Mary de la Rivière Manley, dans l'Angleterre de la première moitié du XVIIIe siècle. Un très grand nombre de ses soixante-dix romans appartiennent au genre épistolaire. *The History of Miss Betsy Thoughtless*, 1751, relève de la méthode adoptée par les Fielding, mais renferme un tel nombre de lettres (soixante-dix-huit en tout) qui font avancer l'action d'une façon décisive, que l'oeuvre doit être comptée parmi les romans épistolaires. La Bibliothèque de l'University of Illinois possède un exemplaire de l'édition princeps, et la Bibliothèque Nationale de Paris conserve la traduction qu'en donna, en 1754, le Chevalier de Fleuriau sous le titre indiqué par Mornet.

15. Le chapitre premier, "servant d'introduction à l'ouvrage," est à la première personne. Elle ne revient plus guère au cours des douze autres chapitres. Il faut néanmoins classer cette oeuvre parmi les *Rahmenerzählungen*.

16. Le tome VII des *Mémoires et avantures* (sic) *d'un homme de qualité qui s'est retiré du monde*. Ce tome continent *L'histoire du Chevalier des Grieux et de Manon Lescaut;* il parut en 1731. Dès 1733, Prévost publia l'oeuvre comme un roman indépendant des *Mémoires*.

17. Schiller (*Xenion*, 13) consacre à l'ouvrage ce distique:

Töchtern edler Geburt ist dieses Werk zu empfehlen,
Um zu Töchtern der Lust schnell sich befördern zu sehn.

Hermes est aussi l'auteur de *Geschichte der Miss Fanny Wilkes* (1766), où l'influence de *Pamela* et surtout de Fielding est visible, et il a écrit les quatre mille pages de *Sophiens Reisen von Memel nach Sachsen* (1769–1773), alors un des livres les plus répandus en Allemagne. L'édition de 1778, que j'ai sous les yeux, est en six volumes: il y a deux cent soixante-six lettres en tout, mais autant de "Fortsetzungen": roman épistolaire comparable, quant à la longueur et quant au succès, du moins en Allemagne, à *Clarissa*.

18. Il s'agit de l'ouvrage le plus volumineux de Wieland—mais qui est loin d'être le seul qu'il ait écrit sous forme de lettres.

19. Rappelons que le premier quotidien français, le *Journal de Paris*, commence à paraître en

1777. Il serait aisé de compiler toute une anthologie avec des citations illustrant l'estime où les auteurs de romans épistolaires tenaient le genre. Quelques exemples suffriront:

—"Rien n'a plu davantage, dans les *Lettres persanes,* que d'y trouver sans y penser, une espèce de roman . . . Ces sortes de romans réussissent ordinairement, parce que l'on rend compte soi-même de sa situation actuelle; ce qui fait plus sentir les passions que tous les récits qu'on en pourrait faire." *Quelques réflexions sur les Lettres persanes,* que Montesquieu rédigea en 1754. Voir *Oeuvres complètes,* éd. de la Pléiade, t.I, p. 129.

—"The distant sounds of music that catch new sweetness as they vibrate through the long drawn valley are not more pleasing to the ear than the tidings of a far distant friend." *The Citizen of the World,* lettre CVI.

—"Weiss Gott—Werther rapporte les paroles de Lotte—wie wohl mir's war, wenn ich mich sonntags so in ein Eckchen setzen und mit ganzem Herzen an dem Glück und Unstern einer Miss Jenny teilnehmen konnte. . . . Der Autor ist mir der liebste, in dem ich meine Welt wiederfinde, bei dem es zugeht wie um mich." L'*Histoire de Jenny,* par Madame de Riccoboni, est un roman épistolaire du type Marianne.   La citation est extraite de la lettre du 16 juin.

—"Une lettre est le portrait de l'âme. Elle n'a pas, comme une froide image, cette stagnance si éloignée de l'amour; elle se prête à tous nos mouvements: tour à tour elle s'anime, elle jouit, elle se repose." *Les Liaisons dangereuses,* lettre CL.

—"The packet (of letters) is a precious one; you will find in it a more lively and exact picture of my life than it is possible, by any other means, to communicate." *Clara Howard,* préface.

—"Die Briefform ist eine der gefälligsten Einkleidungen, wenn man an den andern etwas schreiben will: ihrer bediente sich sogar der hl. Dominikus in seinen Briefen an die hl. Dreieinigkeit, Galen in seinen aus der Hölle an Parazelsus und Omar im Schreiben an den Nilfluss. Ich berühre nicht einmal die unzähligen Menschen, die etwas auf die Briefpost geben. Diese schöne Form der Anschauung, diese niedliche Fassung des Gesundbrunnens der Wahrheit tat der Literatur schon so viele Dienste wie das Postwesen." Jean Paul Richter, *Der Jubelsenior,* Erster Hirten- und Zirkelbrief.

20. Voir aussi C. V. Langlois, *Formulaires de lettres du XIIe, du XIIIe et du XIVe siècle* (Paris, 1890–1897).

21. L'architecture de ce roman est des plus simples, et il y a lieu de croire que Richardson apprit plus, en vue de ses oeuvres ultérieures, par ses *Familiar Letters* que par sa *Pamela.*

22. Voir Charles E. Kany, *op. cit.*

23. En fait, Werther écrit trois fois à Charlotte et il ressort de ces lettres que la jeune fille, elle aussi, correspondait avec son amant. Mais ces échanges de billets ne suffisent pas (malgré la longueur du dernier message de Werther à sa bien-aimée) à altérer le caractère général du roman. On a donc affaire au roman-confidence, au type statique, lorsque les heros principaux de la trame ne prennent pas (ou guère) la plume, ou se contentent d'écrire à des tiers. Humphry Clinker, qui donne son nom au roman, n'écrit pas une seule lettre et n'en reçoit aucune.

24. Il s'agit bien d'une confidence: "N'oubliez jamais que vous m'avez promis de ne jamais dire qui je suis; je ne veux être connue que de vous." Ière partie. Ces sortes de rappels d'une prétendue promesse de secret est un moyen fort courant, dans les romans de ce type, d'attiser la curiosité du lecteur.

25. "Je parlais tout à l'heure de style, je ne sais pas seulement ce que c'est. Comment fait-on pour en avoir un? Celui que je vois dans les livres, est-ce le bon? Pourquoi donc est-ce qu'il me déplaît tant le plus souvent? Celui de mes lettres vous paraît-il passable? J'écrirai ceci de même" (Ière partie).

26. VIe partie. On remarquera que le type statique admet bien plus facilement les descriptions que le type dynamique. Dans *Les Liaisons dangereuses,* par exemple, presque tous les personnages se connaissent: pourquoi, dès lors, les peindre? Dans la cinquième partie, Marianne donne un portrait des plus fins de M. de Climal.

27. Goethe avait à peine vingt et un ans lorsqu'il se mit à composer un premier roman épistolaire. Les quelques pages qui nous en sont restées ne permettent guère de conclusions sur cette phase préwerthérienne et, notamment, on ne saurait définir le type de *Briefroman* qu'il avait choisi. Voir *Goethes Werke,* Gedenkausgabe (Zurich, 1953), t.IV, pp. 263–266.

28. Le laps de temps écoulé entre le moment de l'aventure et celui de la narration peut être plus ou moins long. Mais il n'y a pas lieu de faire ici des distinctions. *Les Confessions du comte de *** sont composées par un auteur dont les souvenirs remontent bien moins loin que ceux de Marianne: l'oeuvre de Duclos et celle de Marivaux relèvent pourtant du même type.

29. L'expression, consacrée par Richardson, de *writing to the moment,* conduit à des abus que Fielding a bien remarqués et, dans sa *Shamela,* fort spirituellement critiqués. Dans la VIe lettre,

l'héroïne réussit ce tour de force qui consiste à rapporter son aventure au moment même où elle a lieu. Elle écrit à sa mère: "Mrs. Jervis and I are just in bed, and the door unlocked; if my master would come—Odsbobs! I hear him just coming in at the door. You see, I write in the present tense, as Parson Williams says. Well, he is in bed between us, we both shamming a sleep, he steals his hand into my bosom," etc. C'est là, évidemment, que l'on peut surprendre les battements du coeur, ce que Richardson préconisait faire par sa méthode. Mais l'auteur de *Clarissa* pratiquait également le *suspense*, qui consiste à interrompre l'action par quelque incident inattendu: l'attention relâchée est endiguée de plus belle par la reprise du récit. Lovelace, après avoir conduit l'héroïne du roman à St.-Albans, mande à Belford: "And now, let me tell thee, that never was joy so complete as mine! But let me inquire—is not my angel flown away? . . . Oh no! she is in the next apartment! Securely mine! —mine for ever!" Procédé fort courant aussi dans les romans épistolaires français; on en trouve un exemple dès la première lettre des *Liaisons dangereuses*, de Cécile à Sophie Carnay. Fin d'un paragraphe: "Adieu, jusqu'à un petit moment." Début du paragraphe suivant: "Comme tu vas te moquer de la pauvre Cécile. . . ." Et celle-ci raconte comment, entre ces deux paragraphes, étant descendue au salon, elle a fait la connaissance d'un cordonnier, alors qu'elle croyait rencontrer son futur mari.

30. Il y a cependant échange de quelques missives par des voies détournées (incluses dans des lettres de tiers).—Werther écrit quatre-vingt-sept lettres à Wilhelm, trois à Charlotte, deux à Albert, et une à la fois à Charlotte et à Albert. Les quelques missives adressées à l'antagoniste, on l'a dit, ne sauraient évidemment affecter la nature du roman qui demeure un roman statique tout comme *Clarissa*. C'est encore la technique de Hölderlin. Dans *Hyperion* il y a en principe une seule série de lettres, signées du héros et adressées à son ami Bellarmin. Mais, au premier livre du tome second, on trouve soudain un échange de lettres entre les héros: treize lettres d'Hypérion à Diotima, qui lui en écrit deux. Il est clair cependant que cette correspondance ne saurait enlever à l'oeuvre son caractère général de roman-confidence. Notons que la fièvre de Werther qui secoua l'Europe non seulement conféra au roman épistolaire un renouveau de force, mais on aima imiter aussi la technique de Goethe. Songeons à *Le ultime lettere di Jacopo Ortis* et à *Obermann*. Il faut noter aussi que les femmes, qui avaient publié en Angleterre, durant les deux premiers tiers du XVIIIᵉ siècle, la majorité des romans par lettres, sans faire, pour cela, de contribution valable à la litterature (exceptons Sarah Fielding et Aphra Behn, celle-ci, pourtant, appartenant au XVIIᵉ siècle), se mettent maintenant à donner dans le genre, un peu partout en Europe, avec un succès plus mérité. On a déjà cité Mme de Charrière, et on parlera de Mme de Staël. Mentionnons *Valérie* de Mme de Krudener, *Claire d'Albe*, de Mme Cottin, sans oublier l'Angleterre, où Miss Burney compose son chef-d'oeuvre à l'âge où Goethe écrivit le sien: *Evelina, or a Young Lady's Entrance into the World*. En Hollande, Betje Wolff et Aagje Deken donnèrent en 1782 leur *Historie van Mejuffrouw Sara Burgerhart*, oeuvre suivie de deux autres romans épistolaires aussi longs que le premier, lesquels, comme lui, connurent quelque retentissement: ces romans ont été traduits en allemand. Dans la liste de Baldensperger, six romans sur dix-huit ont des femmes pour auteurs: preuve péremptoire de leur influence croissante dans la prose d'imagination.

31. L'intérêt des réponses dépend hautement de certaines circonstances de la trame. Dans le cas de notre roman, on ne voit pas en quoi des réponses du docteur Lewis, par exemple, auraient pu contribuer à l'intérêt de l'oeuvre sans en changer la nature.

32. *Werther* contient quatre-vingt-cinq lettres, plus le commentaire de l'éditeur dans lequel s'insèrent des fragments de lettres: quatre-vingt-quatorze documents en tout y compris la traduction d'un poème d'Ossian. Mais le roman de Smollett est trois fois plus volumineux que celui de Goethe.

33. Molière, dans *Monsieur de Pourceaugnac*, fait lui aussi commettre à un personnage inculte des fautes d'orthographe. Dans les réparties du Second Suisse on lit *pandre* pour pendre, *foie* pour fois. Dans une pièce de théâtre le procédé n'a guère de sens—même pour le cas d'un spectacle dans un fauteuil. Mais lorsque Jenkins raconte à Mary Jones que "the squire applied to the mare," le lecteur que la vie académique n'a pas gâté peut avoir quelque raison de sourire.

34. L'ouvrage comprend cent soixante et une lettres et une cinquantaine de correspondances. Trente-sept lettres ont pour auteurs divers personnages dont l'identité et le caractère n'intéressent souvent que fort peu.

35. Paru d'abord dans *Correo de Madrid*, en 1789, l'oeuvre est publiée sous forme de livre, à titre posthume, en 1793.

36. Sur quatre-vingt-dix lettres que contient le roman, dix sont écrites par Nuño, philosophe espagnol, et onze par Ben-Beley, compatriote de Gazel.

37. L'intérêt qu'un confident peut avoir à une discussion est souvent fort limité. C'est la raison pour laquelle, dans le type statique, plus l'action narrée est tragique, plus les réponses sont rares. Il est intéressant d'avoir une correspondance réciproque dans les *Lettres persanes*. Dans *Werther*,

les lettres de Wilhelm seraient sans intérêt majeur, elles risqueraient même de gâter l'oeuvre. *Wilhelm*, de l'écrivain argentin José Domingo Arias Bernal, publié à Buenos Aires en 1943, est une espèce d'épilogue ingénieux au roman de Goethe. (Wilhelm écrit quarte-vingt-deux lettres à Werther, et une à Albert; celui-ci écrit une lettre à Wilhelm.) L'ouvrage de Bernal est sans prétention aucune, ce qui lui confère un certain charme. Mais si chacune de ces lettres de Wilhelm était publiée à la suite de la lettre de Werther dont elle est la réponse, elles réduiraient à la médiocrité un chef-d'oeuvre de la Weltliteratur.

38. Qui est l'auteur du roman? Mon but n'est pas de démêler ici cette question, et je renvoie le lecteur aux critiques suivants: A. Gonçalves Rodrigues, *Mariana Alcoforado—história crítica de un fraude literário*, 1925; E.P.M. Dronke, "Héloïse et Marianne," dans *Romanische Forschungen*, LXXII (1960), 223–256; A. Cioranescu, *"La religieuse portugaise* et *Tout le reste est silence,"* dans *Revue des Sciences Humaines*, fasc. 3, 1963, pp. 317–327.

39. Balzac, dans *La Femme abandonnée*, fait écrire à Mme de Bauséant une lettre qui rappelle telle autre des Lettres portugaises.

40. Lettre V: "Je vous promets de ne vous point haïr." —Plus loin: "Je faut avouer que je suis obligée de vous haïr mortellement." La première phrase, avec sa structure simple, est spontanée, la seconde, de composition complexe, reflète l'artifice.

41. *L'Abbé Aubin*, de Mérimée, contient aussi cinq lettres, adressées par Mme de P*** à Mme de G***. La lettre de l'abbé Aubin à l'abbé Bruneau peut être considérée comme un épilogue. La comparaison de l'oeuvre de Mérimée avec les *Lettres portugaises* ferait bien ressortir les différences fondamentales entre la méthode statique et la méthode dynamique.

42. A comparer avec ce début bien connu des *Confessions* de Rousseau: "Je forme une entreprise qui n'eut jamais d'exemple, et dont l'exécution n'aura point d'imitateur." Du point de vue de la technique, l'oeuvre de Jean-Jacques est un Ich-Roman et aurait pu être publiée, sans la dénaturer, à la manière de *La Vie de Marianne*. Il aurait suffi de faire appel à un confident, à un interlocuteur. Notons les nombreuses lettres insérées dans la IX° et la X° parties.

43. Critique du gouvernement, des écrivains, du théâtre, de l'éducation, telle qu'elle est donnée dans les couvents.

44. New York, 1897, sous le titre de *Letters to an Unknown*.

45. Il était donc parfaitement oiseux de chercher à identifier cette inconnue, et d'avoir découvert qu'il s'agit d'une certaine Mademoiselle Jenny Daquin, de Boulogne, ne représente nullement une contribution à la science littéraire.

46. Herzog reçoit une seule lettre, de Geraldine Portnoy, à qui il en envoie également.

47. La phrase suivante montre le ton de beaucoup de ces lettres: "I should like to know what you mean by the expression 'the fall into the quotidian.' When did this fall occur? Where were we standing when it happened?" (New York, 1964), p. 49.

48. *Op. cit.*, p. 272.

49. *Wjatscheslaw Iwanow*, ouvrage traduit du russe (Vienne, 1949).

50. Sur les *Lettres d'Héloïse et d'Abélard*, et notamment sur leur influence sur *La Nouvelle Héloïse*, voir le commentaire de M. Bernard Guyon, *Oeuvres complètes de J.-J. Rousseau*, t. II, éd. de la Pléiade, 1961, pp. 1336–1341.

51. Barbara envoie à Makar une vintaine de pages dans lesquelles elle fait le récit de son enfance.

52. Il ne saurait être question de donner ici une bibliographie de l'oeuvre. Notons pourtant, d'A. et d'Y. Delmas, *A la recherche des "Liaisons dangereuses"* (Paris, 1964), ouvrage essentiel pour l'étude de l'influence et de la fortune de Laclos et de sa technique, et de Dorothy R. Thelander, *Laclos and the Epistolary Novel* (Genève, 1963), où la méthode des *Liaisons* se trouve soigneusement analysée. Enfin, souvenons-nous des réflexions concernant notre sujet qui ont consignées dans des travaux comme celle de Jean-Luc Seylaz, *"Les Liaisons dangereuses"* et *la création romanesque chez Laclos* (Genève, Paris, 1958). Rappelons enfin l'une des premières études proprement comparatives sur ce roman: "Essai sur les personnages des *Liaisons dangereuses* en tant que types littéraires," par Alfred Owen Aldridge, *Archives des Lettres Modernes*, No. 31 (1960).

53. C'est encore la méthode qu'il emploie dans *Amelia*. Le premier chapitre du livre VIII commence ainsi: "The history must now look a little backwards to those circumstances which led to the catastrophe mentioned at the end of the last book." Voir aussi *Joseph Andrews*, les titres du chapitre 18, livre I, et du chapitre 10, livre II.

54. De même que *Clarissa* participe dans une faible mesure au type dynamique, puisque le roman renferme une très courte correspondance entre l'héroïne et son antagoniste, ainsi *Les Liaisons dangereuses* participent au type statique, puisque toutes les lettres de Cécile adressées à Sophie Carnay sont de pures confidences et ne font en aucune sorte progresser l'action. Il en

est de même de telles lettres des héros principaux narrant des incidents indépendants du système de trames qui s'imbriquent les unes dans les autres.

55. Si on ne compte que les romans à plusieurs voix, Delphine, pour le nombre de lettres (115), tient la seconde place parmi les dames scriptomanes. C'est Clarissa (132) qui tient le record.

56. Une intrigue imbriquée est celle de Mme de Vernon, qui, personne n'en doutait à l'époque, représentait Talleyrand, premier à s'en amuser. On a vu d'emblée quels personnages réels étaient représentés par les heros de Mme de Staël, alors qu'on n'a cessé de speculer sur les modèles de Laclos. Les deux romans sont éminemment destinés à peindre la société contemporaine.

57. Picasso se servant de clous, de ficelles, de papier peint pour en "monter" un tableau n'a donc pas le mérite de l'invention.

58. F.-J. Billeskov Jansen, dans "Les grands romans philosophiques de Kierkegaard," in Revue de l'Université de Bruxelles, No. 3 (avril-mai 1961), p. 10, écrit: "Dans toute sa production littéraire, Kierkegaard aimera l'épisode, c'est-à-dire l'anecdote, l'exemple, la situation dialoguée." L'usage de la lettre pouvait l'aider à satisfaire ce goût.

59. Du naïf au sentimental: voilà bien le développement thématique de Werther, et Schiller ne pouvait trouver d'exemples plus pertinents d'une telle évolution, quand il écrivit Über naive und sentimentalische Dichtung. Or, "sentimentalisch" place le lecteur dans l'orbe ossianique.

60. Il convient de préciser: les oeuvres les plus significatives et les plus personnelles relèvent respectivement de ces types. Mais il est clair que d'autre part Werther a suscité en France des dizaines d'imitations valables de son type, et que ni Rousseau ni Laclos ne sont restés sans écho en Angleterre. En imitant un thème, on a parfois adopté aussi une méthode. En Allemagne, d'autre part, les romans épistolaires offrent d'ordinaire un nombre de correspondances assez restreint, alors qu'on aime à les multiplier en France et en Angleterre. Pamela en offre dix-huit; La Nouvelle Héloïse, vingt-cinq; Sir Charles Grandison, trente-deux; Les Liaisons dangereuses, trente-.six; le Paysan perverti, soixante-huit; Clarissa, soixante-douze.

61. Voir Histoire de la Princesse de Paphlagonie.

62. Ce qui naguère apparaissait comme hautement vraisemblable, comme une "invention heureuse," nous laisse aujourd'hui parfaitement indifférents—ou nous irrite. Les lettres du Paysan perverti portent un titre qui en résume le contenu. Celle du 5 décembre (tome I, Ière partie) est précédée de cette phrase: "J'encourage mon frère." Et on explique: "Ces arguments de lettres sont tous de Pierre R*** et se trouvent écrits de sa main sur le dossier des originaux." Note de l'éditeur. Restif pensait renchérir ainsi sur l'illusion réaliste. Il faut relever aussi la variété des prétextes que les auteurs inventaient pour justifier la publication d'une correspondance. Dans la préface de Hollins Liebesleben (1802), Achim von Arnim déclare: "Ein Freund bat mich auf seinem Sterbebette um die Erfüllung einer Bitte." Et cet ami de prendre sous son oreiller un petit paquet de lettres dont sera fait le roman. Ce n'est qu'un exemple entre cent. Le goût, au XXe siècle, se refuse à de tels subterfuges. Il s'agit maintenant d'un tout autre réalisme. Thornton Wilder, dans l'avertissement de The Ides of March, illustre l'antithèse: "All the documents in this work," dit-il, "are from the author's imagination with the exception of the poem of Catullus and the closing entry which is from Suetonius' Lives of the Caesars."

63. Voyez le titre que Restif de la Bretonne donna a l'un de ses nombreux romans épistolaires: Le Nouvel Abélard ou Lettres de deux amants qui ne se sont jamais vus, en quatre volumes.

64. Nouveau Dictionnaire, t. II, p. 569.

65. Il faut pourtant noter que ce n'est pas là, en général, la préoccupation majeure. Les digressions sont à l'ordre du jour: songeons aux interminables leçons de La Nouvelle Héloïse, ou relisons le titre que Fielding donne à tel de ses chapitres: "A discourse between the poet and the player; of no other use in this history but to divert the reader" (Joseph Andrews, III, 10).

Varieties of Epic Theatre in the Modern Drama

INTEREST in the nature and value of so-called Epic Theatre has mounted with the growing vogue of Bertolt Brecht since World War II, and the literature on Brecht himself has been piling up impressively for the past decade and a half. The present paper is not designed to add directly to that literature; it is my intention, rather, to locate the subject of "Epic Drama" in the stream of efforts to enlarge the scope of modern dramatic art and to invite, rather than consummate, investigations of a number of related topics.

To this end I shall allow myself a number of preliminary generalizations that further study may modify and amplify but is unlikely to contradict. The first of these is that Brecht did not originate modern Epic Theatre; although Brecht's practice and theory have recently given "epic theatre" virtually all of the prestige it possesses in our universities or university theatres, he was not alone— and not even the first—in moving in this direction and drawing attention to it.

Erwin Piscator, born at Marburg, Germany, in 1893, revolting against three years' military service in World War I, exchanged a brief engagement to dadaism for a permanent marriage to politically oriented theatre when he established a short-lived theatre in 1919 at Koenigsberg. It was characteristically called the Tribunal (*Die Tribüne*), and it was there that the director Karlheinz Martin staged Ernst Toller's first play *Die Wandlung,* a lyrical anti-war drama in thirteen rapidly moving, more or less fragmentary, scenes that culminated in a mass scene in which the returning soldier Friedrich, repulsed by his mother and uncle for his conversion to radicalism, starts a revolt with such revolutionary ejaculations as *"Marschiert! Marschiert am lichten Tag!"* and *"zertrümmert die Burgen, zertrümmert, lachend die falschen Burgen."* Piscator next started short-lived ventures such as the Proletarisches Theater in Berlin which lasted until April 1921, and after a year of producing naturalistic plays such as Gorky's *Small Citizen* and Tolstoy's *The Power of Darkness* at the Central-Theater in Berlin in 1921–24, he became the director of the long-established and influential Berlin Volksbühne in 1924 and produced plays of political content and more or less epic form until he broke with that organization in 1927 over his production of Ehm Welk's historical drama, *Storm over Gothland,* an account of a medieval revolt to which Piscator added a politically inspired film sequence. Piscator was accused of arbitrarily injecting propaganda into the work and the film strip was removed by the governing body of the Volksbühne.

Piscator's blending of film and stage drama in this production appears to have been the first successful experiment in giving historical dimension to a play by this means. The author had indicated his intention with a statement on the title page reading "This play does not occur merely in the year 1400," but since he had composed a conventional drama he failed to realize this intention in dramatic scenes. Piscator, in staging the work, resorted to the device of providing contemporary parallels by means of a film-strip. This was to remain a Piscator "epic-theatre" device, and was employed by him during his period of exile in the United States in a provocative production of Sartre's *The Flies* (*Les Mouches*) at the President Theatre, New York, in 1947. After his conflict with the Volksbühne management, Piscator renovated an old theatre in western Berlin, the Theater am Nollendorfplatz and opened his *Piscator-Bühne* in 1927 with a production of Ernst Toller's *Hoppla! Wir Leben* in which he again made considerable use of synchronized filmstrips and staged episodes. The object was to document the traumatic experience of a revolutionary idealist who emerges from eight years of imprisonment into a world run by his socialist comrades that he finds so intolerable that he commits suicide. Since Toller had not done so, Piscator set out to demonstrate what had happened during those eight years to destroy the hopes his hero had once entertained for a "better" world. The premiere on September 3, 1927 ended in a demonstration by the left and resulted in a sharp denunciation of the production as political agitation rather than art.

Important sectors of the press, however, credited Piscator with the creation of a new and extraordinarily vivid mode of dramatic art, while cautioning him to resist the temptations of propaganda. Insisting upon the cause-and-effect relationship between dramatic form and political content, Piscator continued to explore the possibilities of imparting political instruction or criticism in other noteworthy *Piscator-Bühne* productions. From November 1927 to January 1928 he presented a new play, *Rasputin,* by Leo Lania, and as usual, Piscator was not content with the circumscribed—that is, nonepic—character of the play he was going to produce. He saw in it another and more important subject, which he has described as quite simply the destiny of Europe between the years 1914 and 1917. He had been called the real author of *Hoppla! Wir Leben,* and there is indeed hardly a play produced by him in the 1920's that he did not recreate or amplify to such a degree that he could be credited with co-authorship. If Brecht can be called a playwright-director, Piscator may be almost as justifiably described as a director-playwright.

In staging *Rasputin,* Piscator's Epic-theatre leanings led him to take all of Europe for his subject, and to connect the private Rasputin story with the intertwining political and economic factors of the world conflict. To explain the stage production that ensued—an imaginative presentation of multiple action on a globe-like stage—Piscator's play editor Leo Lania, who was apparently the chief author of the final version of the play originally by Alexei Tolstoy, wrote in the program that the aim had been not to present the tragic destiny of a particular hero, but rather to produce a political document about the era. Lania insisted that history could not be divorced from politics and maintained that playgoers wished to see the documents of the past that would illuminate the immediate present. To meet this need, Piscator and his associates added no less than 19 new scenes depicting imperialist machinations to the original seven scenes of Alexei Tolstoy's play. A film strip and a globe-like stage, segments of which were opened to present scenes transpiring in different European capitals, fulfilled Piscator's desire to convert a private tragedy into a public document. And the document was enlarged into a commentary, particularly in the case of the filmstrip, which performed the function of a chorus and addressed the audience directly, calling attention to important historical details, explaining or interpreting them, criticizing the characters' actions, or even haranguing the spectators. The production led to a trial as a result of which Piscator was obliged to eliminate the character "Kaiser Wilhelm II" from the play.

Having carried out the project of an epic documentary with *Rasputin,* Piscator went on to develop an *epic satire* in *The Good Soldier Schweik,* a dramatization of composite authorship based on an uncompleted novel by the then already deceased Czech writer Jaroslav Hašek. (I shall not attempt to unscramble the authorship of the dramatization, originally made by Max Brod and Hans Reimann, modified and augmented by Brecht, Piscator's playreader Gasbarra, Lania, and Piscator himself. There is no complete and definitive text in existence, so far as I know.) This was the first time that Piscator took his material from a novel—a novel of adventure, definable indeed as a picaresque novel except for the fact that its hero Schweik gets into numerous scrapes not as an unmitigated rascal but as a lovable innocent. Schweik's inspired idiocy when he is assigned as an orderly to a lieutenant wreaks havoc with the Austrian army during the World War and makes a hollow mockery of the entire war and of a good deal else besides. Recognizing the satiric possibilities of the work, Piscator allowed it to assume its natural non-Aristotelian character, producing a thoroughly horizontal pattern of incidents strung on the thread of Schweik's comic gaucheness. Since Hašek had not completed the novel, Piscator did not even strain for a conclusion—the play as it stood without a dramatic ending (and it had no Aristotelian "beginning" and "middle" either) was all the action that was needed to expose the absurdities of the Austrian-Hungarian empire and the confusing futility of the first World War.

The dramatic action lay entirely in the movement of the production rather than in any destination sought and arrived at; neither Schweik nor the war had any distinct destination anyway, and that was indeed the point of the satire. Since Schweik, moreover, was a mere cork bobbing on the surface of a world cataclysm concerning which he could have no perspective, movement *alone*—movement without clearly perceived destination—was the essence of this travesty of the state of the war-torn world between 1914 and 1918. The resulting play was inevitably "epic" rather than dramatic in the Aristotelian sense of having a beginning, a middle, and an end. The horizontality of the play was intrinsic— as intrinsic as it is in *Mother Courage,* at the close of which the heroine, who has lost all her children to the war, is still bent upon following camp and hawking her wares. At the same time, Piscator's *Schweik* was no more static than Brecht's *Mother Courage,* since the agitation of the war is a constant pulsation in the play, the individual sections are *events,* and the characters act and are acted upon by individuals and forces. Piscator also achieved a theatrical equivalent in constant stage movement and found both the right technical device and a suitable symbol for it—namely, the treadmill. By means of the tread- mill, everything was kept in movement; and keeping everything in proper flux necessitated expressive curtailments of realistic scenery. Piscator deployed, as Brecht would have done, only partial settings on the stage. He also used film projections, such as the famous caricature drawn by Georg Grosz to represent the army physician who examines the crippled Schweik and pronounces him fit for military service.

Both as a director and play doctor (and in his case the two roles tended to be indistinguishable), Piscator was, then, once more involved in epic dramaturgy by the exigencies of his material and the requirements of his socially engaged art. He was to be attracted henceforth to the novel as a springboard for socially engaged drama, and this interest was later apparent in two dramatizations, with collaborators—namely, Dreiser's *An American Tragedy,* which the Group Theatre produced in New York in the mid-thirties under the title of *The Case of Clyde Griffiths,* and Tolstoy's *War and Peace,* which Piscator first presented at his Dramatic Workshop in New York and subsequently, after returning to Europe in 1951, in France, Germany, and Scandinavia. (It is noteworthy that one of the most highly and deservedly praised productions of the year 1962 in London has been Piscator's *War and Peace,* reworked by an English writer and staged by an English director.) Piscator's penchant for the novelistic stage was also apparent in his New York production of Robert Penn Warren's *All the King's Men* at the President Theatre in January 1948, in which he made con- tinual use of a tiny revolving stage and several ramps for constantly shifting the playing areas.

Each of the first two of these epic plays, however, had a distinctive shape that distinguishes them from both the forced historicity of the *Storm over Gothland* and *Rasputin* productions and the epic comedy of *The Good Soldier Schweik.* *The Case of Clyde Griffiths* assumes the form of a demonstration by means of a court trial. In this dramatization of Dreiser's novel, a Narrator acting as the lawyer for the defense and treating the audience as the jury endeavored to ex- tenuate Clyde's guilt by demonstrating the nature and effect of the forces that collaborated with the immature hero's weak character in encompassing his ruin. The outer form of the play was a trial, but with a difference: Whereas the ordinary trial-drama zealously maintains the illusion of a court trial, Piscator's treatment broke that illusion with the Narrator's speeches to the audience and with the devices of an illustrated lecture; and whereas the average trial play presents a tightly knit action of conflict and discovery in the manner of the *pièce bien faite,* the Piscator dramatization presented a string of episodes as case-history data in the epic-novelistic, largely non-Aristotelian, manner. *The Case of Clyde Griffiths* amounted to an opening up of the trial-drama genre in two senses—in letting the action and the argument spill over the proscenium arch into the audience, thus breaking the tight structure of the well-made-play type of realism, and in visualizing on the stage a series of episodes intended to enlarge Clyde's trial into a trial of his milieu, if not indeed of society as a whole.

Piscator's *War and Peace,* as presented in its final form in London by the Bristol Old Vic, is a radically different type of play. It is a chronicle combining the fate of a single noble family with Napoleon's invasion of Russia. In *War and Peace* we find an intermingling of a novel about people with history. But these artfully arranged snippets from Tolstoy's epic novel became more than a mere adaptation because the episodes were not simply strung together, as they are in a novel. Tolstoy's book underwent a formal modification in agreement with the content of the dramatization, which amounted to an anti-war lecture-demonstration. The play had the usual didactic narrator who assumed the character of a master-of-ceremonies as he defined different playing areas for the private drama and the public action, commented on events, and drew the inevitable anti-war conclusion from his demonstration in an eloquent address to the audience. An additional feature of the work, both as a play and a stage production, was the forthright yet tasteful and dignified way in which the proscenium arch was abolished and the fourth-wall convention ignored. If the genre of *War and Peace* is to be closely defined, we may describe it as a fused private and historical chronicle in the form of a demonstration conducted with complete transparency. We may call the play a complex example of open dramaturgy openly arrived at.

Piscator continued to experiment with epic theatre techniques both in the choice and treatment of plays when he maintained his Dramatic Workshop in New York from 1940 to 1950. One of his most successful productions was *Winter Soldiers,* a drama of resistance to the Nazis in various parts of Europe which contributed to the ultimate defeat of the German army on Russian territory. Written by a young American playwright, Dan James, who was awarded the Sidney Howard Prize, *Winter Soldiers* was an effective epic drama in carrying the action in short scenes occurring either successively or simultaneously in different parts of the European continent. It had the comprehensiveness that Piscator, like Brecht, sought for the theatre. In this case the comprehensiveness was extensive and cinematic; this sequence of episodes constituted a "horizontal epic drama" in the sense in which *Mother Courage* is a "horizontal epic" drama, though a more tightly knit one. *Winter Soldiers* was a *moderate* example of the genre, however, because neither the author of the play nor its stage director, James Light, then an instructor at Piscator's "Workshop," made any effort to theatricalize the production with conspicuous violations of the fourth-wall convention and interpolations of songs, a chorus, a narrator, or a lecture. And the moderateness of the technique was perhaps all to the good, since the representation of the resistance movement on the stage was sufficiently "instructive" without further epic theatricalization and sufficiently "interrupted" by the jaggedness of the resistance-movement scenes not to require additional "distancing" or "alienating" devices; and exhortations in the form of speeches, lectures, or songs would have been quite redundant in the anti-Hitler period of the 1940's.

Winter Soldiers would have been less well received if Piscator had not refrained from overstressing the didacticism to which he was prone. The greatest resistance to epic theatre in New York was to Brecht's early didacticism in the *Lehrstück* genre, which was brilliantly parodied in a skit contributed by the left-wing publicist Emmanuel Eisenberg to the International Ladies Garment Workers' celebrated musical revue *Pins and Needles*. Piscator's addition of a documentary film on the Nazification of Germany to his 1947 production of Sartre's *The Flies,* under his supervision by a member of his staff, Paul Ransom, was deplored as a redundancy. Piscator had resorted to the film sequence in order to draw a contemporary political parallel to Sartre's philosophical, existentialist *Oresteia.* Piscator's tendency to employ stage machinery as far as his slender means would allow, also invited criticism, from his first New York production of *King Lear* on an overworked turntable in 1940 to his staging of *All the King's Men* eight years later. It was one of the weaknesses of both Piscator and Brecht to want to cross all *t's* and dot all *i's* in a script and a production in order to ensure complete comprehension of their argument—a fault against which Piscator was rarely secured by his theatrical talent and from which Brecht was frequently saved by his combination of poetic talent and tough-minded penchant for irony. It was Piscator's special weakness to rely too much upon stage machinery, although it is only fair to report that he was not indissolubly wedded to heavily mechanized productions; one of his most successful productions in New York was a *Twelfth Night,* staged under his supervision by Chouteau Dyer, with exemplary simplicity on a virtually bare stage. It was Piscator's ambition to force through an agreement between modern theatre and the machine age, to make full use of its mechanical resources, and to facilitate the creation of epic drama with "Epic-theatre" means. A statement of this vision of a regisseur-engineer appears in a note contributed by Piscator to my book *Producing the Play,* first published in 1941.

In sum, Piscator, who in his sixty-ninth year has but recently been put in charge of a new theatre being renovated for him in West Berlin which is to rival the Brechtian Theater am Schiffbauerdam in the Eastern zone, contributed a variety of dramatic forms of epic theatre and was, to a degree, Brecht's predecessor. It is significant that his book, *Das politische Theater,* published in 1929, was about to be reissued in Germany in August 1962, and that it should have been put out somewhat earlier in the year by the L'Arche press in Paris in a French translation, *Le Théâtre politique.* The translation was made by the avant-garde playwright Arthur Adamov, who recently abandoned the "theatre of the absurd" school for "epic theatre" with a play about the Paris commune: it was produced in the summer of 1962 under the title of *Spring '71* by the left-wing Unity Theatre of London. Largely unsuccessful in text as well as in the London production, *Spring '71* bears considerable resemblance to Piscator's experiments. It exemplifies a characteristic distinction between epic-theatre technique and the usual history play. An allegorical personage played by a young actress wearing the traditional red cap of Liberty appears at the beginning of the play as well as throughout the text to harangue the audience and inform it about the course of the revolt, to symbolize the conflict and to participate in it at the same time. Thus the fragments of scene are used not in a commonplace narrative sequence, but as projectiles of partisan fervor.

One may feel diffident about the question of chronological precedence, and yet conclude that Brecht had no monopoly on Epic Theatre, although he was without question its leading playwright and, after World War II, also its most celebrated stage director. Moreover, it was to the sum total of successful and unsuccessful experimentation in epic drama that we must look for a determination of the potentialities and pitfalls of Epic Theatre. Piscator's less well known ventures in Germany and the United States give strong evidence of a dramatic movement independent of Brecht's efforts as well as supplementary to it.

Until Brecht came to write his major works after 1940, Brecht's chief contribution to epic drama was *lyrical* rather than dramatic. This is most apparent, of course, in his collaborations with the composer Kurt Weill, *Die Dreigroschenoper* and *Aufstieg und Fall der Stadt Mahogonny*. In this area of theatre, to which Piscator made no particular contribution and for which Brecht was uniquely qualified by his rare poetic talent, he had no peers. A special lyrical realization of "Epic" also appeared in the *Lehrstücke*, notably, *Der Jasager, Der Neinsager, Die Massnahme,* and *Die Ausnahme und die Regel.* These, too, were epic pieces despite their brevity. They illustrated or demonstrated some social idea or some question of tactics with episodes presented singly, as in *Der Jasager* (which should be coupled, however, with *Der Neinsager*), or collectively, as in *Die Ausnahme und die Regel;* Brecht's short plays had in view some issue invoking a larger political sphere of action than the constricted plot of these little plays.

At the same time the crispness of their structure and texture assured the proper esthetic relationship between form and content; the acuteness of the author's argument accorded well with its embodiment in the action and dialogue of the play. The little *Lehrstücke* were miniature epic dramas. They are distinguishable by their compression and telescopic dramaturgy from the "chronicle epic" and the "novelistic" genre represented by Piscator's *Schweik* and Brecht's *Die Mutter,* his dramatization in 1933 of Maxim Gorky's famous novel of the same title.

In this work, too, however, Brecht created a *Lehrstück* of sorts, and a distinctive dramatic form; for instead of merely dramatizing the novel, Brecht inserted lyrical interludes known as "mass chants," with special music composed by Hanns Eisler. In the Theatre Union production given in downtown New York in 1936 the imaginary fourth-wall framed by the proscenium arch was pierced not from within, as when an actor addresses the audience from the stage, but from *without*—that is, from the auditorium. At strategic points in the action a group of actor-singers filed up the stage and delivered appropriate sentiments or comments in unison. These mass chants comprised the choral portions of Brecht's *Mother,* and they served the *Lehrstück* purpose of instructing the audience along with the general "epic theatre" objective of widening the range of a play beyond its plot. At the same time, they were instrumental in promoting the "alienation effect" of Brechtian drama, lowering the emotional temperature of the scenes and reducing identification with Gorky's sympathetic peasant mother whose love for her son turns her into a revolutionary heroine. Students of Brecht will be reminded of Brecht's problem with *Mutter Courage* about a decade later when the role of the camp-following heroine of this latter play was performed so sympathetically in Zürich that he took the precaution of reducing the emotional force of some of the scenes.

That Brecht, as was also the case with later American productions of *Galileo* and *The Good Woman of Setzuan,* paid too dearly for the alienation effect and lost some of the effect on New York audiences was easily noted. The production was not a success even with critics and audiences of the left, and the play appears to have been relegated to an inconspicuous place in the Brecht canon. But the form of the play was fascinating to some observers including myself, then drama critic for *New Theatre* magazine, and Archibald MacLeish. Both of us read papers at a symposium on the play praising the experiment as a means of reintroducing poetry into the modern drama *en bloc* in a novel and viable manner. By comparison with this somewhat aborted drama, *Frau Flintz* by Helmut Baierl, a recent Berliner Ensemble treatment of the conversion of another old-fashioned woman to collectivist ideals in East Germany after World War II, produced in the summer of 1962, was decidedly moderate; the episodes followed each other successively without any pattern of anti-plot and anti-illusionistic interruptions. The structure of Brecht's *Mother* was a veritable blueprint for a chorally augmented epic drama and is another example of its author's important lyrical enrichment of epic theatre. Other examples can be cited. It would be especially profitable to return here to Brecht's *Fears and Miseries of the Third Reich* because some of the most telling dramatic effects are produced by the singing of the *Lied der Moorsoldaten* in a prison scene and by parodies of the "Horst Wessel Song" throughout the play. And the author's reliance on the lyrical element is anything but an evasion of dramaturgy; this work contains many good scenes and includes *The Jewish Wife* and *The Informer,* two superb episodes that have been presented as self-contained one-act plays.

The retention of the lyrical element in Brecht's later work is a well known feature of his technique. I found it tiresome in one, not necessarily conclusive, production of *Der gute Mensch von Setzuan,* the music for which was composed by Paul Dessau, but I found it fairly effective in Washington and London productions of *The Caucasian Chalk Circle* in 1962; and Eric Bentley, who translated *Mother Courage* for a pending Broadway production, made out an extreme case for the importance of the "Songs" in *Mother Courage.* In an essay in Stanley Burnshaw's *Varieties of Literary Experience* (New York University Press, 1962, pp. 60–61), Mr. Bentley makes the point that "the Brechtian song is an individual item, clearly marked off from its content, like an individual number in vaudeville," and repeats his belief that it would be less misleading to declare that in Brecht's plays "the dialogue is an interruption of the songs" than to say that the songs are interruptions of the dialogue. Even if it may be too much to claim that "epic theatre is lyric theatre," it is indisputable that Brecht's most characteristic contribution to epic drama was lyrical.

That contribution was at the same time dramatic and theatrical, and with respect to the forms of Epic drama developed by Brecht and others we are obliged to note that in *Galileo,* for instance, Brecht transformed the conventional genre of biographical drama quite radically. This is apparent when one compares his treatment of Galileo with another well regarded play, Barrie Stavis's *Lamp at Midnight,* the New Stages production which Brooks Atkinson reviewed favorably in the *New York Times* in the 1940's. Atkinson and other New York drama critics, with the exception of Louis Kronenberger then reviewing for the newspaper *PM,* saw little merit in Brecht's play, which was by its author's design the very antithesis of a simple narration and a eulogy. By means of calculated violations of the fourth-wall convention, the use of song as well as demonstration of scientific data, and other "alienating" or "anti-illusionistic" elements in the play, Brecht created a genre of biographical drama in which narrational biography is secondary to demonstration, analysis, and argument.

With this in mind, we are justified in referring to a genre of "epic biography," formally distinguishable from a simple chronicle such as Laurence Housman's *Victoria Regina,* which was originally a haphazard collection of one-act plays about Queen Victoria, and from a more complex play such as Robert Sherwood's *Abe Lincoln in Illinois* which, for all its seeming documentary character in a Lincoln-Douglas debate scene, remains a mere narrative sequence rather than an argument for which the author has found an expressive form.

By comparison with *Abe Lincoln in Illinois,* John Drinkwater's *Abraham Lincoln,* written twenty years earlier, and Norman Corwin's Lincoln-Douglas debate-drama *The Rivalry,* presented in New York twenty years later, were closer to Epic Theatre dramaturgy. The Drinkwater play alternated episodes and a chorus of "Two Chroniclers" speaking verse in unison, and Corwin's play used open dramaturgy and made the Lincoln-Douglas debates the main dramatic feature. Brecht's *Galileo,* nevertheless, is a decidedly more ample and penetrating work than either *Abraham Lincoln* or *The Rivalry;* and Brecht must be credited with having brought biographical drama into the theatre as an *epic* form. *Galileo* is a more fluid, varied, and theatrically original drama than Drinkwater's stiffly patterned play; and *Galileo* combines richer characterization with more penetrating theatricality than Corwin's resumé of Lincoln's political debates.

Mother Courage also constitutes a unique genre. Although it belongs to the quasi-historical genre of Epic Theatre in dealing with The Thirty Years War, it is more personalized in its emphasis than many a chronicle play. It deals primarily with the human beings who both live by war and are destroyed by it. This work, perhaps the most penetrating anti-war play in any language since *The Trojan Women,* expresses the fundamental ambivalence or duality of human nature in an alternation of scenes exposing greed and cowardice with scenes depicting human perseverance and sympathy. The essence of Brecht's chronicle resides in this dramatic pattern or rhythm. And this rhythm is theatrically punctuated by the projections on a front curtain and especially by the "Songs."

It is because of its special structure that *Mother Courage* is distinguishable from the ordinary chronicle play. It differs from a work such as Gerhart Hauptmann's naturalistic Peasants' Revolt drama *Florian Geyer* written in 1896. In Hauptmann's play, the size of the cast and the extensiveness of the action result in an inchoate mass of matter, because there is nothing in the structure of this loose work to hold the parts together. *Florian Geyer* is a much simpler work than the concern with ambivalence allows *Mother Courage* to be, yet Brecht's also loosely tied episodes constitute a comprehensible whole because the dramatic form is a demonstration by strong dramatic and theatrical means. In this work, then, Brecht produced an exemplary epic drama rather than an epic by mere extensiveness or by mere default in failing to observe the Aristotelian dramatic form of a beginning, a middle, and an end. Adamov's *Spring '71,* written almost a quarter of a century later than *Mother Courage,* represents another endeavor to match form and substance; if it is a poor play, it simply proves that it is possible to make a mess of things in *any* form or genre. And if Hauptmann's *The Weavers* and O'Casey's *The Plough and the Stars* are impressive works without benefit of Brechtian theatricalism, if both works have dramatic power and illumination without the dramatic machinery of a Piscator or Brecht, it is an obvious conclusion that there has been no Piscator-Brecht monopoly in epic theatre except possibly in the opinion of extreme partisans. This reflection does not, however, invalidate the view that the presentational, theatricalist, organization of *Mother Courage* does constitute a special form suitable for a dialectical demonstration and dramatic showing, rather than discussion, of its subject. *Mother Courage* is a "pure showing" whereas Giraudoux' non-epic treatment of the Trojan War, for example, is mainly a discussion along urbane Parisian lines; and Shaw's *Saint Joan* is essentially a story which his intellect irradiated with the superb dialectics of the famous tent scene. Anouilh's *The Lark,* it is true, is replete with theatricalist devices, but Anouilh is chiefly playing with theatre while presenting a serious and painful subject. At the other extreme, however, we may find consistency of naturalism, as in *The Weavers,* depriving a play of both a rich texture of characterization (Brecht's is vastly richer in *Mother Courage* than Hauptmann's) and the discussion element Shaw employed so brilliantly in *Saint Joan* and upon which he placed so much emphasis in acclaiming Ibsen as the creator of discussion drama or so-called drama of ideas in *The Quintessence of Ibsenism.*

Brecht's other two major works, *The Good Woman of Setzuan* and *The Caucasian Chalk Circle* also comprise distinct modes of "Epic." They are collectively designated as "parables." *The Good Woman,* written between 1938 and 1941, is a dramatic tale exemplifying the problem of being virtuous in a predatory world. *The Caucasian Chalk Circle,* written in 1944-45, is presented as a legend to illustrate the moral that, as the Singer or Narrator put it, "what there is shall belong to those who are good for it." Both parables, however, are not fortuitous mutations in the Brecht canon but are extensions of the earlier

Lehrstücke, which also illustrated a point by means of a theatrically presented instance. A problematical subject is raised. It is not necessarily answered. It is both raised and answered in *The Caucasian Chalk Circle.* The question raised in *The Good Woman of Setzuan*—the extremely complex problem of goodness in the world as it is—is not answered; it is passed on to the audience.

Two somewhat separate types of drama appear in these parables. We may conclude that *The Caucasian Chalk Circle* is an *"Epic" Morality; The Good Woman of Setzuan* is an *"Epic" Problem Play.* It is not, of course, a well-made-play like Ibsen's *Pillars of Society* because of its theatricalist, quasi-oriental, features, the most striking of which is the heroine's non-naturalistic transformation into her male cousin. It is a shrewdly designed *ill-made* play, and this makes it possible for the play to be truly problematical and ensures the artistic agreement of content and form. If we should call *The Caucasian Chalk Circle* a *Lesson Play* we should have to define *The Good Woman of Setzuan* as a *Question Play.*

Both are modern epic dramas. And both have their limitations or dangers, too. Brecht overcame the chief danger of Morality drama—that of single-tracked lesson-giving in *The Caucasian Chalk Circle* through the open epic form of that play. The structural looseness averted the effect of narrow didacticism, as did also the comic and folksy line of the action. Brecht also successfully combined vivid caricature in depicting the ruling class with affecting characterizations in the case of his humble heroine and her soldier-lover, thus avoiding Morality-Play abstractionism, which is not unknown in Epic Theatre. He also lightened his didacticism by giving it exuberance and folksy theatricality. He did not blend caricature and character, realistic illusion and anti-illusionist detail, but, rather, set these elements side by side, very much as the *pointilliste* dabs one dot of color on the canvas next to a different dot of color instead of mixing them on his palette. Brecht followed the same procedure in his production scheme when he required masks for some characters, such as the Governor's Wife, who is not created as a real person, and dispensed with masks for the servant-girl whose simple human reality is essential to the action and the argument. Brecht, however, was not always so successful in escaping the pitfalls of didacticism, which is apparent in the constricted character of the one-act play *Die Massnahme,* or *The Measure Taken,* written in 1930, and the choppy over-insistence that vitiates the chorus-punctuated dramatization of Gorky's *Mother* and partly accounted for the failure of the Theatre Union production of the mid-thirties. This "weakness from strength," so to speak, accounted for the inadequacy of many an American left-wing drama of the 'thirties that suffered from a so-called *conversion ending,* and also weakened the Berlin Ensemble's recent epic drama *Frau Flintz,* which has the additional faults of diffuseness and failure to make the conversion of its elderly heroine either clear or convincing.

The Good Woman of Setzuan may well leave its audience "hung up," so to speak, so that the play itself becomes problematical, and if it is that for audiences it can prove the same for the venturesome director who stages it. I do not in fact know of any conspicuously successful professional production of this almost a quarter-of-a-century old play in the West; and Brecht himself was apparently troubled by its quizzical character and lack of resolution in dutifully noting the advent of Communist China and declaring that "the province of Setzuan in this parable, which stood for all places where men are exploited by men, is such a place no longer." Nevertheless, it is a genuinely modern type of play in its very inconclusiveness. It is a quizzical drama of failed idealism, of which Ibsen's *Brand* is an epic prototype, Chekhov's *Ivanov* is a naturalistic variant, and Paul Green's *Johnny Johnson,* a play about a Wilsonian Democrat, produced in 1936, is a later "Epic" example. To a degree, however, it is the challenge intrinsic to the unresolved or suspended ending that is important. This is the case in Brecht's play; in Ibsen's lumberingly splendid "epic," *Emperor and Galilean,* in which the reconciliation of the opposites of paganism and Christianity is left for the future; in *Johnny Johnson,* in which the supposed madness of its Wilsonian pacifist puts to shame the unsound sanity of normal men who make war; and in Irwin Shaw's one-act play of the same year (1936), *Bury the Dead,* in which the dead soldiers of a future war step out of their graves in order to seek a fuller life than they had ever had while alive. The range of the suspended, essentially unresolved, Epic type of drama seems large, indeed.

In concluding this summary of epic forms and the problems of dramaturgy encountered in them, it is necessary to observe, of course, that the review is partial and sketchy. For one thing, both Piscator and Brecht insisted that they were following a long-established tradition, evident in the oriental theatre, the classic Greek drama, the medieval mystery-play cycles, the Elizabethan drama, and the romantic theatre that adopted the open Shakespearean pattern of drama from the 18th century *Sturm und Drang* period of *Goetz von Berlichingen* and *Die Raüber* to the late romantic period of Büchner and Gutzkow. This is too large a subject to be treated here. It would also be essential to differentiate between what is and what is not truly modern Epic Theatre; we would have to observe, for instance, that mere epic extension does not make a play an epic drama in the Brechtian sense. Thus Büchner's chronicle of the French Revolution, *Danton's Death,* is a prototype of modern epic and *Oedipus Rex,* Aristotle's example of a perfect tragedy, is *not* an epic drama despite the presence of the choruses. *Oedipus* has a closed structure, *Danton's Death* an open one; it is also "narrative" in the manner of Piscator's *War and Peace* and "documentary" in the manner of *Rasputin* in so far as it gives a kaleidoscopic view of a critical period in history. *Danton's Death* is a composite epic drama possessing the merit of provocativeness and the defect of spottiness and diffuseness. It tells or, rather, shows a many-faceted story, it depicts an historical situation in a variety of scenes, and it flares up into critical scenes of accusation and defense—as in an Epic trial drama. There is no *a priori* reason, of course, why an Epic play should not have a composite structure and style; an "Epic" playwright cheerfully dispenses with the Aristotelian and neo-classic unities. The "composite" Epic play is an obviously acceptable form of modern drama.

Since the advent of Piscator, Brecht, and their associates the leaders of Epic Theatre on the European continent, various degrees and modes of "Epic" have continued to appear in many places—notably in France, where existentialist plays by Sartre and Camus, such as *The Devil and the Good Lord* and *Caligula*, have had marked Epic-theatre features. Successful productions in English are Robert Bolt's Thomas More biography *A Man for All Seasons,* also thriving in New York, and the *War and Peace* London production, in 1962. In the English-speaking theatre, two distinct developments of Epic can be noted in stage drama (aside from musical-comedy chronicles such as Kurt Weill's Broadway failure *Love Life* and Lionel Bart's London success *Blitz*), although attention may also be given to documentary films, which reached their peak in the United States during World War II as well as television documentaries and Epic radio plays, which attained literary distinction in Archibald MacLeish's *The Fall of the City* in 1937 and had rhetorical effectiveness in Norman Corwin's *On a Note of Triumph* produced at the conclusion of World War II.

One type of epic drama intended directly for the stage has been the stage spectacle. In its weakest form, it is currently enjoying a vogue in European countries under the general title of *Son et Lumière.* It is indeed very little more than "Sound and Light" and comprises an open-air historical pageant based on the annals of a particular place such as Notre Dame de Paris or the City of Bruges. A less innocuous form has been the plainly political one represented probably at its worst by staged Nazi demonstrations and perhaps at its best, in literary and theatrical afflatus, by *Mystery-Bouffe,* a mass-spectacle celebrating the Bolshevik Revolution written by the poet Mayakovsky and staged in 1919 by that *Wunderkind* of anti-naturalistic directors, Meyerhold. And a moderate form of dramatic history has been steadily developing in the United States, chiefly in the South, ever since the production, in 1937, of *The Lost Colony,* the first of Paul Green's pageant-plays. Since then Paul Green has written many other pageant-plays, some more epic in quality than others, and he has been joined in this enterprise in outdoor summer theater by other Southern writers, notably Kermit Hunter, the author of the successful Cherokee Indian chronicle *Unto These Hills,* given annually before large audiences at Cherokee (North Carolina), in the Smoky Mountains. The results have been uneven, although Paul Green has maintained a high standard of literary taste in producing these amalgams of historical episodes, recitations, choruses, songs, dances, and spectacles for which Green's generic term "symphonic drama" is not inappropriate.

But if this experiment in American epic theatre has been the most continuous, it is the documentary form that made the greatest impression as a new and vital art form. It materialized as the so-called Living Newspaper and while one cannot urge literary claims for it, it amounted to remarkably dramatic journalism and special pleading. Developed during the Depression period of the 1930's in the work-relief program known as The Federal Theatre, it brought journalists, actors, and technicians together in an endeavor to express the period's analysis of social ills and zeal for social reform. The producers of the "living newspapers" blended narration, action, demonstration, song, and dance; they used both naturalistic and symbolic details at will. They reproduced the façade of a New York slum tenement in *One-Third of a Nation* that could have done justice to David Belasco's spectacular naturalism, and they used nine masks to symbolize the Supreme Court in another production, *Power*. The "living news-papers" favored other formal features, including a sort of minstrel-show inter-locutor or "Little Man" who wants to know why he cannot have decent housing or why electric power is so expensive and a Narrator-lecturer who provides an explanation by means of slides, demonstrations, and scraps of illustrated scenes. The greatest impression that native Epic theatre ever made on the American stage came from these "living newspaper" experiments of the Federal Theatre under the supervision of Hallie Flanagan Davis from Vassar, who later pre-pared a "living newspaper" of her own, $E=Mc_2$, on the subject of the atom bomb, at Smith College and presented it briefly in New York as well. If the "Living Newspaper" came to an untimely end as an epic genre, the reason was not esthetic but economic. It earned high critical praise as a form of theatre despite its slight literary value, but it could not be produced on any impressive scale without federal subsidy. Only one fully implemented "living newspaper," *Medicine Show,* appeared on the New York stage after Congress liquidated the Federal Theatre along with other New Deal welfare projects in 1938. It was also from the Federal Theatre during its last slender lease on life that the American drama acquired its outstanding, if narrowly circumscribed, lyrical epic drama, Marc Blitzstein's song-and-dance satire and paean to social mili-tancy, *The Cradle Will Rock,* which was presented by Orson Welles' Mercury Theatre after the Federal Theatre found it expedient to drop the project it had nursed along.

In England epic drama attracts more attention than it ever did, the attraction resulting in nothing more original, on the one hand, than the biographical chronicle exemplified by John Osborne's *Luther* and Christopher Fry's *Curt-mantle,* and, on the other hand, the effective, theatrically invigorated, drama of *A Man for All Seasons,* which strict proponents of Epic Theatre should be reluctant to endorse wholeheartedly because it doesn't actually go far enough toward illustrating social reality. We are given the sense of the character, Thomas More, but not the issue itself in more than the general terms of his Roman Catholic adherence and other peoples' opportunism. In Germany, Brecht, who died in 1956, has not yet had a successor; the East German author of *Frau Flintz* has made no particular contribution to epic drama and the West German Carl Zuckmayer's *Das kalte Licht* (1955), an account of the treason and detection of Klaus Fuchs the physicist who spied for the Communists, was but a pale reflection of epic drama in 1955 and considerably inferior to his earlier drama of the Nazi period, *Des Teufels General.* In Switzerland, however, epic drama has recently had noteworthy variants in the work of Friedrich Duerrenmatt and Max Frisch (especially in the Morality tragedy of *The Visit* and the parable-comedy of *Biedermann*), so that the further development of Epic forms seems probable even if talent such as Brecht himself possessed is too rare in any period to be anticipated.

In summary it is possible to list at least the following conclusions: Epic drama derives from a tradition that pre-dates the modern period and won new prestige after the neo-classical period with the vogue of Shakespearean open dramaturgy and the rise of Romanticism. But it lacked modern definition and direction until the advent of Piscator and Brecht. It also acquired a dynamic quality in social Expressionism that had some vogue between 1910 and 1925, chiefly in Germany. But the Epic element in such earnest plays as Kaiser's *Gas* and Toller's *Masse-Mensch,* was scattered by expressionist explosions of violence and dissolved in expressionist subjectivity; and the same thing may be observed in more or less dadaist expressions of cynicism and satirical protest, of which Brecht's early plays *Baal* and *In the Jungle of the Cities* and E. E. Cummings' *him* are perhaps the most meritorious examples. When the expressionist wave subsided, Epic Theatre forged ahead with its characteristic forms and found a genius with a dual talent for literature and theatre in Bertolt Brecht. Piscator, Brecht, and others who have been mentioned or unmentioned in this paper produced a number of dramatic forms that have enlarged the scope and enriched the possibilities of modern drama. The end of these ventures has been by no means reached, and they have already been too numerous to be subsumed under a single definition or associated with the single ideological trend of Marxism. Perhaps we can even associate epic theatre with religious drama, as once was the case when the Middle Ages of Faith produced the *mystery* cycles or Passion Plays. Perhaps the Age of Doubt can also produce Epic religious drama, and that this has been the case, in some respects, is suggested by Claudel's Christian chronicle *The Satin Slipper* and Christopher Fry's *A Sleep of Prisoners.* And if these reflections tend to minimize some distinctions and to obfuscate the subject of Epic Theatre with their inclusiveness, such obfuscation may actually be a first step toward clarification. The alternative of limiting application of the adjective "epic" to a single dramatic form is plainly untenable. Certainly, Epic drama, in its widest allowable range of open dramaturgy, has proved to be the only viable non-romantic and unskittish alternative to the constricted dramaturgy of contemporary realism and naturalism.

To arrive at this conclusion, however, is to invite a number of questions. The first is whether "Epic theatre" does not become meaningless unless its application is restricted in one or more respects. That danger is considerable when the term is allowed to embrace pre-modern as well as modern drama because nearly every historical play and non-neoclassic tragedy before Hebbel's mid-nineteenth century *Maria Magdalena* can be designated as "epic drama" in so far as the dramaturgy is presentational, the scope of the presentation is large and varied, and the subject matter is the fate of a ruler, dynasty or nation. Brecht tacitly acknowledged a link with the past when he adapted Sophocles' *Antigone* and Marlowe's *Edward II* or used John Gay's *The Beggar's Opera* as a basis for his *Dreigroschenoper,* and it is worth noting that Piscator chose *King Lear* for his debut as an epic theatre producer-director in New York in 1940. As a matter of fact, Piscator and Brecht *preferred* to identify themselves with the mainsteam of the theatre and the great tradition of presentational drama, which has sanctioned all known devices of open dramaturgy and epic theatre ever since the time of Aeschylus.

The contention that Epic Theatre is anti-Aristotelian did not disturb proponents of "Epic" when they related themselves to the presentational theatre of the past and should not have troubled them, for a good deal of Greek drama, including Aeschylus' Oresteian trilogy, is not "Aristotelian" either. The real difference between the Piscator-Brecht school and the older theatre is ideological rather than esthetic. Even the emphasis on *Entfremdung,* or the "alienation" principle, in Brecht's theoretical writings can be misleading, for presentational comedy has always been more or less "alienating," except in empathic pastoral or romantic scenes; and the formalism of tragedy, in general, not to mention presentational devices such as the Chorus, the *deus ex machina* and the Messenger, has been a "distancing" factor. Therefore, Brecht's term "Epic *Realism,"* with its implication of a materialistic and more or less Marxist viewpoint, is helpful in distinguishing between the Piscator-Brecht type of epic theatre and older presentational styles of theatre.

The term is also helpful in distinguishing the open dramaturgy of a Claudel from that of Brecht. In such baroque work as the chronicle play *Le Soulier de Satin* (1919–1924) and the biographical drama *Le Livre de Christophe Colomb* (1927), undoubtedly uninfluenced by the dramatic art of Piscator and Brecht, the effect is Wagnerian, symbolist, and "magical." If we say that Brecht's *Galileo* and Claudel's *Christopher Columbus* are both epic biographies, we are not saying what *kind* of plays they are except that they are "epic" in certain formal features. Yet it is obvious that the two aforementioned plays "work" on us quite divergently and *affect us* altogether differently. An attempt to take Claudel's plays, as well as those of sundry symbolists, ritualists, and subjective expressionists (Verhaeren, Andreyev, Eliot, Strindberg, O'Neill, Lenormand, et al.), into "epic theatre" on purely formal grounds (and such an effort is made rather strenuously in Marianne Kesting's *Das epische Theater,* Kohlhammer, (Stuttgart, 1959) may, in the last analysis, be commended for comprehensiveness rather than for discrimination.[1] The mystical impetus of Claudel's art, his poetic afflatus (one might call his orotund poetry a form of poetic as well as religious intoxication by comparison with the powerful and ironic *"Sachlichkeit"* of lines by Brecht such as *"Der Grosskönig muss eine neue Provinz haben, der Bauer muss sein Milchgeld hergeben. /Damit das Dach der Welt erobert wird, werden die Hüttendecher abgetragen. /Die Schlacht ist verloren, aber die Helme sind bezahlt worden"*), and the baroque imagination that disposed Claudel toward the grandiose and the grandiloquent alters the essential form of the play. It is not just the surface content, but the inner form of the work that is affected by his mystique; a Claudel epic play becomes in successive parts or as a whole an ecstasy, a plangent oratorio, a solemn rite, or a majestic procession, whereas a Piscator or Brecht drama is essentially a *demonstration* of an idea or point-of-view. To say that *The Satin Slipper* and *Mother Courage* are chronicle and epic plays may be technically correct but tells very little about the distinctive character of these works. Claudel's epic *idealism* produces a work that is essentially an extension of a Calderón *auto sacramentale.* It is fundamentally a different kind of drama than a play produced by Piscator's or Brecht's epic *realism,* despite the similarity of presentational devices, interruption of plot, violation of "fourth-wall" illusionism, structural anti-Aristotelianism, and narrative comprehensiveness.

Efforts to bring other types of work, such as Thornton Wilder's *Our Town* and *The Skin of Our Teeth* and Tennessee Williams' *Camino Real,* within the orbit of "Epic Theatre" must also be viewed with suspicion or hedged about with strong qualifications. They may constitute epic *theatre*, but they are not epic *realism*, and the difference is not simply one of content but of form. Williams' play is merely a "dream-play" analogue to reality, as is indeed Strindberg's *Dream Play* itself. And if we call Wilder's two plays chronicles, which they technically are, we do not touch upon their unique character at all. *The Skin of Our Teeth*, for example, would be more accurately described as two acts of benign extravaganza and one act of domestic drama augmented by *Lehrstück* features, such as the procession of the placard-carrying-figures in Act III. By virtue of its extensive coverage of time and space, its non-Aristotelian structure, and its presentational devices, such as Sabina's address to the audience in Act I, *The Skin of Our Teeth* may be "epic theatre" but is not "epic realism." To a large degree, the play relates itself by means of ingenious anachronisms to vague universals rather than to the particulars of society. Its "Finnegans Wake" type of comic and (in Act II) vaudeville synthesis of the past and present, subordinates content to theatricality. A large part of the play (two out of three acts) operates as a theatrical *tour de force*, and verges on a "theatre for theatre's sake" type of composition. A work of epic realism such as *Mother Courage* differs radically in expressive form from *The Skin of Our Teeth*.

We may conclude, then, that Epic plays can be *organically* very different despite their common non-Aristotelian and "open" structure, depending on the author's organizing principle—that is, on whether the plays are idealistically or materialistically, magically or analytically, romantically or realistically oriented. Claudel actually subordinates the written drama to mime, dance, and spectacle to produce an effect of uncritical and submissive ecstasy or hypnosis. It is precisely because the possibilities of epic theatre have been ample that discrimination among them is important. And in this connection the operative word *realism* in the term "epic realism" should prove especially useful.

NOTE

1. Marianne Kesting, it is only fair to say, acknowledges some distinctions. In her chapter on Claudel, for example (pp. 88–105), she says that *"das Zeitliche wird unter dem Blickpunkt des Ewigen betrachtet"* (p. 99) in *Christopher Columbus*. She admits that *"Claudel bediente sich des epischen Theaters, ausser zum Kommentar, um innere Visionen zu vergegenwärtigen"* (p. 105) and correctly applies the same qualification to Strindberg's *Dream Play*. She also takes note of Claudel's lavish use of atmospheric spectacle, which is actually a characteristic of *symbolist* rather than of epic theatre; and concerning Claudel's heavy reliance on musical effect, a *Wagnerian* rather than epic realistic procedure, she observes that in contrast to Brecht, *"baut Claudel die Musik als 'Fil du récit' ein, welche die Kontinuität der Bühnenhandlung wahrt, während Brecht diese Kontinuität durch die Musik unterbrechen will"*—in order, she might have added, to allow or enable the playgoer's analytical and critical faculty to take over, which is hardly a Claudelian objective. But Marianne Kesting concedes too much similarity in not differentiating sharply enough, in the final analysis, between epic realism and epic symbolism or epic idealism. Herbert Ihering's protest against Claudel's *"Anwendung des epischen Dramaturgie"* is doctrinaire in its rationalism, but has the merit of calling attention to the contrast with epic realism: *"Er . . . verwendet alle Mittel eines revolutionären, eines harten, eines wirklichen Theaters, um religiös zu mystifizieren. Was geschaffen war, um aufzuklären, wird hier dem Glauben unterstellt. Was desillusionnierend gedacht war, dient einer neuen Illusion."* (Quoted in Kesting, p. 89). *The Coral* and the two parts of *Gas* by Georg Kaiser, the expressionist playwright to whom Brecht was rather partial, and Shaw's *St. Joan*, especially in the great pre-trial tent scene between Warwick and the Bishop when they decide to destroy Joan because she is a premature "Nationalist" and "Protestant," are obviously much closer to epic *realism* than Strindberg's *Dream Play* and Claudel's *Satin Slipper* or *Christopher Columbus* despite their patently open structure.

V

Literary Relations

In a sense, literary relations is another term for comparative literature; it is not a part of comparative literature, but comparative literature itself. The subheads under which the articles in this section are grouped could be increased or varied considerably, and some of the articles could logically fit under more than one of the headings.

Literary History. The province of the literary historian is to trace the chronological development of literary culture as a whole, while presenting the general intellectual background of the period or periods he is covering. He stresses major works without neglecting minor. Some scholars even make a distinction between the literary historian and the historical critic. As we have seen, the duty of the literary critic is to analyze specific works and evaluate them esthetically. The historical critic, midway between the literary historian and the literary critic concerns himself, therefore, with both artistic values and historical development. It is much easier to write the history of a single national literature than of all western literature together. As a matter of fact, a comprehensive coverage of the latter subject has never been attempted. Individual periods or even centuries, however, have been treated successfully on the comparative level. Most comparative historical studies are modest in scope and pretentions, and are devoted to strictly limited areas. The article of Schuyler V. R. Cammann well represents the special kind of literary history typical of comparative literature — that requiring an extensive linguistic capability.

History of Ideas. This is a branch of intellectual history developed and brought to perfection by the late A. O. Lovejoy and carried on by the distinguished *Journal of the History of Ideas*. A general discussion of the tenets of its practitioners appears in Philip P. Wiener's article in that journal, "Some Problems and Methods in the History of Ideas" (XXII [1961], 531-548). In contrast to literary history, which attempts to present a comprehensive view of the chronological development of literature, the history of ideas concentrates on single topics such as primitivism, luxury, attitudes toward China, or even the manner in which the arts and sciences have been divided and classified. The essay by Mario Praz in the present collection illustrates what A. O. Lovejoy calls "the presence and influence of the same presuppositions or other operative 'ideas' in very diverse provinces of thought and in different periods" (*Essays in the History of Ideas* [Baltimore, 1948], p. xiv). Professor Praz does not indicate a direct influence by one writer upon another (as Shackleton does in portraying the relationship between Machiavelli and Montesquieu), but he shows how a broad sentiment or feeling expressed by Tasso in heroic poetry of the sixteenth century was transmitted through English poetry to the landscape gardening of the late eighteenth century. A similar parallel between French classical tragedy and the French garden was developed by August Wilhelm Schlegel in his *Vorlesungen über dramatische Kunst und Literatur,* 1809. The article by Professor Praz could equally well appear under the heading, "Literature and the Other Arts."

Mirage. The concept of mirage refers to the impression which one national culture makes upon another through literature. Like the mirage in the desert, this impression may or may not resemble reality. Going beyond the portrayal of national types, such as the stolid Englishman, the volatile Frenchman, or the materialistic American, which are mainly caricatures, the mirage comprises the total effect which one nation makes upon individuals of another. The method was brought to perfection by the French comparatist Jean-Marie Carré. It may be seen in many of his works, including *Les Ecrivains français et le mirage allemand, 1800-1840* (1947). The essay by Harry Levin draws attention to some of the differences between one nation's impression of itself and the impression which it makes upon a neighbor.

Sources and Influences. This has been one of the traditional occupations of scholarship for at least the past century. It is a legitimate and rewarding inquiry to ascertain which have been the most seminal minds in western literary culture and which have been the most receptive to movements from the past. It is also of some significance to ascertain which writers in a contemporary situation react to mutual stimuli. Some critics argue that the search for sources and influences is old-fashioned as if this is enough to discredit the inquiry completely. But even these opponents of influence studies justify the examination of major literary works in order to ascertain the elements which are traditional and those which are unique qualities. One may perhaps go a step beyond and argue that the qualities consciously borrowed from a previous author are those with an already demonstrated efficacy and, therefore of universal esthetic appeal. In the pictorial arts the revealing of similarities in two canvasses in a source and influence relationship is still considered of paramount importance. In comparative literature as well, the recognition of elements of the known in a heretofore unfamiliar situation brings an undeniable satisfaction. Whether this kind of literary detective work throws light on esthetic values is debatable, but that it tells us something concerning the creative process is undeniable. The article by Robert Shackleton goes beyond a discussion of the influence of one writer upon another to reveal the varied intellectual concepts which have been supported historically by the symbolic authority of the two authors with whom he is concerned.

Literature and Society. This is one aspect of the relationship of literature to other aspects of culture. It would be possible to trace social attitudes in the literature of antiquity — as students of the notion of primitivism have already demonstrated. Greek and Roman authors who sang the praises of life in a rural retreat away from the complexities of urban congestion were obviously giving heed to an important social problem. This primitivistic theme is universally considered appropriate for literary study even by those critics who deplore emphasis on elements extrinsic to the work itself — elements such as social and historical backgrounds as well as the author's life. Their opposition is less fervent to the study of literature and art because of the common esthetic bond between the two disciplines, which does not exist in the study of the relations between literature and other disciplines such as psychology, religion, science, and society. *Comparative Literature Studies* has published separate issues devoted to literature and religion and to literature and art. The history of utopian thought belongs as much to literature as it does to philosophy and sociology. A consideration of merely the formal or esthetic features of Plato's *Republic* or More's *Utopia* would be incomplete to say the least. The same could be said of the dramas of Ibsen and Shaw as well as virtually the entire corpus of realism and naturalism. The essay by Martin

Jarrett-Kerr, taken from the special issue on literature and religion, discusses theological and anthropological concepts related to literature and society.

Literature and Science. Some critics argue that it makes little difference whether Milton reflected a Ptolemaic or Copernican view of astronomy in his poetry. They feel that the subject of the cosmos or the external universe is completely irrelevant to poetry in general, including the works of Dante, Milton, and Goethe. The latter, however, took just the opposite view. Goethe was a scientist himself and felt that scientific truth — like all truth — was the proper province of poetry. The essay by Walter J. Ong transcends the biological aspect of evolution to treat the more abstract question of recurrence in the cosmos and its use as a theme for poetry and art.

SCHUYLER V. R. CAMMANN

Christopher the Armenian and the Three Princes of Serendip

IN 1557, A VENETIAN PRINTER named Tramezzino published a small volume of Oriental tales, called *Peregrinaggio di tre figluoli del re di Serendippo.* The title page announced that it had been translated from Persian into Italian by "M. Christoforo *Armeno.*" This little book describing the travels and adventures of the three princes of Serendip became very popular. It was reissued in successive editions in Italy;[1] it was soon translated into German;[2] and it was several times rewritten or imitated in France, though never properly translated there.[3] One of the French adaptations, by a Chevalier de Mailly, was later presented in several European languages, including English.[4]

Horace Walpole, as a child, read Mailly's book, and it was a memory of this that induced him, years later, to coin the word "serendipity." He first used this word in a letter of January 28, 1754, written to his friend Horace Mann, the British Resident in Florence.[5] In that letter he explained it as meaning "accidental sagacity," a quality enjoyed by the three princes, who, as he pointed out," "were always making discoveries by accidents and sagacity of things they were not in quest of"; and he added: "*No* discovery of a thing you *are* looking for comes under this description." The new word was absorbed into our language, and it has enjoyed several cycles of popularity, in the course of which its meaning has gradually changed. Serendipity now is generally understood to mean accidental discovery. However, without the element of sagacity, it has lost its chief ingredient. It was brilliant reasoning, rather than lucky accidents, that characterized the fictional experiences of the three princes.

Interest in the word led back to the original book about the three princes (through association, many people still firmly believe that Walpole actually wrote it) and this interest has led to a number of articles and notes about it in various journals. The proliferation continues on. In the past three years, the

Peregrinaggio has inspired three new books in the United States. Two of these consist of highly elaborate reworkings of the framework story and its seven interior tales, by Elizabeth Jamison Hodges.[6] The third presents the first direct English translation of the old Italian work, with an extensive commentary discussing the background of the book and the word "serendipity."

This last volume, entitled *Serendipity and the Three Princes,*[7] is beautifully printed; otherwise the production is amateur in every sense of that word. Its author-editor, a Chicago attorney named Theodore Remer, undertook to compile it from sheer fondness for the subject. Initial curiosity about the word "serendipity" spurred him to collect information about the word itself, its origin, and its subsequent fate at the hands of popular writers and lexicographers. In the course of this, he discovered that Walpole's inspiration for it had probably been an early edition of Mailly's work,[8] and that the latter had in turn proceeded from the *Peregrinaggio;* then, when he found that the latter had never been translated into English,[9] he persuaded two friends—also amateurs—to undertake its translation.

The subject as a whole is a truly international one, involving an original book in Italian, admittedly translated from Persian, and succeeded by translations and commentaries in French and German. However, the editor lacked the language ability and scholarly background to deal with it in all its details.[10] Attempting to do so, he fell into blunders in the choice of "authorities," and he had the bad luck to choose and overemphasize all the major errors of a certain school of German scholars who had gone off the track in their theories regarding the origin of the *Peregrinaggio.* Lastly, he managed to pass on these erroneous ideas to his translators, giving them serious delusions regarding the nature of the book, and this inevitably crippled their efforts.[11]

The *Peregrinaggio* has had considerable importance in the history of world literature, not only because it was often quoted, and because it inspired a number of other books, but, more importantly, because it served to transmit into the European tradition a whole series of Oriental tales and literary motifs. Unfortunately, the new book distorts this development by denying the earlier stages of this transmission, and—since it was written with an air of confident authority—it has already convinced some influential people that its false ideas are true.[12] In view of this, it seems important to try to correct the errors of this amateur attempt at scholarship, and at the same time to present some newly found facts that help to shed light on the real origin of the *Peregrinaggio.* But, above all, I feel an obligation to restore the memory of the book's maligned and neglected author, whose very name has been dismissed as a fiction.

CHRISTOPHER, THE AUTHOR OF THE *PEREGRINAGGIO*

The title page of the original Italian book, in stating that it was translated from Persian by M. Christoforo Armeno, has a change of typeface for the second word, making it evident that the latter was not a name, but rather a qualifying word or descriptive epithet.[13] At that time, the Armenian people did not usually have surnames,[14] so the translator must have been known simply as "Christopher, the Armenian."

In a rather short and unpretentious preface,[15] after offering praise to God, Christopher stated that he came from Tauris. This is the modern Tabrīz, a city in Northwestern Iran, near the ancient Armenia, still noted for its large Armenian population.[16] He explained that he had heard a great deal about the Europeans—he calls them "Franchi," from the Persian word firangī—and, since they were Christians like himself, he had become very curious to see them.[17] Venice, he said, was the first place he reached in Europe, and he had become fascinated by the city. After some descriptions of particular features of it that appealed to him, contrasting them with memories of the cities in his homeland, he added that he had received much kindness during a three years' residence. It was this, he declared that led him to undertake to do the book, with the help of "a very dear friend," in order to try to repay in part the obligation that he felt toward the people of Venice.

One citizen in particular seems to have been especially kind to him. This was Marc'Antonio Giustiniano, and to him Christopher formally dedicated his book.[18] Giustiniano was a nobleman of wide interests, who owned a press that printed books in Hebrew,[19] and it is quite possible that Christopher, with his ability in Eastern languages, had been able to assist him in his publishing ventures. In any case, the Venetian's interest in the Near East and its peoples doubtless played some part in persuading him to be helpful to the impoverished Armenian.—Christopher must have been very poor indeed, because he admitted in his Introduction that for some three years he had been living in a free room, provided without charge by the charity of the state.

Christopher never named the very dear friend who helped him with the work of translation. This could hardly have been Giustiniano, for he was too busy with other ventures, but it might have been one of Tramezzino's assistants. At this period, Tramezzino was publishing translations of Spanish books, in Latin or Italian,[20] and to do this work he must have needed one or more speakers of Spanish. If one of these had been a man of Moorish or Jewish stock, driven from Spain by the intolerance of the Christian conquerors, he and Christopher—both being expatriates from regions under strong Islamic cultural influence—could have found much in common. But this is only conjecture.

THE PLOT OF THE *PEREGRINAGGIO*

Christopher's book begins by telling that a certain King of Serendippo had three sons. Being very fond of them, he gave them the best possible education. Then, when they were fully trained he tested them, and although their answers pleased him, he feigned anger and banished them, hoping that in other lands they might gain still more experience and wisdom through practical application of their knowledge.

On reaching the land of a king called Beramo (also called Behramo)—which was actually Persia—the brothers met a man who had lost a camel. They described it to him in such detail that he accused them of stealing it. Taken prisoner, they were led before the king. They explained to him how they had deduced the probable appearance of the camel after examining its tracks. He was still dubious, but soon the animal was found, so he freed them. Later, they further impressed the king when he overheard some critical remarks about food and wine that he had given them, and he made them tell the reasons for their deductions. At the same time, they warned him that his Minister was plotting to kill him, and their warning proved true. After these exhibitions of their sagacity, he entrusted them with a difficult mission. He wished them to help him recover "the Mirror of Justice," a family heirloom that an uncle of his had stolen and presented to an Indian queen. Arriving in India, they first subdued a "Fatal Hand" that rose from the sea to trouble the queen's realm, and they further impressed her by solving two riddles (one about dividing some eggs, the· other dealing with a quantity of salt). Thereupon she gave them the mirror.

When the princes returned to Persia, they found King Beramo in great distress. During their absence he had become infatuated with a slave girl named Diliramma, who was an exceptionally talented musician. One day he took her out hunting, and she had teased him into attempting with his bow a most difficult "master shot" that involved pinning a stag's hind foot to its ear. He accomplished this with unusual skill; but, instead of applauding, she ridiculed him. Furious at the thought that he had been insulted in the presence of his nobles, the king ordered that the girl should be exposed in the forest to be devoured by wild beasts. After she had been taken away, however, he realized how much he loved her, and sent some retainers to bring her back. They were unable to locate her because she had been found by an old merchant and had joined his caravan. Without his beloved maiden, the king rapidly declined in health, and nothing satisfied him.

In an effort to help the unhappy king, the three princes suggested that he might find some amusement by building seven palaces of different colors, then installing in each a princess and a storyteller. Perhaps by spending a night in each palace in turn, he might find sufficient enjoyment to help him forget his grief.

The main body of the book, which follows, consists of seven stories or novellas, presenting the tales told on successive evenings by the storytellers in these palaces.

The first tale, delivered in the Silver Palace, describes how the Muslim King of Becher learned from a philosopher how to make his soul leave his body and enter the lifeless frame of another being. The King's treacherous Minister found out the trick, and one day when they were out hunting, he took advantage of it to occupy the king's vacant body when his soul had temporarily left it in order to enter a dead animal. Finally, the king's lost soul was able to return in the body of a parrot. He tricked the Minister's soul into leaving his proper body, then he resumed it, destroyed the soul of his enemy, and enjoyed a happy reunion with his faithful queen, who had meanwhile resisted the advances of the impostor.

The second novella, related in the Purple Palace, tells about the son of the

King of Benesse, who refused to marry until he could find a woman equally fond of hunting. After he had met and married a beautiful huntress, she offended him by an impossible demand, so, after an incident in the hunting field, he commanded that she be fed to some mad dogs. Managing to escape, she found refuge with a monkey trainer, whose clever animal was used to effect her reconciliation with the king.—The whole tale is an obvious retelling, with variations, of the episode between King Beramo and Diliramma; but this time both of the principals engaged in the archery, and the actual feat involved changing a male animal into a female, and vice versa, with several arrows.

The third novella, narrated in a palace decorated with various colors, was located in a city of India called Zeheb. The wealthy lord of that city gave a goldsmith a large amount of gold with which to construct a huge golden lion. A rival smith suspected that the artist had kept back some of the precious metal, but could not be sure unless the lion was weighed. He persuaded his wife to get the artist's wife to ask him how this could be done. The first goldsmith confided to his spouse that the lion could be weighed by placing it in a boat, and marking on the side of the vessel the depth to which it sank; after the image had been removed, the boat could be filled with rocks until it settled to the same mark; then the stones could be removed and weighed individually. His wife indiscreetly divulged the secret to the rival's wife, and the second goldsmith told the noble patron. The weighing was carried out, and the theft was revealed. The guilty goldsmith was then imprisoned in a high tower. Ever resourceful, he told his wife a means for rescuing him; but, while carrying out his plan, he contrived to have her drawn up into the tower to be a prisoner in his place. When she was released by passing travellers and taken before the lord of the city, the latter was highly amused to hear of the clever escape and ingenious revenge. He forgave the goldsmith, who became reconciled with his wife and also with his rival smith.—Next to the story of the three princes themselves, this tale seems to have made the greatest impression on later writers.

The fourth novella, told in the Yellow Palace, relates how Rammo, son of the Sultan of Babilonia, discovered an illicit affair between his stepmother the Queen and the evil Vizier. The guilty lovers, in order to save themselves, contrived to throw the blame on him, and he was exiled. In a distant land, he encountered three men, each of whom taught him a magic trick. Using these arts, he returned unrecognized to his native city and plagued the Vizier by a series of humiliating pranks, including seduction of his daughters, hoping to teach him to mend his ways. Rammo was unable to reform the Vizier, but he ultimately convinced his father that he had been deceived. The guilty pair were banished; the prince married the Vizier's eldest daughter; and when the Sultan died soon after, Rammo ascended the throne.

The fifth novella, narrated in the Green Palace, tells about a King of Hotenne, who distrusted women, but was urged by his counselors to take a wife so the land would have a queen. He selected four suitable candidates and installed each in a separate corner of his palace. With the aid of a silver statue, cleverly constructed so that it would smile when anyone told a lie in its presence, he was warned about three of the girls, and discovered that each was faithless. Accordingly, he arranged a way for each to die while betraying him. The fourth one proved to be a paragon of virtue, and he happily took her as his queen.

The sixth novella, given in the Brown Palace, takes place in a city called Letzer, "in the land of Serger," where a Muslim tyrant ruled. There, a boy named Feristeno and a girl called Giulla, children of two Christian elders, fell in love, and their parents arranged their marriage. The king saw the bride and wanted her for himself. He had Feristeno seized and condemned to death, but the latter escaped with the aid of his tutor's son, named Giassemen, who dug a tunnel into his prison. Meanwhile, the king had brought Giulla to a house in the royal rose gardens, called Giullistano. The couple found a means to communicate by skillfully arranged bouquets of flowers, until Giassemen was able to dig another tunnel from a house owned by Feristeno to her place of confinement. They managed to outwit the tyrant, confusing him by means of the tunnel, which permitted Giulla to run back and forth from the tower to the house, so the king would find her, differently dressed, in each place when he arrived. Finally, they tricked him into letting them leave the country, and when he discovered how completely he had been deceived, he died of shame. After the king's death the couple returned, and helped to Christianize the land.

Eventually—in the course of the seventh tale, told in the Golden Palace— King Beramo learned from the storyteller that his lost Diliramma was still alive, and immediately sent for her. When she returned, he wedded her, and married off the seven princesses. Then he rewarded the three princes of Serendip, who returned to their country. Their aged father was delighted to see them, and on his death the eldest son succeeded to the throne. The second went back to India, to marry the queen whose riddles he had helped to solve. The youngest was recalled to Persia to marry the young daughter of Beramo, and eventually succeeded him as king. With all the threads thus neatly tied, the story ends.

FALSE THEORIES REGARDING THE *PEREGRINAGGIO*

In the mid-nineteenth century, a number of German scholars turned their attention to the *Peregrinaggio,* partly because of the new interest in folk tales and comparative literature. This trend was started by Theodor Benfey, who made a new translation of the 1557 edition into German, although only a brief initial portion was printed during his lifetime, appearing in 1864.[21] Georg Huth followed Benfey, producing a German translation of the rest of the book in three installments, the first of which came out in 1889. He added detailed commentaries on the origins of some of the tales, finding seeming prototypes in classical European or Indian sources.[22] Next, in 1891, Heinrich Gassner republished in full the text of the sixteenth-century Italian original, to make it more widely available to scholars.[23] Profiting from these beginnings, Hermann Fischer and Johannes Bolte, in 1895, jointly issued a new edition of Wetzel's first German translation of 1583.[24] Bolte's extensive commentaries on this discussed again the early origins of the individual tales and motifs, pointing out numerous Indian prototypes. Finally, in 1932, Richard Fick and Alfons Hilka reproduced Benfey's complete translation of the *Peregrinaggio*, which had been left among his unpublished papers, providing a long introduction and some analytical footnotes.[25]

Benfey, in his first examination of the *Peregrinaggio*, had recognized that King Beramo (or Behramo), who played such a key role in the framework of the book, must surely be Bahrām Gūr, the Sasanian king Varhran V, who reigned from A.D. 420 to 440, and had figured prominently in old Persian history, folklore, and legend.[26] Iranian tradition told how King Bahrām had early won fame as a mighty and fearless hunter, and how he had maintained, in seven domed pavillions within his palace, seven storytelling princesses. In fact, these seven maidens and their respective tales had formed the basis for a famous poem by Niẓāmī, called *The Seven Beauties*, or *Haft paiḳar*.[27] Impressed by the obvious correspondences, Benfey initially remarked of the *Peregrinaggio*: "Its form adheres so closely to the *Seven Beauties* that it seems almost to be a reworking of the same by a Christian Persian."[28]

However, on further reflection, Benfey also noted that the seven interior stories in the *Peregrinaggio* did not even remotely resemble those in the *Haft paiḳar*. Moreover, he observed that the story of the three princes describing the unseen camel seemed to be of Arabic origin, even though he knew that the name of their homeland, Serendippo, must have been derived from an old word for Ceylon.

In addition, he felt troubled by the fact that the author had not given them specific names, and had failed to name the country ruled by King Bahrām. This lack of names he considered "un-Persian." He also thought he could detect considerable European influence, especially in the manner of presentation. In the face of these and other problems, Benfey finally concluded that it was doubtful that there had ever been an original Persian book with all this material, to be translated into Italian in sixteenth-century Venice.[29]

Benfey's sweeping judgement regarding the absence of a Persian prototype was parroted by all his successors. Richard Fick carried the ideas even farther in his introduction to Benfey's complete translation. It seemed scarcely credible, he said, that such an attractive collection of stories should not have been discovered in Persian literature if it had ever really existed.[30] Furthermore, since he could not find the name Christoforo Armeno in any Italian or Armenian history or bibliography, he openly doubted that there had ever been such a person.[31] He went on to suggest that the book had actually been composed in Venice, and that the printer Tramezzino himself had perhaps played a part in compiling it.[32]

Fick elaborated this line of reasoning to quite absurd lengths, and his errors were further compounded by the author-editor of *Serendipity*, who uncritically accepted all of Fick's statements, and summed them up with a few additions of his own,[33] as follows:

1) The alleged translator, Christoforo Armeno, existed only on the title page of the *Peregrinaggio*.

2) There was no single source, Persian or otherwise, from which a translation was made by anyone at any time.

3) The name "Serendip" was probably adopted for the locale of the tale because of the big news then current—the conversion of Ceylon to Christianity (about 1552); because it gave the book an exotic and attractive flavor; and because it provided an ancient Indian background.

4) Tramezzino was most likely the compiler of the tales, some of which he improvised, and he should be regarded as the author of the *Peregrinaggio*.

5) The tales, other than those spun by Tramezzino and his circle of noble friends, were of ancient origin, mostly Indian.

Nearly all these points can be rather rapidly dismissed. However, it seems desirable to treat them in some detail in order to make sure that they will not be raised again.

TRAMEZZINO AND CEYLON

The principal argument, the theory that Tramezzino was the author of the *Peregrinaggio,* begins to fall apart when one considers that he was a busy and successful publisher. Records from that time attest that his press was producing numerous books, on a wide variety of subjects.[34] All of this publishing activity would have left him little time to double as an author, even if he had possessed the ability to write well.

Although it seems absurd to question at all the stated authorship, it is even more foolish to make an accusation that this enterprising publisher was guilty of perpetrating a literary fraud for private gain. Michele Tramezzino, already a successful publisher, would hardly have been reduced to writing a book and falsely representing it as a translation from Persian in order to cater to the current vogue for romances. It would have been still less likely for him to try to shape the book to take advantage of an alleged current interest in Ceylon, supposedly aroused by a message that the island had been Christianized by St. Francis Xavier.

In the first place, St. Francis Xavier did not Christianize Ceylon. His first visit to Jaffna, on the northern tip of the island, is said to have brought a considerable number of converts to Catholicism,[35] but this could not by any means be described as the conversion of Ceylon to Christianity, and it does not seem to have created any particular stir in northern Italy. Secondly, publishers of that period were not so hard pressed to produce "timely new books" that they would feel compelled to exploit current "newsworthy" interests. This attitude is a relatively modern one.

Even supposing that an ambitious publisher had wanted to capitalize on St. Francis' temporary success in Ceylon, and assuming that there might have been some enthusiasm for Ceylon in sixteenth-century Venice, this popular feeling would hardly be satisfied by a little book that mentions the place only briefly at the beginning, and again at the very end, without ever describing the island or its inhabitants. The locale of the main story and the greater part of the book is not Ceylon, but Persia. Lastly, if a sixteenth-century Venetian publisher had really been eager to exploit a current interest in Ceylon, he would never have used the word *Serendippo,* as that was a newly-coined name derived from a foreign one, and it would have been meaningless to his fellow citizens.

The term *Serendippo* is so important for any discussion of the *Peregrinaggio* that it deserves a detailed treatment. It would seem that Ammianus Marcellinus, a Greco-Roman writer of the fourth century A.D., was the first to use an obvious variation of the term. In his famous history of the later Roman Empire, *Res gestae,* he spoke of an Indian people called the *Serendivi* who sent ambassadors to Emperor Julian, and they have been identified as having come from Ceylon.[36] (Very likely the term *Serendivi* was ultimately derived from the Pāli *Serumadīpa.*[37]) We do not find the expression used again; but before it dropped from the Latin vocabulary, Roman merchants may have passed it on to the early Arab traders. In any case, the medieval Arabs for several centuries referred to Ceylon as *Sarāndīb.* From them, or perhaps from some common source, the name passed on to the Persians, who spoke of Ceylon as *Serendīp.* Obviously, it was this last term that fathered *Serendippo,* for the Persian variant was the only one to have a final *p* sound.

For some reason still unclear, between the ninth and thirteenth centuries of our era, the Arabs shifted to speaking of the island as *Sīlān,* meaning [Isle of] Gems, and the old name was soon forgotten.[38] The new term was picked up by that much travelled Venetian, Marco Polo, on his visit to Ceylon in 1293, and in his memoirs he spoke of the country as *Seilan,* or *Zeilan.*[39]

At the beginning of the sixteenth century, maps and charts were still representing the island off the southern tip of India under the name of Taprobana—or Taprobane—following the lead of the Alexandrian Greek geographer Claudius Ptolemy, who had made an important set of maps some thirteen centuries earlier.[40] Then, gradually, they began to use the name *Seilan,* or *Zeilan,* with a number of alternative spellings, and the name Taprobana was shifted over to the island of Sumatra.[41]

It is significant that in 1554, three years before he published the *Peregrinaggio,* Tramezzino produced a notable map of the world, which has been praised as the most advanced map of that period. It appeared in two parts, showing the Eastern and Western hemispheres, respectively, and the former contained a rather exact representation of Ceylon.[42] On this, we do not find the island labelled Serendippo; it is simply called Seilan.

The name Serendīp, already obsolete and almost forgotten in the Near East, and apparently never used in Italy, would have been quite meaningless in sixteenth-century Venice. It seems probable that even Christopher did not recognize it as the name of an identifiable place, but merely considered it as a mythical kingdom in a fanciful tale that he was passing on.

It would seem that Europeans in general did not know what—or where—Serendip was, until the end of the seventeenth century. In 1697, Barthélemy d'Herbelot brought out, in one huge volume, an encyclopaedia called *Bibliothèque orientale.*[43] In this, under the entry "Serendib," he defined it as an island in the Indian Ocean, and he added that since Persian geography placed it between the Equator and the First Clime and very near the coast of

India, it was rather certain that this island was the same as that called Seilan or Zeilan.[44]

Even Herbelot was not entirely sure of this attribution, because, in another place, he speaks of "Sarendib, which we believe to be either Zeilan or Simatra."[45] By the mid-eighteenth century, though, any doubts regarding the identity of Serendip with Ceylon seem to have been resolved, at least in educated circles. We know this from a comment by Gibbon[46] and from another of Walpole's letters.[47]

THE QUESTIONED AUTHORSHIP

We have reviewed some of the attempts made by recent writers to deprive Christopher of all credit, not only denying that he wrote the *Peregrinaggio,* but even trying to dismiss his name as a fiction. Their efforts have been so effective that on library catalogue cards for this book, his name is now usually accompanied by a question mark or by that ugly word "spurious."

Actually, the doubters' only substantial argument is a purely negative one. It is simply that modern researches have been unable to find, in the history of sixteenth-century Venice, or in later literary studies on that period, any reference to a Christoforo Armeno—although another Armenian named Christopher is reported to have written a book about Venice at a later time.[48]

There is no good reason why our Christopher's name should have been recorded in any history. Poverty stricken one-book authors are seldom long remembered unless they have had other qualities or deeds to distinguish them. Christopher, by his own admission, was not even an original author, he was simply a poor foreigner who produced a translation. Having such humble status, he would not have been likely to win any recognition at all in that city of proud merchant princes, even at the time when his book was first launched. Writers of fiction, in general, were not highly regarded in sixteenth-century Venice. For example, we know almost nothing about another Venetian author of that period, Gian'Francesco Straparola, although he wrote an even more famous book of popular tales that went into many editions and also was translated in France and Germany.[49] Indeed, we know far more about Christopher as a person, from his own preface, than we do about Straparola.

On the more positive side, we can find in the *Peregrinaggio* many significant details to indicate that it must have been composed by someone who knew Persian. For one thing, the solution of the first riddle sounds coarse and rather far-fetched in Italian—or English—but it would have been an amusing risqué joke in Persian, where the two key words make a pun.[50]

Then, too, we have a number of obvious Persian names, particularly in the sixth tale. Some of these can easily be recognized, such as Giassemen for Jasmin. Others have been italianized by simply adding a suffix like -*eno,* as in the case of the Christian youth named Feristeno, from Fehrist, a common Persian name. Still others have been altered by simply doubling the final consonant and adding -*a* or -*o,* as in the case of Serendippo itself, and the garden called Giullistano, derived from *jullistān* or *gulistān,* meaning "flower garden" or "rose garden" in Persian. A native Italian would scarcely have known these Persian words.

Further evidence for a prototype in Persian, rather than for a fresh compilation in Italian, is provided by other place names. A European writer or storyteller would presumably have taken care to select familiar names of Eastern cities (as the Chevalier de Mailly did, in his imitation of the *Peregrinaggio*), to impart an extra exotic touch to these stories and make them seem more credible as Oriental tales. Yet, one cannot locate any of the place names as given—not even that of Serendippo—on any of the contemporary European maps or charts.

None of the place names in the *Peregrinaggio*—except that of Babilonia (for Babylon, or Baghdad)—could have been easily identified with a known site. However, if we take certain of these names, drop the vowels as given, and introduce new ones, recognizable names sometimes emerge. For example, Hotenne, in the fifth novella, could be reduced to H-T-N, from which we can get Khotan, a major city in eastern Turkestan. (If this seems far-fetched, we shall soon see that Khotan was the locale of the original Persian story.) Similarly, Zeheb, the city of the goldsmiths where the golden lion was made, obviously drew its name from *zahab,* a Persian word for "gold" (derived from Arabic), so it must once have been appropriately named the "City of Gold."

This re-vowelling is no idle word game. Persian books and manuscripts were generally "unpointed." That is, only the consonants were set down, and the reader was expected to provide for himself the correct vocalization from a previous knowledge of the language. (Even in the spoken Persian the vowels are flexible and subject to regional changes.) Christopher, in his modest introduction, made no claims to scholarship. As we have seen, he was apparently a very poor man since he admitted that he had been a charity case for three years, and probably he had never been able to afford any extensive education. Very likely he had had just enough training to provide himself with an elementary skill in reading simple Persian, or *farsī,* so that he could manage account books or handle simple narratives. But this would not have equipped him with the special knowledge necessary to recognize the names of literary or historical figures like Bahrām Gūr, or of places such as Khotan and Serendīp. Furthermore, as a man of Armenian stock, presumably raised bilingually, he might have been instinctively inclined to provide a different set of vowel sounds, and these could have been still further distorted when changed into Italian by the helper he mentioned, to whom he may have actually been dictating. —For, we now know, beyond any question, that Christopher and his helper were indeed working with a definite set of Persian stories, from a well-known book.

THE PROTOTYPE FOR THE *PEREGRINAGGIO*

One may wonder how the nineteenth-century German scholars and their modern successors ever managed to get so far out on their limb of false reasoning. When they were puzzled to find Persian and Indian elements so oddly combined in the *Peregrinaggio,* instead of completely rejecting the idea of a Persian prototype, would it not have been more logical for them to inquire: "Was there any Persian writer, or writer in Persian, who also had close contacts with India?" Had they sought such a person, one outstanding candidate should have instantly sprung to mind.

This was Amīr Khusrau of Delhi, who has been hailed as "the greatest Persian poet that India ever produced," and who was the only writer of Persian in India to attain wide fame beyond the subcontinent.[51] If they had thought of him, there would have been no need to look any further; for it was a well-known work by this famous writer that—either directly or indirectly— must have inspired the *Peregrinaggio.*

Amīr Khusrau, who lived from 1253 to 1325, was the son of a Turkish father and a Muslim Indian mother, and he served as court poet to several kings and princes. Writing poetry came easily for him. As an accomplished musician, he had an ear well attuned to the rhythms and cadence of language, especially the Persian language, and his thoughts presented themselves quite naturally in verse. Having already composed several books of poetry on his own, he decided to undertake an imitation of the *Khamse* of Niẓāmī (d. 1202), written about a century before, which already was considered to be one of the pinnacles of Persian literature. Amīr Khusrau was sometimes criticized, by his jealous contemporaries and by later critics, for "wasting his time on a mere imitation"; but the result of these labors was not just a copy of the earlier work. He took over the basic pattern already established by Niẓāmī, but he altered it freely, presenting old material in a new way, and introducing much that was novel, so that the whole was full of originality.

Niẓāmī's *Khamse,* written between 1171 and 1200, had consisted of five book-lengths poems gathered together in a single volume. One of these poems, the *Haft Paiḳar,* celebrated the life of Bahrām Gūr.[52] King Bahrām, as we have already noted, was a historical ruler of pre-Islamic Iran, one of the most colorful figures in Persian history, and around his memory had clustered a rich accretion of folklore and legends, many of which had been collected in the *Shāhnāme* of Firdausī, completed in A.D. 1010.[53]

Niẓāmī, like Firdausī, dealt with King Bahrām's entire life, but the *Haft paiḳar*—as its title, meaning Seven Beauties, implies—placed special stress on that episode in which he built seven domed pavilions in his palace and installed in each a princess from a different land. Most of the work is taken up by the stories told him by the princesses as he visited each in turn. This convention of presenting a series of tales in an outer frame was very common in Persian literature.

When Amīr Khusrau undertook to do a new version of the *Haft paiḳar,* he began by altering the framework dealing with King Bahrām. Then, for the interior tales, he only once followed Niẓāmī's example. In writing the other six stories, told in the successive pleasure domes, he introduced a new set of tales, several of which were of Indian origin. The completed poem, which he named the *Hasht bihisht,* or "Eight Paradises," thus provides an interesting combination of Persian and Indian tales, set in an old Persian frame, and presented in the Persian language. He finished it in 1302 (A.H. 701).

Amīr Khusrau's *Khamse* soon became popular wherever people could read Persian, and many handwritten copies were produced. One especially notable manuscript was done by the great poet Hafīz, who was born in Shirāz in 1325, the year of the author's death. This was later taken to Tashkent, in Russian Turkestan, where it is still preserved.[54]

In more modern times, Amīr Khusrau's *Khamse* was republished in several editions, both in Persia and in India (or Pakistan); and these, along with numerous illuminated manuscripts, can be found in European and American libraries and museums.[55] However, the entire work has never been translated. Even its most original portion, the *Hasht bihisht*—except for the very free adaptation of it in the *Peregrinaggio*—is known to Western readers only through brief translations of one or two tales, notably, the story of the Three Princes and the Camel-driver.[56]

Back in the seventeenth century, Barthélemy d'Herbelot included in his Oriental encyclopaedia an entry for "Mir Khosrau," listing him as a Persian poet who had done a poem about three Arab brothers who described to a camel-driver the appearance of his lost animal without ever having seen it; and in another place he gave the story in detail, taken from another source, again referring to "Mir Khosrau" and his poem about it.[57] Perhaps it was the description of the three brothers as Arabs that kept people from recognizing them as the three princes from Serendip who had reappeared in the *Peregrinaggio*.

Some two hundred years later, in 1892, another French author, Antoine Lacoin de Villemorin, assisted by Khalil Khan, published a small book re-telling the story of King Bahrām and the princesses of the seven palaces. For this volume, entitled *Jardin des délices,* he drew his material from three different renderings of the well-known epic, by the Persian poets Niẓāmī, Hātifī, and Amīr Khusrau. Like Christopher, he presented a very free recapitulation of King Bahrām's romance with his slave girl as a frame for seven subtales, and these latter he selected out of the three individual sets that were written by the above-mentioned poets. From Amīr Khusrau's *Hasht bihisht* he borrowed the story of the three princes, along with the tale of the Parrot King.[58] Both were very loosely and inaccurately "translated," and unaccountably the princes were again described as Arabs—perhaps because the author and his helper failed to recognize the name Serendip. Poor as it was, this book did help to acquaint more European readers with the work of Amīr Khusrau.

The story of the Three Princes of Ceylon was again retold—somewhat freely—in English, by Mohammad Habib, in a section on the *Hasht bihisht* in his biography of Amīr Khusrau, published in 1927;[59] while the initial portion of the tale was very meticulously translated into English by O. B. Lal in 1896.[60] This last translation is especially important for our study, as it clearly demonstrates the intricacy of Amīr Khusrau's style with its wealth of allusions, showing that a full understanding of this particular tale—and the entire poem—would be very difficult for anyone but a well-trained Persian scholar. Only too clearly does it illustrate the problems that would have faced a man like

Christopher if he were trying to make a direct translation of this complex work.

All the above references to Amīr Khusrau and his story of the three princes had appeared before 1932, when Fick presented his theories regarding the Italian origin of the *Peregrinaggio*. Meanwhile, Hermann Ethé and Johannes Bolte had both listed the *Hasht bihisht* as one of the lineal descendants of the *Haft paiḳar* without suspecting that it might provide a link between the latter and the *Peregrinaggio*.[61]

However, the connection did occur to another European scholar, Albert Wesselski. The latter, an Orientalist in Vienna, published in 1935 an article on the *Haft paiḳar* and its derivatives, in which he neatly demonstrated that many details of the *Peregrinaggio* could be traced directly back to the *Hasht bihisht*.[62] Unfortunately, he himself only knew this book through a scholarly friend in Istanbul, Hellmut Ritter, who sent him brief resumés of its inner tales. Wesselski used this incomplete but factual knowledge to castigate Benfey and to ridicule Fick; but, since he did not possess the original book, he was not able to investigate further, to determine the full extent of the similarities and differences between the *Hasht bihisht* and the *Peregrinaggio*.

A COMPARISON OF THE TWO BOOKS

As a closer examination of the *Hasht bihisht* now seemed necessary to settle some unresolved questions, I undertook to make one, with the expert help of Dr. Ferydoon Firoozi and Mr. Sa'id A. Shirani, who read for me—at different times—two manuscripts in the Princeton University Library.[63] Without their generous assistance, the analyses presented in this section could not have been made.

A preliminary survey quickly revealed that the *Hasht bihisht* had indeed been the primary source for the *Peregrinaggio;* but it also showed that Christopher, in taking his basic material from Amīr Khusrau's poem, had handled it quite freely, making numerous alterations and omitting a lot. Thus, his work must be called an adaptation, rather than a true translation. The *Peregrinaggio* can only be said to have been "translated from Persian into Italian" in a most literal sense: to indicate that the material was transferred, or brought over, from one language into the other.

To be more specific, I soon found that Christopher had in effect turned the *Hasht bihisht* inside out. For example, to make the framework of the *Peregrinaggio,* he used the first of Amīr Khusrau's interior stories—the tale about the three princes of Serendip—in combination with the initial story of King Bahrām, which he greatly abbreviated. In the latter, he used the incident of the master shot as it was told by Firdausī and Niẓāmī (but not by Amīr Khusrau),[64] and he eked out this framework still further by adding a few items from other sources, such as the Fatal Hand, the Mirror of Justice, and the two riddles.[65] Then he lifted two main elements from Amīr Khusrau's original frame in order to construct two new interior tales of his own.

The first of these borrowed elements described another instance of Bahrām's hunting skill, when he caused a male deer to resemble a female one, and vice versa.[66] (Christopher changed the two victims into unicorns, presumably to reduce the number of arrows needed, and hence to make the feat more plausible;[67] but his reference to non-existent beasts produced another implausibility.) He made this adventure the high point of his second novella, which essentially retells the story of Bahrām's expert marksmanship and the banishing of his scornful lady—although the names of the principal characters are never given. This novella was also fleshed out with small incidents from other books.[68]

The second displaced element was Bahrām's reconciliation with Dilārām. Christopher took this from Amīr Khusrau's prologue and expanded it slightly to make his seventh novella.

According to Amīr Khusrau, Bahrām's First Paradise was the hunting field. It was because he spent too much time there, neglecting his Court, that his nobles suggested the building of the seven palaces to house the seven princesses, as a means of keeping him home. Therefore, although the story of the three princes of Serendip was the first interior tale in the *Hasht bihisht,* it was told in the Second Paradise.—Incidentally, Amīr Khusrau never felt it necessary to name his princes, as they were characters in a secondary tale; so Christopher, although he increased their importance, did not feel obliged to name them either. This dispels one of Benfey's chief arguments against a Persian prototype.

We may still wonder why Amīr Khusrau chose to have his three princes come from Ceylon; for, when the same tale appears in certain versions of the *Arabian Nights,* they are described as "sons of the Sultan of Yemen,"[69] and, as we have seen, other writers usually introduced them as Arabs. Perhaps he merely chose Serendīp to fit the poem's meter.

Returning to the *Peregrinaggio,* we find that—with the exception of the second and seventh novellas, already mentioned—Christopher took all of his interior stories from the *Hasht bihisht.*

His first novella, the tale of the king whose soul entered a parrot, adheres closely to the third story in the *Hasht bihisht* (as told in the Fourth Paradise). His third, the tale of the clever goldsmith, faithfully reproduces the second in the *Hasht bihisht* (related in the Third Paradise), except for a change of locale—from Khorasan in Iran, to an unspecified place in India—and the minor variation of having the image to be weighed represent a lion. Amīr Khusrau had carefully followed old Indian tradition in making it an elephant.[70]

Christopher's fourth novella, the tale of Prince Rammo, his evil stepmother, and the adulterous vizier, copies but abridges the very long and amusing story of Prince Rām, the sixth in the *Hasht bihisht* (told in the Seventh Paradise). His fifth, describing the King of Hotenne testing his four consorts by means of the Laughing Statue, very closely follows the seventh, about the King of Khotan, in the *Hasht bihisht* (narrated in the Eighth Paradise). Lastly, his sixth novella, the tale of the girl imprisoned in a tower and rescued through a tunnel, is a rather free adaptation of the fourth tale in the *Hasht bihisht* (told in the Fifth Paradise).

Only one of the interior stories in the *Hasht bihisht* was passed over by Christopher. This was the fifth tale (told in the Sixth Paradise), an eerie account of a wanderer tormented by ghouls and djinns, for which Amīr Khusrau had for once taken his inspiration directly from Niẓāmī, apparently combining the first and fifth stories in the *Haft paikar* and adding some embellishments of his own.[71] (One can see that Christopher's rearrangement of the material in the *Hasht bihisht* was only following a tradition already long established.) The omission of this particular story in the *Peregrinaggio* is quite understandable. This tale of strange apparitions and bizarre delusions, in a desolate wasteland, would have been unusually difficult to translate; also, Christopher may well have felt that it was too exotic, or too firmly based upon Muslim traditions, to be suitable for European readers.

As mentioned above, the *Peregrinaggio's* seventh novella also differed from the *Hasht bihisht*. It consisted merely of a rather slight tale through which the storyteller was able to give King Beramo some news regarding his lost slave girl, thus helping to bring about their reconciliation.

Both Niẓāmī and Amīr Khusrau had effected the reunion of these two chief characters before they began to discuss the princesses in the seven palace-domes, and they had ended their long poems with the mysterious death of King Bahrām in the hunting field.[72] But Christopher saved the reuniting of the lovers for his climax. It would seem that he deliberately wished to conclude the last of his interior stories on another note, emphasizing once more the key theme of reconciliation, which had appeared in the conclusion of each of his other inner tales. Then, in the epilogue, he staged the ultimate reconciliation, when the three princes, having fulfilled their obligations to their host, King Beramo, returned to their native land to be reaccepted by their father, after which each found happiness and prosperity in a different way.

This repeated emphasis on the themes of union, reunion, and reconciliation, which characterizes the *Peregrinaggio*—serving to set it apart still further from its prototype—would seem highly significant for helping us to gain a deeper understanding of its author.

On one level, these recurring themes suggest a longing on the part of a lonely foreigner in a strange land, expressing—consciously, or unconsciously— a nostalgia for his native place, and a strong desire for reunion with his friends and relatives. On another plane, the themes of union and reconciliation might be reflections of a more spiritual longing, such as we find so often expressed by mystic writers like the Sūfī authors of Islam. (Amīr Khusrau was himself recognized as a religious mystic,[73] although that fact is not so obvious in the *Hasht bihisht*.)

Either of these moods—nostalgia for a distant homeland, or spiritual longings for a union of the soul with the Absolute—would have been utterly alien for an Italian businessman in the still prosperous and material-minded atmosphere of sixteenth-century Venice. Thus, they would exclude any remaining claims for authorship by Tramezzino; but they could well have been expected in a homesick Armenian with strong religious feelings.

Indeed, the writer of the *Peregrinaggio* must have been a very pious person, since he began his preface with a moving prayer of adoration to God, in the Persian manner;[74] and in the book itself one of the most noticeable deviations from its Persian prototype is the strong Christian element. This tendency is particularly apparent in the sixth novella, which is loaded with Christian sentiment, to the extent that Amīr Khusrau's colorful and exciting original story is much altered, even rather spoiled as a tale of suspense.

A modern reader's first reaction to all this piety might be to conclude that the writer from the East may have wished to ingratiate himself with devout European readers; or that he may have wanted to make it publicly clear that, in spite of being a foreigner from the Orient, he was still "a good Christian."[75] However, the overall tone of the book makes it seem definite that Christopher was by nature genuinely spiritually-minded.

Yet he was no prude. The *Peregrinaggio* contains a number of ribald tales and incidents. Most of these came directly from the *Hasht bihisht,* but we have noted that he introduced of his own accord a risqué riddle. On the other hand, he did omit a vast amount of sensuality and amorous dalliance that was present in his prototype. Probably the European censors would not have permitted its inclusion; but, although this made the book far more sober than its model, the pruning of much extraneous detail has resulted in faster-paced plots, making for easier reading.

Another divergence from the prototypes is found in Christopher's treatment of the princesses' dwellings. Niẓāmī had them occupying seven domes in one great palace, and Amīr Khusrau gave them seven separate structures within a vast palace complex; but Christopher placed them in seven different palaces, and provided each with a storyteller.[76] He also failed to follow the precedents establishing the colors for the dwellings, their furnishings, and the clothing of the girls themselves.

With Amīr Khusrau, following Niẓāmī, the seven princesses had come from the seven climes or regions of the then-known world. However, each clime was thought to be under the influence of a "planet" (the Sun, the Moon, and the five principal planets of our solar system), while each of these planets was assigned a color, and was assumed to be presiding over a day of the week; so each of his palaces featured the color of the planet appropriate to its occupant.[77] Furthermore, both of the earlier authors had planned their respective stories so that each one, told on the appropriate day of the week, conformed at least in part with the mood or temperament associated with the planet for that day, and contained in it various items bearing—or alluding to—the color of that planet, and hence of the "dome" in which the story was told.[78]

Christopher not only shuffled the stories, as we have seen, but he gave new colors to the palaces and their contents in such a way as to destroy any vestige of their original order and symbolic meanings. One of his palaces, as noted above, did not even have a specific color, but was described as being "of various hues";[79] and nowhere do we find any attempt to associate anything in a tale with the stated color.

Did he do this deliberately? That is, did Christopher perceive the subtle pattern in the original order of colors, linking each with a planet, and then intentionally set out to destroy that order, so as to dissociate himself from Islamic astrology, then falling into disrepute?[80] Or, did he simply fail to recognize the careful planning that his predecessors had devoted to the choice of colors and the selection of appropriate stories to conform to them; and did he then just translate the individual tales at random—possibly according to their degree of difficulty for him—setting down each in the order in which he completed it?

The latter supposition seems the more likely. In fact, one often gets the impression that Christopher may have been recalling stories that he once had read, or even heard, and was just writing them down as they recurred to him. However, we still have the matter of the proper names which look like transcriptions. If they were transcribed, this would imply that he had been using a book or manuscript.

Sometimes, unfamiliar words or names led Christopher into rather grotesque errors. A good example of this is his King of Becher, whose soul left his body and eventually found its way home in a parrot. The name of the ancient Indian king who was the original subject of this tale was Vikramāditya; but when this is transcribed in Persian script it becomes *Bekr-mā-jīt*.[81] Probably through failure to understand this foreign name, Christopher simply took the first syllable of the Persian word and made it into Becher (the *ch* in Italian indicates a sound equivalent to *k* in other languages), then he gave this as the name of the realm. Apparently he also failed to recognize the meaning of *Zahab* as referring to the City of Gold, possibly because it was a literary word, derived from Arabic. Educated Persians generally knew and used many Arabic words and expressions, but it seems that Christopher did not; and his failure to recognize a rather familiar one shows once more his limitations as a translator.

These misunderstood names bring up another point. Neither the name of the Parrot King nor that of the City of Gold appear in the manuscripts of the *Hasht bihisht* that I have personally examined,[82] although they do traditionally belong with the stories in which Christopher placed their misunderstood derivatives. Their presence here, in the right places but in somewhat garbled form, raises some further questions. Did Christopher possess an especially complete manuscript of Amīr Khusrau's book, or perhaps an annotated one? Or, could there have been an intermediate book between the *Hasht bihisht* and the *Peregrinaggio*?[83]

Neither of these alternatives would have been necessary. Although the correspondence between the *Peregrinaggio* and the *Hasht bihisht* is not fully complete, it would have been impossible for a man who was not a scholar to translate the complex Persian poem directly into a European language, so some alterations are to be expected. It is quite obvious that Christopher deliberately made some changes to cater to a European audience, such as his use of the single word king (*re*) to render various Oriental titles (shāh, emīr, etc.), and his suppression of all references to polygamy. It is also possible that he may have added names, or small incidents, from associated material that he may have read or heard elsewhere. Still other changes may have been made with editorial advice or assistance.

One day, an intervening book may still turn up, to provide yet another link in the chain of transmission from Firdausī, Niẓāmī, and Amīr Khusrau to Christopher; but the resemblances between his book and the *Hasht bihisht* are so overwhelming that there can no longer be any doubt that the latter served as basic prototype for the *Peregrinaggio*.

Perhaps it was an awareness of his own shortcomings, and a desire to forestall critical comments, that hindered Christopher from naming his source or sources. On the other hand, he may never have worried about criticism; his principal aim was to entertain his readers, and this he certainly achieved. Anyhow, Christopher, in his *Peregrinaggio*, was in general far more faithful to the main substance of the *Hasht bihisht* than were the various later imitators to his own work.

THE SEQUELS TO THE *PEREGRINAGGIO*

The still-continuing story of the subsequent writings based on the material in the *Peregrinaggio* is especially illuminating, as it shows us western European writers adapting material from Christopher's work as he had adapted from the *Hasht bihisht,* producing a series of adaptations increasingly further removed from the Persian original.

The editor of *Serendipity* listed three French books as translations of the *Peregrinaggio,* but only the third contained even a partial translation. That was the work of the Chevalier de Mailly, previously mentioned.[84] Even he did not get very far; for his book presents only the beginning of the *Peregrinaggio*—its initial frame and the first three novellas—rather loosely paraphrased, with some alterations. Then, without explanation, it suddenly departs entirely from the original. Not only are the succeeding novellas quite new, but Mailly even altered the rest of the framework. King Behram never does get reunited with the slave girl whom he exiled after the hunting incident; whereas her reappearance was an essential element in Christopher's plot. Mailly left this aspect of the framework as a loose end, and proceeded to tack on an exceedingly long and tedious appendage—approximately one-third the length of the whole book—to relate the subsequent· adventures of the three princes after they left Persia.

In addition to these numerous alterations, one immediately notes that Mailly deleted all references to Christianity or religion in general, subjects rather prominently featured in the *Peregrinaggio*. In their place he injected a plethora of classical allusions and sentimental interludes, doubtless considered more likely to appeal to his readers in that age of Humanism and Romanticism.

Mailly's book was essentially only a potboiler, made up of odds and ends of exotic lore, very different in spirit from Christopher's tightly-knit narrative; but it was rather typical of the works turned out in considerable profusion by this strange man, who published some fifteen novels and translations between 1690 and 1724, the year in which he died. Although the Chevalier de Mailly was born into one of the most distinguished noble families of France, and had as his godparents a King and a Queen (Louis XIV and Anne of Austria), he deliberately flouted his high connections; and, since his books were more remarkable for their number than for their content, by the mid-nineteenth century they were no longer read. By then even his personal names had been forgotten, so he is remembered only by his title.[85]

Either Mailly or his publisher arranged to have the book appear with an announcement on its title page saying that it was a translation from Persian. Of course, this was a double deceit. The beginning of the book was merely an unacknowledged translation of part of Christopher's Italian *Peregrinaggio,* while the rest was simply made up by the author—though he drew some of his material from other writers—and his own work was totally un-Persian in thought and in feeling.

Whatever one may think of it now, Mailly's book must have enjoyed a certain popularity in the eighteenth century. It was twice published in French during his lifetime, then after his death it was reprinted in an anthology, and it was translated into several other languages.

Whoever translated Mailly's book into English for William Chetwood's edition of 1722—his name is never stated—managed to convey the style and spirit of it rather adequately. But he did make some very naïve blunders in translation, which indicate that he must have been an Englishman not too well acquainted with the French language.

For example, Mailly described how the owner of the lost camel again met the three princes as they were sitting in the shade (*ombre*) of a plane tree, at the edge of a beautiful fountain. The Englishman translated the passage to say: "The next day he again overtook the young princes who were at Ombre on a plain by the side of a pleasant fountain."[86] Again, in one of the sub-tales introduced by Mailly, a Grecian lady announced that she had a magnificent house in the suburb (*faubourg*) of Corinth, and the Englishman presented this as "a magnificent house at Faubourg near Corinth."[87] These mistakes are amusingly similar to some made by Christopher in his rendering of place-names.

Mailly's book was translated into German in 1723, under the title *Der persianische Robinson,* since Robinson Crusoe's name—by then internationally known—served as a popular catchword to suggest any kind of imaginary travels. Its title page announced that it had been translated from Persian into French and then into German,[88] again disregarding Christopher's prior translation and Mailly's extensive additions. A Danish translation from the German one appeared six years later, carrying the title *Amazonte,* from the name of the heroine in Mailly's final novelette.[89] In 1766 there was also a Dutch translation, apparently taken directly from the French one, although its title page also announced, "translated from the Persian."[90]

The remaining two French works inspired by the *Peregrinaggio* were even farther removed from the original. In 1610, François Béroalde de Verville published a long rambling book called *L'Histoire véritable ou le voyage des princes fortunez*,[91] the plot of which obviously owed some details to the *Peregrinaggio*, though the story as a whole was very different. Then in 1712 the other, called *Les Soirées bretonnes*, was issued by the prolific author Thomas Simon Gueulette, who was famous in eighteenth-century France as a teller of imaginary tales.[92] Although this also borrowed details from the *Peregrinaggio* for its quaint and confused plot, it, too, was very remote from the original.

The author-editor of *Serendipity* listed both these books among the translations of the *Peregrinaggio*, but neither was a translation in any sense. Neither of them ever refers to such characters as King Beramo and Diliramma, or the three princes, or even the land of Serendip. In short, both lie outside the mainstream of transmission, and they deserve mention only as examples of Christopher's influence on later writers.

Gueulette, who was quite notorious for his borrowings from other authors, more than once drew ideas from the *Peregrinaggio*, for he used further details from it in another book known as the *Contes tartares*.[93]

Voltaire's satirical novel *Zadig* included an amusing episode in which the hero identified *two* lost animals without having seen either,[94] and Benfey and his followers assumed that this must have been inspired by Mailly's account of the three princes of Serendip describing the lost camel.[95] However, this is a questionable case. Voltaire need not have obtained his ideas from Mailly. He is known to have consulted Herbelot's encyclopaedia for other Oriental elements in *Zadig*, and he could have found the story of the three princes there, taken from another source.[96] On the other hand, it is obvious that William Hauff drew directly from Voltaire—and not from any version of the *Peregrinaggio*—for his fable about "Abner the Jew, who had seen nothing," since Hauff mentions the same two animals that Zadig had identified (a stallion and a bitch) and gave them similar distinguishing marks.[97]

Another author who unquestionably borrowed from the *Peregrinaggio* was the Venetian playwright Carlo Gozzi. His use of material from two of Christopher's subtales, for a play done in 1762,[98] suggests a sustained interest in the *Peregrinaggio* in Venice, where it had first appeared.

These various references by no means exhaust all the European writings that have derived—directly or indirectly—from the *Peregrinaggio* in the period from the seventeenth to the nineteenth century. But we have doubtless said enough to demonstrate that Christopher's book exerted a widespread and continuing influence in Europe.

In America, public interest in the book about the three princes seems to have begun with a brief précis or resumé of Benfey's complete translation of the *Peregrinaggio* by Francis B. Sommer, published in 1959 in one of the *Ohio Valley Folk Publications*.[99] This merely retold the basic story very briefly, in a couple of mimeographed pages. However, the introduction expressed again the too-familiar skepticism regarding its authorship. It said: "The attributed author, Christoforo Armeno (the Armenian), claims to have translated this work from the Persian into Armenian and then into Italian; but it is doubtful that he ever existed."[100] Here we have again the false conception of the Benfey school, with an added twist that is equally without foundation. Of course it was unnecessary for Christopher to take the middle step of translating into Armenian, and he never claimed to have done so. As a man from Tabrīz, he would have had Persian as his primary language.

The first complete book in English on the three princes, since Chetwood's translation of Mailly, was *The Three Princes of Serendip,* written by Miss Hodges.[101] (In fact, she admitted that the Chetwood version had been one of her sources of inspiration.[102]) In writing this, she took only the framework of the narrative that had appeared in the *Peregrinaggio,* using the incidents regarding the three princes and King Bahrām to build the basic plot of "a story book intended for children." Although she was only making an adaptation of what was already a very old story-cycle, her approach was quite modern in its attempts to interweave the factual with the fantastic. Hoping to impart a stronger degree of authenticity, she inserted the results of considerable research into Singhalese, Indian and Persian, history, geography, and culture almost to the point of overloading the fragile plot, but she managed to retain something of the romantic quality of a fairy tale, and used it to carry a worthy moral.

Since she was intentionally using only the basic frame, without the novellas, this book says nothing about the tales narrated in the seven palaces, beyond a brief mention that the stories had been told. Also, she simplified even the basic frame by deleting a few of the lesser incidents, and made it a vehicle for another, quite different kind of narrative, involving a quest which is only achieved at the very end.

By contrast, Miss Hodges' second book, *Serendipity Tales,*[103] was composed primarily of six of the seven stories that made up the core of the *Peregrinaggio,* with an additional one of her own on a pseudo-Chinese theme. Unfortunately, the total product was not very successful. The tales as she has presented them seem as decadent and overdrawn as the accompanying illustrations, which are "exotic" pen-and-ink sketches in the style of Aubrey Beardsley; and the sheer weight of strange, outlandish names for people and places makes a top-heavy load, far too great for these slight tales to bear. (We can now see how wise Amīr Khusrau and Christopher both were in resisting the temptation to give names to everybody and every thing; they realized the importance of well-paced plots.) One can only say that this second book seems a bore even for adults, and it could scarcely hold the interest of children.

THE NEW ENGLISH TRANSLATION

We have seen that the recent book called *Serendipity* made some highly erroneous statements about the *Peregrinaggio,* its background, its author, and its literary descendants. What can we say about its other portion, "the first direct English translation"?

Although the Borsellis' new translation of the *Peregrinaggio* was not done strictly word for word, and they have taken some questionable liberties in supplying extra words, or adding occasional interpretations of their own which are not strictly accurate, on the whole their rendering reads quite well as a quaint, semi-medieval collection of Italian folktales with an Oriental setting. The trouble is, the stories in the *Peregrinaggio* were not Italian folk tales!

The general effect of quaintness stems partly from their insistence upon rendering most of the dialogue in stilted or archaic English. Here is an example: " 'Goodness, tell me by your faith, modest maid, who are you? Of whom are you the daughter?' he asked."[104]

Apparently they assumed that such language would better reproduce the flavor of sixteenth-century Italy, as they imagined it; but it removes the stories even farther from their original Oriental milieu, as well as destroying any last elements of realism.

Other faults were caused by the translators' obvious inability to visualize the scenes which they were trying to recreate. For example, in two instances, a key element in the plot of a hunting tale is the king's use of a pellet-bow to accomplish a long-distance shot. A pellet-bow is a small but powerful form of cross-bow, intended to shoot a small round projectile with considerable speed and directness. However, in both places, the translators have rendered *arco da pellote* as "slingshot."[105] This mention of a child's toy, ineffective at any real distance, adds an unintentional comic note to what was originally intended as a spectacular display of long-range accuracy.

Then, another tale describes how a faithless consort had been accustomed to swimming across a river to meet her lover, keeping herself afloat by clinging to a large watertight jar. When the king discovered that she was betraying him, he arranged to have an unbaked jar substituted for the one she usually relied on; so when she took it out upon the river, it disintegrated, leaving her to drown. Here, the translators, lacking a clear mental picture of the situation, merely said: "The unfired vase sank because it was unable to hold the water and she too sank with it."[106]—Obviously the purpose of the jar was not to hold water, but to keep it out, so it could serve as a float.

Again, when they described the Indian king ordering the lion image, they said he gave the goldsmith "ten thousand gold coins of that land (called golden pesos)."[107] The *Hasht bihisht* had said that the king gave him a thousand *man* of pure gold, a *man* being a Persian weight, and Christopher had translated the word *man* as *peso,* meaning "weight," although he increased the amount to ten thousand weights of gold (*diecimila pesi d'oro*).[108] The error of turning these weights into *pesos* seems doubly absurd because a *peso* was an exclusively Spanish unit of currency, confined to Spain and its overseas possessions. Therefore it was totally unsuitable in an Asian tale.

Mistakes like these are not vital in themselves, and it may seem petty to cite them. When there are quite a number of them, however, the effect is cumulative, and the net result is a poor translation by modern standards.

The editor of *Serendipity* announced that he had deliberately sought a translator who was not familiar with the *Peregrinaggio* nor acquainted with any translations of it. Was he trying to maintain the amateur status of his book—not realizing that that was a serious weakness—or was he merely defending in advance the work of inexperienced translators?[109] Even if the Borsellis had had no previous knowledge of the book beyond what the editor had told them regarding the alleged authorship by Tramezzino, etc., it should have been their obligation to consult the previous translations before publishing theirs. In particular, they should have examined the one by Theodor Benfey, who was a careful translator, in spite of his own misguided views on the origin and authorship of the *Peregrinaggio*. A preliminary comparison with his work would have quickly exposed a number of weak points that could have been caught and corrected before publication.

Finally, the translators provided some unintentional irony by a long letter to the editor of *Serendipity,* which he presents in his book, discussing the style of the *Peregrinaggio*. Apparently having been assured in advance that the latter had been written by the publisher Tramezzino, and not by "a mythical Armenian," they tried to explain the style and form of the work as the product of an Italian author of the Renaissance. However, the elements that they singled out happen to be typically Persian literary traits.

They remarked upon the "synonymous adjectives in pairs," "elaborately fashioned sentences" that "run on and on almost endlessly," and a general lack of punctuation.[110] All of these familiar Persian characteristics appear in the *Hasht bihisht,* and Christopher must have been so steeped in the style that it was only natural for him to continue to use it. In Amīr Khusrau's book, one also meets a constant tendency for direct discourse to lapse suddenly into indirect, a trait that greatly bothered the translators. In addition, they complained about finding that pronouns do not always agree with their antecedents and "a female animal may become a male without the benefit of the transfiguration magic so common in the Novella[s]."[111] These particular features, too, were certainly to be expected: Persian has no distinctions of gender, and Christopher was being forced to translate from a language familiar to him, which lacked gender, into a language probably still somewhat strange to him in which gender was stressed. All these features that troubled the Borsellis merely emphasize that the author of the *Peregrinaggio* was an ex-citizen of Iran, working with truly Persian tales, thus providing further vindication for Christopher.

CONCLUSION

We have seen that a number of modern scholars and popular writers have considered the *Peregrinaggio* to be an original work, probably written by the publisher Tramezzino, from which sprang a number of derivative books. However, investigation has shown that it was itself an adaptation, only a link in a series of derived works: the fourth—or perhaps the fifth[112]—in a line that began with Firdausī's *Shāhnāme* of A.D. 1010 and ended with Miss Hodges' second book in 1966.

We also saw that in the course of this transmission, successive authors set out to copy or imitate a predecessor, but invariably they went on to use their own imagination to produce what were essentially new books. The Chevalier de Mailly and Miss Hodges—not to mention the author of the *Peregrinaggio*— were each working in that old tradition, and in spite of their alterations and even distortions of the borrowed material, they all deserve credit for trying to adapt old stories to the tastes of new readers in their respective periods.

While reviewing the *Peregrinaggio* itself and comparing it with its undoubted prototype, the *Hasht bihisht,* we learned enough about its author, Christopher the Armenian, to confirm his identity and to reveal him as an authentic person. In his own autobiographical remarks, in the Preface, he appeared as a very human individual, a former resident of Tabrīz in Iran, then living in Venice and fond of his new home, a very poor man, who was grateful to those who had helped him. Internal evidence in the text itself has further shown us that he must have been a rather religious man—though sometimes given to earthy humor—and that he was probably quite homesick for Asia. Obviously, he was not much of a scholar; but he seems to have had a rather wide acquaintance with Persian poetry and literature, and he was so deeply imbued with Persian language traits that these hampered his Italian. He certainly did not do a good translation by modern standards, but that probably was not expected; in any case, it would have been most difficult to translate Amīr Khusrau's complex poetry directly into any European language. He did do a rather good job of presenting the substance of the *Hasht bihisht* in a highly readable form, and his fast-moving plots display considerable ability at condensation and synthesis. On the whole, his book shows a good measure of creativity.

Christopher did not invent the Three Princes of Serendip, as has often been stated. It was Amīr Khusrau who gave this name to the anonymous heroes of an already-ancient tale. But, by giving them greater importance in his book, he raised them from minor figures to a position of relative prominence in world fiction, and he did introduce them to the West.

As for the *Peregrinaggio's* successors, the Chevalier de Mailly's book may seem a very poor copy of it—almost a parody—while the Chetwood translation of Mailly is sometimes ridiculous for its misreadings; yet, viewed in the broader perspective of international literature, as links in a chain that reaches back more than a thousand years into two great civilizations of Asia, both of these later works take on a special significance, as do the books of Elizabeth Hodges, thus far the last in the long, long line.

It must now be clear that Michele Tramezzino should be remembered primarily as an industrious printer who labored to make foreign works available to his cosmopolitan-minded fellow citizens in sixteenth-century Venice; while Christopher the Armenian should regain full credit for his authorship, for his part in the transmission of Asian stories and ideas, and for his clever reworking of old materials. But the highest praise should be reserved for Amīr Khusrau, whose genius united the Persian and Indian traditions and gave new life to old tales as he passed them on.

UNIVERSITY OF PENNSYLVANIA

NOTES

1. Later Italian editions of the *Peregrinaggio* appeared in Venice in 1577, 1611, 1622, and 1628, and in Turin in 1828. See Hermann Fischer and Johannes Bolte, "Die Reise der Söhne Giaffers," *Bibliothek des Litterarischen Vereins in Stuttgart*, Vol. 208, Tübingen, 1896, p. 177.

2. The first German translation, by Johann Wetzel, a Swiss, appeared in Basel in 1583. It was reissued in 1599, and reworked by Carl von Libenau in 1630. Fischer and Bolte republished Wetzel's book in 1896. (See previous note.)

3. The French authors generally just imitated the *Peregrinaggio*, adapting some of its motifs for incidents in what were new and different books. They never attempted a complete translation into their language.

4. Chevalier de Mailly, *Le Voyage et les aventures des trois princes de Serendip*, first appeared in Paris in 1719, and was reprinted in Amsterdam in 1721. It was again reprinted in Paris and Amsterdam in 1788, in an anthology called *Voyages imaginaires*, edited by C. G. T. Garnier. The English edition, entitled *The Travels and Adventures of Three Princes of Serendip*, was published in London by William Chetwood, in 1722. (The name of the translator is never given.)

5. See *The Yale Edition of Horace Walpole's Correspondence*, edited by W. S. Lewis, Vol. 20, New Haven, 1960, p. 407. It is now assumed that Walpole had read the 1721 edition of Mailly's work, printed in Amsterdam. See *ibid.*, note 3.

6. Elizabeth Jamison Hodges, *The Three Princes of Serendip*, Atheneum Press, New York, 1964, and *Serendipity Tales*, New York, 1966.

7. *Serendipity and the Three Princes, from the Peregrinaggio of 1557*, edited by Theodore G. Remer, University of Oklahoma Press, Norman, Oklahoma, 1965.

8. See note 5, above.

9. As mentioned above, in note 4, the only English version of the *Peregrinaggio* was the Chetwood translation of Mailly's book; but Mailly had merely produced an adaptation of the Italian original, in no sense a real translation.

10. The editor of *Serendipity* frankly admits (on p. 9) that he was not equipped with a knowledge of any of the languages necessary for this particular project; and, although he says he worked on the historical material for eight years, helped by various friends who translated for him portions of the commentaries on the *Peregrinaggio*, they seem to have skipped the footnotes, into which the commentators had placed most of their more valuable leads.

11. The translators, Mr. and Mrs. Augusto Borselli, were apparently persuaded by the editor into thinking that the *Peregrinaggio* was not really a translation from a Persian book, but an original product of 16th century Italy. The translation, its rendering into English, and their comments on the original text, were all colored by this false premise. This will be discussed further.

12. One of the first to be misled was Professor W. S. Lewis, the famous editor of the Walpole letters, who wrote an introduction to *Serendipity*, stating that in future he would refer his numerous correspondents to this book (p. viii).

13. The title page for the 1557 edition of the *Peregrinaggio* is reproduced in *Serendipity* on p. 50.

14. Except for noble clans like the Pakradoonis, who had regular family names, most Armenians down into the 20th century had no real surname. Children just used their father's given name with the suffix *-ian*, and the next generation changed this accordingly.

15. The original preface in Italian was reproduced by Bolte, *op. cit.*, pp. 5-8, at bottom of each page. The overly-suspicious editor of *Serendipity* thought that this preface was written by an Italian and that it contained "satire on the social order of Venice" (p. 8). Both suppositions are unwarranted.

16. On a recent visit to Tabrīz, the writer was surprised at the large number of shop signs bearing Armenian names.

17. Failing to recognize the words derived from Persian, the Borsellis translated *Franchi* as "the French people," and *Franchia*, which meant "the land of the *Firangi*" i.e., Europe, as "France," thus distorting the original meaning.

18. For the original dedication, in Italian, see Bolte and Fischer, *op. cit.*, pp. 3-5, bottom of each page.

19. See Horatio F. Brown, *The Venetian Printing Press*, New York and London, 1891, p. 106.

20. *Ibid.*, p. 101. Tramezzino's work with Spanish books is also mentioned in the *Imprimatur* for the 1557 edition of the *Peregrinaggio*.

21. This brief beginning, with a long introduction, appeared in Benfey, "Ein alter christlich-persischer Roman: Die Reise der drei Söhne des Königs von Serendippo," *Orient und Occident*,

Vol. 3, no. 2, Göttingen, 1865, pp. 257-288. It did not go beyond the princes' first encounters with King Bahrām, before he sent them on the mission to India.

22. Georg Huth, "Die Reise der drei Söhne des Königs von Serendippo: ein Beitrag zur vergleichenden Märchenkunde," *Zeitschrift für vergleichende Literaturgeschichte*, N.F., Vol. 2, 1889, pp. 404-414; Vol. 3, 1890, pp. 303-330; Vol. 4, 1891, pp. 174-202.

23. In *Erlanger Beitrage zür englischen Philologie*, Vol. 10, Erlangen, 1891.

24. See references in notes 1 and 2, above.

25. Theodor Benfey, "Die Reise der drei Söhne des Königs von Serendippo," with introduction and notes by Richard Fick and Alfons Hilka, in *Folklore Fellows Communications*, no. 98, Helsinki, 1932, pp. 3-170.

26. A long poetic account of the legendary life of Bahrām Gur appeared in the *Shahname* of Firdausī, completed in A.D. 1010. This has been translated by Arthur George Warner and Edmond Warner, in *The Shāhnāma of Firdausī*, London, Vol. 6, 1912, and Vol. 7, 1915.

27. The *Haft paikar* was translated into English by C. E. Wilson, London, 1924. The editor of *Serendipity*, being unaware of this, presented a clumsy translation of a passage in German describing one of the incidents in the *Haft paikar*, which Benfey had taken from an early 19th century German author (*Serendipity*, pp. 180-182), and in this all the names appear in highly distorted forms.

28. See *Kleinere Schriften von Th. Benfey*, edited by Adalbert Bezzenberger, Berlin, 1892, Vol. 2, p. 197.

29. Benfey, in *Orient und Occident*, Vol. 3, p. 261, and *passim* to p. 270.

30. Introduction to Benfey's translation, in *F. F. Communications*, no. 98, p. 9.

31. *Ibid.*, pp. 9 and 10.

32. *Ibid.*, p. 10.

33. *Serendipity*, pp. 47-48.

34. H. F. Brown, *Venetian Printing Press*, p. 101.

35. St. Francis Xavier's success was only temporary. His converts were soon persecuted and even massacred, until those who remained were eventually brought under Portuguese protection. c.f. Harry Williams, Ceylon, *Pearl of the East*, London, n.d., p. 334.

36. See Ammianus Marcellinus, *Res Gestae*, translated by John C. Rolfe, in the *Loeb Classical Library*, Cambridge, Mass., 1937, Vol. 2, p. 212, for the original Latin text; p. 213 for the English translation; and also p. 212, note 1.

37. See Dines Andersen, *A Pāli Glossary*, Copenhagen, London, and Leipzig, 1907, p. 277. See also note 46, below. Contrast with this evidence the particularly confused paragraph in *Serendipity* (on p. 30), which says, "We can reasonably assume that "Serendip" is not Arabic . . . neither is it likely that it is derived from the Pali *serumdipa*."

38. This change of names is discussed by Sir Henry Yule, in *The Book of Ser Marco Polo*, London, 1871, Vol. 2, p. 254, note 1; though some of his statements seem very out of date.

39. See Giovanni Battista Ramusio, *Delle navigationi et viaggi*, Venice, 1559, Vol. 2, p. 53.

40. For the development of maps of that area, see A. E. Nordenskiold, *An Essay on the Early History of Charts and Sailing Directions*, translated by Francis A. Bather, New York (1964). The original work appeared in Swedish in 1897, under the title *Periplus: utkart till sjöböckeras äldsta historia.*

41. The result of this change can be observed on Tramezzino's famous map, referred to in the following note.

42. Tramezzino's map is reproduced in Nordenskiold, *op. cit.*, 1964 ed., Fig. 66, p. 147.

43. Barthélemy d'Herbelot (de Moulainville), *Bibliothèque orientale*, first published in Paris, in 1697. It was reissued in 1776.

44. *Ibid.*, 1697 ed., p. 806. Berthelot went on to say, "In fact, since the name of Dib or Div, in the Indian language signifies an island, the name of Serendib does not mean anything else than the Isle of Seran, or Selan." His philological knowledge may not have been too sound, but his reasoning was fairly accurate. We can easily imagine a combination of *Seruma* and *dīpa*—probably Serumdīpa—with the *m* soon changing to *n* for euphonic reasons, and final *a* being lost, to give *Serundip*, from which the suffix *-dīp* was finally dropped, as well. It is slightly more difficult to explain how *Serun* or *Seirun* got changed to *Seilan*, but there is clearly a connection between them.

45. *Bibliothèque orientale*, 1697 ed., p. 392b.

46. See Edward Gibbon, *History of the Decline and Fall of the Roman Empire*, New York, 1826 edition, Vol. 2, p. 361, text and note 6.

47. See Horace Walpole's letter to the Countess of Upper Ossory, on Feb. 14th, 1796, in the *Yale Edition of Horace Walpole's Correspondence*, Vol. 34, New Haven, 1965, pp. 212-213.

48. For a somewhat confused reference to the second Armenian Christopher, see *Serendipity*, p. 45, note 17 (continued on p. 46).

49. Of Straparola, we only know that he was born in Caravaggio, towards the end of the fifteenth century; that he wrote *Le piacevole notte*, a compilation of much older tales, together with some poems; and that he died in Venice in 1557. See the *Dizionario enciclopedico italiano*, Rome, 1960, Vol. 10, p. 743, or the *Grande dizionario enciclopedico*, Turin, 1962, Vol. 12, p. 165. Since he was a contemporary of Christopher, Benfey suggested that he might have been the helper mentioned in the Preface to the *Peregrinaggio* (in *Orient und Occident*, Vol. 3, p. 267). However, this assumption was based on the false supposition that Christopher's stories were, at least in part, old Italian stories of the same kind as those published by Straparola, so it seems untenable.

50. When the Indian queen presented the problem of how to divide a set of five eggs evenly, without breaking any, the third prince gave three to her and one to her Minister, keeping one himself. Then he told her that they were now equally divided. When the queen challenged him, he explained to her that he and the Minister each had two more inside their trousers. The answer to this second riddle sounds crude or even shocking in Italian, or English; but it would have been more subtle in Persian, which has several words that mean both "egg" and "testicle," for example: *khāya* or *baiza*. As far as I know, this particular pun would not be possible in any western European language.

51. Amīr Khusrau's proper name was Jamīn ud-Dīn Abu'l-Ḥasan; but he has been more generally known as Amīr Khusrau Dehlawī. For two detailed studies of his life and work, see Mohammad Habib, *Hazrat Amīr Khusrau of Delhi*, Aligarh Muslim University Publications, Bombay, 1927, and Mohammad Wahid Mirza, *The Life and Works of Amīr Khusrau*, Calcutta, 1935.

52. See note 27, above.

53. See note 26, above.

54. See Jan Rypka, *Iranische Literaturgeschichte*, Leipzig, 1959, pp. 250-251, and A. J. Arberry, *Classical Persian Literature*, New York, 1958, p. 330.

55. A number of manuscripts of Amīr Khusrau's *Khamse* were beautifully illustrated, but unfortunately some of these have been cut up to obtain their pictures. See Binyon, Wilkinson, and Gray, *Persian Miniature Paintings*, London, 1933, p. 95, no. 78, for a set of such paintings attributed to the great Bihzād. A superbly illustrated *Khamse* of Amīr Khusrau, composed in the 17th century, is in the Philadelphia Art Museum (Collection of S. S. and Vera White).

56. J. G. T. Graesse, in *Trésor de livres rares et précieux*, Vol. I (Dresden, Geneva, London and Paris, 1859), while discussing the *Peregrinaggio*, remarks, "A Russian translation of this novel composed in the course of the 14th century although unpublished proves its antiquity." However, when one consults the reference for this confused statement, a work by N. M. Karamsin, one finds nothing at all relevant. Of course, that would be too early for a translation of the *Peregrinaggio*, but there is nothing in the work cited to suggest a translation of the *Hasht bihisht* either.

57. *Bibliothèque orientale*, 1697 ed., pp. 121a and 582b. Actually, Herbelot was quoting the story from another Persian work; but its details are essentially the same as those in the *Hasht bihisht*, except for the nationality of the princes, and it may have been borrowed from the latter.

58. A. Lacoin de Villemorin and Dr. Khalil Khan, *Le Jardin des délices*, 2nd edition, Paris, 1897, pp. 149-162 (the Three Princes), and pp. 165-185 (the Parrot King).

59. *Op. cit.*, pp. 77-85.

60. O. B. Lal and J. Prasada, *Complete Key to the Persian Entrance Course for 1897-1898* (for the University of Allahabad), Allahabad, 1896, pp. 72-84.

61. See C. H. Ethé, "Firdausis Yusuf und Zulīkhā," in the *Proceedings [Verhandlungen] of the Seventh International Orientalist Congress, Vienna, 1886*, Vienna, 1888, Semitic section, p. 35, V. 2; and Bolte, *op. cit.*, pp. 205-206.

62. Albert Wesselski, "Quellen und Nachwirkungen der Haft Paikar," *Der. Islam*, Vol. 22, no. 2, 1934, pp. 106-119.

63. See the *Descriptive Catalogue of the Garrett Collection of Persian, Turkish, and Indic Manuscripts . . . in the Princeton University Library*, London, 1939, pp. 6-7, nos. 13 and 14.

64. See A. G. and E. Warner, *The Shāhnāma of Firdausi*, Vol. 6, p. 383-384, and C. E. Wilson, *Haft Paikar*, Vol. 2, p. 84. Nizāmī changed the animal to an onager, or *gur*. It is impossible to give more specific references to the *Hasht bihisht*, as the manuscripts do not have numbered pages.

65. Riddles are common in Persian literature, as in the story-cycle that inspired *Turandot;* and the "Mirror of Justice" was mentioned in Amīr Khusrau's story of the Parrot King, so Christopher apparently took it from an interior story to enrich his frame.

66. Warner, *Shāhnāma*, Vol. 6, p. 383.

67. To strike off the male unicorn's horn and to provide the female with an arrow "horn" would require only two arrows; whereas one would need four to do the same kind of thing to a stag and a doe, and assuming the latter were in flight, this second feat would seem impossible.

68. Although the sub-tales sound familiar, this time it is more difficult to locate specific sources.

69. See V. Chauvin, *Bibliographie des ouvrages arabes,* Vol. 7, Liège and Leipzig, 1903, p. 158; and note the many further references given.

70. The "Weighing of the Elephant" theme recurs in the Chinese story about Ts'ao Ch'ung. Actually, it is an old Indian motif that came to China through Buddhism. See E. Chavannes, *Cinq cents contes et apologues extraits du Tripitaka chinois,* Paris, 1911, Vol. 3, pp. 4-5, where he presents an old Buddhist tale containing this theme, which was translated into Chinese in A.D. 472. Amīr Khusrau set the story of the Goldsmith in Khurasan (Northwestern Iran), but Christopher put it back into India. The reasons for these shifts of scene are not known.

71. One can sense the flavor of Amīr Khusrau's fifth tale by reading the fifth tale of Nizāmī, C. E. Wilson, *Haft Paikar,* Vol. I, pp. 189-213. As the planet for that day (Wednesday) was ·Mercury, both writers described a phantasmagoria with mercurial changes of visions and ideas.

72. Bahrām spurred his horse into a rocky cavern and disappeared. His body was never found. Both Nizāmī and Amīr Khusrau followed the description of his death with a section of moral reflections, but the stories as such ended with his passing.

73. See M. Habīb, "Life and Works of Amīr Khusrau," *Muslim Review,* Vol. I, no. 4, Calcutta, 1927, p. 3.

74. Amīr Khusrau begins the *Hasht bihisht* with an invocation to Allah, and a dedication to his princely patron. Similarly, Christopher began the *Peregrinaggio* with an invocation to God, and a dedication to Giustiniani.

75. In that period, at the beginning of the Counter Reformation, feelings ran high, and Christopher may have felt himself under suspicion; but though this thought may have been present in his mind, its influence on his writing was probably only secondary.

76. In the *Hasht bihisht,* as in the *Haft paikar,* the princesses themselves had told the stories.

77. C. E. Wilson, in *Haft Paikar,* Vol. 2, p. 123, note 1,147, comments that Nizāmī, in establishing his order of the climes, did not follow any of the customary systems but was quite arbitrary; however, he did take the days in the usual sequence, paying due attention to the proper planets and their traditional colors, and so did Amīr Khusrau, as follows:

1. Saturday,	subject to		Saturn, black.
2. Sunday,	"	"	The Sun, yellow.
3. Monday,	"	"	The Moon, green.
4. Tuesday,	"	"	Mars, red.
5. Wednesday,	"	"	Mercury, turquoise (blue).
6. Thursday,	"	"	Jupiter, sandalwood (pale tan).
7. Friday,	"	*	Venus, white.

In European languages, the names for the days of the week still show survivals of this order, inherited from the Classical World. English preserves traces in Saturday, Sunday, and Monday, but it is more obvious in the French: lundi, mardi, mercredi, jeudi, vendredi.

78. The miniature painters of Old Persia vied in producing sets of seven pictures, each showing one of the palaces with its dome, its furnishings, and the clothing of its inmates, all done in variations of a single hue. The Freer Gallery, in Washington, D.C., has some fine examples.

79. The palace in Christopher's third novella.

80. Since the days of Alfonso the Wise, in the 13th century, many Europeans have been fascinated by Muslim planetary lore. However, the activities of such people as Agrippa of Nettesheim—as described in Book II of his *De Occulta philosophia* (1531), esp. Chapter 22—indicate the debased kind of magical practices to which this tended to lead, and they help to explain the wrath of the ecclesiastical authorities against the practitioners, who tried to use planetary influences to evil ends.

81. King Vikramāditya was also the hero of a whole cycle of Indian tales that were translated into Persian, and from Persian into French. The French translation, by Baron Lescallier, entitled *Le Trône enchanté* was published in New York in 1817. A copy of this rare work is preserved in the Jefferson Library at the University of Virginia.

82. My informants in Princeton remarked that the manuscripts we were examining had many lacunae. Oriental copyists frequently made mistakes, and sometimes they left out words or ideas that they could not understand.

83. Wesselski, *op. cit.,* p. 112, assumed that there actually was an intermediate book. Perhaps there was; but, as I am trying to show, the differences between the *Peregrinaggio* and the *Hasht bihisht* could largely be accounted for without having to posit a missing volume.

84. See reference in note 4, above.

85. For a brief sketch of the Chevalier de Mailly's life, and a list of his books, see Pierre Larousse, ed., *Grand dictionnaire universel du XIX⁰ siècle,* Paris, n.d., Vol. 10, p. 948. (The editor of *Serendipity* refers to him throughout as "De Mailly"; this is equivalent to speaking of the Duke of Devonshire as "Of Devonshire," and is poor form.)

86. Chetwood translation (see reference in note 4, above), p. 9.

87. *Ibid.*, p. 117.

88. Bolte, *op. cit.*, p. 196, reproduces the oddly spelled wording found on the title page of this German edition of Mailly's book.

89. *Ibid.*, p. 197.

90. The title page of the Dutch translation was reproduced by Benfey, in *Orient und Occident*, Vol. 3, p. 260.

91. François Béroalde de Verville, *l'Histoire véritable, ou le voyage des princes fortunez*, Paris, 1610.

92. T. S. Gueulette, *Les Soirées bretonnes*, Paris, 1712. This was reprinted in *Le Cabinet des fées*, Geneva and Paris, 1786, Vol. 32. See Bolte's comments on both these books, *op. cit.*, p. 195.

93. Gueulette, *Les Mille et un quart d'heures; Contes tartares*, Paris, 1715; reproduced in *Cabinet des fées*, Geneva 1787, Vols. 21, p. 496, and 22, pp. 9, 89.

94. See Voltaire, *Zadig, ou la destinée*, edited by Georges Ascoli, Paris, 1921, Chapter 3, pp. 13-17. (*Zadig* itself was written in 1749.)

95. For Bolte's comment see *Orient und Occident*, Vol. 3, p. 264. See also Benfey, in *Orient und Occident*, Vol. 3, p. 264.

96. See reference in note 58, above, and note that the story repeated by Herbelot might still have derived from Amir Khusrau's *Hasht bihisht*.

97. Wilhelm Hauff, "Märchen von Abner der Juden, der nichts gesehen hat," *Werke*, Vol. 4, pp. 142-152. This is in a collection called *Deutsche National-litteratur*, Stuttgart, n.d.

98. Carlo Gozzi, in *Il Re cervo* (1762), used both the Transference of the Soul motif, from the first novella about the King turned parrot, and the Smiling Statue motif from the fifth novella, to provide incidents in this comedy. See Carlo Gozzi, *Opere teatro e polemiche teatrali*, Giuseppe Peronio, ed., Milan, 1962, pp. 170-236.

99. F. B. Sommer, "The Three Princes of Serendip, a Précis on an Old Tale," *Ohio Valley Folk Publications*, N.S., no. 17, Chillicothe, Ohio, 1959.

100. Although public interest in the *Peregrinaggio* seems to have begun with Sommer's brief article, he was not the first American to comment on the *Peregrinaggio*. See Martha Pike Conant, *The Oriental Tale in the Eighteenth Century*, New York, 1908. In this book (her Ph.D. dissertation for Columbia University), she rather quickly dismissed the *Peregrinaggio*—which she knew only from Mailly, Chetwood's translation of Mailly, and Bolte's comments—regarding it as a "pseudo-translation," supposedly Oriental but actually Italian.

101. See reference in note 5, above.

102. Hodges, *op. cit.*, pp. 155-156.

103. See reference in note 5, above. On page 177 of *Serendipity Tales*, she echoes the prevalent misconception, speaking of the *Peregrinaggio* as "ascribed to 'M. Christoforo Armeno,' a name scholars think pseudonymous."

104. *Serendipity*, p. 106. Actually, this scrap of conversation represents a painfully literal translation of the Italian original, in a kind of "Olde Englyshe" style. It is typical of the dialogue throughout the translation.

105. *Ibid.*, pp. 75 and 98.

106. *Ibid.*, p. 135.

107. *Ibid.*, p. 108, has two instances of the misuse of the word *pesos*.

108. *Peregrinaggio*, 1557 edition, p. 39.

109. *Ibid.*, p. 35. In another case (on p. 42), the author-editor defended an atrocious, overly-literal translation of a passage from German, saying, "The pertinent portions of this Introduction have been translated here from German into English with little or no editing in order to preserve its quaint flavor."

110. *Ibid.*, pp. 164-165. Old Persian manuscripts had no punctuation at all; so Christopher would not have been accustomed to using it.

111. *Ibid.*, pp. 165-166.

112. If perchance there had been an intermediate work between the *Hasht bihisht* and the *Peregrinaggio*, the latter would be the fifth in the line of transmission. But see note 83, above.

MARIO PRAZ

Armida's Garden

ABSTRACT

Tasso belongs to a line of geniuses, including, *e.g.*, Montaigne and Diderot, in whom we detect striking anticipations of romantic attitudes. In the *Gerusalemme* we find episodes (that of Olindo and Sofronia and the other of Tancredi and Clorinda) in which a peculiar sense is clearly discernible of painful pleasure (*algolagnia*) closely related to a well-known aspect of romantic sensibility. This aspect of Tasso "goes together with other manifestations of his sensibility which all point in the same direction," as the use of the *non so che* to express "a quantity of still undefined feelings which later blossomed into romantic attitudes," the awareness of the spell of ruins and of vast deserted places, and most of all the taste for comely negligence, which he transferred from oratory (as recommended by Longinus' *On the Sublime,* section 22), to female beauty and to the garden (*Gerusalemme*, XVI, stanzas 9-10), thus "making a first step towards the creation of the 'natural' or picturesque garden that became an English specialty during the eighteenth century." Tasso's lines "indicate a revolution in taste which became general during the seventeenth century," that idea of elegant disorder which was stressed by Ben Jonson in a song included in *The Silent Woman* and by Herrick's charming lines "A sweet disorder in the dress."

The search for forerunners and anticipations, though rich in surprises, is fraught with obvious dangers.* The critic often isolates a passage from its context, and gives it a weight it does not possess, like those art-historians who discover unexpected landscapes in the background of fifteenth-century altar-pieces. Some time ago this kind of search was undertaken for the metaphysical

* This was the Henry Rowlatt Bickley Memorial Lecture delivered at St. Hugh's College, Oxford on June 6th, 1967.

trend in English literature, but the widest beating that has ever been made for anticipations concerns the romantic period: there is a whole literature about inklings and forerunners of the romantic sensibility, as, since the application of the historical method to literary criticism, every generation has ransacked the past for pedigrees of its present attitudes, and while the early romantics found a father in Shakespeare, the decadents exhumed all the texts of the past which bore a resemblance to their way of feeling. One need only read passages of Huysmans' *A rebours,* about the books to which went Des Esseintes's admiration, to see what passionate interest even then worked that shock of recognition which establishes links between kin souls throughout the course of history. T. S. Eliot imagined a metaphysical tradition running through three phases, and found brothers in the poets of Dante's circle, in Donne and his school, and in Baudelaire, Rimbaud, Laforgue; nowadays, in a climate thick with anxiety and ambiguities, the interest of critics is focussed on the mannerist period with its vacillating creeds, changing colours, serpentine forms, and strange mixture of abstract and concrete.

There are geniuses of the past who seem particularly liable to this kind of investigation; their common trait, which in a sense explains this persistent interest of later ages in them, is their many-sidedness, restlessness and fundamental ambiguity, so that it is even possible to quote them in support of opposite views, and in any case of the most impressive anticipations: Montaigne, Tasso and Diderot belong to this class.

In Montaigne Jean Rousset [1] has seen a forerunner of the baroque sensibility because of his volubility, his wavering and mobile personality, and the mark of *variété et étrangeté* stamped on all his works: a fortuitous assemblage of *grotesques et corps monstrueux,* polymorphous figures conceived according to an idea of disorder which art had not envisaged and mastered so far. But the random arrangement of thoughts, the indulgence in whims and extravagant images, the candid avowal of personal idiosyncrasies, make of Montaigne also one of the forerunners of the romantic essay as it took shape in Charles Lamb.

Diderot, also, was a many-sided personality; in his universal and prophetic brain there were present the seeds and more than the seeds of many later developments, so that Delacroix and Baudelaire, no less than David, saw themselves mirrored in him. He had learned from Sterne the art of smoothly gliding from one subject to the other, of achieving a flow out of an innumerable scintillation of little waves: in so far he is a typical writer of the rococo period. In *Le neveu de Rameau* digressions, secondary dialogues inserted incidentally into the main one, scenes, either real or imaginary, are recorded, the speaker apostrophizes himself. In the *Supplément au voyage de Bougainville* the first and second interlocutors report bits of conversation in their repartees, and the first one sketches a quarreling scene between an actor and his wife; the author himself intervenes in the dialogue, and this is the strangest trait of all, because the first interlocutor is introduced as the author of the *Père de famille*, i.e. Diderot himself, who in this case is split into two characters. *Jacques le fataliste*, modelled on *Tristram Shandy*, is, like its prototype, no novel at all in the traditional sense of the word. On the other hand Diderot responded most of all to the grandeur, the majesty of the simplicity of the ancients, despised the petty graces and sugary affectations of that very rococo style of which in other respects he was a typical representative; he proposed to bring back a sober and dignified taste to a frivolous society, and drew inspiration from the example of Socrates for the conduct of his own life. Philosophy had not extinguished the impulses of feeling in him; he was capable of magnanimous outbursts and not insensitive to certain cruel, violent, dionysiacal (to use Nietzsche's word) aspects of the ancient world, and to those "charms of horror which inebriate the strong" (and one understands why the eighteenth century enthusiasts of the Laocoön should find sublimity in Dante's espisode of Ugolino, that mediaeval Laocoön); but he appreciated also the new, tragical element introduced by Christianity.

We find in him the genuine source of that neoclassicism which later, when it was crystallized in a formula, degenerated into a pompous vacuity; but at the origin, that idea of an antiquity felt as a school of virtue capable of inflaming the heart, those ruins seen as the natural abode of great spirits, had the flavour of real life, not of an academy. There was in him that very aspiration to the simple, the absolute, the geometrical, which animated the great revolutionary architects Ledoux, Boullée, Lequeu, Friedrich Gilly. A man of the theatre, an archaeologist and digger, a philosopher, historian and poet, in the lively picture Garat gives of him when he visited him in 1779, he is seen shifting his conversation from one subject to the other with a mercurial lightness, with a harmonious versatility which stamp him of the same line of geniuses as Montaigne.

Diderot could be claimed by the classicist and the romantic with equal right, Tasso can be pronounced a mannerist, a forerunner of the romantics, and, in the field of the visual arts, be likened to the most diverse painters without gross impropriety. G. C. Argan [2] and Ferruccio Ulivi [3] are reminded of Tintoretto for certain effects of light and shadow, particularly of the Santa Maria Egiziaca of the Scuola di San Rocco, with its fabulous Oriental background. Elsewhere, in the *Sette Giornate del Mondo Creato*, Tasso shows a delight in semi-precious stones and in that type of sophisticated allegory which is a manneristic trait of the painters, Jacopo Zucchi in particular, who decorated the Studiolo of Palazzo Vecchio in Florence for Francesco I Medici. That he might be compared to such different artists as Tintoretto and Zucchi, and even to a Northern painter who has affinities with Zucchi, Bartholomew Spranger, should not be a matter of surprise, because Tasso, to use a psycho-analytical term, was a schizophrenic. But after all the parallels with painters indicate little more than a vague *air de famille;* within the field of literature certain nuances of sensibility are much more significant.

The age of Tasso, it is true, was filled with the spirit of Counter-reformation, which insisted on the beauty of martyrdom for the Faith and adorned the altars of churches with gloomy, gory paintings: but the fact that Tasso wrote some of his more moving passages when describing circumstances in which Beauty and Death are intimately connected, reveals in him characteristics which the Baroque artists were to exploit frequently for love of contrasts, and in which the romantics were to indulge when they gave the reins to that type of sensibility. To Tasso's eyes pain seemed to throw beauty into relief, and martyrdom to wring from it pathetic accents. It has been observed by Donadoni [4] that Olindo, bound to the stake beside his beloved, though ostensibly a martyr for the Faith, speaks only the language of ardent love and longing much more concrete than the usual Petrarchan allusions to a metaphorical love's sacrifice. In Tasso imminent death seems to inspire love with a new thrill, and Sofronia, her tender arms bound with cruel cords, as she gazes upon her lover with pitiful eyes, appears more beautiful and more desirable now that she is threatened with martyrdom. Olindo rejoices to be consort of the funeral pyre:

> Ed oh mia morte avventurosa a pieno!
> Oh fortunati miei dolci martiri!
> S'impetrerò che giunto seno a seno
> L'anima mia ne la tua bocca spiri. . . .[5]

One wonders whether here Tasso expresses the same emotion which inspired in Gustave Flaubert the more explicit words of the *Tentation de Saint-Antoine*, at the point where the Saint, as he flagellates himself, is transported in imagination to the side of his beloved, Ammonaria the martyr:

J'aurais pu être attaché à la colonne près de la tienne, face à face, sous tes yeux, répondant à tes cris par mes soupirs; et nos douleurs se seraient confondues, nos âmes se seraient mêlées (*Il se flagelle avec force*). Tiens, tiens! pour toi, encore!—Mais voilà qu'un chatouillement me parcourt. Quel supplice! quelles délices! ce sont comme des baisers. Ma moelle se fond! je meurs.

There is an opportune note in the stage direction: "L'ombre des cornes du Diable reparaît." Flaubert had no illusion about the Christian value of Antony's act. Nor was Chateaubriand deceiving himself when he made René attribute to Céluta the words: "Mêlons des voluptés à la mort." Whether Tasso had illusions about Olindo's feelings cannot be said with certainty. Donadoni, at any rate, quite rightly observes that "the episode shows a fundamental part of the poet's nature; it was essential for him that he should not hesitate to give expression to one of the most profound and painful instincts of his soul." He also justly remarks upon the substantial similarity of the subject with that of Tancredi, who slays, without recognizing her, his beloved Clorinda, the sister—both lesser and greater—of Camilla of the *Aeneid*. In this episode, too, tragedy adds a more subtle pathos to beauty:

> Ma ecco omai l'ora fatale è giunta,
> Che 'l viver di Clorinda al suo fin deve.
> Spinge egli il ferro nel bel sen di punta,
> Che vi s'immerge, e 'l sangue avido beve;
> E la veste, che d'òr vago trapunta
> Le mammelle stringea tenera e leve,
> L'empie d'un caldo fiume. Ella già sente
> Morirsi, e 'l piè le manca egro e languente.
> . . . . . .

Amico, hai vinto: io ti perdon . . . perdona
Tu ancora . . .
. . . . . .
In queste voci languide risuona
Un non so che di flebile e soave
Ch'al cor gli scende, ed ogni sdegno ammorza,
E gli occhi a lagrimar gli invoglia e sforza.
. . . . . .
D'un bel pallore ha il bianco volto asperso,
Come a' gigli sarian miste viole:
E gli occhi al cielo affissa; e in lei converso
Sembra per la pietate il cielo e 'l sole:
E la man nuda e fredda alzando verso
Il cavaliere, in vece di parole,
Gli dà pegno di pace. In questa forma
Passa la bella donna, e par che dorma.[6]

The full significance of Clorinda's death becomes apparent in
the light of Erminia's heartbroken longing to be killed by Tancred.
Erminia (Canto VI, stanzas 84-85) mingles the idea of imprisonment and death with that of love, in a very characteristic manner:

E forse or fòra qui mio prigioniero,
E sosterria da la nemica amante
Giogo di servitù dolce e leggiero;
E già per li suoi nodi i' sentierei
Fatti soavi e alleggeriti i miei.

O vero a me da la sua destra il fianco
Sendo percosso, e riaperto il core,
Pur risanata in cotal guisa al manco
Colpo di ferro avria piaga d'Amore:
Ed or la mente in pace e 'l corpo stanco
Riposeriansi. . . .[7]

And when Erminia at last finds Tancredi again, he looks like
a dead and bloodless corpse after his duel with Argante (Canto
XIX, stanzas 106 et seq.):

De le pallide labra i freddi baci
Che più caldi sperai, vuo' pur rapire;
Parte torrò di sue ragioni a morte,
Baciando queste labra esangui e smorte.
Pietosa bocca . . .
. . . . . .
Lecito sia ch'ora ti stringa, e poi
Versi lo spirto mio tra i labri tuoi.
. . . . . .

Rinvenne quegli . . .

. . . . . .

Aprì le labra, e con le luci chiuse
Un suo sospir con que' di lei confuse.[8]

Erminia, the emotional creature drunk with tears, is, as has been observed,[9] Tasso himself.

Elsewhere, in the *Aminta*, Silvia's beauty is made poignant through the painful condition to which she has been reduced by the satyr. Here too the lover is near the distressed beauty, this time not to die with her or to kill her, but to deliver her from the ropes with which the satyr has tied her to the tree. And again in the *Aminta*, there is the scene in which the shepherd, a martyr for love, comes back to life beneath Silvia's kisses, so that his suicide

. . . sotto
Una dolente imagine di morte
Gli recò vita e gioia.[10]

The outward aspect of these subjects—martyrdom for the Faith (in the case of Olindo and Sofronia), ignorance as to the real nature of the adversary (in that of Tancredi and Clorinda), defence against the assault of the satyr (in that of Aminta and Silvia)—may for a moment obscure the source of Tasso's inspiration which is the same in all these episodes—an inspiration which can be traced to a peculiar sense of painful pleasure closely related to that which was going to appear in many of the Romantics.

'Tis the melodious hue of beauty thrown
Athwart the darkness and the glare of pain,
Which humanize and harmonize the strain.[11]

An examination of Tasso's own life from this point of view might further confirm this theory. Perhaps he experienced pleasure at feeling himself a victim, perhaps he enjoyed his imprisonment as much as he suffered from it; and the stratagem by which he terrified his sister with the news of his own death was the act, certainly, of a disturbed mind, but may have been the act of a man who was an epicure in pain.

Tasso is a forerunner of all those romantics whose peculiar sensibility demanded the death of the heroine, from Chateaubriand's Velléda:

Aussitôt elle porte à sa gorge l'instrument sacré: le sang jallit. Comme

une moissonneuse qui a fini son ouvrage et qui s'endort fatiguée au
bout du sillon, Velléda s'affaisse dans le sang—

to Maurice Barrès' Simone (in *Un amateur d'âmes*) who kills
herself:

Et les tendres gémissements que lui imposait sa blessure se mêlant à
leurs aveux demi-étouffés, elle mourut en pressant contre ses petits seins
éclaboussés de sang les mains de l'ami de son coeur.

This romantic aspect of Tasso is by no means an isolated trait,
it goes together with other manifestations of his sensibility which
all point to the same direction.

One of the ways of expressing a quantity of still undefined feelings which later blossomed into romantic attitudes, was the use
of the phrase *je ne sais quoi*. It first appeared as a symptom in
the course of the seventeenth century in the fifth of Father Bouhours' *Entretiens d'Ariste et d'Eugène* (1671). In this fifth dialogue, entitled *Le je ne sçai quoi*, Eugène says: "Les Italiens qui font
mystère de tout, employent en toutes rencontres leur *non so che*:
on ne voit rien de plus commun dans leurs Poëtes";[12] and Ariste
adds that "le je ne sçai quoi a beaucoup de vogue parmi nous",
and that "nous sommes en cela aussi mysterieux que nos voisins."
Pascal (*Pensées,* lxvi) seems to trace the expression to Corneille
(see for instance *Rodogune,* I, v); it occurs in Menestrier's *Art des
Emblèmes,* 1662, in the Sieur de Chaumels's *Devises panegyriques
pour Anne d'Autriche,* 1667, and many other seventeenth-century
texts; it was employed by Marivaux and Montesquieu.[13] Finally
Rousseau found in the term *romantique* the appropriate word to
define that elusive and indistinct thing which hitherto had been
vaguely expressed by *je ne sais quoi* ("Enfin ce spectacle a je ne
sais quoi de magique, de surnatural, qui ravit l'esprit et les sens"—
Nouvelle Héloïse). The romantic character of the *je ne sais quoi*
is further confirmed by a passage about *Les Mystères* in Chateaubriand's *Le Génie du christianisme:*

Il n'est rien de beau, de doux, de grand dans la vie, que les choses
mystérieuses. Les sentiments les plus merveilleux sont ceux qui nous
agitent un peu confusément. La pudeur, l'amour chaste, l'amitié vertueuse,
sont pleines de secrets. On dirait que les coeurs qui s'aiment s'entendent
à demi-mot, et qu'ils ne sont que comme entr'ouverts. L'innocence à son
tour, qui n'est qu'une sainte ignorance, n'est-elle pas le plus ineffable
des mystères. . . .

The majority of the instances quoted from the Italian by Bouhours comes from Tasso. Tasso did not invent the expression himself. Agnolo Firenzuola used it in his dialogue *Delle bellezze delle donne,* 1541, and Dante, before him, had already used it, but only in two cases—*Paradise,* III, 59, and *Convivio,* IV, 25—apropos of an aesthetic or emotional ineffability, and Petrarch in this sense once (son.: "In nobil sangue"). It was Tasso, however, who gave currency to the expression, using it many times in his major poem to indicate emotions in their first stirrings.

In the thirty-seventh stanza of the Second Canto of the *Jerusalem* it is used to describe the feeling of the king who has condemned Olindo and Sofronia to be burnt alive, at the spectacle of the tender and heroical exhortations of the generous couple which move the attending crowd to tears:

> Un non so che d'inusitato e molle
> Par che nel duro petto al re trapasse;
> Ei presentillo e si sdegnò, né volle
> Piegarsi e gli occhi torse, e si ritrasse.[14]

In the fifth stanza of the Twelfth Canto, Clorinda advises Argante to join her in a foray against the Christians, and tells him that for some time her restless mind, perhaps inspired by God, has been meditating "un non so che d'insolito e d'audacée", where the *non so che* renders the *aliquid* [15] of the Virgilian source of this passage (*Aeneid,* IX, 186: "Aut pugnam aut aliquid iamdudum invadere magnum/mens agitat mihi"); this is not so significant, but the other instance from the same canto, about the intonation of the words of dying Clorinda which, as we have seen, melts Tancredi's heart ("un non so che di flebile e soave") is indicative of Tasso's sensibility; also in this case the expression is modelled on the Latin, for Lucretius had said (*De rerum natura,* IV, 1125-26):

> . . . Medio de fonte leporum
> Surgit amari aliquid, quod in ipsis floribus angat.

The *non so che* occurs in the following canto (XIII, 40) to indicate the bewildered state of mind of Tancredi in the enchanted wood:

> Fremere intanto udia continuo il vento
> Tra le frondi del bosco e tra i virgulti,
> E trarne un suon che flebile concento
> Par d'umani sospiri e di singulti;

> E un non so che confuso instilla al core
> Di pietà, di spavento e di dolore.[16]

In Canto XVII, st. 57, we find the expression used to indicate a faintly descried source of light ("Ed ecco di lontan a gli occhi loro/Un non so che di luminoso appare"), and in Canto XX, 1, a dimly emerging shadow ("un non so che da lunge ombroso scorse"), in XX, 51, an indistinct sound ("Ma odi un non so che roco e indistinto"); but Tasso in most cases uses the expression, as I said, to denote the initial stage of an emotion, particularly a soft one. So in *Gerusalemme*, XIX, 94, it is used to describe Erminia's sudden falling in love with Tancredi:

> Allora un non so che soave e piano
> Sentii, ch'al cor mi scese, e vi s'affisse,
> Che, serpendomi poi per l'alma vaga,
> Non so come, divenne incendio e piaga.[17]

The Latin source of this passage, *Aeneid*, IV, 66, describes the same process, but without the *aliquid* corresponding to the *non so che*, to denote the mysterious character of the influence:

> Est mollis flamma medullas
> Interea, et tacitum vivit sub pectore vulnus;
> Uritur infelix.

In a similar way in *Aminta* (I, ii. 87 ff.) the protagonist describes his early attraction to Silvia:

> A poco a poco nacque ne'l mio petto,
> Non so da qual radice,
> Com'erba suol che per se stessa germini,
> Un incognito affetto.[18]

The *non so che* in the *Torrismondo* is employed to convey a sense of foreboding in which we seem to catch an early hint at Maeterlinck's much more articulate technique. Says Alvida in that tragedy (I, i, 25, 29-30):

> Temo ombre e sogni
> . . . .
> e temo, ahi lassa!
> Un non so che d'infausto o pur d'orrendo . . .[19]

and (III, vi, 193): "Io temo, ahi lassa!"

In all these cases, then, Tasso introduces a further element of mystery into the description of ambiguous appearances or feel-

ings, whereas Dante, in a similar case, had been content to say
(*Purgatory*, VII, 79 ff.):

> Non avea pur natura ivi dipinto
> Ma di soavità di mille odori
> Vi facea uno incognito e indistinto.[20]

There are other instances to show that Tasso, working on the
suggestion of Virgil and Dante, stressed certain effects and in many
cases added to them a further thrill.[21]

Thus in the *Gerusalemme conquistata* (III, 26 ff.) we find a nocturnal scene which could be perfectly at its place in a Gothic tale:

> Non lunge, quai veggiam fantasmi o larve,
> Poi che nascoso è lo splendor diurno,
> Tale un corrier ne l'ombre oscuro apparve
> Per non diritte vie cheto e notturno:
> Ed ove il maggior lume occulto sparve,
> Spiegan tremuli rai Giove e Saturno.[22]

Such traits denoting in Tasso a responsiveness to effects which were
to form the characteristic elements of romantic sensibility, have
frequently been noticed by the critics. And Tasso's novelty in this
field did not escape the most aware of his contemporaries, because
Tintoretto's painting inspired by the episode of Clorinda's death
(Chicago, Logan Collection) has been not arbitrarily defined by
Argan: ". . . perhaps the first romantic picture in the whole history of painting," [23] not only romantic because of its dramatic
structure, which culminates in the languishing face and pale hand
of Clorinda shown in full light, in contrast with the dark storm-
tossed tree and the sullen overcast sky, but chiefly because of the
concentration of the interest of the painter in the expression of the
feelings of the persons represented. And certainly, if Lucan in his
Pharsalia (III, 399 ff.) had given Tasso the idea of the enchanted
wood:

> Lucus erat longo numquam violatus ab aevo
> Obscurum cingens connexis aëra ramis
> Et gelidas alte summotis solibus umbras.
> Hunc non ruricolae Panes, nemorumque potentes
> Sylvani, Nymphaeque tenent; sed barbara ritu
> Sacra Deum, structae diris altaribus arae
> Omnisque humanis lustrata cruoribus arbos—

if, for the description of the congregating witches Tasso antici-
pates Salvator Rosa, and for the bleeding cypress has used the

same source which inspired to Dante the sad forest of suicides, i.e. *Aeneid* III, 26, the pathetic situation of Tancredi wounding the supposed ghost not of a companion (Polydorus, in Virgil) or a stranger (as in Dante), but of his very beloved he had unwittingly killed, is worthy, to say the least, of the most romantic of the Elizabethans, John Webster.

Tasso's predilection for gloomy settings, like that forest, is probably the reason why he placed in the gloomy North, Scandinavia ("quella orrida regione, dove sei mesi de l'anno sono tenebre di perpetua notte") [24] the scene of his tragedy *Torrismondo* (based on a theme which was going to fascinate the romantics, the incest motif illustrated by the unwitting couple Torrismondo—Alvida), though there are no touches of local colour there for the landscape, but only for the customs (the description of the festive games in II, vi, 32-104, derived from Olaus Magnus); and also this interest for the Scandinavian North was a novelty in Tasso's time, and became current in Europe only at the time of Gray and Collins. It was Collins in fact who mentioned Tasso in his *Ode on the Popular Superstitions in the Highlands* in which he recalls his impression on reading the episode of Tancredi in the enchanted wood:

> How have I trembled, when, at TANCRED's stroke,
>   Its gushing blood the gaping cypress pour'd;
> When each live plant with mortal accents spoke,
>   And the wild blast up-heav'd the vanish'd sword!
> How have I sat, when pip'd the pensive wind,
>   To hear his harp, by British FAIRFAX strung.
> Prevailing poet, whose undoubting mind
>   Believ'd the magic wonders which he sung!
> Hence, at each sound, imagination glows;
>   Hence his warm lay with softest sweetness flows:
> Melting it flows, pure, num'rous, strong and clear,
> And fills th'impassion'd heart, and wins th'harmonious ear.

Another pre-romantic trait of Tasso is his awareness of the spell of ruins. There is the twentieth stanza in the XVth Canto of the *Jerusalem* about the ruins of Carthage. Tasso's passage, in fact, does not state much more than the commonplace *concetto predicabile* about the vanity of human things witnessed by ruin, an idea which Shelley was to convey in a memorable way in his sonnet on Ozymandias:

> Giace l'alta Cartago: a pena i segni
> De l'alte sue ruine il lido serba.
> Muoiono le città, muoiono i regni;
> Copre i fasti e le pompe arena ed erba;
> E l'uom d'esser mortal par che si sdegni:
> Oh nostra mente cupida e superba! [25]

Tasso in this case had drawn on a passage of Sannazaro's Latin poem *De partu Virginis*.[26] In both poets the Christian meditation on the caducity of things seems on the verge of the elegiac mood which is fully developed in the famous passage at the beginning of the third scene of Act V of *The Duchess of Malfi:* "I do love these ancient ruins," in its turn indebted to Montaigne (III, 9) and to Cicero (*De finibus*, V, i and ii: "quacunque enim ingredimur in aliquam historiam vestigium ponimus"). Indeed it is all a matter of stress and inflection, for even Webster's conclusion apparently repeats the Christian tag:

> But all things have their end:
> Churches and cities (which have diseases like men)
> Must have like death that we have.

All these pre-romantic features are however not so important for the history of taste as a hint one finds in the description of Armida's garden in Canto XVI of the *Gerusalemme* (stanzas 9-10):

> L'arte, che tutto fa, nulla si scopre.
> Stimi (sì misto il culto è col negletto)
> Sol naturali e gli ornamenti e i siti.
> Di natura arte par che per diletto
> L'imitatrice sua scherzando imiti.[27]

This passage owes not a little to Longinus' treatise *On the sublime*, in which however the same principle was applied to eloquence. In his twenty-second section Longinus says that the best writers have recourse to *hyperbata* or transpositions and displacements in the order of things to be said, so as to imitate passion, whose language shows a certain amount of disorder, ". . . as if stirred by restlessness, as by an inconstant wind, they change words in a thousand ways, and feelings, and the ordinary course of speech; in so doing they imitate the acts of nature. For art is perfect just when it seems to be nature, and nature successful when art underlies it unnoticed." [28]

Now Tasso adopted Longinus' advice both in his juvenile *Discorsi dell'arte poetica* (composed about 1564, published 1587) and in his

late *Discorsi del poema eroico* (published 1594 but composed between 1575 and 1580):

> I versi spezzati, i quali entrano uno nell'altro . . . fanno il parlar
> magnifico e sublime.[29]

> E 'l cominiciar il verso da casi obliqui suole esser cagione del medesimo
> effetto nel parlare, il quale si può chiamar obliquo, o distorto, come in
> que' versi: "Del cibo, onde 'l signor mio sempre abbonda, Lacrime e
> doglia, il cor lasso nudrisco." [30]

> L'antipallage similmente, che si può dire mutazione de' casi, può
> accrescer la magnificenza del parlare.[31]

> Si può annoverar con questo il pervertimento dell'ordine, quando si
> dice innanzi quel che dovrebbe esser detto dopo; perché al magnifico
> dicitore non si conviene una esquisitta diligenza.[32]

> E la trasposizione delle parole, perch'ella s'allontana da l'uso comune
> . . . E 'l perturbar l'ordine naturale, posponendo quelle che dovrian
> esser anteposte . . . E l'*hyperbaton,* che si può dir distrazione, o inter-
> ponimento.[33]

Now Tasso applied this very principle to female beauty, with a
suggestion from Ovid (*Amores,* I, 14, 21):

> Tum quoque erat neglecta decens, ut Threcia Bacche,
> Cum temere in viridi gramine lassa iacet.

In the sonnet: "S'arma lo sdegno e 'n lunga schiera e folta" he
praised

> Bellezza ad arte incolta, atti soavi. . . .[34]

And he did the same in his description of Sofronia in the *Gerusalemme,* who "sua beltà non cura" (II, 14):

> Non sai ben dir s'adorna, o se negletta,
> Se caso od arte il bel volto compose;
> Di natura, d'Amor, de' cieli amici
> Le negligenze sue sono artifici.[35]

But Tasso's applying the same idea of comely negligence to the
garden had far-reaching consequences. It is said that the Royal Park
of Turin, inaugurated by Emanuele Filiberto and finished by Carlo
Emanuele I of Savoy (of which only the description survives in
Theatrum Sabaudiae) inspired Tasso's garden of Armida, but in
any case by fitting to this latter Longinus' precepts for the perfect
orator, Tasso made a first step towards the creation of the "natural"
or picturesque garden that became an English speciality during the
eighteenth century.

Of course the first stimulus came to the English gardeners from the landscapes of Lorrain and Poussin and Salvator, and from what the travellers reported about the gardens of the East, the mysterious taste of *sharawadgi*. The development of the English art of gardening has been many times traced, by Christopher Hussey in his standard work on the Picturesque, and by others. But Tasso's lines indicate a revolution in taste which became general during the seventeenth century. Perhaps this revolution was, to use a current phrase, in the air. Because already before the publication of the *Gerusalemme*, in a poem attributed to Jean de Bonnefon, included by J. C. Scaliger in the *Anthologia latina* published with *Publii Virgilii Maronis Appendix*, Lyons 1572, we read an exhortation to a lady, Basilissa, not to dedicate over much attention to the dressing of her hair and not to use cosmetics, for a neglectful simplicity pleases best.[36]

Ben Jonson paraphrased this Latin poem in a song included in *The Silent Woman:*

> Still to be neat, still to be drest,
> As you were going to a feast;
> Still to be powder'd, still perfumed;
> Lady, it is to be presumed,
> Though art's hid causes are not found,
> All is not sweet, all is not sound.
>
> Give me a look, give me a face
> That makes simplicity a grace;
> Robes loosely flowing, hair as free;
> Such sweet neglect more taketh me
> Than all th'adulteries of art;
> They strike mine eyes, but not my heart.

Robert Herrick, in his turn, developed the idea in one of the most charming lyrics of the Caroline period:

> A sweet disorder in the dress
> Kindles in clothes a wantonness:
> A lawn about the shoulders thrown
> Into a fine distraction:
> An erring lace, which here and there
> Enthralls the crimson stomacher:
> A cuff neglectful, and thereby
> Ribbons to flow confusedly:
> A winning wave, deserving note,
> In the tempestuous petticoat:

> A careless shoe-string, in whose tie
> I see a wild civility:
> Do more bewitch me than when art
> Is too precise in every part.

It may seem a far cry from Tasso's modest Sofronia, whose negligent attire surpassed the skill of art, to this tempestuous apparition in the Baroque manner. For Herrick's frivolous mood reminds us of the deep emotions the draperies of Bernini's statues are supposed to suggest. The artistic result is of the same kind: a significant movement instead of beautiful stillness, a puzzling charm, a *non so che* shared by both Sofronia and Herrick's delightful *coquette*.

The principle of asymmetry which was eventually to bring to such oddities as Donne's *Autumnall* in praise of a woman no longer young, or as the picturesque charm of the old parson's daughter mentioned in Uvedale Price's *Distinct Characters of the Picturesque and Beautiful* (1801), whose cross-eyes and uneven teeth were considered picturesque qualities, that principle of asymmetry which was going to proclaim that "plus belle que la beauté est la ruine de la beauté", and educate the eye to appreciate the aesthetic qualities of ruins, found in Tasso's sensibility the earliest response, and the lines on Armida's garden: "L'arte che tutto fa, nulla si scopre", and what follows, echoed in Boileau's line (*Art poétique,* II) apropos of the Pindaric ode: "Chez elle un beau désordre est un effet de l'art", and in the Marquis de Girardin's definition (in *De la composition des Paysages*) of a landscape, where "l'art sans se montrer nulle part, a parfaitement secondé la nature".

The Marquis de Girardin had laid out a landscape garden in the English style round his *château* at Ermenonville, and had asked the advice of the English gardner poet William Shenstone. The place is known in literary history for its association with Rousseau who had chosen it (under the fictitious name of Clarens) as the ideal setting for the idyl of Julie and Saint-Preux in *La Nouvelle Héloïse*. Elsewhere Rousseau too echoed Tasso's lines on Armida's garden in his criticism of the formal gardens:

L'erreur des prétendus gens de goût est de vouloir de l'art partout, et de n'être jamais content que l'art ne paraisse . . . Que signifient ces allées si droites, si sablées, qu'on trouve sans cesse, et ces étoiles par lesquelles, bien loin d'étendre aux yeux la grandeur d'un parc, comme on l'imagine, on ne fait qu'en montrer maladroitement les bornes? [37]

The Marquis de Girardin erected in the grounds of Ermenonville a Pyramide du philosophe dedicated to the four pastoral poets Theocritus, Virgil, Gessner and Saint-Lambert, and a Temple de la Philosophie in proximity of a lake, where each column had the name of a great writer. Alexandre de Laborde's description, in *Description des nouveaux jardins de la France*,[38] says that the temple was never finished, and many columns were waiting for new geniuses to give them a name: in 1808 it was in ruins, a fact which "might offer ample matter for satire" because "it was the philosophers of 1793 who most contributed to demolish it". The names of the famous writers written on the columns are not given by Laborde, but we would be surprised if Tasso's name was absent, for it is to him after all that the earliest idea of the landscape garden in Europe can be traced.

It all began from a precept of rhetoric that Tasso adapted to gardening, then, as Horace Walpole remarked: "The setting sun and the long autumnal shades enriched the landscape to a Claude Lorrain".[39] For, according to Walpole, three new Graces, Poetry, Painting and Landscape Gardening had to unite in order to dress and adorn Nature. And if one reflects that the present aspect of the English countryside was the creation of that supreme tailor of Nature, Lancelot Brown, who, if he did not plant all the trees one admires now in England, certainly surveyed all of them, so that after his intervention no one could have thought that those scenes created by him had not been always there, such as they had come out of the hands of divine Providence, if one keeps this in mind, might not one apply to England Tasso's lines on Armida's garden, and transform Kipling's famous line "Our England is a garden"[40] into: England is Armida's garden? For, contrary to what Kipling says (" And such gardens are not made by singing . . ."), this garden was actually created by the singing of the Italian Amphion, Torquato Tasso.

MARIO PRAZ · *University of Rome*

NOTES

1. *La littérature de l'âge baroque en France, Circé et le Paon* (Paris: Corti, 1953), pp. 236–37.
2. "Il Tasso e le arti figurative," in *Torquato Tasso*, by various hands (Milan: Marzorati, 1957), pp. 209 ff.

3. *Il manierismo del Tasso e altri studi* (Firenze: Olschaki, 1965).

4. *Torquato Tasso,* I, p. 234.

5. "And ah, my death, fortunate to the full! Ah, happy my sweet martyrdom! If I obtain that, joined with thee breast to breast, I may exhale my soul into thy mouth. . . ."

6. "But lo, the fatal hour is arrived that the life of Clorinda must to its end. He thrusts the point of the steel into her fair bosom: it sinks deeply and greedily drinks her blood; and her garment which, embroidered with fair gold, gently and lightly enfolds her breasts, is filled with the warm stream. Already she feels she is dying, and her feet, weak and languishing, fail to support her. . . . 'Friend, thou hast conquered: I pardon thee. . .pardon thou me in thy turn. . . .' In these languid words echoes something mournful and sweet which pierces to his heart and extinguishes all resentment, and excites and compels his eyes to weep. . .Her white face is overspread with a lovely pallor, as though violets were mingled with lilies: she fixes her gaze upon the sky; and sky and sun seem turned towards her with pity: and raising her bare, cold hand towards the knight, she gives him, instead of words, the pledge of peace. In this manner passes the fair lady, and it seemed that she slept."

7. "Perhaps even now he might be my prisoner here, and would sustain his loving foe's sweet and light yoke of servitude; already, through his bonds, I would feel my own made kinder and lighter. Or else, should his right hand have smitten my own side, and opened again my breast, the wound of the steel would at least have healed in such wise Love's wound: my mind and my weary body would rest at last in peace."

8. "From his pale lips cold kisses, which I longed to feel more ardent, do I yet wish to snatch; I will wrest from death part of its rights by kissing these wan and bloodless lips. . . .'Piteous mouth. . .Allow me now to embrace thee and then to pour out my spirit between thy lips'. . . .He came back to life . . . he opened his lips, and with eyes closed mingled a sigh with hers."

9. Donadoni, *op. cit.,* I, p. 260.

10. " . . . beneath a mournful image of death brought to him life and joy."

11. Shelley, *On the Medusa of Leonardo da Vinci.*

12. 1721 edition (Paris: Delaulne), p. 320.

13. See Giulio Natali, *Storia del 'nom so che',* in *Lingua nostra,* XXI, 2 (1951), pp. 45-49.

14. "Something unusual and soft seems to penetrate the hard heart of the king; he felt it coming, and spurned it; neither did he want to yield and turned his eyes away and withdrew".

15. The Latin *nescio quid* is found however in Saint Augustine, quoted by Bouhours: "Hoc nosse primitus, et christiano corde tenere debemus, non ad praesentis temporis bona nos factos esse christianos, sed ad *Nescio Quid,* quod Deus iam promittit, et homo nondum capit."

16. "Meanwhile he heard the wind continuously sighing among the branches and the shrubs of the forest, and draw a sound out of them which seemed a plangent concert of human sighs and sobs, and filled the heart with I do not know what confusion of pity, terror and pain".

17. "Then I felt something sweet and tender invade my heart and stick there; then insinuating itself into my yearning soul it became, I do not know how, a fire and a wound."

18. "Little by little there was born in my heart, I do not know from what root, like a grass born without seed, an unknown passion."

19. "I fear shadows and dreams. . . . I fear, woe is me! something either inauspicious or horrible."

20. "Not only had Nature painted all complete,/But of a thousand fragrancies had made/One new and indistinguishable sweet" (Lawrence Binyon's translation).

21. See Giovanni Getto, *Interpretazione del Tasso* (Napoli: Edizioni Scientifiche Italiane, 1951), pp. 456 ff.

22. "Not far away, similar to ghosts or apparitions when the splendour of the day hides itself, a messenger appeared in the dark shadows, silent and enwrapped in the night through devious paths, and in the place where the major light had concealed itself, Jupiter and Saturn display tremulous rays."

23. *Op. cit.*, p. 218.

24. Tasso's words in dedicating *Torrismondo* to Vincenzo Gonzaga. *Opere minori in versi* ed. A. Solerti (Bologna: Zanichelli, 1895), III, p. 195. Cf. *Torrismondo*, I, iii, 115-120.

25. "The once high Carthage lies down: the shore hardly shows the mark of its high ruins. Cities die, kingdoms die; grass and sand cover the glories and splendours; and man seems to be indignant at his own mortality. O, the cupidity and pride of our souls!"

26. Devictae Carthaginis arces
  Procubuere: iacentque infausto in litore turres
  Eversae. Quantum illa metus, quantum illa laborum
  Urbs, dedit insultans Latio et Laurentibus arvis!
  Nunc passim, vix reliquias, vix nomina servans
  Obruitur propriis non agnoscenda ruinis.
  Et querimur genus infelix humana labare
  Membra aevo, cum regna palam moriantur et urbes.

27. "Art, which does everything, remains hidden. There is such a mixture of culture and neglect, that you imagine that the ornaments and the lay-outs are only natural. It seems as if nature was playing at imitating her own imitator, art."

28. ". . . οὕτως παρὰ τοῖς ἀρίστοις συγγραφεῦσι διὰ τῶν ὑπερβατῶν ἡ μίμεσις ἐπὶ τὰ τῆς φύσεως ἔργα φέρεται. τότε γὰρ ἡ τέχνη τέλειος ἡνίκ' ἂν φύσις εἶναι δοκῇ, ἡ δ' αὖ φύσις ἐπιτυχὴς ὅταν λανθάνουσαν περιέχῃ τὴν τέχνην."

29. The breaking of the lines, so that they pass into each other . . . makes for magnificence and sublimity" (Tasso, *Prose diverse*, ed. Guasti, 1875, Vol. I, p. 219).

30. "Beginning a line with oblique cases usually produces the same effect in the speech, which may therefore be called oblique or distorted, as in those lines: 'Of the food of which my lord has always plenty, tears and sorrow, I feed my wearied heart.' " (ibid, p. 223).

31. "Similarly anthypallage, that is the substitution of one case for another, may increase the magnificence of the speech." (ibid., p. 222)

32. "One may cite alongside the reversal of the order, when one says before what should be said after; because a fastidious precision does not suit a magnificent speaker." (*Ibid.*, p. 232; cf. p. 55: "Per non incorrere nel vizio del gonfio, schivi il magnifico dicitore certe minute diligenze"—"In order to avoid the defect of turgescence, the magnificent speaker ought to dispense with a minute accuracy").

33. "And the transposition of words, because it departs from the common usage . . . And the alteration of the natural order, postponing words which should be placed in front . . . And the *hyperbaton,* which may be called a pulling apart or interposition of words, or clauses." (ibid., p. 233)

34. "Beauty artfully neglected, a sweet demeanour."

35. "You cannot tell whether she is adorned or neglected, whether chance or art made up her beautiful face; her negligences are artifices of nature, of Love, and of the friendly skies."

36. "Semper munditias, semper, Basilissa, decores,
semper compositas arte recente comas,
et comptos semper cultus, unguentaque semper,
omnia sollicita compta videre manu
non amo. Neglectim mihi se quae comit amico
se det et ornatus simplicitate valet.
Vincula ne cures capitis discussa solutis
nec ceram in faciem: mel habet illa suum.
Fingere se semper non est confidere amori;
quid quoque saepe decor, cum prohibetur, adest?"
37. Quoted by E. Malins, *English Landscaping and Literature* (London: Oxford University Press, 1966), p. 76.
38. Paris, de l'Imprimerie De Delance, 1808.
39. In a letter to Miss Mary and Miss Agnes Berry, 16 Sept. 1791, referring to the view from Strawberry Hill; quoted by Malins, *op. cit.*, p. 121.
40. *The Glory of the Garden.*

France-Amérique:
The Transatlantic Refraction

T IS NOW THIRTY YEARS since Bernard Faÿ inaugurated a chair in American Civilization at the Collège de France. By assisting at his lectures, almost in the literal sense of the idiom, Gertrude Stein was returning the extravagant compliments with which he had recently prefaced a translation of her turgid autobiographical novel, *The Making of Americans.* Younger Americans then at the Sorbonne found themselves occasionally crossing the Rue Saint-Jacques for that weekly reunion. Those were the opening months of the New Deal at home, and the sprightly lecturer succeeded in relaying its atmosphere of excitement. Yet, though he was nothing if not *au courant,* his course was geared to the clichés and cadres of a French academic syllabus. It never reached the régime of Franklin D. Roosevelt, at least not while I was attending; but I well recall that, in its vivid evocation of Theodore Roosevelt, a dynastic note was already sounded. T.R. was presented as a Grand Monarch, with a Spanish Question of his own, and Oyster Bay as his Petit Trianon. Just as Louis XIV patronized Molière, Racine, and Boileau, so our *roi soleil* had his court circle, whose common forename—conveniently for purposes of note-taking—alliterated with Harvard: Henry James, Henry Adams, and Henry Cabot Lodge. The rest was much in the same vein: familiar words to an unrecognizable tune. The stranger it sounded to us, and the farther it deviated from its sources in fact, the better it adapted to its new climate of preconception.

Bernard Faÿ has since disappeared into an oblivion which he sought and earned, after a desperate effort to exert his mediating talents during the German occupation. I mention him now, not merely because he exemplifies that distortion which distance lends to the view, but because his approach is happily uncharacteristic. A long and percipient line of French observers, stemming from Tocqueville, has viewed America not as a repetition of the feudal past, but as an adumbration of the democratic future. We might note that, as France itself has moved closer to those *Scènes de la vie future,* in the phrase of Georges

Duhamel, the reports of its *voyageurs* have become increasingly severe. But, the more they have been put off by what they can only regard as the irrational elements in American life, the more they have been fascinated by the reflection of those elements in American literature. Far from minimizing the cultural differences, French critics have been notably receptive to the uniqueness of our major writers. Melville and Hawthorne, misunderstood in their homeland more often than not, met with contemporary appreciation from Philarète Chasles and Emile Montégut. Faulkner made a serious critical impact, before his compatriots had fully awakened to him, through the translations of Maurice-Edgar Coindreau. Books by American authors have figured early and continuously in the English curricula of the French universities, where scholars have done more to interpret them than in any other country except our own, and not excluding Great Britain.

One country's image of another is likely to depend on its image of itself, particularly when its culture is as highly organized and systematically diffused as that of France. Our culture, from that vantage point, has seemed both antithetical and complementary. Thus our first ambassador, Benjamin Franklin, came to personify the *philosophes'* answer to the *ancien régime.* Conversely, it was the French emigrant, Crèvecoeur, who voiced Europe's hope for the United States as a place of asylum and a melting-pot of races. Chateaubriand dramatized the antithesis between the New World and the Old through the contrasting figures of the noble savage, Chactas, and his world-weary interlocutor, René. The significant contrast, in the American episodes of Chateaubriand's *Mémoires d'outre-tombe,* was between his social criticisms and his romanticized landscapes. Perhaps because civilization could have but one center, for Frenchmen, they have been peculiarly susceptible to the attractions of the uncivilized. Their taste for the primitive and the exotic was aptly gratified by the Leatherstocking Novels. Cooper himself preferred to treat more civilized material, but his reading public wanted more Indian-fighting; consequently, his treatment of it became more and more idyllic. D. H. Lawrence draws an amusing picture of *"Monsieur Fenimore Cooper, le grand écrivain américain,"* dreaming about the pathless forest in a Parisian boudoir.[1] The situation might serve as a paradigm for Franco-American literary relations: for Americans who go abroad only to rediscover themselves, and for cosmopolites who welcome them on condition that they remain outlanders.

The striking exception is Poe, who has indeed been taken to the bosom of French poetry, albeit on the problematic assumption that he was ostracized in his native land. His America was described by Baudelaire as "a vast cage, a big counting-house"—a large-scale application of those bourgeois influences which European artists were engaging themselves to flout.[2] More than his work, the legend of his life made him a generic literary hero, gallicized and virtually canonized by the diaeresis superimposed on his name: *Poë, poète, poésie.* The philistines were the *Eux* of Mallarmé's sonnet, while he remained the *Lui-même,* whose tomb would become a monument for all *poètes maudits.* Most of his own Gallic touches are superficial, such as the nonexistent Rue Morgue; but it seems pertinent that, when he chose to elucidate his mysteries, he chose Paris as their setting; and his paragon of ratiocination had to be a Frenchman, Monsieur C. Auguste Dupin. The cycle of the Symbolistes, which drew inspiration from Poe, counted among its adherents two Franco-Americans, Stuart Merrill and Francis Viélé-Griffin, and was rounded out by an Anglo-American epilogue in the person of T.S. Eliot. The light that it reflected back on its origin was not primitivism so much as decadence. A storm of black snow, reported from Michigan, seemed to the Goncourt brothers highly appropriate for "the land of Poe."[3] Baudelaire had resolved the paradox by declaring that America was "young and old at once."[4] Possibly, as Lawrence would speculate, it had rotted before it was ripe.[5]

Southward, it could become a symbol of overripe tradition. Out of ancestral nostalgia Julien Green could raise a backdrop for *Sud,* where a psychological melodrama culminates in the outbreak of the Civil War. Yves Berger's recent novel, *Le Sud,* covers more ground, since it imposes a storybook Dixie upon an actual Provence, and—for geographical rather than sexual reasons—names its heroine Virginie. Yet the original idyll of youthful freshness, the recurrent sentimental dream of *la vie des fauves,* is not altogether lost today. It could be rediscovered in Chicago by Simone de Beauvoir, retreating from the café dialectic of *Les Mandarins,* which is dedicated to Nelson Algren. To Michel Butor, whose quest for novelty has driven him across most of the states in *Mobile,* the variety encountered is precisely as rich as the assortment of ice creams at Howard Johnson restaurants. However, the patterns of ordinary existence, with their neon lights and jazz rhythms, no longer differ widely from one hemisphere to another. And the technological style of our epoch, whether or not we call it Americanization, has been reshaping artistic forms everywhere. Walt Whitman pioneered in liberating formal verse. Claude-Edmonde Magny's study of American novelists, which in turn has affected French fiction, *L'Age du roman américain,* might almost have been entitled *L'Age du roman cinématographique.* But Jean-Paul Sartre, hailing John Dos Passos as the inventor of this technique, simply reveals his own lack of conversance with Dos Passos' model, Joyce's *Ulysses.*

Shortly after the last war, on the occasion of his single visit to the United States, M. Sartre argued very frankly: "There is one American literature for Americans and another for the French."[6] Exercising their categorical flair, the French have established a twentieth-century canon, *Les Cinq Grands,* comprising Faulkner, Hemingway, Dos Passos, Steinbeck, and Caldwell.[7] With due respect for all five, most American critics would look upon them with varying degrees of admiration. Most of us were rather surprised when John Steinbeck, following Faulkner and Hemingway, received the Nobel Prize in Literature. We should not have been; we should have recalled that its first recipient was the banal Sully-Prudhomme, and that the Swedish Academy is not more immune to provinciality and propaganda than any other self-appointed literary authority. We could appreciate the sociological interest behind its first award to an American; for, though Sinclair Lewis may seem homespun to us, he manifested a certain exoticism for Europeans—as the Hungarian critic, Jean Hankiss, pointed out.[8] But the laureation of Pearl Buck—which was more of a recognition for China—demonstrated that well-meaning international sympathy, even at a second remove and without artistic distinction, could be the sole criterion. In Russia it is not surprising to see the party line determine the vogue of foreign as well as Soviet books. Some writers, like Jack London, gain more honor in other countries than their own: Maupassant, Anatole France, and Romain Rolland have exported better than they have endured in France.

The novels on Dr. Sartre's five-name shelf, he maintains, have taught his compatriots—Camus, for example—the lesson of action. The French are by no means unaware that our literature contains other works in a more analytic genre; but, having invented that genre, they feel they have little to learn about it from us. Hence the up-to-date *Histoire littéraire des Etats-unis* of Cyrille Arnavon emphasizes the rougher and readier aspects at the expense of Henry James's "Byzantinism."[9] James, of course, had learned many technical lessons from the French masters, and generously acknowledged them in his criticism. Like Henry Adams, he assumed the posture of a pilgrim genuflecting before the shrines of Gothic tradition. His vocation had been confirmed by a vision, his boyish dream-adventure of the Louvre, wherein the Galerie d'Apollon became his "bridge over into Style."[10] The esthetic spectacle of Paris, glittering before Strether like an iridescent jewel, held its ethical hazards, to be sure. James's American master, Hawthorne, on his brief and belated trip through France, had registered a comparable reaction to his initial *table d'hôte*. Hawthorne had decided that English cooking is "better for one's moral and spiritual nature," since it leaves you in no doubt that "you are gratifying your animal needs." Whereas, "in dealing with these French delicacies, you delude yourself into the idea that you are cultivating your taste while satisfying your appetite."[11] Puritanism has seldom armed itself more sternly against less vicious temptations.

James, in a novel like *The American* or a tale like "Madame de Mauves," worked out classic parables of the encounter between American innocence and continental sophistication, always conceived from the standpoint of a neophyte venturing beyond his depth. Guile at first hand, the accumulation of power, the mechanics of intrigue, the dynamics of enterprise, and the specific pitfalls of worldly experience may have seemed to subsist beneath his novelistic notice; all the more reason for admiring that writer whom he considered to have made the most of such themes, Balzac. Curiously enough, Balzac seems also to have been the novelist best represented among the books read by Melville during his silent years. One of the most emphatic of his frequent pencillings underscores a description of New York in *The Two Brothers,* an English translation of *La Rabouilleuse:* "a place where speculation and individualism are carried to the highest pitch, where the brutality of self-interest attains to cynicism, where man, essentially isolated, is compelled to push his way for himself and by himself, where politeness does not exist . . ."[12] Melville had tackled the Balzacian problem of the young provincial struggling against the metropolis in *Pierre,* with equivocal results. The traditional vehicle of our nineteenth-century fiction, the romance, did not lend itself to the complex realities of modern circumstance. The process of adapting the form to the subject had to be helped by recourse to the French naturalists; Edward Eggleston was inspired by Taine, Frank Norris by Zola, and finally Theodore Dreiser by Balzac.

It was as the habitat of natural man that our continent had originally appealed to the French. Yet our men of letters, inhibited by nineteenth-century notions of gentility, sometimes envied the freedom of their Gallic *confrères* to explore all manner of subjects. James wrote a letter to Howells, after a heady evening in the circle of Flaubert, wistfully confiding that Edmond de Goncourt's forthcoming yellowback would set out to investigate—if I may quote James verbatim—"a whorehouse *de province.*"[13] This would not do, as he hardly needed to comment, for the readers of *The Atlantic Monthly.* Half a century afterward, after the First World War, it would be the Americans who were breaking through the barriers of polite constraint and the French who were beginning to follow a transatlantic initiative. Doubtless those barriers had meanwhile been breaking down further. The point of intersection between the two literatures was Paris during its brilliant period of *l'Entre-deux-guerres.* Writers and artists of both nationalities, and of many others, fraternized there with consequences which have continued to fructify. Expatriation was an ideal apprenticeship for the lost-and-found generation of Hemingway. Henry Miller felt more at ease amid the seedy bohemianism of the Latin Quarter than in returning homeward to *The Air-Conditioned Nightmare.* Since the Second World War, *The Paris Review* has offered a showcase for promising newcomers, along with a forum for advice from their elders; but, in contrast to the footloose exploits of the 'Twenties, it is bound to seem elegiac and secondhand.

Our theme has had no definitive resolution, nor is it reducible to an explicit formula. Howard Mumford Jones's study, *America and French Culture,* deals comprehensively with political, religious, and social backgrounds.[14] It is not Professor Jones's fault that, in the six years since his volume appeared, there has been no second volume dealing with the American reception of French literature. There are a number of parallel studies from the other side, which would seem to show that intercultural exchange is contingent and episodic by nature. Meetings of first-rate minds are as rare as renderings by first-rate translators, and such shocks of recognition deserve to be studied for their own sake. The shift in atmospheric conditions, when moving between the hemispheres either way, produces a refraction which must be allowed for and reckoned with by Comparative Literature. Generalizing broadly about our literary interrelationship, we might say that the eastward trend across the Atlantic has been largely a traffic in images, whereas the ideas have tended to cross in the other direction. This means that our debt to France is primarily intellectual, a reckoning of methods borrowed by craftsmen or attitudes developed from ideologues. It is more than counterbalanced at the popular level by the credit—if not the discredit—that we have gained from France's interest in America as a perennial series of illustrations and impressions, an unending source of color and anguish, vigor and jargon, invention and syncopation.

The mirage of a Nouvelle France in this hemisphere, though it can still be momentarily conjured up by the nationalistic rhetoric of an André Malraux, began to fade away when Jefferson purchased the Louisiana Territory. Nor could there be any serious danger of an invasion which would leave the French culturally subservient, so long as their language is officially guarded by their Academy, and M. Etiemble wages his private war on Americanisms. The mutual attraction of the two cultures is that of opposites: ours has had a centrifugal movement, as well as an outward perspective, where theirs has had a centripetal tendency, along with an inside viewpoint. Consequently, others have always turned to them for precepts and examples of refinement, while their more robust spirits have frequently sought to escape from the effeteness of their own conformities. The avenues of escape have been pointing westward ever since Montaigne animadverted upon a South American cannibal. The American influence could be described, in the terminology of the Russian Formalists, as that process of deliberate estrangement characteristic of —and necessary to—all literatures when they have reached a stage of fixed conventions, facile elegance, and overfamiliarity. Then they must renew their energies by being rebarbarized, and that is where America seems to come in. According to the aphorism of Mirabeau, an audience of foreigners constitutes a "living posterity."[15] Should that make us skeptical in referring ourselves to the future, or should it give us pause when we next attempt to evaluate a book from abroad?

HARVARD UNIVERSITY

NOTES

1. D. H. Lawrence, *Studies in Classic American Literature* (New York, 1930), p. 70.

2. Edgar Allan Poe, *Œuvres en prose traduites par Charles Baudelaire*, ed. Y. G. Le Dantec (Paris, 1951), p. 1014.

3. Edmond and Jules de Goncourt, *Journal*, ed. Robert Ricatte (Paris, 1955), II, p. 418.

4. Baudelaire, *op. cit.*, p. 1062.

5. Lawrence, *op. cit.*, p. 55.

6. Jean-Paul Sartre, "American Novelists in French Eyes," *Atlantic Monthly*, CLXXVIII (August, 1946), p. 114.

7. Thelma M. Smith and Ward L. Miner, *Transatlantic Migration: The Contemporary American Novel in France* (Durham, 1955).

8. Jean Hankiss, *La Littérature et la vie: Problématique de la création littéraire* (São Paulo, 1951), p. 163.

9. Cyrille Arnavon, *Histoire littéraire des Etats-unis* (Paris, 1953), p. 297.

10. Leon Edel, *Henry James: The Untried Years* (Philadelphia and New York, 1953), p. 70.

11. Nathaniel Hawthorne, *Passages from the French and Italian Note-Books* (Boston and New York, 1897), p. 17.

12. I owe this quotation—transcribed from Melville's copy of the Katherine Wormsley translation now in the New York Public Library—to Mr. Walker Cowen, whose Harvard dissertation on Melville's marginalia should be published before too long.

13. Leon Edel (ed.), *The Selected Letters of Henry James* (New York, 1955), p. 66.

14. Howard Mumford Jones, *America and French Culture, 1750–1848* (Chapel Hill, 1927).

15. H.-G. Riqueti, Comte de Mirabeau, *Collection des Travaux*, ed. Etienne Méjan, (Paris, 1792) III, p. 196.

ROBERT SHACKLETON

Montesquieu and Machiavelli:
A Reappraisal

THE NAMES of the President of the Parlement of Bordeaux and of the Florentine Secretary have often been linked together, both in the realm of the history of literature and ideas, and in relation to practical politics. A nineteenth-century political writer, Maurice Joly, a fighter for freedom and a victim of oppression, died by his own hand in 1877, having published thirteen years before, almost clandestinely, a *Dialogue aux enfers entre Machiavel et Montesquieu*. This robust political pamphlet in the form of a dialogue of the dead, originally directed against Napoleon III, was plagiarized curiously in the *Protocols of the Learned Elders of Zion* and met a more honorable and more suitable fate in being reissued in 1948 by the publishing house Calmann-Lévy in a collection directed by Raymond Aron and entitled *Liberté de l'esprit*. It was to support a different cause that Marc Duconseil published in 1943 his *Machiavel et Montesquieu: recherche sur un principe d'autorité*. This is an attack on democracy inspired by the ideologies dominant on the European continent in the year of its publication, and it is certainly best forgotten. But at least, when considered along with Joly's *Dialogue aux enfers,* it shows how varied are the causes served by a confrontation or comparison of Montesquieu and Machiavelli. These two philosophers have each been the object of the most widely differing interpretations. Each has been regarded as reactionary, each as progressive; but however habituated one has become to paradoxes of judgment, one is still surprised to be reminded that, for all his Whig loyalties, it was to Montesquieu that Macaulay ascribed "a lively and ingenious, but an unsound mind" and Machiavelli whom he called "judicious and candid."

The study of the relationship of two persons who are both, in a sense, *sub judice* could perhaps throw some light on each of them; and assessing Montesquieu's attitude and debt to Machiavelli is an important task and one which has been effectively undertaken already. It is the aim of this paper to clarify, to correct, and to add to what has been written on Montesquieu's debt to Machiavelli, and to do so especially by using the method of chronological study of Montesquieu's manuscripts.

The essential work on this subject is E. Levi-Malvano, *Montesquieu e Machiavelli* (Paris, 1912). This monograph supersedes everything previously written on the subject and is itself far from being superseded. The author, known also to eighteenth-century specialists for his researches on the *Encyclopédie* in Tuscany, knew well the works of both Montesquieu and Machiavelli. He had access to documents at Bordeaux which are subsequently lost and have only recently come to light again; and if sometimes he announces as certain an influence which is probable, and as probable one which is just possible, his work is still solid as well as suggestive. Since then important contributions have been made by Friedrich Meinecke in *Die Entstehung des Historismus* (Munich, 1959; first edition 1936), by V. De Caprariis in his article "I 'Romani' del Saint-Evremond" (*Rivista storica italiana, 1955*), and by Sergio Cotta in his *Montesquieu e la scienza della società* (Torino, 1953) as well as in his translation, *Lo Spirito delle leggi* (Torino, 1952). Interesting suggestions have been made by J. H. Whitfield in his *Machiavelli* (Oxford, 1947). Some new facts were disclosed in my *Montesquieu: A Critical Biography* (Oxford, 1961). An important article, "Montesquieu, lecteur de Machiavel" by A. Bertière, appeared in the *Actes du Congrès Montesquieu* [of 1955] (Bordeaux, 1956). Finally, all serious work on Montesquieu owes much to the critical edition of *L'Esprit des lois* of J. Brethe de La Gressaye (Paris, 1950–61).

Levi-Malvano had been able to set eyes on the catalogue of the library of La Brède, made under the direction of Montesquieu. This catalogue was subsequently lost, rediscovered in 1950,[1] and published in 1954.[2] It is thus possible to correct Levi-Malvano's list of editions of Machiavelli owned by Montesquieu. This I do on the strength of the manuscript catalogue and, in two cases, from the actual books which I have seen at La Brède. I have further identified, so far as possible, the works in question in the Machiavelli bibliography of Gerber.[3] Montesquieu's holdings were as follows:

1. *Princeps.* Ursellis, 1600, 12°. This Latin translation by Tegli contains also Possevino's *Judicium de Nicolai Machiavelli et Joannis Bodini quibusdam scriptis,* the *Vindiciae contra tyrannos,* and an anonymous treatise entitled *De jure magistratuum in subditos et officio subditorum erga magistratus,* which is a translation of a French work *Des droits des magistrats sur leurs sujets, publié par ceux de Magdebourg.* The first edition of Tegli's translation of the *Principe* appeared in 1560. (Cf. Gerber, III, p. 74, no. 7).

2. *Discours politiques sur les Décades de Tite-Live.* Amsterdam, 1692, 12°. The further description *traduit par A.D.L.H.* (*sc.* Amelot de La Houssaye) is inaccurate. Amelot did not translate the *Discorsi,* and this French rendering was by Tétard or Testard, a Huguenot doctor or minister living in exile in Holland. (Cf. Gerber, III, p. 56, no. 1, where the translator is not named).

3. *Le Prince.* Amsterdam, 1684. 12°. Translated by Amelot de La Houssaye. (Gerber, III, p. 53, no. 2). This copy is still present at La Brède.

4. *Discours de l'état de paix et de guerre.* [Paris, 1614]; followed by *Le Prince.* [Paris], 1613; followed by *L'Art de la guerre.* Paris, 1614, 8°. This is incorrectly described in the catalogue, where the presence of the translation of the *Discorsi* has not been noted. The first title page in the volume is misplaced

and mentions only *L'Art de la guerre,* though the first work in the volume is the *Discours.* My description is based on the actual book, which is still at La Brède. (Gerber, III, p. 42, no. 1, which identifies the translators as Gohory for the *Discours,* Gaspard d'Auvergne for the *Prince,* and Charrier for *L'Art de la guerre.*)[4]

5. *Disputationum de re publica quas discursus nuncupavit, libri tres.* Mompelgarti, 1589. 8° (Cf. Gerber, III, p. 82, no. 1).

6. *Opere.* Nell'Haya, 1726. 4 vols. 12°. (not in Gerber).

All six of these entries appear in the catalogue in the same handwriting, which is that of secretary *d,* the Abbé Duval.[5] This means that all these works were acquired before the end of 1731; and since the last entry, for the edition of 1726, though in the same hand is clearly a later addition and is written in a different ink, it would be reasonable tentatively to conclude, on the basis of frequent analogies in the catalogue, that the first five works were the original stock of the library and that Montesquieu acquired the sixth between its date of publication (1726) and 1731. It is seen, then, that it was not until 1726 at the earliest that he possessed the works of Machiavelli in Italian, and that previously he owned *Il Principe* and the *Discorsi* in Latin, two French translations of the *Principe,* two of the *Discorsi,* and one of *L'Arte della guerra.* It should be added that the *post mortem* inventory of his library in Paris (as opposed to La Brède) lists, in the uncommunicative manner of the day, "neuf volumes in-douze, dont Machiavel,"[6] and that the library of the Academy of Bordeaux, frequently used by Montesquieu, was rich in editions of Machiavelli, the catalogue of 1790 listing as many as ten editions published before 1750, of which it is not possible to say which were translations and which the original Italian.[7]

How did he use these abundant resources? In answering this question it will be fruitful to divide his life into chronological phases and to begin with the earlier years of his life, preceding his departure on his travels in 1728.

The first sign of awareness of the works of Machiavelli which Montesquieu displays occurs in his first surviving work, the *Dissertation sur la politique des Romains dans la religion,* which (though it was not published until 1796) he read to the Academy of Bordeaux in 1716. Levi-Malvano's demonstration of Montesquieu's extensive utilization of the *Discorsi* in this work is conclusive. Those chapters of the first book of the *Discorsi* where the religion of the ancient Romans is discussed are so close in general theme and argument to Montesquieu's ideas that when verbal resemblances are added there can be no reasonable doubt of the President's indebtedness. The praise given to Numa for instituting religion in Rome, the discussion of the auguries, the mocking of reliance placed on the behavior of a chicken, the viewing of religion as a means of social discipline—all are cases where Montesquieu and Machiavelli meet, and their meetings are more striking when the French translation of the *Discorsi* by Testard, rather than the original Italian, is compared with Montesquieu's text. For example:

> Numa, voyant donc un peuple féroce, et voulant le réduire à se soumettre aux lois de l'Etat, et à savoir vivre en paix, il se tourna du côté de la religion, parce que

> c'est une chose absolument nécessaire, pour conduire un peuple et pour conserver une république; et il ordonna si bien les choses que, pendant plusieurs siècles, il n'y eut point d'Etat où la crainte de Dieu régnât tant que dans celui-ci (*Discours,* I, xi, in *Oeuvres,* La Haye, 1743, I, pp. 82–3)

> Ce ne fut ni la crainte ni la piété qui établit la religion chez les Romains, mais la nécessité où sont toutes les sociétés d'en avoir une . . . . . Romulus, Tatius, et Numa asservirent les dieux à la politique: le culte et les cérémonies qu'ils institu-èrent furent trouvés si sages que, lorsque les rois furent chassés, le joug de la reli-gion fut le seul dont ce peuple, dans sa fureur pour la liberté, n'osa s'affranchir. (Nagel III, p. 38; Pléiade I, p. 81)

A more striking case, not cited by Levi-Malvano and not to be explained by a common indebtedness to Livy, occurs in Chapter xxv of the first book of the *Discorsi:*

> Comme il se faisait tous les ans un sacrifice à Rome, qui ne pouvait être fait que par la personne du roi, et les Romains ne voulant pas que le peuple trouvât que l'absence des rois eût apporté aucun changement à une institution ancienne, ils créèrent un chef de ce sacrifice, qu'ils appelèrent Roi sacrificateur, et ils le soumirent au souverain pontife. (*Oeuvres,* I, p. 154)

> Les rois de Rome avaient une espèce de sacerdoce: il y avait de certaines cérémonies qui ne pouvaient être faites que par eux. Lorsque les Tarquins furent chassés, on craignait que le peuple ne s'aperçût de quelque changement dans la religion; cela fit établir un magistrat appelé *rex sacrorum,* et dont la femme était appelée *regina sacrorum,* qui, dans les sacrifices, faisaient les fonctions des anciens rois. (Nagel III, p. 48; Pléiade I, p. 90)

Montesquieu's utilization of the *Discorsi* in 1716 is clear and evident.

It is surprising also, and the obscurity of these earliest years of Montesquieu's life permits one only to speculate on the circumstances which drew him to the *Discorsi*. Perhaps they included the reading of Saint-Evremond's *Réflex-ions sur les divers génies du peuple romain,* where many points of encounter with Machiavelli appear. Perhaps the Italian Abbé Oliva, his friend in these early years, recommended the book to him. Perhaps, likelier still, he had read the famous article *Machiavel* in Bayle's *Dictionnaire historique et critique.*[8] But in the years following the *Dissertation* this interest in the *Discorsi* was to suffer an eclipse. Cotta has drawn an interesting and suggestive parallel between the allegory of the Troglodytes in the *Lettres persanes* and a passage in the *Discorsi*[9]*;* and *Pensée* 184, dating probably from about 1726, cites Machiavelli's warning against sudden changes in States.[10] But Montesquieu's thought is tak-ing now an orientation which leads it to attitudes very different from those of the Florentine Secretary.

In the years around 1725 Montesquieu's major intellectual concern was to refute the doctrines of Hobbes and Spinoza, and in particular to attack the notion, with which their doctrines were by an over-simplification equated, that justice and right lay simply in the positive law of the civil magistrate. In oppo-sition to this view Montesquieu, at this stage of his career, greatly stressed the concept of natural law and showed, in the only partially extant *Traité des devoirs* of 1725, a great indebtedness to Pufendorf. He argued, as he had already argued in the *Lettres persanes,* that justice was anterior to human society and existed independently of all human conventions, that there was a rationally based moral law to which all—and not least princes—were subject, and that politics must be held incompatible with morality, reason, and justice.[11] The author of *Il Principe* could not, in these circumstances, be regarded otherwise than as a teacher of evil, and Montesquieu, in *Pensée* 207 (c. 1727), referring to a passage in the *Lettres persanes,* specifically deplores the *Machiavélistes.* And though Montesquieu (as Cotta astutely points out)[12] agrees tacitly with Machiavelli in regarding politics as an autonomous discipline, his opposition to *raison d'Etat* and utilitarianism and of course to political dissembling is intense at this stage of his career.

In this opposition and in the consequent opposition to the author of *Il Principe,* Montesquieu was in harmony with his friends and contemporaries in France. The role in French thought of *Télémaque* was completely opposed to Machiavellianism,[13] and the influence of Fénelon was strong in the salon of Madame de Lambert, of which Montesquieu was an habitué. Ramsay, deducing a political system from the writings of Fénelon in his *Essai de Politique* (1719), the Abbé de Saint-Pierre with his cult of *bienfaisance* and his *Projet de paix perpétuelle,* and their associate in the Club de l'Entresol, the Marquis d'Argenson, can all be regarded as opponents of Machiavelli. Nor did this attitude end in the early part of the century. The Marquis d'Argens writes in the *Lettres juives* that if he were a monarch he would order the burning of the works of Machiavelli since he seeks to enslave truth to interest[14]; Legendre de Saint-Aubin, a modest compiler but not destitute of intelligence, describes the Florentine as "ce maître fameux d'une politique criminelle."[15] The eighteenth century's standard biographical dictionary accuses him of teaching murder and poisoning[16]; Moreri says, "les maximes de sa politique sont extrêmement dangereuses."[17] Niceron, an imperturbable scholar, gives the lie to the defenders of Machiavelli.[18] Nor does Diderot, in the article *Machiavélisme* in the *Encyclopédie,* or Jaucourt, in the article *Florence,* write differently. The general attitude of the French Enlightenment to Machiavelli was hostile.[19] He was the supporter of despotism, the apologist for *raison d'Etat,* and the advocate of deceit; and as the Enlightenment was to condemn him, so did Montesquieu condemn him during the first years of the personal reign of Louis XV.

This was not, however, his final attitude. In 1728 Montesquieu departed on travels which took him to Italy and to England, and he returned to France in 1731. He then proceeded to write, first the *Considérations sur les causes de la grandeur des Romains et de leur décadence,* and then the first books of *L'Esprit des lois;* and these are impregnated with the influence of the Florentine Secretary.

The extent of this influence has been sufficiently demonstrated by Levi-Malvano for it to be unnecessary to rehearse his evidence here. Two examples, from many adduced, may suffice; they are examples from the *Discorsi,* that former source of inspiration to which Montesquieu now returned.

First:

> Je soutiens qu'il était nécessaire d'abolir la royauté à Rome, ou que, ne le faisant pas, l'Etat serait en très peu de temps devenu faible et de nulle valeur. (*Discours,* I, xvii; *Oeuvres,* 1743, I, p. 119)

> Il devait arriver de deux choses l'une: ou que Rome changerait son gouvernement,
> ou qu'elle resterait une petite et pauvre monarchie. (Nagel I, C, p. 354, Pléiade II,
> p. 71)

The second example:

> Il est, ce me semble, nécessaire de parler des brouilleries qu'il y eut dans Rome
> depuis la mort des Tarquins jusqu'à la création des Tribuns, et de dire ensuite
> quelque chose contre l'opinion de ceux qui soutiennent que cette république fut si
> sujette aux séditions et si remplie de désordres, que si sa bonne fortune et la valeur
> de ses soldats n'eussent pas suppléé à ces désordres, c'eût été une république
> inférieure à toutes les autres. (*Discours*, I, iv, in *Oeuvres*, 1743, I, p. 30)

> On n'entend parler, dans les auteurs, que des divisions qui perdirent Rome; mais
> on ne voit pas que ces divisions y étaient nécessaires, qu'elles y avaient toujours été
> et qu'elles y devaient toujours être. (Nagel I, C, p. 414, Pléiade II, p. 119)

And one example not cited by Levi-Malvano:

> Les Romains ne négligèrent rien pour se faire des intelligences dans les pays qu'ils
> voulaient conquérir, afin qu'elles leur servissent de porte pour y entrer, et ensuite
> de moyens pour les conserver. (*Discours*, II, i, in *Oeuvres*, 1743, I, pp. 342–3)

> Ils ne faisaient jamais de guerres éloignées sans s'être procuré quelque allié auprès
> de l'ennemi qu'ils attaquaient, qui pût joindre ses troupes à l'armée qu'ils
> envoyaient. (Nagel I, C, p. 396, Pléiade II, p. 104)

These examples are only indications. The debt of Montesquieu in the *Con-sidérations* to the *Discorsi* of Machiavelli is most extensive both in general lines of thought and in points of detail. The mode of thought, the nature of the questions raised, the moralistic approach to history—all these indicate a revival of an interest and a sympathy which had been evident at the time of the *Dissertation sur la politique des Romains dans la religion* but which subsequently had not merely dwindled but had been effaced by an adhesion to a simple, traditional, superficial anti-Machiavellianism. What factors brought about this change of attitude?

One interesting possibility has been indicated in the fascinating article already mentioned, "Montesquieu, lecteur de Machiavél," by A. Bertière. Louis Machon had been secretary to Richelieu, at whose request he had indited an *Apologie pour Machiavelle*.[20] This work, still unpublished, selected from the canon of Machiavelli passages among those which had been held most reprehensive. He divided his text into twenty-three chapters, each headed by a maxim extracted, in thirteen cases from the *Discorsi*, in ten cases from *Il Principe*, using the translations of Gohory and Gaspard d'Auvergne respectively. His *Apologie* is at the same time a vigorous defense of Machiavelli and a work of personal and independent reflection with Machiavelli's text as a starting point.

The manuscript of the *Apologie pour Machiavelle* is to be found in the municipal library of Bordeaux, where it bears the shelfmark 935. The detailed comparison of the text of Machon with the works of Montesquieu does, to say the very least, establish a *prima facie* case that Montesquieu knew and used the *Apologie pour Machiavelle*. Bertière has effected this comparison with skill and caution and has taken care not to exaggerate the finality of his conclusion. But a consideration of such passages as that where Machon compares Tiberius and Louis XI, which Montesquieu likewise does in his *Réflexions sur le carac-*

tère de quelques princes, argues strongly for Montesquieu's knowledge of the manuscript of Machon. Bertière is unable to suggest a date at which Montesquieu read the *Apologie pour Machiavelle;* but he has established for the relevant period the history of the manuscript. It was to be found in the library of the Pontac family until the death, in 1694, of the son of Arnaud de Pontac. Then it passed into the hands of the Marquis de La Tresne and was in 1707 bought by the *conseiller* Duplessis or Duplessy. On his death at an unknown date it was acquired by a bookseller, Bergeret, from whom it was purchased by Barbot; and in 1747 it was given by Barbot, with the rest of his library, to the Academy of Bordeaux. With all these families Montesquieu was well acquainted: Pontac, Le Comte de La Tresne, Duplessy, Barbot. He was particularly friendly with the Duplessy family, especially with Madame Duplessy whose father-in-law Pierre-Michel was the purchaser of the manuscript,[21] and above all with Barbot who was a close ally and from whom he borrowed books. Even if it can be proved that Pierre-Michel Duplessy was dead in 1724,[22] nothing conclusive can come from that investigation about the date of Montesquieu's seeing the manuscript.

More useful information is arrived at by another approach. Bertière has listed seven borrowings by Montesquieu from the *Apologie* which seem more decisive than the others. These seven occur in different works of the President. Two of them are later than the rest: *Pensée* 1794, which is subsequent to 1748, and a passage from Book X of *L'Esprit des lois* which can be dated from the handwriting of the manuscript as belonging to the years 1741–3. The other three passages come from *Pensée* 540, from the *Réflexions sur le caractère de quelques princes,* and from *Pensée* 1302. These passages can be dated, with all necessary reserve, in 1730–3, 1731–3, and approximately 1738, respectively.[23] If to these can be added a less conclusive general borrowing in the collected fragments known as *Les Princes,* it appears that Montesquieu took cognizance of the manuscript of Machon's *Apologie pour Machiavelle* in the early years of the fourth decade of the century. These are the years immediately following his return from England, the years of the preparation of the *Considérations sur les Romains.* If this demonstration, which cannot be held final, gives at least tentative assurance, then Montesquieu's reading of Machon, as proved by Bertière, falls into a coherent and balanced pattern.

To understand the other elements in this pattern, it is necessary to note that though the reputation of Machiavelli in France, even with the relatively advanced thinkers, was unsavory, opinions abroad were different. Writers outside the limits of France, even when French themselves and using the French language, were often favorable. The article *Machiavel* in Bayle's dictionary has already been mentioned. Written with ambiguities characteristic of the author, it offered material for a friendly and sympathetic interpretation. And Bayle likewise, in his review in the *Nouvelles de la République des lettres* in 1687 of Amelot de La Houssaye's translation of *Il Principe,* had expressed surprise at the number of those who believed that Machiavelli was advocating a dangerous policy for princes to pursue; it was, on the other hand, from princes that he learned his policy and he was narrating and not approving.[24] The other two principal French-language journals of Holland had made their comment on the Florentine Secretary. Le Clerc's *Bibliothèque universelle*,[25] reviewing Testard's translation of the *Discorsi*, had quoted the preface's contention that the maxims of the Inquisition were far worse than those of Machiavelli; the *Histoire des ouvrages des savants*,[26] discussing the same work, begins its essay with the words, "Le nom de Machiavel effarouche d'abord les gens," and goes on to show that this judgment is unjust, alluding once again to the comparison between the Inquisition and Machiavelli. More than half a century later the exiled Prosper Marchand was to defend Machiavelli in his *Dictionnaire historique*.[27] The Protestant sympathy for Machiavelli was naturally not less marked in England, and indeed he had had his protagonists of note in the seventeenth century, starting with Bacon, who, opposing the current of hostility of the Elizabethan age,[28] had written, "we are much beholden to Machiavel and others, that write what men do and not what they ought to do."[29] Of the political writers of the later seventeenth century several were indebted to Machiavelli. Even of Locke it has been said[30] that he, rather than Hobbes, "could perhaps be looked on as Machiavelli's philosopher." The more radical thinkers had a greater debt to Machiavelli. To Harrington's *Oceana* have been attributed, as its three bases, "ancient prudence, Machiavelli the retriever, and Venice the exemplifier"[31]; and certainly the work is strongly marked with the imprint of the *Discorsi*. The classification of Commonwealths into two groups, "the one for preservation, as Lacedemon and Venice, the other for increase, as Rome," and the division of governments into absolute monarchy, aristocratic monarchy, and commonwealth are both derived by Harrington from Machiavelli, and both bear close affinity to Montesquieu's system.[32] Montesquieu could not fail to hear of Harrington during his stay in England; he was acquainted with his works, possessed the first edition of the *Oceana*, cited it twice in *L'Esprit des lois*,[33] and inevitably had his recollection of Machiavelli refreshed by reading it. And it was the author of the *Discorsi* rather than of *Il Principe* that Harrington presented to him.[34]

The debt to Machiavelli of Algernon Sidney is more marked still. The Florentine is cited in relation to several problems, especially in connection with corruption in governments and virtue in princes, and particularly in passages which express thoughts that Montesquieu was later to develop. The Abbé Dedieu, while indicating some resemblances between Sidney and Montesquieu, was inclined to minimize the possibility of influence.[35] But since his day it has been discovered that Montesquieu had made a written analysis of the works of Sidney (which had been translated into French in 1702). Without that knowledge, indeed, some similarities are so marked as to argue for Montesquieu's knowledge of Sidney. Such a case is found in relation to corruption in a despotic State:

> Nothing can better illustrate how far absolute monarchies are more subject to . . . venality and corruption than the regular and popular governments, than that they are rooted in the principle of the one, which cannot subsist without them; and are so contrary to the others, that they must certainly perish unless they defend themselves from them. (*Discourses concerning Government*, London, 1704, p. 184)

> Le principe du gouvernement despotique se corrompt sans cesse, parce qu'il est corrompu par sa nature.
>
> Les autres gouvernements périssent, parce que des accidents particuliers en violent le principe. (*Lois*, VIII, 10)

Other passages are closely akin to both Machiavelli and Montesquieu. Sidney's Section XIV declares, "No sedition was hurtful to Rome, till through their prosperity some men gained a power above the laws," an idea expressed by the Florentine in the *Discorsi* (I, 4). An echo of Machiavelli and a foretaste of Montesquieu alike are found in these words:

> All human constitutions are subject to corruption, and must perish, unless timely renewed and reduced to their first principles.[36]

Before traveling to England Montesquieu had spent almost a year in Italy. He entered on the road from Graz to Venice early in August 1728, and left by the Brenner at the end of July 1729. He had acquired sufficient skill in the language to write it as well as to read it. His stay in Tuscany might well have revived his interest in Machiavelli; and his visit to Naples is still likelier to have done so, especially if he made the acquaintance of Paolo Mattia Doria whose work *La Vita civile* abounds in echoes of the author of the *Discorsi*.[37] But Machiavelli's fame in the early eighteenth century was greater in England than in his own country; and when Montesquieu was plunged into the excitement of English political controversy, he found Machiavelli cited again and again. Not only did he read his name repeatedly in such republican writers of the previous age as Harrington and Sidney, but also he found him frequently quoted in the current pamphlets of party politics. Extracts from Bolingbroke's polemical journal *The Craftsman* appear so frequently in Montesquieu's notebook the *Spicilège* as to make it clear that the President was a regular and attentive reader, and indeed the genesis of Montesquieu's doctrine of the separation of the powers appears to be found in that journal.[38] In *The Craftsman* for 27 June 1730 one reads:

> Though I would not advise you to admit the works of Machiavel into your canon of political writings; yet since in them, as in other apocryphal books, many excellent things are interspersed, let us begin by improving an hint taken from the Discourses of the Italian Secretary on the first decade of Livy.
>
> He observes that of all governments those are the best which, by the natural effect of their original constitutions, are frequently renewed or drawn back, as he explains his meaning, to their first principles; and that no government can be of a long duration where this does not happen from time to time, either from the cause just mentioned or from some accidental cause.

These words, quoted in a journal which Montesquieu is known to have read, as they had been quoted by Sidney in his *Discourses* which Montesquieu likewise is known to have read, are strikingly similar to his own:

> Quand une république est corrompue, on ne peut remédier à aucun des maux qui naissent, qu'en ôtant la corruption et en rappelant les principes. (*Lois*, VIII, 12)

Machiavelli's own words were these:

> E' cosa più chiara che la luce, che non si rinovando questi corpi, non durano. Il modo di rinovargli è . . . ridurgli verso i principii suoi. (*Discorsi*, III, i, in *Opere*, Nell'Haya, 1726, III, p. 282)

And in the translation of Testard:

> Il est manifeste que, si ces grands corps ne se renouvellent point, il faut qu'ils périssent. La manière de les renouveler, . . . c'est de les ramener à leurs principes. (*Oeuvres,* 1743, II, p. 2)

Is it not clear that it was the English reading of Montesquieu which rekindled his interest in Machiavelli? There are three further relevant passages in the *Spicilège,* the notebook which Montesquieu took with him on his travels. One of these includes the name Machiavelli under the heading "Livres originaux que j'ai à lire." [39] All the books listed being by non-French authors, the meaning would appear to be that the books are to be read in the original text, not in translation or vicariously through commentaries. Doubtless this text, probably dating from 1731, is connected with Montesquieu's acquisition of his first Italian edition of Machiavelli, the Hague edition of 1726. About the same time the *Spicilège* quotes a fairly long paragraph from the *Istorie fiorentine,* the text being clearly Montesquieu's own translation from the Italian original.[40] Finally, the *Spicilège* includes the entry:

> Machiavel n'a parlé des princes que comme Samuel en a parlé, sans les approuver. Il était grand républicain. (Cleland).[41]

Cleland was a friend of Pope, Chesterfield, and Arbuthnot, and was known to Montesquieu in England.

After his return to France, Montesquieu applied himself unremittingly to his literary tasks. The *Considérations sur les Romains,* the *Réflexions sur la monarchie universelle,* and the chapter on the English Constitution were his first occupations. These finished and (in the case of the *Considerations*) published, he began the enormous task of preparing *L'Esprit des lois.* He worked quietly and secretively, so that only his closest friends were aware of what he was engaged on: his son; Guasco and Cerati who were Italians; and Barbot who owned the manuscript of Machon's *Apologie pour Machiavelle.* As he pursued his labors the works of the Florentine Secretary were never far from his mind. He read them in whatever edition was at a given moment most convenient: sometimes in Italian, as was just now seen; frequently (as verbal similarities show) in French; from time to time—perhaps, indeed, most often of all—in Latin.[42] It was in the years following the publication of the *Considérations* and after the composition of the essay on the British constitution, and not before, that the first books of *L'Esprit de lois* were written.[43] It was then that Montesquieu stressed the utility of *brigue* in the republic, as Machiavelli had done before. It was then that he argued for the return to the principles of government as a remedy for corruption in a State; it was then that he stressed the dependability of the people in making election: "le peuple est admirable pour choisir ceux à qui il doit confier quelque partie de son autorité" (*Lois,* II, 2). This reliance on Machiavelli continues through the following decade, both on points of detail and on points of substance. If meanwhile Frederick the Great, assisted by Voltaire, produced a refutation of Machiavelli, even relying in some measure on Montesquieu's own writing for his arguments,[44] the President is undeterred. He is advancing, in relation to Machiavelli, a new attitude, more sophisticated than the simple condemnation produced by others, and based on wider reading.

It is not, of course, an attitude of adulation without alloy. He remains hostile to the simple, bare doctrines of *Il Principe*. He reproaches Machiavelli for his infatuation with Cesare Borgia.[45] He remarks with approval that *le machiavélisme* is waning in France.[46] But when he wishes, in a letter to Madame Du Deffand, to praise her friend Hénault, he compares him with Machiavelli.[47] And when he seeks to praise liberty in the *Pensées,* he selects words—"ce bien qui fait jouir des autres biens"—strangely reminiscent of the *Discorsi*'s words, "la liberté consiste à pouvoir jouir de son bien en sûreté." [48]

It is possible to sum up Montesquieu's attitude to Machiavelli and the help derived from his doctrines. Factual information about Roman and Italian history is derived from the *Discorsi* and the *Istorie*. Much is taken from him in relation to the social and historical role of religion in the State, and Montesquieu's empirical, utilitarian attitude to religion as a social phenomenon came from the Italian. Montesquieu's pragmatic attitude to climate and terrain is in part inspired by Machiavelli, and this borrowing of ideas reaches its peak in the *Considérations* and in the years immediately following their publication.

The role of Machiavelli's influence in the elaboration of *L'Esprit des lois* is important but limited. The great, synthesizing principles of the masterpiece owe little to the Italian. Montesquieu's study of historical causation greatly transcends Machiavelli's as does the range of his documentation. It is in the preliminary books of *L'Esprit des lois,* where Montesquieu examines his three governments, monarchy, despotism, and the republic, that Machiavelli's mark is most felt; but not in the description of despotism, where Montesquieu seeks non-European examples; only briefly in the description of monarchy, for he did not need to go to the Florentine to study the French *parlements* and fundamental law.[49] Indeed, in a passage which he excised from *L'Esprit des lois* he expressly accuses Machiavelli of confusing monarchy and despotism:

> C'est le délire de Machiavel d'avoir donné aux princes pour le maintien de leur grandeur des principes qui ne sont nécessaires que dans le gouvernement despotique, et qui sont inutiles, dangereux, et même impraticables dans le monarchique. Cela vient de ce qu'il n'en a pas bien connu la nature et les distinctions; ce qui n'est pas digne de son grand esprit.[50]

It was on the republic that Montesquieu thought Machiavelli a greater authority, and it was his pronouncements on the republic, contained in the *Discorsi,* which he mainly utilized. But the importance of Machiavelli's influence on Montesquieu exceeds the role, in Montesquieu's thought, of the republic, which, though it is more than peripheral, is primarily a dialectical complement to more important things. Reading Machiavelli stimulated Montesquieu to reflect on the extent and on the limits of personal policies in the history of States, on historical causation, and above all on the relation between history and politics. In seeking this inspiration in Machiavelli, in turning to the *Discorsi* as well as to *Il Principe,* Montesquieu was giving a modern and mature orientation to the French Enlightenment, and the occasion for his doing so was in significant measure afforded by his stay in England.

OXFORD UNIVERSITY

NOTES

1. See Robert Shackleton, "Montesquieu: Two Unpublished Documents," *French Studies,* IV (1950).

2. *Catalogue de la bibliothèque de Montesquieu,* ed. L. Desgraves (Genève and Lille, 1954).

3. A. Gerber, *Niccolò Machiavelli. Die Handschriften, Ausgaben, und Uebersetzungen seiner Werke im 16. und 17. Jahrhundert,* 3 vols. (München, 1912–13).

4. The La Brède copy of this edition of the *Discorsi* has a number of underlinings and two marginal annotations. These are not in a known hand, and the incidence of the passages in question throws no light on Montesquieu's reading.

5. See Shackleton, "Les Secrétaires de Montesquieu," in *Oeuvres complètes de Montesquieu,* ed. A. Masson, 3 vols. (Paris: Nagel, 1950–55) I, xxxv–xliii. The volumes of this edition are referred to below as Nagel, I, II, and III. The *Oeuvres complètes,* ed. R. Caillois, 2 vols. (Paris: Bibliothèque de la Pléiade, 1949–51), are referred to as Pléiade, I and II.

6. *Catalogue de la bibliothèque de Montesquieu,* p. 243.

7. Bibliothèque municipale de Bordeaux, MS. 834; see also P. Barrière, *L'Académie de Bordeaux* (Bordeaux and Paris, 1951), p. 105 ff.

8. See Shackleton, "Bayle and Montesquieu," in *Pierre Bayle, le philosophe de Rotterdam,* ed. P. Dibon (Amsterdam, 1959); and cf. S. Cotta, *Montesquieu e la scienza della società* (Torino, 1953), pp. 24–25, where the influence of Bayle is viewed as having been greater than that of Machiavelli.

9. Cotta, p. 309.

10. Nagel, II, p. 65; Pléiade, I, p. 1460; cf. *Discorsi,* I, p. xvi.

11. Nagel, III, p. 165; Pléiade, II, p. 112.

12. Pléiade, II, p. 203, and *Lo Spirito delle leggi,* I, pp. 20–21.

13. See A. Cherel, *La Pensée de Machiavel en France* (Paris, 1935), pp. 201–241.

14. *Lettres juives* (La Haye, 1738), II, p. 298.

15. *Traité de l'opinion* (Paris, 1735), V, p. 276.

16. Chaudon, *Nouveau dictionnaire historique-portatif* (Amsterdam, 1769), III, p. 8.

17. *Le Grand dictionnaire historique* (Amsterdam, 1740), VI, p. 11.

18. "Amelot de La Houssaye," *Mémoires pour servir à l'histoire des hommes illustres* (Paris, 1736), XXXV.

19. Cf., inter alia, A. Panella, *Gli Antimachiavellici* (Firenze, 1943), pp. 84–93.

20. See also K. T. Butler, "Louis Machon's *Apologie pour Machiavelle*—1643 and 1668," *Journal of the Warburg and Courtauld Institutes,* III (1939–40), pp. 208–227.

21. See A. Grellet-Dumazeau, *La Société bordelaise sous Louis XV et le salon de Mme Duplessy* (Bordeaux and Paris, 1897).

22. E. Féret, *Statistique générale . . . du département de la Gironde* (Bordeaux and Paris, 1889), III, *Première partie: Biographie,* 218. Duplessy's son is stated to be *conseiller* in 1724, having presumably succeeded his father.

23. These dates are based primarily on the handwriting of the manuscripts. See the bibliography in Shackleton, *Montesquieu, a Critical Biography* (Oxford, 1961), pp. 400–408, and Shackleton, "Genèse de l'*Esprit des lois,*" *Revue d'histoire littéraire de la France,* LII (1952), pp. 425–438.

24. *Oeuvres diverses* (La Haye, 1737), I, pp. 740–741.

25. Vol. XX (*suite*), 1693 (seconde édition, Amsterdam, 1698), pp. 328–332.

26. *Juillet,* 1691 (troisième édition, Rotterdam, 1698), pp. 483–485.

27. "Anti-Machiavel" (La Haye, 1758).

28. See M. Praz, *Machiavelli in Inghilterra* (Roma, 1943).

29. *Advancement of Learning* (1605), in *Philosophical Works,* ed. J. M. Robertson (London, 1905), p. 140.

30. P. Laslett, ed. *Two Treatises of Government,* by John Locke (Cambridge, 1960), p. 87.

31. Z. S. Fink, *The Classical Republicans* (Evanston, 1945), p. 54. See also R. Polin, "Economique et politique au XVIIe siècle: l'*Oceana* de James Harrington," *Revue française de science politique,* II (1952), pp. 24–41.

32. Harrington, *Oceana and Other Works* (London, 1747), pp. 147 and 275.

33. *Lois,* XI, p. 6, and XXIX, p. 19.

34. Cf. Fink, p. xi: "The Machiavelli of the *Discourses* . . . had, I made bold to assert, far more influence in English political thought in the seventeenth century than the Machiavelli of *The Prince.*"

35. J. Dedieu, *Montesquieu et la tradition politique anglaise en France* (Paris, 1909), pp. 314–326.

36. *Discourses,* p. 103.

37. See Shackleton, "Montesquieu et Doria," *Revue de littérature comparée,* XXIX (1955).

38. See Shackleton, "Montesquieu, Bolingbroke, and the Separation of Powers," *French Studies,* III (1949).

39. Spicilège § 561 (Nagel, II, p. 847; Pléiade, II, p. 1369).

40. Spicilège §513 (Nagel, II, p. 831;.Pléiade, II, p. 1353).

41. Spicilège §529 (Nagel, II, p. 836; Pléiade, II, p. 1358).

42. One direct quotation can come only from the Latin of the *Discorsi*. This is the phrase "peu sont corrompus par peu" (*Lois,* VI, 5). The Italian reads, "pochi fanno sempre a modo de' pochi"; Testard's French, "le petit nombre agit toujours comme font les petites compagnies"; the Latin text, "ubi pauci judices sunt, facile a paucis corrumpi queant" (*Discorsi,* I, 7). A second case occurs in a reference to *Discorsi,* I, 55, where Montesquieu's "sac" corresponds more readily to the Latin "arca" than to the Italian "coffre."

43. See *Montesquieu, a Critical Biography,* p. 265.

44. See *L'Anti-Machiavel par Frédéric II,* ed. C. Fleischauer, *Studies on Voltaire and the Eighteenth Century,* V (Geneva, 1958).

45. *Lois,* XXIX, p. 19.

46. *Lois,* XXI, p. 20.

47. Nagel, III, p. 1383.

48. *Pensée* 1574 (Nagel, II, p. 453; Pléiade, I, p. 1430). Cf. *Discours,* trans. Testard, I, p. 16, in *Oeuvres,* I, p. 113.

49. Cf. *Discorsi,* III, p. 1.

50. Nagel, III, p. 580; Pléiade, II, p. 996.

MARTIN JARRETT-KERR, C. R.

The Conditions of Tragedy

"**W**HAT THEN IS TRAGEDY**? If no one asks me, I know; if I wish to explain it to one that asketh, I know not." So might one paraphrase St. Augustine's famous remarks about time.[1] Maybe our best approach to an explanation is to see what are some of the conditions which, in the main traditions of literature, are essential to or destructive of the composition of tragedy.

We can recognize perhaps two boundaries: to the left and to the right. The boundary on the left is that of de-humanization. It is represented, some will feel, in an extreme form in the French "anti-novel." Alain Robbe-Grillet, a scientist by training (expert in tropical agriculture, which is not irrelevant to his writing), obviously owes a great deal to Sartre's *La Nausée* and his well-known distinction between the *en-soi* and the *pour-soi*. But Robbe-Grillet criticizes Sartre (and Camus too) for yielding to sentimentality. They are guilty, he says, of using metaphor; and a metaphor is either a capitulation or a falsehood.[2] When you talk of the "majesty" of a mountain or of a village "nestling" in a valley, you are writing anthropomorphically, i.e., you are guilty of the pathetic fallacy. But it is just this that leads to tragedy and ultimately to the illicit creation of a God: If you begin by using metaphor, you may end by believing in God, because God is no more than the most generalised form of the pathetic fallacy. God is a projection of the human sense of misery:

> I call out. No one answers. Instead of concluding that no one is there—which might be quite simply an ascertainable fact, dateable, localised in space and time—I decide to behave as if someone were there, but someone who, for reasons unknown, refused to answer. From now on the silence which follows my appeals is no longer a *true* silence: It is endowed with a content, a depth, a soul. . . . Ought I to go on calling out? . . . Should I use a different set of words? Again I try . . . but I very soon realise that no one will answer. Yet the invisible presence that I continue to create by calling out forces me to go on forever breaking the silence with my unhappy cry. . . . In the end, my distraught consciousness translates my exasperated loneliness into a high fatality and a promise of redemption.[3]

The kinship between this mood and that of Samuel Beckett's plays and novels is clear, but it is precisely this that Robbe-Grillet wants to deliver us from. Instead he offers us *le nouveau roman*, which is written in such a way as to discard the old "sacrosanct psychological analysis," and invites the reader

> to look at the world which surrounds him with entirely unprejudiced eyes. . . . Around us, defying the clutter of our animistic or protective adjectives, things *are there*. Their surfaces are clear and smooth, *intact*: neither doubtfully glittering, nor transparent.[4]

This is why the cinema is the most authentic art form today, for it moves us away from the "universe of signification" (psychological, social, functional) and can stress the sheer *thereness* of familiar gestures and objects. Instead of what the Marxist critic Roland Barthes has called "the romantic heart of things," a dubious kind of inwardness, ordinary objects lose their ambivalence, their secrecy. The hero, too, of this new kind of novel is, literally, "all there." The traditional hero is constantly being distorted, overwhelmed, even destroyed by the author's interpretations of him; he is never fully there—he is "relegated to an intangible *elsewhere*, ever more remote and indistinct, the hero of the future"; but the new hero will "stay put"—it is the commentators who appear to be otiose, even dishonest. Away go the old myths of profundity—"Ah, vous croyez encore à la nature humaine, vous!" cries Robbe-Grillet contemptuously. Man is just a behavior-pattern at a given moment. "Soul-states"—hate, love, etc. —are sloppy metaphors. The artist's business is not to provide an explanation but to "create an object."

The result in Robbe-Grillet's novels is predictable. Every event, object, person in them is described as with a slide rule on a drawing board. For instance, this scene, visible from the dining room in *La Jalousie*:

> The corner window has both leaves open—at least partly. The one on the right is only ajar, so that it still covers at least half of the window opening. The left leaf, on the other hand, is pushed back towards the wall. . . . The window therefore shows three panels of equal height which are of adjoining widths: in the centre the opening, and on each side, a glass area comprising three panes. In all three are framed fragments of the same landscape: the gravel courtyard and the green mass of the banana trees. . . . Franck's big blue sedan, which has just appeared here, is also nicked by one of these shifting rings of foliage, as is A . . .'s white dress when she gets out of the car.[5]

This is not the place for a lengthy discussion of Robbe-Grillet. But it is significant that even Marxist critics disagree among themselves about him. Roland Barthes praises him, precisely because he rejects tragedy: "Tragedy is merely a way of retrieving human unhappiness, of subsuming it, and thus of justifying it in the form of necessity, wisdom or purification. It is precisely this process that we must reject today: we must search for a technical method of avoiding the traps which tragedy lays—for nothing is more insidious than tragedy."[6] On the other hand, the East German Marxist critic Ernst Fischer finds fault with this *nouvelle vague* for the same reason. He points out— referring to modern cybernetics for comparison—

> how closely the "anti-novel" corresponds to these neo-positivistic ideas and to what a striking extent the people in these novels are reduced to the "black box" of cybernetics, where only the relations of input and output matter and never the nature and essence of man. False philosophical conclusions from the revolutionary

discoveries of cybernetics have linked up with a literary method which, in certain individual instances, may be as useful as behaviorism is in science but which, as a whole, not only describes the dehumanization of man but actually invests this dehumanization with the character of inescapable finality.[7]

Whether, then, we praise or blame Robbe-Grillet for inventing a method which makes tragedy impossible, he clearly provides us with the left-hand boundary. There is no tragedy possible where there is no "human nature" distinct from the rest of nature. Actually, in his attempt to escape anthropomorphism, Robbe-Grillet gives us, I think, only a sort of flat, universal theriomorphism—or better, entomomorphism: his eye for insects is significantly acute.

The boundary on the right is marked by any doctrine which makes suffering and sorrow ultimately unreal. It is, for instance, often held that Christian doctrine does so and that, therefore, no Christian tragedy is possible:

> An actor who has often played the role of Becket (in *Murder in the Cathedral*) put the matter succinctly: "I know I am being murdered on the stage, but not once have I really felt dead."[8]

I do not know that Mr. Eliot ever claimed that his play was a tragedy. There is no doubt, however, that the anonymous author of the eleventh- or twelfth-century play *Christus Patiens* thought it a proper Christian successor to Euripides. And Milton thought so, too. In his Preface to *Samson Agonistes*, i.e., in his own defense, he says that "Gregory Nazianzen, a Father of the Church, thought it not unbeseeming the sanctity of his person to write a Tragedy, which he entitled, *Christ Suffering*." (Perhaps it does not much matter that Milton is some eight centuries out.) The play is called a "Passion according to Euripides," is 2,640 lines long, and is made up of lines (about one in three) ingeniously lifted from seven of Euripides' plays. It begins after the betrayal of Christ and ends after the Resurrection; it has a chorus of Galilean women; there are five messengers, one of whom recites a dialogue between Pilate, the chief priests, and the guard from the sepulchre. The Virgin is the main figure, but Christ, St. John, St. Joseph of Arimathea, Nicodemus, and Mary Magdalene also appear. The play opens with a travesty of the Prologue to *Medea*. Medea had said:

> Ah would that Argo ne'er had winged her way
> To Colchis through the blue Symplegades,
> That ne'er in glens of Pelion had fallen
> Those pines likewise beneath the axe!

In *Christus Patiens* the Virgin's opening speech is:

> Ah would the snake had never entered Eden,
> That in its glens the serpent ne'er had hid!

For the trial of Christ some of the lines are borrowed from the trial of Orestes, and (even more daringly) for Christ on the cross, the lines describing Peleus caught up in the fir-tree (from *The Bacchae*). The Epilogue ends with the unambiguous words:

> Here is a drama true, not wrought of lies,
> Nor smeared with the dung of half-wit tales of old.[9]

No doubt the play is worthless. But even if it were not, it would raise the question whether a drama which includes a hero's death, but ends with a resurrection and a vindication, can be a tragedy. I think that we certainly have to contest Corneille's description of *Polyeucte*—"Polyeucte, Martyr: Tragédie Chrétienne en cinq actes." For, even more explicitly than Beckett, Polyeucte desires martyrdom:

> J'ai l'ambition, mais plus noble et plus belle:
> Cette grandeur périt, j'en veux une immortelle,
> Un bonheur assuré, sans mesure et sans fin,
> Au-dessus de l'envie, au-dessus du destin.

The hero's death not only assures him heavenly bliss, but also effects the conversion of his wife Pauline, who is literally baptized in his blood; the conversion of his father-in-law Felix, who then spares Pauline the death-penalty; and the softening, if not (one is led to expect) the ultimate conversion, of Sévère himself, to whom Polyeucte bequeathes his wife.

The play is skillful, powerful, and moving; and the poetry is both resonant and sharp. But there is a tension, if not a contradiction, at the heart of it. Insofar as it has a certain classical, tragic grandeur, it is because Polyeucte has a Promethean kind of defiance, if not bravado, which is less than fully Christian. (Give him a chance, you may say: he is baptized only between Act II and Act III, an hour or so before his death. He has hardly had time to grow into Christian humility! But that is to bring Bradleyan psychology to a classical drama.) On the other hand, insofar as the notion of martyrdom is linked to the notion not only of heavenly glory but also of spiritual effectiveness in this world—the blood of the martyrs is the seed of the Church—that is, insofar as the play is authentically Christian, it ceases to be a tragedy in the classical sense. It may be this very tension which gives the play something of its unique greatness in the Corneille corpus. But at least it defines for us the right-hand borderline of tragedy.

But granted that tragedy must operate within these two boundaries, does this help us much in defining itself? Let us try working towards the center from the borders.

First from the left. We have seen that Robbe-Grillet deliberately rejects tragedy and, with it, the notion of the personal. But is there not an element of the "impersonal" in great classical tragedy? Is this not the meaning of the swing away from Bradley: for instance, in Professor Stoll's denial of all relevance of psychology to Shakespeare's characterizations? Critics, says Stoll, have overlooked "a central Aristotelian principle and indulged too much in thoughts about Shakespeare's characters."[10] No doubt this extreme view overlooks the extent to which Aristotle's own principles logically lead to some concern for characterization. "There should be nothing improbable among the actual incidents" in a tragedy; and though the plot is more important than the characters, these must be "good," "appropriate," "life-like," and "consistent." True, "a convincing

impossibility is preferable to an unconvincing possibility."[11] But the wholly un-
believable or monstrous character would not do. There is indeed something of
a swing back toward Bradley today. Professor Empson says, "There was a
fashion for attacking 'character-analysis,' especially in Shakespeare, which I
have taken some time to get out of."[12] And Mr. John Bayley has even defended
the kind of question represented by Morgann's "Was Falstaff really a coward?"
and ridiculed in Professor L. C. Knights' *How Many Children Had Lady Macbeth?* Is this sort of query

> really quite so absurd as it sounds? Its great virtue . . . is that it takes for granted
> the scope and completeness of Shakespeare's tragic setting. . . . There is a sense
> in which the highest compliment we can pay to Shakespeare is to discuss his great
> plays as if they were also great novels.[13]

This involves Mr. Bayley in defending *Othello* against its detractors—particularly Mr. Eliot and Dr. Leavis. Their premise is

> that a great play should be impersonal, that the quirks and undercurrents of indi-
> vidual psychology should be swallowed up in a grand tragic generality. It is
> significant that admirers of this impersonality in Shakespeare find it at its height
> in *Antony and Cleopatra,* which is of all his plays the closest to its source. The
> admired qualities are already implicit in Plutarch. . . . Already the theme is
> noble, archetypal, while that of *Othello* might well have been turned into comedy,
> as Shakespeare converted similar tales in *Much Ado* and *All's Well.* The nature
> of this gap between story and play, and the steps taken to span it, are ignored by
> the purists of tragic completeness.[14]

This is percipient. Yet I believe that the "purists" were basically right. It was
Shakespeare's peculiar genius to lift the naturalistic, without too much disturb-
ance or distortion, into the conventional and thereby to give it a greater, because
a more classical, stature, and at the same time to bring the conventional, by
occasional natural touches, down from the pillared archways and pediments into
living contact with surrounding human existence. The gap between his sources
and the plays he makes of them does not consist in that the sources are conventional, stylized, whereas Shakespeare's resulting plays are concrete, psychologically convincing. The gap consists in that the sources are (usually) trivial,
pedestrian, or artificial (whether naturalistic or conventional), whereas the
plays are resonant with the music of greatness and permanence. It *is* a distraction
to ask how many children Lady Macbeth had, just as it would be a fatal distraction to ask whether Jocasta had had any husbands before Laius and Oedipus.
And if one looks at *Oedipus the King,* and then at what Seneca, Corneille, and
Dryden made of it, one sees that it is the compression, the simplicity, the lack
of irrelevant incident or psychologizing about incident and character which
give it its greatness.

I conclude that, though the total de-personalizing of man marks the left
boundary of tragedy, a relative "impersonality" or distance—by which themes
loom larger than the men who play in them—is not destructive of tragedy, but
indeed has been (so long as the men are recognizable as men, and not puppets
or symbolic ghosts) a mark of the greatest tragedies we have known.

We have worked towards the center from the left boundary. Now let us move in from the right. The boundary itself has been expressed in different ways:

> Goethe: Tragedy disappears to the degree that an equitable settlement is possible.
> Karl Jaspers: The believing Christian no longer recognizes tragedy as genuine. Redemption has occurred and is perpetually renewed by grace.
> I. A. Richards: The least touch of any theology which has a compensating Heaven to offer the tragic hero is fatal.

We have agreed that a *Polyeucte* or a *Murder in the Cathedral* is outside the bounds of genuine tragedy. But the relevance of Christian (or of any "redemptive") theology to the possibility of tragedy is a more delicate issue.

Mr. George Steiner states roundly that "the Christian vision of man leads to a denial of tragedy,"[15] and that "real tragedy can occur only where the tormented soul believes that there is no time left for God's forgiveness."[16] But the implication of this, as Professor E. J. Tinsley acutely points out, is that "Christian orthodoxy is universalist." Indeed, he suggests that

> Some sense of original sin is essential to the tragic sentiment, which sees man as both victim and culprit. The weakening of this doctrine inside theological circles because it was thought to be tied up with the literal acceptance of the Adam and Eve myth and incompatible with the idea of evolution, and outside because it was often confused with Augustinian notions of original guilt, has been a potent factor in making the present climate of thought much less favourable to the tragic sense.[17]

To put the point—or rather, the two points—concretely: a martyrdom can never be a tragedy, but a damnation can. *Doctor Faustus* can be regarded as a fair sample of Christian tragedy—as, indeed, can *Macbeth*—because they both carry a great load of Catholic dogma on their backs and yet do not flinch at the full tragic possibilities of man. There is, of course, a difference between *pre-* and *post-Christum,* in the nature of tragic expression: but it is a difference within the notion of tragedy, not a difference between tragic and non-tragic. Mr. Steiner, for instance, contrasts the Greek view of destiny with that of the Old Testament:

> The wars recorded in the Old Testament are bloody and grievous, but not tragic. They are just or unjust. The armies of Israel shall carry the day if they have observed God's will. . . . They shall be routed if they have broken the divine covenant. . . . The Peloponnesian Wars, on the contrary, are tragic. Behind them lie obscure fatalities and misjudgments.[18]

This may be true of the wars; but I do not believe it proves that there can be no tragedy except where there is a Greek notion of *Atè*. Indeed, when he later compares the Elizabethans with the Romantics, Mr. Steiner says that in the former

> A tragic rift, an irreducible core of inhumanity, seemed to lie in the mystery of things. The sense of life is itself shadowed by a feeling of tragedy. We see this in Calvin's account of man's condition no less than in Shakespeare's.[19]

Yet some accounts of the difference between Greek and Elizabethan would imply that tragedy is possible only with the former. Mr. W. H. Auden says:

> Greek tragedy is the tragedy of necessity: i.e., the feeling aroused in the spectator is "What a pity it had to be this way"; Christian tragedy is the tragedy of possi-

bility, "What a pity it was this way when it might have been otherwise.". . . . The hubris which is the flaw in the Greek hero's character is the illusion of a man who knows himself strong and believes that nothing can shake that strength, while the corresponding Christian sin of Pride is the illusion of a man who knows himself weak but believes he can by his own efforts transcend that weakness and become strong.[20]

Mr. Auden is actually contrasting Greek tragedy with a novel like *Moby Dick;* but what he says would apply equally to Shakespeare, and indeed he does later mention *Macbeth*. His conclusion is that Greek tragedy is inescapably pessimistic:

> The pessimistic conclusion that underlies Greek tragedy seems to be this: that if one is a hero, i.e., an exceptional individual, one must be guilty of hubris and be punished by tragic fate; the only alternative, and not one a person can choose for himself, is to be a member of the chorus, i.e., one of the average mass; to be both exceptional and good is impossible.[21]

The mention of the chorus is interesting, because in quite another context the theologian Reinhold Niebuhr had asked:

> What would the hero of tragedy do without these weeping, appreciating and revering spectators? This necessity of pity from the lesser who keep the law for the greater who break it out of inner necessity, is the symbol of an unresolved conflict in the heart of Greek tragedy. It does not know where the real centre of life lies, whether in its law or in its vitality. Therefore the weak law-abiders must honour the strong law-breakers, lest the latter seem dishonourable.[22]

Now this judgment on Greek civilization—for that is what it is—seems to me a theological judgment which does not arise out of the situation of the Greek theater as such. I happen to agree with it, but it is an extraneous judgment, not a literary one. The same is true, though less so, of Auden's description of the essential "pessimism" of Greek drama. If we could put ourselves in the sandals of the Greek spectator at a performance of *Oedipus* or *Medea,* should we come away at the end with "pessimism" as our prize? If by "pessimism" we mean "despair of the world, of fate, of the gods," surely this is the emotion to which *catharsis* is supposed to be applied. Perhaps in the long run it is not the rather abstract and generalized notions of a particular people's theology that will best illuminate the works of art they produce, but the more hazy, symbolic forms through which they think their theology. And these may be similar to those of other peoples in a way which brings an imaginative agreement over a wide area.

Let us widen the area still more and see what happens. Teilhard de Chardin as far back as 1923 wrote: "I feel more and more strongly the necessity to free our religion from everything in it that is specifically Mediterranean."[23] This goes for more than religion. It is significant that Brecht drew, for some of his plays, on Japanese and Chinese sources. Let me take an Indian one, Kalidasa's *Shakuntala* (probably fifth century). I read it twelve years ago or more, but was fortunate to see a performance of it by an Indian cast in Johannesburg in 1956. It is based on a legend from the Mahabharata, but the legend has been expanded, embroidered, and made more dramatic. It may seem irrelevant to a discussion of tragedy, for it is a kind of fairy-tale comedy—indeed, all Indian plays must traditionally have a happy ending, and this puts them outside our right-hand boundary. But, abstracting from that convention for a moment and disregarding the *deus ex machina* conclusion (a charioteer of Indra comes down to take the hero Dushyanta off to battle with demons, and it is in the land of the gods, apparently, that the recognition and the reconciliation between Dushyanta and Shakuntala take place), we can in fact find potentially tragic moments in the play. Shakuntala, a lovely virgin, has married King Dushyanta, who saw her when he was hunting in the forest. When pregnant, she comes to the capital to remind him of their marriage. But because of a curse put on them both by an irascible sage, Durvasas, who was annoyed about a minor failure in hospitality, the King does not recognize Shakuntala. When he does remember her, she has departed from the court and has been snatched into heaven.

In spite of this supernatural conclusion and the reconciliation, the play does show some of the characteristics of Greek drama. King Dushyanta, looking back at the crisis, says of his wife, Shakuntala:

> My memory failed me, and I rejected her. In so doing I sinned against Kanva [i.e., Shakuntala's ward] . . . . But afterwards when I saw the ring, I perceived that I had married her.

(The ring was to have been the means by which Shakuntala would prove to him her identity, but part of the curse was that she should lose it in the Ganges. After she has vanished, the ring is found and brought to the King.)

> *Kashyapa* (father of the gods: reassuring him): My son, do not accuse yourself of sin. Your infatuation was inevitable. . . .
> *Dushyanta:* Then I am free from blame!
> *Shakuntala* (to herself): Thank heaven! My husband did not reject me of his own accord. He really did not remember me. I suppose I did not hear the curse, in my absent-minded state, for my friends warned me most earnestly to show my husband the ring.

The supernatural element is not surprising, since Shakuntala herself was half-supernaturally born: A royal sage was getting so holy with ascetic practices that the gods became jealous of his sanctity. They sent a nymph, Menaka, to tempt him, and Shakuntala, born of this holy man and the nymph, was the result! Yet basically the ingredients are those common to all classical drama: Fate decrees the original situation; then, not fully aware of what you are doing, you break a law; and then Nemesis (a henchman of Fate) guides the course of events within the given situation. Finally there is a *dénouement,* which may be tragic or happy, and though you will be blamed only for that segment of the resulting evil for which you are really responsible, you will suffer out of proportion to that blame. But take courage! For either the sorrow will be lifted (comedy), or at least its significance for man will be shown and can be accepted (tragedy).

I know nothing of Japanese and Chinese drama. But I do know that African folklore and ritual can throw an interesting light on our European dramatic tradition. Dame Sybil Thorndyke has written of the remarkable reception she and her husband had from Africans (Negroes of South Africa) when playing

Medea in Johannesburg, and I can confirm this, having sat among the African audience at the time. Back in 1899 Mary Kingsley wrote about the African convert to Christianity who was troubled by the theme of *Job*—why do the righteous suffer?—

> . . . I see the temptation to return to those old gods—the gods from whom he never expected pity, presided over by a god that does not care. All that he [the African, in his anxiety] had to do with them was not to irritate them, to propitiate them, to buy their services when wanted, and above all to dodge and avoid them, while he fought it out and managed devils at large.[24]

And an anthropologist, Professor Meyer Fortes, has written an illuminating study, *Oedipus and Job in West African Religion*,[25] which shows the form of and the social way of coping with the themes of Oedipus and Job among the Tallensi of West Africa. He says that the central conception of Oedipus, the "Oedipal principle," "is best summed up in the notion of Fate or Destiny," and the "Jobian principle" is summed up in that of "Supernatural Justice."[26] Now among the Tallensi many evils (accidents to men, above all barrenness in women) are due to an evil pre-natal Destiny; this can be met only by sacrifices to the paternal ancestors, who will put things right. The parallel with Sophocles is exact—up to a point; but beyond that point there is divergence. For whereas for Oedipus there is no reconciliation possible, the Tallensi victim has a chance, viz., by restoration of the right relationship to his ancestors. Of Oedipus, Professor Fortes says:

> His fate is evil; it enters into his life at the very beginning through his being rejected by his parents when they cast him away. He survives only because he is accepted by substitute parents. . . . But his fate catches up with him. He is finally overwhelmed by his fate because he unknowingly violates the basic norms of filial relationship. His tragedy can be described as that of a man blindly seeking to achieve his legitimate place in society, first as son, then as husband, father and citizen, against the unconscious opposition of an inborn urge to avenge himself by repudiating his parents, his spouse, and his children. When he succumbs to this fate he shows his revulsion against himself by mutilating his own eyes, and so blotting out his relationship with his kin and his society. He dies in exile, almost like a ghost departing from this world rather than like an ordinary man.[27]

But the Tallensi would provide a means of countering Oedipus' pre-natal Fate. And so, perhaps, like the Indians, they would not have allowed of ultimate tragedy.

What is common to these diverse examples are the two elements: (a) you are not wholly responsible for your fate; therefore your suffering is undeserved, quixotic from man's point of view: *Moral*—puny man must respect what is greater than he. But (b) you are partly responsible for what you make of your fate, even for part of the fate itself; therefore if you are to keep your self-respect, you must do something about it (repent, sacrifice, accept): *Moral*—puny man is still valuable for his freedom.

And this is relevant to the last question we must ask: what is the future for tragedy in the West? Mr. Steiner reminds us that the main reason for the decline (he calls it the death) of tragedy is the coming of Rousseauist optimism, which

> . . . cannot engender any natural form of tragic drama. The romantic vision of life is non-tragic. In authentic tragedy, the gates of hell stand open and damnation is real. The tragic personage cannot evade responsibility. To argue that Oedipus should have been excused on grounds of ignorance, or that Phèdre was merely prey to hereditary chaos of the blood, is to diminish to absurdity the weight and meaning of the tragic action.[28]

And he says percipiently of Ibsen that, though the greatest dramatist of the past two hundred years, he

> . . . starts where earlier tragedies end, and his plots are epilogues to previous disaster. Suppose Shakespeare had written a play showing Macbeth and Lady Macbeth living on their black lives in exile after they had been defeated. . . . We might then have the angle of vision that we find in *John Gabriel Borkman*.[29]

And the reason why the tragic dimension is missing from Chekhov is simply because Chekhov was a physician, "and medicine knows grief and even despair in the particular instance, but not tragedy."[30] If the recent past is thus unpromising, what of the future? Mr. Raymond Williams, critic, historian, and novelist, has put the contrasting views in a dialogue. First, the view that tragedy has no future:

> When man is his own measure, or, worse, when the attributes of God are transferred to man or to life, you simply cannot have tragedy. . . . Tragedy [in the sense of] the bare facts of suffering and death, of course still exists. But tragedy as a form which can interpret them significantly is only a memory. When, as with the Greeks and Elizabethans, there was an order beyond human life, the bare facts could be illuminated and transcended, because there were facts beyond them to which they could relate.[31]

But another character replies:

> We have abandoned the tragic universe, and we've lived past the tragic hero. [But] we have reached, definitively, the tragic society. . . . Tragedy has, if you like, broken out of its frame. . . . Yeats spoke of tragedy as breaking the dykes between man and man, and I have always remembered the phrase and been moved by it. But did he only mean sympathy? . . . That is real, but not only that. And I have been moved . . . by men's actual solidarity in suffering: a coming together, and a giving, that seem absolute, while they last. . . . [In this shared suffering] which of these, in the end, can be the individual, and which society? . . . The tragedy seems to be, our tragedy seems to be, in the images of connection.[32]

Something of the same emphasis is in Brecht, who replaces human *nature* by human *relations:* who claims in his plays to offer us his personages in such a way that we deduce their character from their actions—instead of the traditional theater "which derives its action from the nature of the characters."[33]

We have, however, seen reason to doubt whether this account of "the traditional theater" does justice to it—whether Brecht is not reacting against the idealistic-psychological interpretation of romantic criticism. Brecht's own program for his theater would, if carried out, take him over our left-hand boundary of tragedy—the de-personalized. His success as a playwright lies in the fact that he does not carry out his program: that his sense for the human person in the human situation is too powerful to remain trapped in the bulldozer jaws of doctrinaire Marxism. The reason, again, why *Waiting for Godot* is the one play of Samuel Beckett's that stands out from the sad ash cans (and audiences have registered this), is because here, in the face of Beckett's metaphysical conclusions, his sense of human life, his sheer power to make people laugh (not just sick laughter, either), are at full play and show him, Beckett, to be imaginatively still within the human family.

The banal conclusion is this: that tragedy will survive only so long as the artist does not work against the grain of common human nature; conditions of man and society may be such that it can survive even then only in an attenuated form; but survive it will, so long as man is man. And perhaps we shall find it re-emerging most forcefully in those countries where a total political authority tries to encompass the total human person—tries and fails. For (and it is a Marxist critic who writes this) "Man, being mortal and therefore imperfect, will always find himself part of, and yet struggling with, the infinite reality that surrounds him."[34]

PRIORY OF SAINT PAUL,
LONDON

NOTES

1. *Confessions*, Book XI, Part XIV.
2. See his articles in *Nouvelle Revue Française*: "Une Voie pour le roman futur," *NRF*, IV (July 1956), 77-84, and "Nature, humanisme, tragédie," *NRF*, VI (October 1958), 580-604. See also J. G. Weightman, "Alain Robbe-Grillet," *Encounter*, XVIII (March 1962), 30-39.
3. "Nature, humanisme, tragédie," pp. 590-591. Cited by Weightman, p. 32.
4. "Une Voie pour le roman futur," pp. 80-81.
5. *Jealousy* (New York, 1959), pp. 47-48.
6. Cited by Weightman, p. 31.
7. *The Necessity of Art: A Marxist Approach* (Baltimore, 1963), p. 200.
8. George Steiner, *The Death of Tragedy* (London, 1961), p. 341.
9. Cited in Frank L. Lucas, *Euripides and His Influence* (New York, 1963), p. 86.
10. See Elmer E. Stoll, *Art and Artifice in Shakespeare* (Cambridge, 1933) and "Poetry and the Passions," *PMLA*, LV (December 1940), 979-992.
11. Humphrey House, *Aristotle's Poetics* (London, 1956), *passim*.
12. *Milton's God* (London, 1961), p. 69.
13. *The Characters of Love* (London, 1960), pp. 41 ff.
14. *Ibid.*, p. 137.
15. Steiner, p. 6.
16. *Ibid.*, p. 332.
17. *Christian Theology and the Frontiers of Tragedy* (Leeds, 1963), pp. 19 ff.
18. Steiner, p. 6.
19. *Ibid.*, p. 16.
20. "The Christian Tragic Hero," *New York Times Book Review*, December 16, 1945, p. 1. Cited in William K. Wimsatt and Cleanth Brooks, *Literary Criticism: A Short History* (New York, 1957), p. 55.
21. *Ibid.*
22. *Beyond Tragedy* (New York, 1937), p. 165. Cited in Thomas R. Henn, *The Harvest of Tragedy* (London, 1956), pp. 160-161.
23. Letter of 27 May 1923.
24. *West African Studies* (1899). Cited in Olwen Campbell, *Mary Kingsley* (London, 1957), p. 130.
25. Oxford, 1959. Professor Fortes is Professor of Social Anthropology at Cambridge University.

26. Fortes, p. 11.
27. *Ibid.*, pp. 70 ff.
28. Steiner, p. 128.
29. *Ibid.*, pp. 296 ff.
30. *Ibid.*, p. 302.
31. "Dialogue on Tragedy," *New Left Review*, Nos. 13-14 (January-April 1962), 26-27.
32. *Ibid.*, pp. 34-35.
33. Martin Esslin, *Brecht: A Choice of Evils* (London, 1959), p. 118.
34. Fischer, p. 223.

WALTER J. ONG, S. J.

Evolution, Myth, and Poetic Vision

> . . . They say,
> The solid earth whereon we tread
>
> In tracts of fluent heat began,
>   And grew to seeming-random forms,
>   The seeming prey of cyclic storms,
> Till at the last arose the man.
>   . . . Arise and fly
>   The reeling Faun, the sensual feast;
>   Move upward, working out the beast
> And let the ape and tiger die.—(Tennyson, *In Memoriam*, CXVIII)

THE INFLUENCE OF DARWIN upon the poetic and artistic imagination has become a commonplace, documented by a large assortment of studies from Lionel Stevenson's *Darwin among the Poets* (1932) through Georg Roppen's *Evolution and Poetic Belief* (1956). And yet, surveying the work of the creative human imagination today, one is struck by the slightness of creative drive connected with an awareness of evolution, cosmic or organic. It is not that the poets refuse to accept evolution. They render lip service to it. But it does not haunt their poetic imaginations.

One of the great evolutionary philosophers of our day, Father Pierre Teilhard de Chardin, has been accused of writing often as a poet. But we are hard put to find poets who make creative use of evolutionary insights comparable to Teilhard's. Teilhard faces forward, into the future, as, in its brighter moments, does the rest of our world, permeated as it is with evolutionary thinking. But the poets and artists tend to exalt the present moment when they are not facing the past. There is here certainly some kind of crisis concerning the relationship of the poet or artist to time.[1]

The situation is complicated by the fact that today's poets and artists generally are acutely aware of the continuing development of art itself. The existence of a self-conscious *avant-garde* makes this plain enough. Poetry, together with art generally, has a sense of its own domestic time. But cosmic time, as this has been known since the discovery of evolution, is another matter. Most poets and artists are not much interested in it, even when they are most intently concerned with man, who exists in this time. Writers who do deal with larger patterns of development in time tend to slip into thinly veiled sensationalism, as does George Bernard Shaw in *Back to Methuselah,* or sensationalism not so thinly veiled, as in George Orwell's *1984,* or they handle cosmic time not very successfully, as does Hart Crane, or half-heartedly, as does T. S. Eliot. One feels that, in the last analysis, the poet and artist are not very much at home in an evolutionary cosmos.

The basic issue between poetry and evolutionism is seemingly the need in poetry, as in all art, for repetition. The drives toward repetition show in poetry in countless ways—in rhythm, in rhyme, in other sound patterns, in thematic management and plotting (Joyce plots *Ulysses,* which for all practical purposes is a poem in the full sense of this term, to match Homer, as Virgil in a different way plotted the *Aeneid*). Even the key to all plotting, recognition, is a kind of repetition, a return to something already known.
In "Burnt Norton" T. S. Eliot writes:

> And the end and the beginning were always there
> Before the beginning and after the end.[2]

Finnegans Wake is a serpent with its tail in its own mouth, the *ouroboros*: the last words of the book run back into its first words.

The preoccupation of poetry and of art in general with repetition is shown at its deepest level in the constant resort to the natural cycle of the year: spring, summer, autumn, winter. Mircea Eliade has shown the tremendous drive of this cycle within the human consciousness in his book *The Myth of the Eternal Return*. Indeed, the cosmic myth of the seasons, with its lesser parts, its contractions, expansions, and other variations and projections (the succession of day and night, the imaginary Hindu *kalpa* of 4,320,000,000 solar years, Yeats's elaborate hocus-pocus in *A Vision*), dominates the subconscious so thoroughly that one can speak of it simply as natural symbolism—all nature symbolism comes to focus here—or even as *the* myth, for, in effect, there is no other. Professor Cleanth Brooks, distinguishing interest in history from interest in nature, notes that in modern poets "the celebration of nature is not tied to a cyclic theory."[3] It is my conviction that it need not be. But even in the writers Professor Brooks cites, such as Dylan Thomas, there is a discernible hankering for cyclicism; and in others he cites, such as Wallace Stevens, who shows keen interest in non-cyclic change, one finds less than a wholehearted welcome of a truly historic view. As we shall see, in place of the continuities of history one finds in Stevens rather a discontinuous series of states of chaos, each separately resolved by the imagination, each resolution, in a sense, being a kind of repetition of foregoing resolutions, with no recognizable progress.

In a perceptive study Professor Northrop Frye has recognized this fact, proffering a classification of the archetypes of literature based on the natural cycle of the year because "the crucial importance of this myth has been forced on literary critics by Jung and Frazer."[4] Professor Frye's first phase is the "dawn, spring and birth phase," concerned with the hero, revival and resurrection, creation, and the defeat of the powers of darkness, and having as subordinate characters the father and the mother. This, he states, is the "archetype of romance and of most dithyrambic poetry." The second phase is that of "zenith, summer, marriage or triumph." Here we are concerned with apotheosis, the sacred marriage, and entering into Paradise, and with the subordinate characters of the companion and bride. This is the archetype of comedy, pastoral, and idyll. The "sunset, autumn and death" phase is the third, concerned with the dying god, violent death and sacrifice, and the hero in isolation. The traitor and the siren are subordinate characters, and this phase is the archetype of tragedy and elegy. The fourth and last phase is the "darkness, winter and dissolution phase," with its floods, return of chaos, defeat of the hero—the *Götterdämmerung,* accompanied by the ogre and the witch as subordinate characters. This is the archetype of satire, as instanced in the conclusion of *The Dunciad.*

Waiving questions as to the applicability of the details of this structure to the actuality of poetry and art, we can see that Professor Frye is presenting us here with something on the whole both real and powerful. Moreover, as he himself observes in the same place, the natural cycle not only touches poetry in terms of its themes, imagery, and characters, but also in more pervasive terms, such as that of rhythm itself, which appears essential for art, verbal or visual: "Rhythm, or recurrent movement, is deeply founded on the natural cycle, and everything in nature that we think of as having some analogy with works of art, like the flower or the bird's song, grows out of a profound synchronization between an organism and the rhythms of its environment, especially that of the solar year."

Everyone can recognize the actuality of these rhythms, too. Spring does come back each year. Day succeeds night, and night day. Men are born and die. There are, however, certain problems here in establishing rhythmic patterns. The likening of man's life to a cycle, for example, is based on an all too obvious distortion: there is *some* likeness between the helplessness of an old man and that of an infant, but to mistake one for the other one would have to be out of one's mind —here the cyclic myth has asserted its compelling power in consciousness and made plausible in our assessment of human life a pattern which is really not there: the life of an individual actually ends quite differently from the way it began. One can think otherwise only by blotting out certain facts.

The same is true with regard to groups of men taken as groups. In an article a few years ago, I pointed out in some detail that the likening of the "life" of a nation or empire or of a culture or people or tribe to the life even of an individual man, and *a fortiori* to a perfect cycle in which the end is the same as the beginning, is quite indefensible and utterly contrary to fact, although by leaving out of consideration certain obvious facts, by proper selectivity, a certain analogy, very loose, between a nation and an individual and a much feebler analogy between the history of a social group and circular movement can be made out.[5] But, on the whole, these analogies probably deceive more than they inform. The

Roman Empire "fell" (returned to the starting point from which it had presumably "risen") only in a very loose sense. It "died" only in a very loose sense, too, for it had never really been conceived and born as a human being is. The institutions of the Roman Empire are still all around us and in us, more widespread today than ever before; the descendants of its citizens are extraordinarily active over a greater expanse of the world than ever before, as mankind becomes more and more unified. Much as a circular area, say, a foot in circumference, can be discerned on an absolutely blank blackboard simply by disregarding the rest of the blackboard, so rise-and-fall or birth-and-death patterns can, of course, be discerned in events in the stream of time by proper selectivity. But what do such patterns explain? We like the rise-and-fall pattern probably less because it informs us about what is actually going on in the world than because it is, after all, a pattern, and the simplest pattern of all, imposed on the field of history, noteworthy for its lack of pattern. The attraction of periodicity operates largely from within the human psyche.

What sort of actuality do the cycles of nature have when we view them in terms of what we know of the universe since the discovery of cosmic and organic evolution? In the last analysis, they do not have much. Rhythms are approximations. Perfect cycles, exact repetitions, recurrences of identical starting points, are not really to be found. Although each winter is succeeded by spring, every year is actually different from every other if we look to details. What lengthier rhythms there may be—several years of drought and several of floods —are not really exact cycles, but approximations of cycles which gradually alter. On the whole, the global climate is changing in some kind of linear-style pattern, for the evolution of the earth is progressing toward an end-point quite different from its beginning. In the cosmos as we now know it, there is no real repetition anywhere, for all is in active evolution. One sees repetition only in the rough, where one does not examine more closely. But the universe is being examined more closely all the time. Weather patterns, to stay with our example, are being fed into computers to give us the remarkably accurate forecasting which has developed over the past decade or so. Climatic changes are being studied as they really occur over telling expanses of time, not as impressionistic constructions fabricated out of the limited experiences in one man's lifetime, inaccurately recalled.

Of course, there is a human dimension to the universe, and in the dimensions of one life, rhythms of repetition humanly identifiable and humanly satisfying are to be found. But the human dimension today also includes a great deal of abstract, scientific knowledge—for science is nothing if not a human creation, since it exists only within the human mind. Our abstract, scientific knowledge, which is now entering so thoroughly into planning as to be eminently real as well as abstract, includes a knowledge of the evolution of the cosmos and of life. This means that, in conjunction with an immediate experience of approximate recurrence, we experience also, if we are alert to the world in a twentieth-century way, an awareness of the fact that recurrence does not stand up *in detail*. Quite literally, in the modern physical universe, nothing ever repeats itself. Least of all does history.

The classic model for cyclic repetition, when it was rationalized, had been the supposedly immutable path of the sun around the earth. Now we know not merely that the earth moves around the sun, but also that it moves in a path, not circular but elliptical, which is gradually changing its form, in ways which are measurable. The stars are not changeless, but in full evolutionary career. So is our solar system. And the elements themselves are dismembered and reconstituted in the process of cosmic evolution.

One can still project a cyclic model of perpetual repetition upon actuality, pretending that everything now happening happened before an infinite number of times and will happen again an infinite number of times. But study fails to reveal any warrant within actuality itself even for the model. Even if we are living in a so-called "throbbing universe," which expands to a maximum and then over billions of years reverses and contracts to a single, unimaginably hot super-atom only to explode and expand again, all the evidence we have around us from the universe itself suggests that the pattern of events in the second explosion will be different from that in the first. To cap all this anti-repetitiveness is the appearance of human life itself in the cosmic process. For each man is a unique individual, utterly different from his fellows, all of them, no matter how many they are. The difference is not merely genetic. It is conscious, as can be seen in identical twins, who have the same genetic structures but quite different consciousness, the one "I" utterly distinct from the other. Each of us knows he is unique—that no one else experiences this taste of himself which he knows directly, a taste, as Gerard Manley Hopkins put it, "more distinctive than . . . ale or alum." No one in possession of his wits is concerned that one of the other three billion or so persons in the universe today is identical with himself. For each man knows his own induplicability and interior inaccessibility. In simply knowing himself, each knows that his interior landscape is unique and open only to his own mind. With man at the term of the cosmic and organic evolutionary process, we thus are aware of the universe in its entirety as building up to maximum unrepeatability, self-conscious uniqueness, singularity folded back on itself.

With this kind of awareness, what remains of recurrence as a foundation for poetry and art? We are, of course, as we have seen, still acutely conscious of approximate recurrence to a degree: there is, after all, the evident succession of spring, summer, autumn, winter, repeating year after year. But this basic repetition, and all that goes with it, is no longer at the heart of life in the way in which it used to be. It has been displaced. It is now eccentric. A somewhat sentimental account explains the displacement by urbanization and industrialization: large numbers of men now live far from the wilds of nature or the domesticated life close to nature on the farm. But, more radically, the displacement has come about by the intellectual discovery of the cosmic facts, which are known to persons in rural areas as well as in the cities: we live not in a cyclic, perpetually recurring, but in a linear-type time. I say "linear-type" rather than "linear" because time, being nonspatial, is not entirely like a straight line, either. But it is like a straight line rather than a circle in the sense that events in time end at a different point from that at which they begin. (Whether they are really "strung out" like points on a line is another queston: in fact, they are not.) My life at its end is different from what it was at its beginning. The universe, even now, is different from what it was five billion years ago and gives evidence of continued progressive differentiation from its initial stage and all subsequent stages.

The displacement of the sense of recurrence as the dominant human awareness is, I believe, a major crisis, and probably the major crisis, in the arts today. The displacement does not, of course, affect everyone in society equally. The sensibility of millions of persons, even in highly technologized societies, is doubtless still dominated by a feeling for recurrence which is functionally little different from that of their ancestors two hundred years ago, at least in many areas of life. They do feel the spring, summer, autumn, and winter as a real part of themselves. But even they are undoubtedly affected more radically than they are consciously aware by the psychological structures of society today, particularly by the stress on planning, whether economic or social or industrial or international or interplanetary. Planning means the conscious control of mind over the elements in nature and spells the end of the dominance of quasi-cyclic experience. With planning, matters end up differently from the way in which they began. Moreover, with modern technology, the effect of the seasons—basic to sustaining a sense of recurrence—has been blunted in ways which are sure to be telling, if only subconsciously, for all. A heated and air-conditioned building is pretty much the same in summer and winter, and more and more persons, educated and uneducated, are spending more and more time in such buildings. Transportation, formerly so much affected by the movement of the seasons, is more and more independent of this movement. In technologized societies menus are increasingly the same the year round, or can be. On television one can see skiing in the middle of one's own summer and aquaplaning in midwinter. The difference between night and day, for practical working purposes, has long since disappeared from major areas of human existence. One has to gloss the text "The night cometh when no man can work" to make it comprehensible to a swing-shift worker in an assembly plant. Even the most unreflective are affected by this detachment of life from the rhythms of nature.

A fortiori the poets and artists are affected. And they know it. In accord with their deeply felt desire for up-to-dateness, which is the desire to speak for man in our time and is itself an anti-cyclic or post-cyclic phenomenon, contemporary poets generally will give at least lip service to the eclipse of recurrence as a central human experience. But how far is poetry affected by this lip service? Poets in English and some other languages continue to use rhyme—although it is significant that they no longer use it so often as they once did. They continue to use lines of more or less matching lengths—although again they do so less than they used to. Occasionally, in fits of desperation, they may resort to bongo drums. But here again, although jazz is indeed relevant to modern living precisely because of its apotheosis of rhythm, resort to jazz is regarded more and more as an escape, if a necessary one. Primitive man banged his drums to attune himself to cosmic harmonies. Modern man resorts to jazz to get away from it all.

The real crisis, however, for modern poets occurs in the images of which they can avail themselves and of course in stylistic and structural devices of repetition where these intersect with or otherwise engage the imagery of a poem. The old reliable cosmological imagery of recurrence appears less and less serviceable. What sort of enthusiasm could be brought today, for example, to the creation of a work such as Edmund Spenser's "Epithalamion," where, if we can believe Professor Kent Hieatt's fantastic calculations,[6] the day and year are represented by the twenty-four stanzas and 365 long lines of the poem, the apparent daily movement of the sun relative to the fixed stars is figured in other line-totals, and at one point the ratio of light to darkness at the time of the summer solstice, when the action of the poem takes place, is properly signaled to the reader? One can, of course, cite Joyce's *Ulysses*—but here the relevance of cosmic imagery is indirect. It is maintained by literary allusion rather than by direct feeling for nature. Joyce builds out of Homer, and countless others, not out of "nature" directly. Of course Spenser builds out of other poets, too, for he is filled with literary allusion. But with him cosmology itself is also more directly operative. Milton, here, is a key figure. *Paradise Lost* was built on a cosmology no longer viable in Milton's day, but clung to deliberately by Milton for poetic reasons. My point is that poets and artists generally today are faced with a crisis similar to Milton's, and even deeper than his was. The polarization of literary dispute around the figures of Milton and Joyce in the mid-twentieth century is perhaps symptomatic: both Milton and Joyce face cosmological problems, and both retreat from them.

Awareness of the modern cosmological crisis in poetry has seldom come to the surface of the contemporary sensibility, and a case for modern "cosmic poetry," with some of the marks of the older recurrence-based patterns, has in fact been made in *Start with the Sun,* by James E. Miller, Jr., Karl Shapiro, and Bernice Slote.[7] The authors of this book also show how, more or less in association with the drift to old cosmic themes, another emphasis is capital in many modern poets: the stress on the esthetic moment, on "creativity," on the instant of "epiphany." This emphasis, which has an obvious Coleridgean as well as Symbolist and Imagist background, deserves attention here, for it throws great light on the poet's relationship to the sense of cosmic time itself. Mircea Eliade has shown that the primitive sense of time, particularly of sacred time, involves a psychological need to recover the beginning of things.[8] Early man—and we can assimilate to early man all mankind generally, more or less, until the psychological effect of typography had entered deep into the subconscious and established a new relationship toward records, the past, and time—early man felt time and change as somehow involving degeneration, a moving away from a perfect "time" at the beginning, a time which was really not a time but an extra-temporal condition, the so-called "time" of mythological existence. The events of mythology—for example, Athena's springing from the head of Zeus, Dionysus' dismemberment by the Maenads—were not the sort of things for which one could supply dates. (As has frequently been noted by scholars, the Biblical accounts of origins involve a different, contrasting sense of time, even when the Biblical accounts are obviously influenced by extra-Biblical mythology.)

Time poses many problems for man, not the least of which is that of ir-resistibility and irreversibility: man in time is moved ahead willy-nilly and cannot actually recover a moment of the past. He is caught, carried on despite himself, and hence not a little terrified. Resort to mythologies, which associate temporal events with the atemporal, in effect disarms time, affording relief from its threat. This mythological flight from the ravages of time may at a later date be rationalized by various cyclic theories, which have haunted man's philosophizing from antiquity to the present. In the wake of romanticism, how-ever, we find a new refuge from the pressure of time in the cult of the here-and-now esthetic experience, the esthetically achieved moment which gives a sense of expanded existence and of a quasi-eternity. Georges Poulet, in *Studies in Human Time,* Frank Kermode in *Romantic Image,* and others elsewhere have elaborated various ways in which this sense of escape from time is managed, from the French writers leading up to Proust on through various American writers: Emerson, Poe, Emily Dickinson, T. S. Eliot, and others. Post-romantic estheticism depends in great part on the sense of this esthetic moment, different from and more valuable than experiences in ordinary time. We find this sense particularly acute in the Bloomsbury esthetic growing out of and around G. E. Moore's *Principia Ethica,* which influenced so typical a modern writer as Virginia Woolf. James Joyce's doctrine of "epiphany," of course, belongs in this same setting. And the influence on the New Criticism is evident: the poem as "object" is assimilated to a world of vision, which is a timeless world by com-parison with that of words and sound. An esthetic of "objective correlatives," whatever its great merits, to a degree insulates poetry from time. Up to a point all poetry provides an esthetic refuge from "real" time, but earlier poetic theory, even that expounding poetry as divinely inspired and thus different from ordinary talk, generally lacks this exaltation of a moment of "realization" which is so commonplace today.

The stress on the moment of realization, on epiphany, under one of its aspects, can thus actually be a dodge to avoid the consequences inherent in the knowl-edge we have that we live in an evolving universe. It can provide a means of escaping from the real—that is, from cosmic on-goingness—a latter-day time-shelter, replacing the primitive's mythological refuge. This is not to say that the older attempts to escape from time have been entirely abandoned. The quest for a lost Eden, the "radical innocence," which Professors R. W. B. Lewis, Ihab Hassan, and others have discerned in American writers particularly, revives some of the old mythological routines. But this quest for a lost Eden, although real enough, must today be looked for closely to be found. Writers do not openly advertise that their creative drives are being powered by a quest for a lost Eden. They often do talk openly about the value of the esthetic moment.

Once we are aware of the psychological issues here, it is possible to discern some fascinating perspectives in modern poetry. Those which we shall here employ are related to Professor Cleanth Brooks's division, already adverted to, between poets preoccupied with history (related to evolutionism) and those preoccupied with nature (related, as we have seen, to cyclicism). But they refine this division further, as I believe. We can view poets in three groupings, not always too neatly distinct, but, given the proper reservations, highly informative concerning the poet's problem of relating to the known universe.

There are, first of all, those poets who are consumed with the imagery of the old cosmic mythology to such an extent that it rather effectively dominates their entire outlook. Such would be, for example, D. H. Lawrence, Dylan Thomas, Lawrence Durrell, and Robert Graves. The suggestion of cyclicism takes various forms here, but common to them all is at least preoccupation with fertility (or its opposite, sterility). Indeed, the present cult of sex (often clearly an obsession) in literature appears from the point of vantage we occupy here to be a flight from time comparable to the fertility ceremonials of primitives, but more desperate because our sense of the evolutionary nature of actuality makes time more insistent today than ever before. Radical innocence is sought more frenetically because we are more aware of its inaccessibility.

In the case of Lawrence, the cult of sex and death—which yields such beauties as "Bavarian Gentians"—is linked with a nostalgia for the past and conscious revivals of old chthonic images, such as the serpent, which were supposed to restore modern man to his lost Eden. Dylan Thomas immerses himself more spectacularly in nature imagery. "Fern Hill" runs on in a riot of time and fertility symbols: apple boughs, the night, time, barley, "all the sun long," grass, sleep, owls, the dew, the cock, "Adam and the maiden," the new-made clouds, "in the sun born over and over," sky blue trades, morning songs, "the moon that is always rising," "time held me green and dying." This stirring poem is a litany of life and death, in its cosmology still of a piece with Lucretius. Lawrence Durrell celebrates the mysteries of sex with a sophisticated neopagan fervor, having little to do with a sense of man's present position in the cosmos he is taking over more and more, although Durrell does have some sense of temporal progression in the evolution of social groupings. Graves protracts what he takes to be ancient continuities into the present.

> Is it of trees you tell . . .
>
> . . . .
> Or of the Zodiac and how slow it turns
> Below the Boreal Crown,
>
> . . . .?
>
> Water to water, ark again to ark,
> From woman back to woman:
> So each new victim treads unfalteringly
> The never altered circuit of his fate,
> Bringing twelve peers as witness
> Both to his starry rise and starry fall.[9]

Here one notes strong, and doubtless deliberate, suggestions of the old wheel of fortune, so well known to students of the Middle Ages and so revealing of the pagan cyclicism which haunted the medieval mind. Other poets deeply involved in various ways in chthonic, cyclic themes are Edgar Lee Masters and, most of all, Yeats. Indeed, Yeats is so spectacularly and desperately anti-evolutionary that there is little point in discussing him here. But it is worth noting that in *A Vision,* "Byzantium," and elsewhere his cyclicism comes patently and directly from his poetic needs.

The work of poets such as these, deeply involved in sex, fertility rituals, and, by the same token, death, could perhaps be described as Dionysian; and, by contrast, an evolutionary view, which takes full cognizance that history and time do not fold back on themselves but move resolutely forward with the mysterious upthrust evident in the ascent from protozoans to man, could be described as Apollonian. Perhaps all poetry must be in some way Dionysian because of its sources in the subconscious. But one hesitates to make this judgment if only because one suspects that the Nietzschean division into Dionysian and Apollonian is itself the result of a flight from time. Nietzsche's own cyclicism suggests that his thought, whatever its other brilliances, was not relating itself to the full facts of an evolutionary cosmos.

A second group of poets is related to time in another way. These are the poets adverted to above who attempt to solve the problem of time by greater concentration on the pure esthetic moment. In his *Studies in Human Time* Georges Poulet beautifully describes the way in which Emily Dickinson presents in her poetry moments without past and without future except insofar as the future threatens the loss of the moment.[10] Each poem is a moment of experience which releases us from time:

> Safe in their alabaster chambers,
> Untouched by morning and untouched by noon,
> Sleep the meek members of the resurrection,
> Rafter of satin, and roof of stone.[11]

Miss Dickinson does not flee evolutionary time by resort to the seeming endless recurrences associated with a cult of the Earth Mother. She simply dwells in the instant and attempts to protract it. In this, her work is an early example of what would become a regular style, particularly from the Imagists on, a style revived by many poets at the present moment. The cult of the esthetic moment (or epiphany) marks to a greater or lesser degree the poetic performance and beliefs of James Joyce, Edith Sitwell, Conrad Aiken, Wallace Stevens, E. E. Cummings, William Carlos Williams in his more Imagist phases, and countless others. To a greater or lesser degree it permeates the contemporary consciousness from the heights of the New Criticism down to the level of the most unimaginative beatnik writers. Ezra Pound, with his own complicated sense of history, shows its influence, most evidently in his constant cry to "make it new"— although this exhortation has other implications also. In his poetry and poetic theory, Wallace Stevens, despite his predilection for change, bypasses the development of the universe as such and views existence—poetically conveyed— as a series of disconnected esthetic mergings of imagination and chaos. And the newer generation of poets—James Wright, Robert Bly, Donald Hall, Howard Nemerov, John Knoepfle, and others—may repudiate their predecessors on other scores, but they show, if anything, an even more intense devotion to the esthetic moment, often very intimately conceived.

The drift toward the old chthonic fertility cycles (more noteworthy in the Old World poets, at least until very recently) and the retreat into the esthetic moment (discernible on both sides of the Atlantic) are complemented by a third tendency in modern poetry, a disposition actually to accept linear-type change and even to demand it as a condition of poetic activity. This disposition is more marked among American poets than among British and Irish, a fact which is of course related to the nature of the American experience. Whitman is obviously a striking expositor of this experience, with his attitude of total acceptance toward being and his sense of a dynamic present, diverging toward past and future and uniting and equalizing them. Probably more than the somewhat doctrinaire and clinical acceptance of evolutionism which one meets with in early British writers such as Tennyson, George Bernard Shaw, and H. G. Wells, or even Swinburne, Whitman's sense of participation in the ongoing work of the universe appears to acclimate evolutionism to the poetic world. But does it really succeed? Poulet is quite right in noting that Whitman's is "an enunciation, at once successive and cumulative, of all that has been, and of all that will be."[12] "The universe is a procession with measured and perfect motion," Whitman announces.[13] But, unlike Péguy's comparable procession, which as Poulet again explains, has a termination, Whitman's procession simply advances, occupying worlds and times, but never changing anything, never getting anywhere. In fact, in Whitman we find little if any attention to the inner dynamism of evolution itself; what Teilhard has called the "inwardness" of things, the drive within the evolutionary process which moves from the externally organized original cosmos to the cosmos known and more and more controlled from the interior of man's person,[14] is missing from Whitman.

This is not to say that there is no historicism at all in Whitman. Whitman comes off one of the best in his awareness of the one-directional process of history, for his sense of a dynamic present, diverging toward the past and future and uniting and equalizing them, as well as his sense of the uniqueness of the individual imply a sense of the evolutionary, essentially nonrepetitive movement of time.[15] And yet, Whitman, too, is trapped by the old cyclicism, as, for example, in "Song of the Answerer":

> They bring none to his or her terminus or to be content and full,
> Whom they take they take into space to behold the birth of the
>   stars, to learn one of the meanings,
> To launch off with absolute faith, to sweep through the ceaseless rings and never
>   be quiet again.[16]

In the last analysis there is little or nothing in Whitman to differentiate past and future. Whitman's is still a cult of the present moment, temporally expanded, with little real anguish. For him the present does not grow out of the past, nor the future out of the present. Past, present, and future simply coexist— and all too peacefully. The universe and Whitman's appetite, as Poulet notes, exactly equal one another. How can anything happen when so much bland satisfaction reigns? Whitman has little of the dissatisfactions of the reformer or the future-oriented man.

But if he is not especially concerned about improving things, other American poets more typically are—William Carlos Williams, for example, who insists, dramatically in his *In the American Grain* and by explicit assertion in many other places, that it is the business of the present in America to reconstitute its past and to improve its poetic language and hence its poetic realization of actuality.[17] It is interesting that Williams does not think much in terms of degeneration or decadence (which often reveal a cyclic model in the sub-conscious): the plight of Americans is not that they have defected from their past but rather that they are only now in a position to lay hold of it reflectively and effectively for the first time, since it now is old enough really to be a past to them. Williams dedicates *Paterson* to this enterprise of recovery, which in a way does look ahead. Yet the time which Williams deals with does not unfold, nor does it thrust forward. The present is authenticated by the past and the future lies as a potential in past and present, but there is little adventure in facing what is to come, little sense of unattained horizons ahead. Such a sense, of course, is not necessary for the writing of poetry, but it would seem to be some-thing which could be included in poetic awareness.

One discerns comparable attitudes in Hart Crane. Crane's vision, conceived in *The Bridge,* is born of his sense of his own moment in history, in time, at the dawn of the machine age. His reactions are not querulous, but positive, like those of Whitman, whom he eulogizes. Crane's confident assertion of faith in the future of industrial America hints at a feeling for linear, evolutionary time. But his compulsion to create the "American myth" drives him toward more cyclic views to fulfill his need for a pattern, and we find in the "Ave Maria," for example, a fascination with the old cosmic movements and with cyclic patterns in a variety of forms:

> Of all that amplitude that time explores,
>
> . . . .
>
> This disposition that thy night relates
> From Moon to Saturn in one sapphire wheel:
> The orbic wake of thy once whirling feet,
> Elohim, still I hear thy sounding heel!
>
> White toils of heaven's cordons, mustering
> In holy rings all sails charged to the far
> Hushed gleaming fields and pendant seething wheat
> Of knowledge,—round thy brows unhooded now
> —The kindled Crown! acceded of the poles
> And biassed by full sails, meridians reel
> Thy purpose—still one shore beyond desire! [18]

The fascination with cyclic patterns echoes in the last line of "To Brooklyn Bridge": "And of the curveship lend a myth to God."

Crane's representation of history is more interiorized than Whitman's expan-sive canvases, but his quest for a stabilizing myth, a symbolic structure which will somehow catch the historical process in poetic toils, draws him back at times into something like primitive cyclicism. Crane had read Oswald Spengler. At other times, perhaps under the influence of P. D. Ouspensky, he retreats from the flow of time into a mythical eternal present which alone exists but is parceled out to man piecemeal.

Crane is typically American in his determination to try to make poetic sense of history. Other Americans show a similar concern. Allen Tate, Robert

Penn Warren, William Carlos Williams, Archibald MacLeish, and Robert Lowell, for example, have felt compelled at least from time to time to build poetry around historical events which have appeared to them as part of their own life-worlds—the Civil War for Tate and Warren, the New Jersey city of Paterson for Williams, for MacLeish American *miscellanea,* New England for Robert Lowell. All these poets evince a distinctly open-end or linear-type view of time. They are helped by the fact that the American past they turn to is a recorded, truly historical past, free to all intents and purposes of prehistory and of prehistory's cyclic tow. (The exception which must be made for the native American Indian prehistory is relatively minor.) Another American, Robert Frost, shows the same open-endedness in his own less explicitly historical, more anecdotal concerns. There is little if any mythical reconstruction in Frost. No cyclic nostalgia shows, for example, in the typically courageous, forward-looking poem "An Old Man's Winter Night." Nevertheless, in the particular perspectives we are considering here, it appears that the achievements of these poets are often limited. Their historical mood is predominantly retrospective. It may seem strange to suggest that history can be anything other than retrospective, and yet we know so much history now that we rightly feel the knowledge of the past driving us into the future. I am not saying that these or other poets should be obliged to treat history otherwise than as they have, for they have done exceedingly well in following each his own genius. Nor do I intend to suggest that anyone should opt for a fatuous view of pure progress as man's destiny in his earthly future. I am only saying that these poets cannot be cited as having caught up in their poetry the entirety of present-day man's real time sense.

Even Pound and Eliot, whose personal and poetic journey from the United States back into Europe was a quite conscious re-entry into history, have not provided a point of view in which one can assimilate a full historical and evolutionary vision to a poetic one. Pound piles historical incident on historical incident. His "Cantos" read as a vast pastiche of eyewitness accounts, overheard conversations, and reflections from everywhere out of the past, with Ecbatana and the ancient Near East jostling what Pound in "Canto XXVIII" styles "solid Kansas." But the impression one gets is not of the development of history so much as it is of a present in which all this history is caught up and somehow moved out of time. "Time is the evil. Evil," "Canto XXX" cries. Eliot's great essay on "Tradition and the Individual Talent," with its sensitive description of the relationship of past, present, and future, provides one of the purest examples of truly historical thinking in our century, and the line from "Burnt Norton" which states, "Only through time time is conquered," is a gnomic expression of the condition of both history and transcendence. And yet, the same "Burnt Norton" opens with a quotation from Heraclitus which states, "The way up and the way down are one and the same," focuses, especially in its part II, on the image of whirling movement ("There is only the dance"), and concludes with the lament, "Ridiculous the waste sad time/Stretching before and after." It is noteworthy that the Heraclitian fragment, "The way up and the way down are one and the same," strongly suggests cyclic fatalism (return to point of departure or inability to leave it) and by no means says the same thing as does Eliot's much advertised other source, St. John of the Cross, or the Gospel source on which St. John relies, "He who exalts himself will be humbled, and he who humbles himself will be exalted." The words of Jesus incorporate a dialectical movement missing in this somewhat paralyzing quotation from the Greek sage. All in all, in his poems and plays (for example, *Murder in the Cathedral,* Acts I and II) Eliot interlaces references to historical, evolutionary time with references to cyclic patterns so frequent and intense as virtually to immobilize the historical. Geoffrey Bullough has pointed out Eliot's preference for "formal patterns" over Bergson's open-ended *élan vital.*[19]

In a sense the point thus far made in this study might be seen as predictable. The poetic theorists from Aristotle through Sir Philip Sidney and beyond always knew that poetry and history were at root incompatible—despite the fact that, as we are well aware today, the poetic imagination has often been stimulated by historical events, proximate or remote. But the point here is precisely that such theory is no longer adequate. The incompatibility of poetry and history is today a more desperate matter than it used to be. A sense of history, seen as evolutionary development, has now become an inevitable dimension of all reflective human existence, and if the very feel for evolutionary development is unassimilable by poetry, then poetry cannot compass one of the most profound and intimate of modern experiences.

A sense of history, which is of a piece with a sense of an evolutionary cosmos, is a sense of the present as growing out of a past with which we are in some kind of verifiable contact, and a sense that the present differs from this past with which it connects and that the future will differ from both present and past. It is a sense of continuity and difference, each reflecting the other, such as Eliot so well expounds in "Tradition and the Individual Talent." We have seen the basic reason why such a sense poses a problem for poets: it undercuts structures dear to them, first by downgrading recurrence as such, making what repetition there is only approximate and somewhat incidental, and secondly by making the present not only a present but also a sequel and a prelude. The problem may not appear pressing when we experience only a single poem, but when we look at the entire body of work of a poet, either in its larger themes or images or in the theory which it at times consciously—perhaps often too consciously—shows forth, the problem, as we have seen, is urgent indeed. A significant drift toward either cyclicism or the isolated moment is unmistakable in modern poetry.

The poet has always been ill at ease, to some degree, in the world of actuality. Poetry is imitation, as the ancients well knew. Admittedly, poetry as such cannot be history. But it must be human, and the urgent question today is whether it must write off the modern experience of evolutionary historicity, whether it can even talk about this experience without betraying itself as poetry. This unresolved question, I believe, is what, deep in the subconscious, in great part underlies the *malaise* of poets and their friends today, occasioning the complaint that poets are outsiders more than they used to be, discarded by "modern society," a seemingly unrealistic complaint, since it appears probable that never have poets been more read and more courted than in our present technological United States. The basic question is: Can poetry face into continuous nonrecurrence as such and assimilate it without distorting it? Can it be that the poet (and the artist generally) feels himself an outsider today less because he has been actively expelled from modern society than because he has failed to make his own one of its deepest insights, its sense of historical time and its drive into fulfillment in the future?

We have noted above the American poets' share in the American sense of drive into the future. This sense holds some promise of change. Further promise of change is to be found in the Christian world view itself, which calls for specific attention here because it has been the source of so much of modern man's sense of history. For the Christian, both the universe and the life of the individual man end in quite different states from those in which they began. Time makes a difference. Time tells. Christian teaching urges no one to try to recover a lost Eden. Salvation lies ahead, at the end of time. And Adam's sin, which drove man from the Garden of Eden, is even hailed in the Holy Saturday liturgy of the Roman Catholic Church as *felix culpa,* "happy fault," because it gave God occasion to send His Son Jesus Christ to redeem man. The promise of the future is thus greater than that of the past. Christian (and Hebrew) teaching underlines the nonrepetitiveness of actuality and by the same token the importance of the unique, unrepeatable, human self, the human person. Christianity, like evolutionary thinking, is anticyclic.

Many of the modern poets who espouse an open-end view of time also give evidence of more or less explicit Christian influence—Allen Tate, Robert Lowell, Richard Wilbur, and W. H. Auden would be examples in point, although I do not believe that any of them has fully solved the problem of assimilating our modern sense of time to the artistic medium. There is however another poet generally classified as modern who is especially worth looking into here for the directness—and precocity—with which he has faced into the problem of time, historicity, and the human person living in time. The grounds on which he faces the problem may be too explicitly Christian to solve the problem for some. Yet there is, I believe, something to learn from him. This poet is Gerard Manley Hopkins, an artist who, although he apparently had read little if any Darwin, is still, I believe, more at home in history and in an evolutionary cosmos than most other modern or near-modern poets, although he is not quite aware of his own entire at-homeness here. His Catholic dogmatic background simply fitted him for an evolutionary time-sense despite the fact that the initial steps toward evolutionary thinking caused no little consternation in Catholic and other religious circles.

The key passages in Hopkins for our present purposes are in "The Wreck of the Deutschland." In this poem Hopkins is dealing with the significance of a horrifying event, a wreck in which a German ship, the *Deutschland,* outward bound from Bremen, foundered on shoals in the North Sea during a storm and was stranded for thirty hours without help, with great loss of life and with the most horrible suffering and distress. In one rescue incident, a seaman, lowered on a rope from the rigging to help a woman or child drowning on the deck, was dashed by a wave against the bulwarks and decapitated. The next morning, according to the *Times* report, "when daylight dawned, his headless body, detained by the rope, was swaying to and fro with the waves."[20] Among the.details which he picked up from the *Times* accounts, Hopkins focuses on one particularly: "Five German nuns, whose bodies are now in the dead-house here, clasped hands and were drowned together, the chief sister, a gaunt woman 6 ft. high, calling out loudly and often, 'O Christ, come quickly!' till the end came."[21] The central movement in Hopkins' thought in his poem turns on his inquiry into what this nun meant in her cry, "O Christ, come quickly!" He explores many possibilities—was she asking for rescue? For death as a relief for herself and all those around?—and finally settles for the cry as one of recognition and acceptance. This horrible visitation, this agonizing, not even private but involved with the agony of all those around her, was the real advent of Christ Himself in this nun's life: here she would meet Him in her death, and she called out for Him to come and take her "in the storm of his strides." She sees Christ not as an avenger, but as God, her Lover, and in his love as "the Master/*Ipse,* the only one, Christ, King, Head:/He was to cure the extremity where he had cast her;/Do, deal, lord it with living and dead." This was the point—unknown until now—to which her life had been building up, and she was ready, for she had known that God's coming need not be gentle, that He is present not only in "the stars, lovely-asunder" or in "the dappled-with-damson west," but in all the events in history, even the most horrible, out of which He can bring joy. Hers was a faith which could see God in everything—in disaster as well as joy, indeed most of all in her own death—and never waver in its confidence in Him. Had not St. Paul asked in the *Epistle to the Romans* (8:35, 37), "Who shall separate us from the love of Christ? Shall tribulation, or distress, or persecution, or hunger, or nakedness, or danger, or the sword? . . . But in all these things we overcome, because of him who has loved us."

What we note here is a sense of history at perhaps its highest possible pitch. Hopkins, as we find in his theoretical observations, was devoted to the "instress" of things, to uniqueness itself, to what made each thing itself only, other, different from all else. His poetry everywhere testifies to the intensity of his love for variety, for "all things counter, original, spare, strange," as he puts it in "Pied Beauty." Hopkins connected his interest in the uniqueness of things with the thought of his thirteenth-century predecessor at Oxford, Duns Scotus, but interest in the unique was beyond a doubt far more intense and explicit in the post-romantic Englishman than in his medieval compatriot, who was necessarily far less sensitized to history by his age than Hopkins by his. Hopkins, in fact, is clearly a proto-existentialist in his preoccupation with the singular and the singularity of existence, with "my selfbeing, my consciousness and feeling of myself, that taste of myself, of *I* and *me* above all and in all things, which is more distinctive than the taste of ale or alum."[22] His sonnet "As kingfishers catch fire, dragonflies draw flame" announces a kind of self-definition in action: "Whát I dó is me." But his fascination with the unique and his sense of historicity is shown perhaps most strikingly by the way in which in the "Deutschland" he has fixed on the consciously accepted death of a human being—the utterly unique culmination of an utterly unique existence—as the very focus of existence and meaning.

He relates this death to the action of God's grace—the free gift of God which establishes the unique relationship between each unique individual and God. But grace itself, Hopkins insists, is an historical event. It does not come from heaven, direct from God's existence beyond time. Hopkins knows this will shock but presents it as a central Catholic teaching:

> Not out of his bliss
>   Springs the stress felt
> Nor first from heaven (and few know this)
>   Swings the stroke dealt—
> Stroke and a stress that stars and storms deliver,
> That guilt is hushed by, hearts are flushed by and melt—
>   But it rides time like riding a river
> (And here the faithful waver, the faithless fable and miss).[23]

It is clear from the preceding lines of the poem that the "stress" is God's grace, the pressure he exerts on man's life (firm, delicate, mysterious, in Hopkins' image, like the pressure of the streams trickling down from the surrounding hills which hold the head of water in a well up to its level). This grace, "delivered" through the universe in the violence of storms as well as in the interior movements of consciousness which bring the sinner to repentance and hope, does not come directly from God in eternity ("his bliss") but only in history through Jesus Christ, who was and is both God and man, and as man a real material figure identifiable in actual cosmic time. Hopkins goes on about grace:

> It dates from day
>   Of his going in Galilee;
> Warm-laid grave of a womb-life grey;
>   Manger, maiden's knee;
> The dense and the driven Passion, and frightful sweat;
> Thence the discharge of it, there its swelling to be,
>   Though felt before, though in high flood yet.

The grace at work in the world today comes into the present through the historical life of Jesus Christ—His Incarnation, birth, and, most of all, His passion and death. Even the grace given fallen man antecedent to Christ was given in view of Christ's coming into historical time.

"It dates." This is the scandal. Hopkins' uncanny appreciation of the drives in the human psyche which make it. want to dissociate itself and what it values from time is evident in the fact that he recognizes the scandal of time, which creates difficulties even for believers. "Here the faithful waver." For it seems indecent that an Almighty God would tie Himself so firmly into the flux of things, focusing His definitive visitation of man at one single brief period, the lifetime of Jesus Christ, and spreading all out from there. Equally uncanny is Hopkins' deep appreciation of the psychological mechanism of the old cosmic mythologies. Far ahead of his time, writing as though he had read Professor Eliade, he states with precocious insight that myths are nothing less than an attempt to escape from time, to make significance dateless. "The faithless fable and miss." They do not see the movement of grace in life as something that "rides time like riding a river." They try to find meaning by escaping from time.

Written in 1875, only sixteen years after the appearance of *The Origin of Species* and without any discernible direct Darwinian influence, "The Wreck of the Deutschland" actually makes use of a theme assimilable to an evolutionary sense of time, an "open-end," developmental structuring of events more explicitly and downrightly than any other poem of comparable size or importance which I know of since Darwin. The presence of grace has proved, in the Christian sense of history, to be a presence curiously of a piece with the presence which man himself feels in the universe since knowledge of cosmic and organic evolution has shaped his deeper attitudes toward his life-world. Hopkins' open-end view of time is focused in the world of the human person and of grace, which lives in persons, rather than in the more material world of cosmic and organic evolution. To this degree his view remains underdeveloped. Hopkins was not greatly taken with Darwin's discoveries, although perhaps he would have been had be lived longer. But his world is open to them; indeed, it would welcome them, with the sense of the uniqueness of things to which these discoveries can give and have given rise.

Hopkins is certainly not the only poet who is influenced by a Christian sense of God's grace operating in real historical time on persons each of whom is unique. Many other poets, most of them far less consciously, are influenced by the same open-ended historicism, as Professor Brooks has pointed out in *The Hidden God*. Such open-ended historicism is part of the Hebreo-Christian heritage, which in fact was perhaps a necessary condition for Darwin's seeing what he saw: it appears unlikely that a sensibility overconditioned by cyclic views would have been gripped, as Darwin was, by evolutionary patterns. But to say that open-ended historicism and the related evolutionary outlook are at home in the Christian world view is not to say that earlier poets, even the most Christian, entirely succeeded in accommodating a truly Christian sense of time to their poetic sensibilities. Professor Brooks has suggested that "with the breakup of the Christian synthesis, nature and history have tended to fall apart."[24] We have to be careful about imputing to past ages a Christian synthesis. If such a synthesis should include a sense of man's real place in the real physical universe of time and space, as apparently it should, there has been not only no valid Christian synthesis in the past but not even a moderately good synthesis. You cannot have a valid Christian synthesis based on a false cosmology or even on a notably defective one. We must face the fact that earlier cosmologies were both defective and, in many crucial points, false. Nature was never until recent times effectively conjoined with history. The problem today is not to restore an old union but to implement a new one. This problem, the present study suggests, is not particularly distressing to the Christian who understands his heritage in the depths at which it can now be understood. But it is a grievously distressing problem for the poet and artist of our time as poet or artist—whether he be Christian or not—and one from which most poets and artists, consciously or subconsciously, retreat. In other words, it is easier for the Christian as such than for the poet or artist as such to subscribe in the depths of his being to an evolutionary universe. It is also easier, *mutatis mutandis*, for the Jew, since the Old Testament sense of time and the New Testament sense of time are of a piece, although the entry of God into time and history is less intense without the New Testament doctrine of the Incarnation.

The plight of the modern poet and artist is truly extreme. The poet or artist is acutely ill at ease in our present life-world. The earlier life-world belonged to the poets largely because it was so largely constructed out of the archetypal images which poetry and art tend to favor. If to a degree the modern world has rejected the poet, the poet also often has rejected the modern world because it demands a reorganization of his sensibility which is utterly terrifying. If the poet speaks for his age, he tends to speak for those who turn away from the characteristic awarenesses of modern man concerned with history and time.

With some exceptions, in his sense of time and history and of the succession of events, the poet thus has tended to be an aborigine, a primitive. Some maintain that the poet or artist must continue always to be such. I do not believe that he can afford to do so. Of course, no one can prescribe how a poet must speak. If, however, the poet is going to speak for modern man, he is going to have to take into account somehow man's total consciousness, even though this entails a reorganization of his own psyche and of the entire tradition of poetry so drastic as to fill us with utter terror. Very possibly the archetypes in the psyche are themselves in process of being reorganized under pressure of present discoveries. How subconsciously archetypal can archetypes be when they are the objects of knowledge as conscious as that which we bring to them today? Let us be honest in facing the future of poetry and art and man. What will poetry be like ten thousand or one hundred thousand years from now? Will man be able still to live with his once fascinating little dreams of recurrence?

SAINT LOUIS UNIVERSITY

NOTES

1. In another context, but using some of the material used here, I have treated this subject in the study "Myth or Evolution? Crisis of the Creative Imagination," *McCormick Quarterly*, XVIII, Special Supplement (Jan., 1965), 37-56. This previous study was read as a paper at a colloquium on "Myth and Modern Man" sponsored by McCormick Theological Seminary in Chicago on October 22, 1964, with other papers by Paul W. Pruyser, Mircea Eliade, and Schubert M. Ogden. The present study is a revised and enlarged version of a lecture given on May 11, 1964, for the Thirty-First Peters Rushton Seminar in Contemporary Prose and Poetry at the University of Virginia. For material in both these studies I wish to acknowledge help from papers and discussion by members of a 1964 St. Louis University graduate seminar on modern poetry and evolutionism: John K. Crane, Sister Mary Ruth Gehres, O.S.U., Elaine K. Halbert, Judith Hoemeke (Mrs. Gerald A.), Leah Jansky (Mrs. Radko K.), Barbara Lawrence, Lannie LeGear, Young Gul Lee, Catherine Manore, John A. Marino, Sister Mary Joan Peters, O.S.F., Barbara Quinn, Mary Slackford, Sister Dorothy Marie Sommer, C.PP.S., Norman J. Stafford, Doris Stolberg, and Alice Zucker.

2. T. S. Eliot, *Collected Poems 1909-1962* (New York, 1963), p. 180.

3. Cleanth Brooks, *The Hidden God: Studies in Hemingway, Faulkner, Yeats, Eliot, and Warren* (New Haven, 1963), p. 130.

4. Northrop Frye, "The Archetypes of Literature," in *Myth and Method,* ed. James E. Miller, Jr. (Lincoln, Neb., 1960), p. 155.

5. Walter J. Ong, "Nationalism and Darwin: A Psychological Problem in Our Concept of Social Development," *Review of Politics,* XXII (1960), 466-481.

6. *Short Time's Endless Monument: The Symbolism of Numbers in Spenser's "Epithalamion"* (New York, 1960). See also Alastair Fowler, "Numerical Composition in *The Faerie Queene,*" *Journal of the Warburg and Courtauld Institutes,* XXV (1962), 199-239, and the same author's *Spenser and the Numbers of Time* (New York, 1964).

7. *Start with the Sun: Studies in Cosmic Poetry* (Lincoln, Neb., 1960).

8. Mircea Eliade, *The Myth of the Eternal Return* (New York, 1954), *passim;* cf. the same author's *The Sacred and the Profane* (New York, 1957) and *Patterns in Comparative Religion* (New York, 1958).

9. Robert Graves, "To Juan at the Winter Solstice" (1946), *Collected Poems 1959* (London, 1959), p. 212.

10. Georges Poulet, *Studies in Human Time,* trans. Elliott Coleman [with an Appendix, "Time and American Writers," written for the translated edition] (Baltimore, 1956), pp. 345-350.

11. *The Poems of Emily Dickinson,* ed. Thomas H. Johnson (Cambridge, Mass., 1955), p. 151 (n. 216).

12. *Studies in Human Time,* p. 344.

13. *The Complete Poetry and Prose,* ed. Malcolm Cowley (New York, 1948), I, p. 120.

14. Pierre Teilhard de Chardin, *The Phenomenon of Man* (New York, 1959) and *The Divine Milieu* (New York, 1960), *passim.*

15. See *Studies in Human Time,* pp. 342-345.

16. Quoted by Bernice Slote in *Start with the Sun,* p. 238.

17. See, for example, his "Author's Note" contributed to *Modern Poetry: American and British,* ed. by Kimon Friar and Malcolm Brinnin (New York, 1951), p. 545.

18. Hart Crane, *Collected Poems,* ed. Waldo Frank (New York, 1946), p. 8.

19. Geoffrey Bullough, *Changing Psychological Beliefs in English Poetry* (Toronto, 1962), pp. 226-227.

20. "The Historical Basis of 'The Wreck of the Deutschland' and 'The Loss of the Eurydice,' " Appendix [giving the text of the *Times* reports], in *Immortal Diamond: Studies in Gerard Manley Hopkins,* ed. by Norman Weyand (New York, 1949), p. 368.

21. *Ibid.,* pp. 367-368.

22. I have pointed out this existentialist strain in Hopkins in a review in *Victorian Studies,* III (1960), 305-308.

23. "The Wreck of the Deutschland," in *Poems of Gerard Manley Hopkins,* ed. W. H. Gardner, 3d ed. (New York, 1948), p. 57.

24. Cleanth Brooks, *The Hidden God,* p. 129.

NOTES ON CONTRIBUTORS

HASKELL M. BLOCK is Professor of Comparative Literature at Brooklyn College and Executive Officer of the doctoral program in Comparative Literature of the City University of New York. He served as Visiting Professor of Comparative Literature at the University of Illinois in 1966-1967. He is the author of *Mallarmé and the Symbolist Drama* and co-editor of *Masters of Modern Drama*. His article from *Comparative Literature Studies* has been reprinted in a collection edited by S. G. Nichols, Jr. and R. B. Vowles, *Comparatists at Work*.

SCHUYLER V. R. CAMMANN holds degrees from Yale, Harvard, and Johns Hopkins. He is Professor of East Asian Studies in the Graduate School of the University of Pennsylvania. His books include *China's Dragon Robes* and *The Land of the Camel*.

FREDERICK W. DILLISTONE graduated from Oxford University with Honors in Mathematics in 1924. He later became Doctor of Divinity in 1951. He was Dean of Liverpool Cathedral 1956-1963 and is now Fellow of Oriel College, Oxford. His books include *Christianity and Communication* and *Christianity and Symbolism*. His article from *Comparative Literature Studies* has been reprinted in an anthology edited by George A. Panichas, *Mansions of the Spirit*.

LILIAN R. FURST was educated at the Universities of Manchester, Paris, Zurich, and Cambridge (Girton College). She has taught German at Queen's University of Belfast and is now Senior Lecturer in Comparative Literary Studies at the University of Manchester. Her article from *Comparative Literature Studies* has been reprinted in her book *Romanticism and Perspective*.

JOHN GASSNER, born in Hungary and educated in New York, was for many years Sterling Professor of Dramatic Literature at Yale University. He is author of *Masters of the Drama, The Theatre in Our Times,* and *Form and Idea in the Modern Theatre.* His article from *Comparative Literature Studies* has been reprinted in *Directions in Modern Theatre and Drama.*

Ihab Hassan is Benjamin L. Wait Professor of English and Chairman of the Department at Wesleyan University. He is author of *Radical Innocence* and *The Literature of Silence.*

Martin Jarrett-Kerr, C. R. was educated at Oxford University and has been Vice-Principal of the Theological College of the Resurrection in Yorkshire. His books include *D. H. Lawrence and Human Existence, François Mauriac* and *Studies in Literature and Belief.* His article from *Comparative Literature Studies* has been reprinted in *Mansions of the Spirit,* edited by George A. Panichas.

François Jost was educated at the University of Fribourg and the Institut de Littérature Comparée at the Sorbonne. He has taught at Fribourg and Colorado and is now Professor of French and Comparative Literature at the University of Illinois. He has published two volumes of *Essais de littérature comparée* as well as *La Suisse dans les lettres françaises au cours des âges,* and *Jean-Jacques Rousseau suisse.* His article from *Comparative Literature Studies* has been reprinted in his *Essais de littérature comparée.*

Harry Levin is Irving Babbitt Professor of Comparative Literature at Harvard University, and chairman of the Department of Comparative Literature. He has been President of the American Comparative Literature Association. His various publications include *The Gates of Horn: A Study of Five French Realists, The Myth of the Golden Age in the Renaissance,* and *James Joyce: A Critical Introduction.* His article from *Comparative Literature Studies* has been reprinted in a collection of his essays, *Refractions.*

Rocco Montano has been professor at the University of Naples, Harvard University, Johns Hopkins University, Catholic University of America, and the University of Maryland. He is now Professor of Italian and Comparative Literature at the University of Illinois. His books include *Storia della poesia di Dante,* and *L'estetica del rinascimento e del barocco.*

Edwin M. Mosley is Professor of English and Provost at Skidmore College. His books include *Pseudonyms of Christ in the Modern Novel, The Outsider as Hero and Anti-Hero,* and *F. Scott Fitzgerald: A Critical Essay.* His article from *Comparative Literature Studies* has been reprinted in *Mansions of the Spirit,* edited by George A. Panichas.

Grigore Nandris received his Ph.D. at Cracow University and later studied in Paris at the Ecole Pratique des Hautes Etudes. In 1926 he became Professor of Slavonic Philology in the University of Cernăuti, and in 1948 he was appointed to the first Chair of Slavonic Philology in the School of Slavonic and East European Studies in the University of London. He has published many books on Slavonic philology.

Walter J. Ong, S.J., is Professor of English at Saint Louis University and has been visiting professor at New York University and the University of Chicago. His books, which represent critical explorations of literature, culture, and religion, include *The Barbarian Within, In the Human Grain,* and *The Presence of the Word.* His article from *Comparative Literature Studies* has been reprinted in a collection of essays by various authors edited by M. E. Marty and D. G. Peerman, *New Theology No. 5,* as well as in his own *In the Human Grain.*

MARIO PRAZ, K.B.E., Hon. D.Litt. Cambridge (England), Paris (Sorbonne), and Aix-Marseilles, has held the Chair of Italian at the Universities of Liverpool and Manchester and the Chair of English at the University of Rome. His books translated into English include *The Romantic Agony, The Hero in Eclipse, The Flaming Heart,* and *The House of Life.*

ALLAN RODWAY took the English Tripos at Cambridge just after World War II and has since taught at the University of Nottingham, where he is now Reader in English.

ROBERT SHACKLETON, Fellow of Brasenose College, Oxford, since 1946, now occupies the office of Bodley's Librarian. He holds honorary degrees from the Universities of Bordeaux and Dublin, is a Fellow of the British Academy and Corresponding Member of the Academy of Bordeaux, and has been President of the British Society for French Studies and of the International Comparative Literature Association. He has published a critical edition of Fontenelle's *Entretiens sur la pluralité des mondes,* and *Montesquieu, a critical biography.*

RENÉ WELLEK, educated at Charles University in Czechoslovakia, is Sterling Professor of Comparative Literature at Yale University. He has been President of the American Comparative Literature Association. His books include *Immanuel Kant in England, The Rise of English Literary History,* and *A History of Modern Criticism.* His article from *Comparative Literature Studies* came out almost simultaneously in a collection of his articles, *Concepts of Criticism.*

BIBLIOGRAPHY

I. Works Concerned with the Methods
of Comparative Literature

Baldensperger, Fernand, and Werner P. Friederich. *Bibliography of Comparative Literature*. Chapel Hill, 1950. A Supplement appears annually in *Yearbook of Comparative and General Literature*. Bloomington, Indiana: University of Indiana Press.

[Carré, Jean-Marie] *Connaissance de l'étranger. Mélanges offerts à la mémoire de Jean-Marie Carré*. Paris, 1954.

Cioranescu, Alejandro. *Principios de literatura comparada*. Universidad de La Laguna, 1964.

Corstius, Jan Brandt. *Introduction to the Comparative Study of Literature*. New York, 1968.

Deugd, Cornelis de. *De Eenheid van het comparatisme*. Utrecht, 1962.

Etiemble, René. *Comparaison n'est pas raison*. Paris, 1963.

Friederich, Werner P., and David Henry Malone. *Outline of Comparative Literature from Dante Alighieri to Eugene O'Neill*. Chapel Hill, 1954.

Guyard, Marius-François. *La Littérature comparée*. Paris: 1951.

Jeune, Simon. *Littérature générale et littérature comparée. Essai d'orientation*. Paris, 1968.

Nichols, Stephen, Jr., and Richard B. Vowles. *Comparatists at Work. Studies in Comparative Literature*. Waltham, Mass., 1968.

Rousseau, André-Marie, and Claude Pichois, *La Littérature comparée*. Paris, 1967.

Rutgers University, Faculty of Comparative Literature. *Syllabus of Comparative Literature*. New York, 1964.

Stallknecht, Newton P., and Horst Frenz. *Comparative Literature: Method and Perspective*. Carbondale, Illinois, 1961.

Trousson, Raymond. *Un Problème de littérature comparée. Les Etudes de thèmes. Essai de méthodologie.* Paris, 1965.

Van Tieghem, Paul. *La Littérature comparée.* Paris, 1931.

Weisstein, Ulrich. *Einführung in die Vergleichende Literaturwissenschaft.* Stuttgart, 1968.

Wellek, René, and Austin Warren. *Theory of Literature.* New York, 1949.

II. PROCEEDINGS OF THE INTERNATIONAL COMPARATIVE LITERATURE ASSOCIATION

Venezia nelle letterature moderne. Atti del Primo Congresso dell'Associazione Internazionale de Letteratura Comparata. A cura di Carlo Pellegrini. Florence, 1955.

Comparative Literature. Proceedings of the Second Congress of the International Comparative Literature Association at the University of North Carolina. Edited by Werner P. Friederich. Chapel Hill, North Carolina, 1959. 2 vols.

Proceedings of the IIIrd Congress of the International Comparative Literature Association. 'S-Gravenhage, Holland, 1962.

Proceedings of the IVth Congress of the International Comparative Literature Association. Edited by François Jost. The Hague, 1966. 2 vols.

III. JOURNALS

Arcadia. Zeitschrift für vergleichende Literaturwissenschaft. Germanistisches Seminar der Universität Bonn, Bundesrepublik Deutschland.

Books Abroad. Norman, Oklahoma: University of Oklahoma Press.

Comparative Literature. Eugene, Oregon: The University of Oregon.

Comparative Literature Studies. Urbana, Illinois: The University of Illinois Press.

Hikaku Bungaku [Journal of Comparative Literature]. Comparative Literature Society of Japan.

Hikaku Bungaku Nenski [Etudes de la littérature comparée]. University of Tokyo.

Mosaic. Winnipeg, Canada. The University of Manitoba Press.

Revue de Littérature Comparée. Paris, Librairie Marcel Didier.

Rivista di letterature moderne e comparate. Firenze: G. C. Sansoni Editore.

Yearbook of Comparative and General Literature. Bloomington, Indiana: Indiana University Press.

Zagadnienia Rodzajów Literackich [Les Problèmes des genres littéraires]. Warsaw, Poland: "Ars Polona."